D. H. Lawrence and the Trembling Balance

D. H. Lawrence and the Trembling Balance

James C. Cowan

THE PENNSYLVANIA STATE UNIVERSITY PRESS
University Park and London

To Judy and Hal
in search of the honorable beasts

Library of Congress Cataloging-in-Publication Data

Cowan, James C.
    D.H. Lawrence and the trembling balance / James C. Cowan.

    p. cm.
    Includes bibliographical references.
    ISBN 0-271-00692-7
    1. Lawrence, D. H. (David Herbert), 1885–1930—Criticism and
interpretation. I. Title.
    PR6023.A93Z62317   1990
    823'.912—dc20   89–39019

It is the policy of The Pennsylvania State University to use acid-free
paper for the first printing of all clothbound books. Publications on
uncoated stock satisfy the minimum requirements of American National
Standard for Information Sciences—Permanence of Paper for Printed
Library Materials, ANSI Z39.48–1984.

Contents

Abbreviations

References to the works of D. H. Lawrence are cited parenthetically in the text by abbreviated title and page numbers. Where it is available, the Cambridge edition is quoted; where it is not, other editions are cited. Cue titles refer to the following editions of primary sources:

AR   *Aaron's Rod.* Edited by Mara Kalnins. Cambridge: Cambridge University Press, 1988.

A   *Apocalypse and the Writings on Revelation.* Edited by Mara Kalnins. Cambridge: Cambridge University Press, 1980.

CL   *The Collected Letters of D. H. Lawrence.* Edited by Harry T. Moore. 2 vols. New York: Viking Press, 1962.

CP   *The Complete Poems of D. H. Lawrence.* Edited by Vivian de Sola Pinto and F. Warren Roberts. New York: Viking Press, 1971.

CSS   *The Complete Short Stories of D. H. Lawrence,* vol. 3. London: William Heinemann, 1955.

EME   *England, My England and Other Stories.* Edited by
             Bruce Steele. Cambridge: Cambridge University
             Press, 1990.

EC   *The Escaped Cock.* Edited by Gerald M. Lacy. Los
             Angeles: Black Sparrow Press, 1973.

EP   *Etruscan Places.* In *Mornings in Mexico* and *Etruscan
             Places.* London: William Heinemann, 1956.

FU   *Fantasia of the Unconscious.* In *Psychoanalysis and
             the Unconscious* and *Fantasia of the Unconscious.* In-
             troduction by Philip Rieff. New York: Viking Press,
             Compass Books, 1960. 51–225.

FLC   *The First Lady Chatterley.* New York: Dial Press,
             1944.

JTLJ   *John Thomas and Lady Jane.* New York: Viking
             Press, 1972.

K   *Kangaroo.* London: William Heinemann, 1955.

L   *The Ladybird.* In *Four Short Novels by D. H. Law-
             rence.* New York: Viking Press, Compass Books,
             1965.

LCL   *Lady Chatterley's Lover.* New York: Grove Press,
             1959.

Letters   *The Letters of D. H. Lawrence.* Edited, and with an
             Introduction, by Aldous Huxley. New York: Viking
             Press, 1932, reprinted 1936.

Letters MS   *Letters from D. H. Lawrence to Martin Secker, 1911–
             1930.* [London]: Privately printed, 1970.

Letters 1   *The Letters of D. H. Lawrence.* Vol. 1: *September
             1901–May 1913.* Edited by James T. Boulton. Cam-
             bridge: Cambridge University Press, 1979.

Letters 2   *The Letters of D. H. Lawrence.* Vol. 2: *June 1913–
             October 1916.* Edited by George J. Zytaruk and
             James T. Boulton. Cambridge: Cambridge University
             Press, 1981.

Letters 3   *The Letters of D. H. Lawrence.* Vol. 3: *October 1916–
             June 1921.* Edited by James T. Boulton and Andrew
             Robertson. Cambridge: Cambridge University Press,
             1984.

Letters 4 *The Letters of D. H. Lawrence*. Vol. 4: *June 1921–
March 1924*. Edited by Warren Roberts, James T.
Boulton, and Elizabeth Mansfield. Cambridge: Cam-
bridge University Press, 1987.

Letters 5 *The Letters of D. H. Lawrence*. Vol. 5. *March 1924–
March 1927*. Edited by James T. Boulton and Lindeth
Vasey. Cambridge: Cambridge University Press,
1989.

LG   *The Lost Girl*. Edited by John Worthen. Cambridge:
Cambridge University Press, 1981.

MEH   *Movements in European History*. Edited by Philip
Crumpton. Cambridge: Cambridge University Press,
1989.

Paintings *Paintings of D. H. Lawrence*. Edited by Mervyn Levy.
New York: Viking Press, A Studio Book, 1964.

P   *Phoenix: The Posthumous Papers of D. H. Lawrence*.
Edited by Edward D. McDonald. New York: Viking
Press, 1936, reprinted 1968.

P II   *Phoenix II: Uncollected, Unpublished, and Other
Prose Works by D. H. Lawrence*. Edited by Warren
Roberts and Harry T. Moore. New York: Viking
Press, 1968.

PS   *The Plumed Serpent*. Edited by L. D. Clark. Cambridge: Cambridge University Press, 1987.

PO   *The Prussian Officer and Other Stories*. Edited by
John Worthen. Cambridge: Cambridge University
Press, 1983.

PU   *Psychoanalysis and the Unconscious*. In *Psychoanalysis and the Unconscious* and *Fantasia of the Unconscious*. Introduction by Philip Rieff. New York: Viking Press, Compass Books, 1960.

QR   *The Quest for Rananim: D. H. Lawrence's Letters to
S. S. Koteliansky, 1914–1930*. Edited by George J.
Zytaruk. Montreal and London: McGill–Queen's Uni-
versity Press, 1970.

R   *The Rainbow*. Edited by Mark Kinkead-Weekes.
Cambridge: Cambridge University Press, 1989.

RDP   *Reflections on the Death of a Porcupine and Other Essays.* Edited by Michael Herbert. Cambridge: Cambridge University Press, 1988.

SL   *Sons and Lovers.* Edited, with an Introduction and Notes, by Keith Sagar. Harmondsworth, Middlesex, U.K.: Penguin Books, 1981, reprinted 1986.

St. M   *St. Mawr and Other Stories.* Edited by Brian Finney. Cambridge: Cambridge University Press, 1983.

SCAL   *Studies in Classic American Literature.* New York: Viking Press, Compass Books, 1961.

SM   *The Symbolic Meaning: The Uncollected Versions of "Studies in Classic American Literature."* Edited by Armin Arnold. New York: Viking Press, 1964.

STH   *Study of Thomas Hardy and Other Essays.* Edited by Bruce Steele. Cambridge: Cambridge University Press, 1985.

T   *The Trespasser.* Edited by Elizabeth Mansfield. Cambridge: Cambridge University Press, 1982.

TI   *Twilight in Italy.* New York: Viking Press, 1958.

WP   *The White Peacock.* Edited by Andrew Robertson. Cambridge: Cambridge University Press, 1983.

WMH   *The Widowing of Mrs. Holyroyd.* In *The Complete Plays of D. H. Lawrence.* London: William Heinemann, 1965.

WL   *Women in Love.* Edited by David Farmer, Lindeth Vasey, and John Worthen. Cambridge: Cambridge University Press, 1987.

Acknowledgments

My work on D. H. Lawrence has never been carried out alone. In addition to the two people named in my dedication, I am especially indebted to Michael Squires and Daniel J. Schneider for their comments on the manuscript. Mike Squires, whose dialogue with me on Lawrence has been marked by a strong sense of professional commitment and personal integrity, repeatedly challenged me to establish the terms of my argument and to clarify my position. Dan Schneider, whose critical interchanges with me on Lawrence have been mutually valuable and rewarding, has broadly informed my own understanding of Lawrence's psychology and symbolism. Both men have contributed substantially to the form my ideas have taken in this book.

I am indebted to Dennis Jackson for more than two decades of personally satisfying and professionally productive association in several ventures relating to Lawrence, and especially for his service to Lawrence scholarship in assuming the editorship of *The D. H. Lawrence Review*. I am grateful to Keith Cushman, Howard M. Harper, and Judith Ruderman for an ongoing, happy, and stimulating exchange of ideas and feelings on Lawrence; and to L. D. Clark and George J. Zytaruk for the benefit over many years of their generous knowledge of Lawrence. I also want to thank Philip M. Griffith,

Ian S. MacNiven, Charles Proudfit, and Julius Raper for their help-
ful comments on various parts of the manuscript. Finally, I acknowledge a special debt to Joanne Trautmann Banks, who first challenged me to explore the relations between literature and medicine,
and to Charles Rossman, who first encouraged me to write this book.
All of these people have supported my work in many ways beyond
those mentioned in these brief acknowledgments. I thank them all
for the impetus of their critical insights; I value them even more for
the shared warmth of their friendship.

Beyond my particular debt to these individuals, I am grateful
more generally to the community of Lawrence scholars within which
my work has been carried out. Among the professional rewards of
editing *The D. H. Lawrence Review* and two volumes of bibliographi-
cal abstracts (published as *D. H. Lawrence: An Annotated Bibliography of Writings about Him*, vols. 1 and 2), and chairing a series of
MLA seminars that were the matrix out of which the D. H. Lawrence Society of North America emerged, is the opportunity they
afforded me by learning from virtually every author whose contributions were presented in these forums. The major personal reward for
me was that through these scholarly ventures I was privileged to
work with colleagues in Lawrence studies throughout the world.

I acknowledge the assistance of a National Endowment for the
Humanities Summer Stipend, which supported my initial research
on Lawrence, Jung, and alchemy for chapter 10.

Portions of this book have appeared, in different form, in several
scholarly journals and books. The original version of chapter 2 was
published as "D. H. Lawrence's Dualism: The Apollonian-Dionysian
Polarity and *The Ladybird*," in *Forms of Modern British Fiction*, ed.
Alan W. Friedman (Austin: University of Texas Press, 1975), 73–99.
Some portions of chapters 4 and 6, extensively revised, had their
genesis, respectively, in sections of "Lawrence's Criticism of Melville," *Melville Society Extracts*, no. 17 (February 1974): 6–8; and
"D. H. Lawrence and the Resurrection of the Body," *D. H. Lawrence:
The Man Who Lived*, ed. Robert B. Partlow, Jr., and Harry T. Moore
(Carbondale and Edwardsville: Southern Illinois University Press,
1980), 94–104; the latter was also published in *Healing Arts in
Dialogue: Medicine and Literature*, ed. Joanne Trautmann (Carbondale and Edwardsville: Southern Illinois University Press, 1981),
55–69. Chapter 7 is an expanded form of "Lawrence and Touch,"
D. H. Lawrence Review 19 (Spring-Summer 1985–86): 121–37. Chapter 8 is slightly revised from "Phobia and Psychological Development in D. H. Lawrence's 'The Thorn in the Flesh,'" in *The Modern-*

ists: Studies in a Literary Phenomenon, Essays in Honor of Harry T. Moore, ed. Lawrence B. Gamache and Ian S. MacNiven (Rutherford, N.J.: Fairleigh Dickinson University Press, 1987), 163–70. Chapter 9 is revised from "Lawrence's Phoenix: An Introduction," *D. H. Lawrence Review* 5 (Fall 1972): 187–99. Chapter 11 is a revised and expanded form of "Lawrence, Joyce, and the Epiphanies of *Lady Chatterley's Lover,*" *D. H. Lawrence's "Lady": A New Look at "Lady Chatterley's Lover,*" ed. Michael Squires and Dennis Jackson (Athens: University of Georgia Press, 1985), 91–115. Chapter 12, published in its original form as "The Function of Symbols and Allusions in D. H. Lawrence's *The Man Who Died,*" *American Imago* 17 (Fall 1960): 241–53, appeared in vastly revised form as "Allusions and Symbols in D. H. Lawrence's *The Escaped Cock,*" in *Critical Essays on D. H. Lawrence,* ed. Dennis Jackson and Fleda Brown Jackson (New York: G. K. Hall, 1988), 174–88. I am grateful to the editors and publishers of these journals and collections for permission to adapt the material for this book.

Finally, I wish to thank Gerald Pollinger, Laurence Pollinger Ltd., and the Estate of Mrs. Frieda Lawrence Ravagli for permission to quote from Lawrence's published works in the editions cited.

Introduction

Projective Identification and Imaginative Empathy

Much of this book deals with ideas and issues that were intensely personal for D. H. Lawrence, as they are for me—physiological balance, psychic resilience, and creative change; the antinomies of existence; the role of the artist, and the movies as a popular art; psychoanalysis and the unconscious; the human body, the etiology of illness, and the restoration of health; touch in human relationship; phobia and psychological growth; the alchemy of transformation; epiphanic insight; a revisionist view of Christian myth and doctrine; and the resurrection of the flesh in sexuality. In confronting these ideas and issues, the critic inevitably brings to bear more than the conventional tools of literary scholarship and the intellectual constructs of modern literary theory. Textual reading of any kind places the reader in an object relation to the author. Lawrence's way of presenting these ideas and issues, in addition to his subject matter itself, makes him more susceptible than most writers to the reader's unconscious participation in the reading process. In extension of one aspect of critical theory and as an introduction to my own reading of Lawrence, I want to consider briefly the contributions to reader response of the differing psychic mechanisms of projection, projective identification, and imaginative empathy.

According to Sigmund Freud, projection is a primitive mechanism by which "internal perceptions of emotional and thought processes can be projected outwards in the same way as sense perceptions; they are thus employed for building up the external world, though they should by rights remain part of the *internal* world." Projection functions as a defense against unconscious conflicts by attributing one's own unconscious impulses, attitudes, feelings, and perceptions to people or objects in the world outside oneself, but "it also occurs where there is no conflict."[1] It may be hypothesized that the greater the ambiguity of the literary field, the more it will serve as a stimulus for the projective interpretations of readers. But as Norman N. Holland has shown, even a relatively straightforward description, such as the tableau of Emily and her father in William Faulkner's "Rose for Emily," evokes differing projective responses from different readers.[2]

Holland suggests that the literary work through its form "acts out defensive maneuvers for us: splitting, isolating, undoing, displacing from, omitting (repressing or denying) elements of the fantasy."[3] In *5 Readers Reading,* Holland relates individual responses to the reader's own "psychological processes, that is, to his search for successful solutions within his identity theme to the multiple demands, both inner and outer, on his ego." After examining the language of several critics, Holland concludes: "Not only do equally skilled readers show the usual variations in interpreting conscious themes and meanings; they also reveal in their wordings that they are creating the story and its meanings for themselves out of different unconscious materials."[4] The fact that Holland's five subjects were not untrained, naïve readers but advanced undergraduate English majors suggests that their "defensive and adaptive strategies" in reading may be representative of most of us. If responses to literature are routinely projective, the implications for criticism are far reaching.

It is easy to see many critical readings, including one's own, as examples of projective response, involving at times the early developmental (more primitive) defense mechanisms of splitting and projective identification, first described by Melanie Klein in an effort to define more explicitly the projective process that occurs prior to the establishment of firm delineation between self and object. As Hanna Segal, in her elucidation of Mrs. Klein's psychoanalytic theory, describes the mechanism of projective identification, "parts of the self

---

1. Freud, *Totem and Taboo, Standard Edition,* 13:64.
2. Holland, *5 Readers Reading,* 4.
3. Holland, *The Dynamics of Literary Response,* 189.
4. Holland, *5 Readers Reading,* 128, 48.

and internal objects are split off and projected into the external object, which then becomes possessed by, controlled and identified with the projected parts."[5] According to Melanie Klein, who replaces the traditional concept of developmental stages with the less time-bound concept of early structural "positions," this kind of splitting is characteristic of "the paranoid position," in which boundaries between self and other remain confused, and angry, aggressive components of the self are kept at bay by attributing them to the other. The "paranoid position" is followed by a working-through process in "the depressive position," in which boundaries between self and other are more stable, and self and objects are recognized as both good and bad. The other can be hurt and the self depressed in relation to that hurt. In Mrs. Klein's terminology, a "position" is "a mental space in which one is sometimes lodged," "an always available state, not something one passes through."[6] The positions are experienced in relation to human objects, internal or external. These early interpersonal relationships are the substrata for the individual's reality perceptions regarding the world of affective ties. According to Mrs. Klein, hatred against bad parts of the self, originally directed against the mother from "the paranoid position," in subsequent object relations is directed against another object, which is then felt as persecutory. But good parts of the self also are expelled and projected into the other in developing good object relations or identifying the ego ideal.[7] Here perhaps is an emotional basis for the reader or critic either to overidealize or to be overthreatened by a given artistic work.

Since its introduction by Melanie Klein, efforts by the psychoanalytic community to standardize the meaning and usage of the term *projective identification* have produced no unanimity. Otto F. Kernberg, an object relations theorist whose work has centered in borderline personality disorders, applies the term only to persons in whom the very primitive defense mechanism of splitting characterizes the psychic structure. For Kernberg, projective identification is followed and basically replaced by projection, a more mature defense based in

5. Segal, *Introduction to the Work of Melanie Klein*, 27.
6. Mitchell, ed., in Klein, *The Selected Melanie Klein*, 28, 116. According to Mitchell, Mrs. Klein, who had used the term "position" as early as 1930, first deployed it in this sense in her paper "A Contribution to the Psychogenesis of Manic-Depressive States" (1935), 116–45. Melanie Klein's theory of the two early positions is set forth in "Notes on Some Schizoid Mechanisms" (1946), 176–200. Subsequently, accepting W. R. D. Fairbairn's conception of "the schizoid position," Mrs. Klein adopted "the paranoid-schizoid position" as the term for the first of these states (1952).
7. Ibid., 183–84.

repression rather than splitting and requiring the presence of firm ego boundaries.[8] W. W. Meissner, despite initial reservations about its usefulness, concludes that the concept of projective identification has a "legitimate place" but advocates limiting its scope to its original Kleinian meaning as "an intrapsychic mechanism . . . in which the self or some part of the self is projected into the object" with which this part of the self then becomes identified.[9] Joseph Sandler, who finds the concept valuable, believes it describes a process that cuts across all levels of development and thinks that it need not be tied to the Kleinian model of psychological development.[10]

In spite of the differences in approach to this terminology, all agree that the process serves the function of *control* of unconscious feeling states by attributing these feelings to the other, who may be a real human object or a fantasy representation of that object. With such feelings safely attributed to the other, the individual seeks to control unwanted aspects of the self through a lived-out relationship with the other as external object, or through a fantasy relationship with the other as internal object.

When the interaction is with an internal object on the fantasy level, Joseph Sandler characterizes the process as "*first stage projective identification.*" In this case, "the parts of the self put into the object are put into the fantasy object, the 'internal' object." This stage of projective identification involves "shifts and displacements in mental representation or in fantasy" for the purpose of "regulating unconscious feeling states," by controlling the object to gain "the unconscious illusion that one is controlling the unwanted and projected aspects of the self."[11] Viewed in this light, the act of reading, which processes the text through the reader's internal world, where it is experienced concretely in imaginative terms on various levels of unconscious fantasy, establishes a situation that is conducive to first-stage projective identification.

Sandler also describes second- and third-stage projective identification. These concepts, which have evolved from clinical practice, are used in describing the psychoanalytic therapist's relationship to the projective identifications brought by the patient to the therapy

8. Kernberg, "Projection and Projective Identification," 796. In the revised form of this article in *Projection, Identification, Projective Identification,* ed. Sandler, 93–115, the same distinction is made in different language in a corresponding passage, p. 94.

9. Meissner, "Projection and Projective Identification," in *Projection, Identification, Projective Identification,* ed. Sandler, 53, 42. See also the earlier form of this material in Meissner's "Note on Projective Identification."

10. Sandler, "The Concept of Projective Identification," 14–17.

11. Ibid., 19–29.

situation. In Sandler's conception, the self and the other are related through the constellation of the unmet self needs that the patient brings and that anticipate a particular response from the therapist as significant other. The therapist's own identification with and response to the patient's projective identification represents "*second stage projective identification.*" The therapist's ability to experience and to contain those identifications for working through is referred to as "*third stage projective identification.*" These concepts are of particular importance in analytic discussions of transference and countertransference.

W. W. Meissner, like Sandler, distinguishes radically between intrapsychic and interpsychic projective identification: "In the one-body context, both the projection and the identification take place in one mind: the projection takes place in relation to the subject's own object representation, and the ensuing identification takes place entirely as an intrapsychic event. In the two-or-more-body context, the projection takes place in one mind while the identification(s) take place in other minds."[12]

The transference experience that I see as operative in reading is universal. As Heinrich Racker expresses it, "Every real external object acquires the meaning of one or another part of the ego (and id), or of one or another of the internal objects, this meaning depending on the constellatory disposition of the moment and on the external object's real characteristics."[13] Although the text is itself already a displacement on the part of the author, it clearly serves as the medium through which the author (or his characters) can function as external object, and neither textual reading nor the projective identification of the reader requires the author's literal presence to complete the transaction. In fact, I have chosen to use the term *projective identification,* rather than *projection,* to describe the process of unconscious control of one's own unresolved affective needs because of its implication that those needs occur in an interpersonal context, one informed by early relationships with a significant other. By placing the process of projective identification in this larger framework rather than limiting it to the primitive mechanism of early development or borderline states, Joseph Sandler provides the basis for understanding its operation in the literary arena. To paraphrase Racker's observation on countertransference, the reality of the text is answered by the reality of the reader's response. The critic, from the meanings that his own person and work, and the

12. Meissner, "Projection and Projective Identification," 43–44.
13. Racker, *Transference and Countertransference,* 64.

impact of the text, have for him, responds with "real feelings, anxieties, defences, and desires."[14]

Even a relatively sophisticated reader may identify an early introjected object, or part object, of his or her own internal world, either a good object or a persecutory one, with a writer like Lawrence and then respond to the writer and his work, at least in part, as to that object. That, I think, is the operative psychic mechanism behind what L. D. Clark noted in most of us at the D. H. Lawrence Festival in Taos in 1970: "each person has his own image of Lawrence and in the end reveals his allegiance to that image alone."[15] We are all adept at rationalizing and defending our own "critical" positions, of course, but sometimes that "position" may be an earlier one, considerably earlier. Such responses, though articulated as literary criticism with all its accoutrements, actually derive from the critic's own internal world, which may contain pockets of affectively charged boundary confusions, an unclear demarcation between self and other that will significantly color the critical response. In any case, when the external object is a literary artist, this kind of projective response, unlike imaginative empathy, has other purposes besides the ostensible one of literary criticism.

Imaginative empathy as a literary concept is related to what John Keats calls "*Negative Capability,* that is, when a man is capable of being in uncertainties, mysteries, doubts, without any irritable reaching after fact and reason."[16] Alfred Margulies draws a parallel between Husserl's use of "phenomenological reduction" and Freud's use of "free association" as means of "experiencing freshly," then relates both to "negative capability." Citing Keats's statement that the poet "has no Identity—he is continually in for— and filling some other Body—,"[17] Margulies draws on his own experience as a psychoanalyst to show that the goal which Keats pursued "of feeling himself into the reality of the other, as if to illuminate the object contemplated from within," is an essential quality not only for the poet but also for the psychoanalytic psychotherapist to bring to his encounter with the other. Margulies describes "two broad steps toward the goal of sharing the world of the other": first, "the setting aside of expectations or presuppositions, the avoidance of concluding" about the other, and then, the projection of one's own consciousness into the other by means of imagina-

---

14. Ibid., 60.
15. Clark, "The D. H. Lawrence Festival," 45–46.
16. Keats, *The Letters of John Keats,* 1:193.
17. Ibid., 1:387.

tive empathy. "The first step corresponds to the negative capability, the second to *Einfühlung*."[18]

Many psychoanalysts, employing their empathic ability as one of their principal analytic skills, have drawn on their clinical experience to define empathy and its limits for their own psychoanalytic practice. For Ralph R. Greenson, empathy is a mode of knowing through "emotional closeness," an intimate, non-verbal form of establishing contact," a regressive phenomenon derived from the preoedipal period and "related to the more or less controlled regressions seen in creative individuals." It is "a means of establishing contact with a lost love object" or "an attempt at restitution for the loss of contact."[19] In the definition of Heinz Kohut, "empathy as 'vicarious introspection' . . . is the capacity to think and feel oneself into the inner life of another person. It is our lifelong ability to experience what another person experiences, though usually, and appropriately, to an attenuated degree."[20] Kohut's phrase "vicarious introspection" recognizes an element of projection of personal content that makes the empathy possible. But criticism, like the empathic process in psychoanalysis, necessarily involves as well an essential element of psychic distancing that moves beyond projection toward understanding and interpretation, in the critic's formulating and articulating an interpretation of his own self-experience in response to the text. As George S. Klein explains the psychoanalytic principle, "the analyst relies upon a perceptual process, still little understood, which Polanyi has called 'indwelling,' and Home 'cognitive identification,' in which the analyst reconstructs the subject's orientations by dwelling within the patient's experiences and behavior while standing back from them sufficiently to enable him to detect configurations of intention, especially disavowed ones, that the patient is living out in his experiences and movements."[21] There

18. Margulies, "Toward Empathy: The Uses of Wonder," 1031. Margulies further elaborates these ideas in *The Empathic Imagination*, chap. 1.

19. Ralph R. Greenson, *Technique and Practice of Psychoanalysis*, 382–83. Greenson believes that the capacity for empathy, an essential quality for the psychotherapist, cannot be taught but that those who have it can be taught how to use it effectively. See his "Empathy and Its Vicissitudes" (1960), in *Explorations in Psychoanalysis*, 147–61.

20. Kohut, *How Does Analysis Cure?*, 82. Kohut, for whom "[e]mpathy is the operation that defines the field of psychoanalysis" (174), gives a sensitive and humane treatment of the subject in his chapter "The Role of Empathy in Psychoanalytic Cure" (172–91). See also his theoretical essay "Introspection, Empathy, and Psychoanalysis: An Examination of the Relationship Between Mode of Observation and Theory," in *The Search for the Self*, 1:205–32.

21. George S. Klein, *Psychoanalytic Theory*, 27.

are, of course, substantive differences among the fields of poetry, psychoanalysis, and criticism, one of them being that the writer is not a patient and the critic is not in position to enter into a therapeutic relationship with him. But allowing for appropriate distinctions among the three fields, the quality of imaginative empathy seems to me to be as essential for the critic as for the poet and the psychoanalytic psychotherapist.

Projective identification begins as a primitive mechanism of defense. In that form Hanna Segal calls it "the earliest form of empathy" and says it "provides the basis for the earliest form of symbol formation."[22] Joseph Sandler explains this principle by suggesting that the earliest "state of primary confusion between self and object . . . (usually called primary identification) is one which persists in modified form throughout life, and which can provide the basis for the capacity for empathy." Sandler and W. G. Joffe postulate that in secondary identification an empathic process occurs, characterized by a momentary return to the "primary confusion" of an undifferentiated boundary state "whenever an object is perceived or its representation recalled. What happens then is that the boundaries between self and object become imposed by a definite act of inhibiting and of boundary-setting." A similar process, I believe, is involved when the reader is exposed to a new encounter with the text. As Sandler and Joffe suggest, the capacity to suspend defensiveness and return to "this genetically early state . . . must surely provide the basis for feelings of empathy, for aesthetic appreciation, for forms of transference and countertransference in analysis." This momentary state of oneness provides the bridge between self and object before "the ego function of disidentifying" restructures the boundaries.[23]

An important concept relative to empathy is Heinrich Racker's useful distinction between concordant and complementary identification. In concordant identification, the identification with the individual's immediate self-experience provides the basis for one's sense of the enduring experience of the other. In complementary identification, unconscious identification with the internal object representation communicated by the other interferes, at least temporarily, with one's "intention to understand." In concordant identification, one "coexperiences, to a corresponding degree, . . . the impulses, anxieties, and defences" communicated in the other's self-representation. In complementary identification, one defensively coexperiences the internal objects being projected by the other. According to Racker, the

22. Segal, 36.
23. Quoted in Sandler, "The Concept of Projective Identification," 25–26.

two are "closely connected": "to the degree to which the analyst fails in the concordant identifications and rejects them certain complementary identifications become intensified. It is clear that rejection of a part or tendency in the analyst himself—his aggressiveness, for instance—may lead to a rejection of the patient's aggressiveness . . . and that such a situation leads to a greater complementary identification with the patient's rejecting objects, toward which this aggressive impulse is directed." Since the analyst's identifications are "a sort of reproduction of his own past processes," which are being repeated in "response to stimuli from the patient," an empathic outcome of his complementary identifications in a successful concordant identification (his "understandings" of the patient) depends on the analyst's having achieved some understanding of his own self experience, in particular of his own early development and internal objects.[24]

Psychologically, in textual reading, complementary identification, by evoking a negative response to particular elements in the text, may arouse strong feelings of aversion (the text as persecutory object), of being controlled by the text to the extent of feeling victimized by what one perceives as the writer's imposing his projective identifications on the reader. Similarly, an excessively positive response to particular elements in the text may lead to strong feelings of admiration or idealization (the text as ideal object), emerging in the form of overidentification with the writer or elevation of him to the extent of discipleship in a cult of devotees. In either case, an empathic concordant outcome of these initially unconscious complementary identifications requires the same kind of self-awareness and insight on the part of the critic as on the part of the analyst concerning one's own internal objects and psychological processes. Lawrence, more than any other modern writer, has been the object of both negative and positive overidentifications. Negative responses to particular elements in his texts have labeled him in turn a pornographer, a primitivist, an atavistic enemy of civilization, an ignorant opponent of religious orthodoxy, a fascist, a pervert, and a sexist, while positive responses to other elements have labeled him a sexual liberator, a righteously angry iconoclast, a political or religious guru, a Salvator Mundi, and a profound psychologist of sex. Empathy involves the ability of the reader to suspend judgment temporarily in order to experience both the complementary and concordant aspects of the identification and to come to a balanced perception of the text and the authorial presence behind (or within) it. Empathic understanding of a given author represents a concordant

24. Racker, 134–35, 175.

identification based in wide knowledge of his work rather than in selective sampling designed to reinforce either the persecutory or the idealized object of the complementary identification.

Using the model of "interactional communications," Michael H. Tansey and Walter F. Burke describe empathy in psychoanalysis as the outcome of an interactional process with the patient's projective identifications, involving a unitary sequence of three phases. If critical reading may be seen as analogous to the analytic situation, then the text projected by the author corresponds to the patient's projective identification. The critical reader is then in the position of the analyst, who receives, internally processes, and responds to the communication, reflecting understanding and appropriate interpretation of what has been communicated. In Phase I: *Reception,* the receiver of the communication or projective identification purposely suspends usual boundaries and assumes a state of openness, of primary identification. This state, characterized by "freedom from memory and desire," allows the receiver to have "aroused within himself a specific set of self-representations and their associated affective states" in response to the other's projective process. At the point at which one experiences the affective pressure from the interaction, the identificatory experience is marked by an affective signal, and the communication is received. An empathic outcome depends on the receiver's "ability to tolerate the pressure or pull of the interactional communication," and his "capacity to tolerate the temporary modification of his self experience." Phase II: *Internal Processing,* involves the receiver's "development of working models of the self-representations of both the other person and himself" in order to achieve insight on "possible empathic connections" between the experience of the two. The basis for the working models is the receiver's ability to identify himself with the other through the felt experience of both the concordant and complementary aspects of the other's projective identification. Phase III: *Communication,* involves the receiver's responding to the communication. This response may range from silent reflection, through the formulation of interpretations based on his understanding of the experience that has been received, to "explicit references to some connection between the . . . self-experiences" of both parties.[25] I suggest that this "radically mutual process" of empathy, though stated in the unpoetic language of interactional communications theory and applied to the empathic process of the psychoanalytic therapist's response to the patient's

25. Tansey and Burke, "Projective Identification and the Empathic Process," 42–69, espec. 52, 53, 58, 60, 62, 64.

projective identification, is directly relevant, with appropriate modifications, to the process by which imaginative empathy is achieved in critical reading, with the critic taking the role of the empathic analyst.

The quality of empathy allows one in part to suspend the prejudgments of one's own unconscious agenda, even as one learns also, in Laurentian terms, to trust the tale rather than the teller (*SCAL* 2), to read between the lines of the artist's conscious, didactic meaning and to grasp the unconscious wish fulfillment or "myth-meaning" underneath, in order to enter into an empathic alliance with the writer that makes accessible what Lawrence saw as the potentially restorative or therapeutic function of art. It would be idle to suggest that the critic either can or should cease using his own internal world in organizing his response to the external world. But for the encounter with the literary artist as other to become useful for criticism, the critic must grow beyond *unwitting* projective identification that remains unconscious and unanalyzed, beyond merely defending one's view of the artist as the external embodiment of either the idealized object or persecutory object of one's own internal world and manipulating him as one's own special Lawrence. The sensitive critic will bring to the encounter an empathic quality derived, in a sense, it is true, from his or her own intensely felt personal experience, but experience that has been worked through (or is being worked through in relation to the literary work), understood and incorporated as earned insight, so that the critic can maintain the self-awareness, psychic distance, and neutrality necessary to encounter Lawrence's otherness and avoid the pitfall of merely projecting one's own inner world upon the ambiguity of the literary field. The empathic reader in the critical encounter temporarily suspends his own boundaries in order to have the opportunity to grow and change as he again differentiates from the literary field. Through psychic distancing, he maintains a sense of the organic whole, which partially checks his complementary identifications with particular elements in the text by demanding that he relate everything in it to the controlling center, thus enabling him to encounter the otherness of the writer and the impersonality of the work of art. The "true artist" brings the materials that inform the critical encounter by connecting the reader to the affective structures that govern our lives and define our needs. If the artist is Lawrence, he puts one in touch with the feelings and instincts of one's own deepest self.

According to Arnold Goldberg, empathy may be thought of in terms of either closed or open systems of exchange. Some forms of textual reading, he says, seem to derive from an effort to categorize empathy or understanding through a closed system, involving codes, systems of delivery, and translations and concerned with transferring facts or feelings from one source to another. The effort to categorize empathy by an open system, on the other hand, involves "such issues as shared meanings, intersubjectivity, and free exchange. Thus every fact is constantly being modified by input from other parts of the system." As Goldberg explains, "In textual analysis, the difference is of a reader's reading a book in a fixed rendering of its contents versus reading as an almost different person as he or she changes from day to day."[26] Why isn't this simply projection or projective identification in a different guise? Because here the reader is neither unknowingly projecting repressed material that is too intolerable to admit into consciousness nor splitting off unwanted or idealized parts of the self and projecting them into the artist by an unconscious mechanism that allows one to possess and manipulate the fantasy image of the writer as the embodiment of the internal object by those projected parts of the self. Instead, the reader, with self-awareness of the ongoing dynamic processes affecting his perceptual apparatus, makes his whole self available to the encounter with the artist in full knowledge that his own capacities for empathy and insight change and vary with the experiences and condition of his self as organism.

The kind of critical reading I propose, though it maintains a respect for the artist's integrity and ultimately for the boundaries of his artistic utterance, is not reducible to extraspection of the text considered solely as objective artifact. The act of reading itself internalizes the text, so that some degree of introspection is necessary to complete the transaction between artist and critic. In other words, the critical reader himself is part of the system. Some awareness and understanding of his own internal world enables him to function within the system by responding, relatively speaking, empathically rather than only projectively. The principal objective control that the critic brings to the reading is his conscious critical theory, but this is not enough to prevent his also bringing along additional baggage filled with his unconscious needs, prejudices, fears, and expectations—in short, the objects of his own internal world. It requires great sensitivity, self-awareness, honesty, and tact to avoid strewing the contents of this baggage over the literary field and then reading it back as if it were there all along. Critics, like other readers, do project their own meanings and then negotiate, but if the

26. Goldberg, *A Fresh Look at Psychoanalysis*, 108–9.

critic is relatively self-aware, acquainted with the self-contents that he or she is bringing to the encounter with the writer, the negotiated meaning need not be a gross, unconscious, and uninformed projective identification.

If I did not see some parts of myself in Lawrence, I would not have stayed with him for so long. My recognition of parts of my own life and being in him has enriched my response to his work. On an immediate level, such reader response may begin in primary identification marked by a state of "primary confusion" of boundaries between self and object. But I try to avoid merely transferring my needs and responses to Lawrence and then presenting in criticism those parts of myself as if they were his. While I have often used what I know from my own human existence, which necessarily includes the introjected objects of my inner world, I have tried to avoid confusing myself with Lawrence or my objects and experience with his. I have tried, in other words, to move beyond the "primary confusion" of boundaries toward secondary identification as empathic connection. My attempt has been, however imperfectly, to understand Lawrence's own ideas and feelings, to approach his writings openly, without too many preconceptions of my own, to see *him*.

No one develops the capacity for empathy without experiencing empathic understanding from others as well as the pain and separation introduced into such empathic relationships by one's own projective identifications. In Lawrence's psychoanalytic theory of the unconscious, the human individual needs the balance not only of forces within the self but also of creative relationship with the empathic other. Giving his own revisionist reading of Christ's statement "Man doth not live by bread alone" Lawrence says, "He lives even more essentially from the nourishing creative flow between himself and another or others" (*PU* 46).

On my part, I want to acknowledge the creative influence, at once both deeply personal and intellectual, of two people, my wife, Judith R. Cowan, and Harold L. Frazier, both of them medical doctors and psychiatrists. From the outset, my work has been indebted most to Judy Cowan, who for three decades has made a place in our home for D. H. Lawrence. Whatever critical insights I may have to offer come out of this central relationship and reflect the benefit of countless discussions with her. While my critical limitations are my own, my life with her has enabled me sometimes to see beyond them. My relationship with Hal Frazier and his with me have been characterized by mutual authenticity and commitment. His empathy with me has supported my growth in understanding the personal issues and objects that I have brought to the encounter with others, including my critical encounter with Lawrence, and has enabled me sometimes to feel my way beyond my own egoistic needs toward imaginative empathy. The "nourishing creative flow" between myself and these two people is profoundly significant in my life. I cannot encapsulate what my bond with either of them has meant to me; that is something I must live out in the "trembling balance" of my daily existence. This book is dedicated to them with my love and thanks for being who they are.

1

The "Trembling Balance": Homeostasis, Resilience, and Creative Change

In "Morality and the Novel," D. H. Lawrence says, "Life is so made, that opposites sway about a trembling centre of balance" (*STH* 173). Philosophy, religion, and science, he believes, all attempt to nail things down with fixed laws designed to stabilize the equilibrium. The novel, however, presents the living quality of the relationship between the opposites: "The novel is the highest complex of subtle interrelatedness that man has discovered." Thus, "morality in the novel" does not consist in nailing down fixed truths but in "the trembling instability of the balance" (*STH* 172). For "of all the art forms," he adds, "the novel most of all demands the trembling and oscillating of the balance" (*STH* 173).

The balance Lawrence suggests is not a static polarity of any two opposites but the delicate, dynamic equilibrium of life. His emphasis is not upon entities mechanistically associated in simple dichotomy but upon the organic relationship of those entities in all its subtle fluidity and complexity. The function of art, he says in "Art and Morality," "is to reveal things in their different relationships" (*STH* 166). In "The Novel," Lawrence declares: "We have to choose between the quick and the dead. The quick is God-flame in everything. And the dead is dead" (*STH* 182–83). As he elaborates: "the quickness of the quick lies . . . in a certain weird relationship between that which is quick and—I don't know; perhaps all the rest of things. It seems to consist in an odd sort of fluid, changing, grotesque or beautiful relatedness" (*STH* 183).

Lawrence, like Henri Bergson and William James, sees reality in flux rather than in fixity. Lawrence's statement that the novel is a discovery "far greater than Galileo's telescope" is not intended as hyperbole. "The novel is the highest form of human expression so far attained" precisely "[b]ecause it is so incapable of the absolute" (*STH* 179). In "Why the Novel Matters," in distinguishing between the abstract or absolute truth of the saint, the philosopher, and the scientist, and the "simple" truth of the novelist, Lawrence reiterates the "trembling" quality of the balance: "The novel is the one bright book of life. Books are not life. They are only tremulations on the ether. But the novel as a tremulation *can* make the whole man-alive tremble" (*STH* 195).

The true function of the novel, Lawrence believes, is not to serve a didactic purpose but to help us to get in touch with our own feelings by learning to listen to them. In "The Novel and the Feelings," he affirms that this form alone can express the "whole stormy chaos of 'feelings,' " not the standard emotional concepts, such as love, fear, and anger, but the genuine "feelings" in both their instinctual roots and their particularity. Thus, the novel serves an educative function by helping us "to educate ourselves, not by laying down laws and inscribing tablets of stone, but by listening":

> But listening-in to the voices of the honorable beasts that call in the dark paths of the veins of our body, from the God in the heart. Listening inwards, inwards, not for words nor for inspiration, but to the lowing of the innermost beasts, the feelings that roam in the forest of the blood, from the feet of God within the red, dark heart. [*STH* 205]

As Lawrence elaborates in "The Spirit of Place,"

> Art has two great functions. First, it provides an emotional experience. And then, if we have the courage of our own feelings, it becomes a mine of practical truth. We have had the feelings *ad nauseam*. But we've never dared dig the actual truth out of them, the truth that concerns us, whether it concerns our grandchildren or not. [*SCAL* 2]

The conception of life that Lawrence presents in these essays is as an open system in a condition of growth and flux, which maintains an organic equilibrium characterized as a "trembling balance" both within the organism and between the self and the other or between the individual and the environment. Lawrence's insistence that science, among other branches of knowledge, attempts to stabilize the equilibrium by establishing fixed laws is applicable only to closed systems, not to the more advanced scientific thinking of Lawrence's own day, though even the more theoretical science, such as Albert Einstein's relativity theory and Werner Heisenberg's uncertainty principle in physics, sought to understand these processes rationally. To illustrate their similarities and their differences, I want to draw a parallel between Lawrence's concept of the "trembling balance" of organic life and the physiological concept of homeostasis defined by his contemporary, the physician and physiologist Walter B. Cannon (1871–1945):

> The highly developed living being is an open system having many relations to its surroundings—in the respiratory and alimentary tracts and through surface receptors, neuromuscular organs and bony levers. Changes in the surroundings excite reactions in this system, or affect it directly, so that internal disturbances of the system are produced. Such disturbances are normally kept within narrow limits, because automatic adjustments within the system are brought into action, and thereby wide oscillations are prevented and the internal conditions are held fairly constant.[1]

In keeping with his conception of the body as an open system, Cannon avoids the term "equilibrium," which scientifically has an "exact meaning as applied to relatively simple physico-chemical states, in closed systems, where known forces are balanced." Rather, he uses the term "stasis," without its usual connotations of immobility and stagnation, to mean a "condition—a condition which may vary, but which is relatively constant." Cannon suggests that "the means employed by the more highly evolved animals for preserving uniform and stable their internal economy" may be generally applicable "principles for the establishment, regulation and control of steady states" in "other kinds of organization—even social and industrial—which suffer from distressing perturbations."[2]

As one of the fathers of modern physiology, Cannon attempted to

1. Cannon, "Organization for Physiological Homeostasis," 251–52.
2. Cannon, *The Wisdom of the Body*, 24–25. This book synthesizes and distills Cannon's body of work on homeostasis.

quantify homeostatic functioning in experimental investigations of the physiological bases of hunger and thirst, the influence of the endocrine glands on metabolism, and the function of adrenal secretion in the chemical regulation of body temperature.[3] Cannon shares with Lawrence a view that structures of the autonomic nervous system play a central role in the maintenance of balance: "As an interofective system exerting its influence on the activities of the viscera the autonomic must necessarily be intimately involved in the preservation of that stability and constancy of the internal economy of the organism which we have called homeostasis."[4] In calling for further investigations to establish the principles of physiological homeostasis, Cannon sets forth six tentative but definite scientific postulates, the application of which would ultimately enable the medical practitioner to predict homeostatic functioning and thus to make appropriate interventions to restore dysfunctional homeostatic systems and promote change in the direction of health.[5]

Lawrence's writings reveal his awareness of physiological homeostasis, but always with an acute sensitivity to life's mystery and with ultimately religious questions about its purpose. In *The Rainbow,* when Ursula Brangwen focuses the light on the field in her microscope and sees a single-celled "plant-animal lying shadowy in a bound-

---

3. See Cannon and Washburn, "An Explanation of Hunger," 441–54; Cannon, "Croonian Lecture. The Physiological Basis of Thirst," 283–301; Cannon, "Some General Features of Endocrine Influence on Metabolism," 1–20; Cannon and Querido, "The Rôle of Adrenal Secretion in the Chemical Control of Body Temperature," 441–54.

4. Cannon, *The Wisdom of the Body,* 261.

5. Cannon, "Physiological Regulation of Normal States: Some Tentative Postulates Concerning Biological Homeostatics," 246–47. The scientific purpose of Cannon's investigations is clear in the six postulates, which are stated as follows:

> 1. In an open system, such as our bodies represent, composed of unstable structure and subjected continually to disturbance, constancy is in itself evidence that agencies are acting or are ready to act to maintain this constancy. . . .
> 2. If a homeostatic condition continues, it does so because any tendency towards a change is automatically met by increased effectiveness of a factor or factors which lessen the change. . . .
> 3. A homeostatic agent does not act in opposite directions at the same point. . . .
> 4. Homeostatic agents, antagonistic in one region of the body, may be cooperative in another region. . . .
> 5. The regulating system which determines a homeostatic state may comprise a number of cooperating factors brought into action at the same time or successively. . . .
> 6. When a factor is known which can shift a homeostatic state in one direction, it is reasonable to look for automatic control of that factor or for a factor or factors having an opposing effect.

less light," she recalls an earlier conversation with Dr. Frankstone, a woman physicist, who, viewing life as a closed system analogous to electricity, questions whether any "special mystery" should be attributed to it: "May it not be that life consists in a complexity of physical and chemical activities, of the same order as the activities we already know in science?" (*R* 408). But Ursula has already begun to see her professors not as "priests initiated into the deep mysteries of life and knowledge" but as "only middle-men handling wares they had become so accustomed to that they were oblivious to them." Hence, her formal education seems merely "a second-hand dealer's shop, and one bought an equipment for an examination" (*R* 402–3). Now she considers Dr. Frankstone's hypothesis critically: "Electricity had no soul, light and heat had no soul" (*R* 408). Identifying herself as an organism like the living cell on her slide and tentatively accepting the scientific concept of a physiological balance, Ursula asks first the nature of the homeostasis and what the homeostatic forces are:

> Was she herself an impersonal force, or conjunction of forces, like one of these? She looked still at the unicellular shadow that lay within the field of light, under her microscope. It was alive. She saw it move—she saw the bright mist of its ciliary activity, she saw the gleam of its nucleus, as it slid across the plane of light. What then was its will? If it was a conjunction of forces, physical and chemical, what held these forces unified . . . ? [*R* 408]

Then she goes beyond the physiological concept to add "and for what purpose . . . ?" Ursula wonders whether the point of the homeostasis can be only the existential aim of self-preservation and self-assertion:

> For what purpose were the incalculable physical and chemical activities nodalised in this shadowy, moving speck under her microscope? What was the will which nodalised them and created the one thing she saw? What was its intention? To be itself? Was its purpose just mechanical and limited to itself? [*R* 408]

Finally the microscope becomes the lens that illuminates Ursula's vision of a mystery lying beyond even existence: Self-realization was a consummation by which one's individual identity is seen as infinite.

> It intended to be itself. But what self? Suddenly in her mind the world gleamed strangely, with an intense light, like the

nucleus of the creature under the microscope. Suddenly she had passed away into an intensely-gleaming light of knowledge. She could not understand what it all was. She only knew that it was not limited mechanical energy, not mere purpose of self-preservation and self-assertion. It was a consummation, a being infinite. Self was a oneness with the infinite. To be oneself was a supreme, gleaming triumph of infinity. [R 408–9]

Ursula's epiphany, I want to suggest, differentiates the scientific conception of physiological homeostasis articulated by Walter B. Cannon from Lawrence's idea of the "trembling balance." The real distinction is not, as Lawrence may have supposed, between a static and a dynamic world view, or between a mechanistic and an organic vision of life, or even between a closed system and an open one. For there is really no substantial disagreement on *what* life is: Both Cannon and Lawrence see it as a dynamic, organic, and open system. The distinction, rather, is between a scientific methodology that examines life rationally and asks *how,* and a religious perspective that experiences life intuitively and asks *why.* Ursula's question *why* reaches toward some kind of transpersonal answer. It is significant that her question is not answered *God* in the traditional sense her forebears would have understood, nor even *the Church* as her father might have answered, but *the self in darkness,* with its Laurentian connotations of instinct and intuition and behind them the unknown god. If one conceives of man's knowledge as a small circle of light surrounded by a vast outer darkness encompassing the unknown, as I think both Cannon and Lawrence did, then either one can seek to know the unknown rationally and empirically by means of investigation designed to explain *how* things work, or one can open oneself to experience of the unknown intuitively through empathy that affords insight on the meaning and purpose of existence. This is how Ursula conceives the matter:

That which she was, positively, was dark and unrevealed, it could not come forth. It was a seed buried in dry ash. This world in which she lived was like a circle lighted by a lamp. This lighted area, lit up by man's completest consciousness, she thought was all the world: that here all was disclosed for ever. Yet all the time, within the darkness she had been aware of points of light, like the eyes of wild beasts, gleaming, penetrating, vanishing. And her soul had acknowledged in a great heave of terror, only the other darkness. This inner circle of light in which she lived and moved, wherein the trains rushed and the factories ground out their machine-produce and the plants and the animals worked by the light of science and knowledge, suddenly it seemed like the area under an arc-lamp, wherein the moths and children played in the security of blinding light, not even knowing there was any darkness, because they stayed in the light. [R 405]

The "trembling balance" is not only between homeostatic physiological forces but also between the known and the unknown, light and darkness, the moths of the mind and the "honorable beasts" of the blood.

Ursula's dawning sense of the self in darkness is echoed in the "Benjamin Franklin" essay in Lawrence's recognition, again in the context of education, of a distinction between the ideal self "playing the patient ass in a tweed jacket" and another, more fundamental self:

Is Yale College going to educate the self that is in the dark of you, or Harvard College?

The ideal self! Oh, but I have a strange and fugitive self shut out and howling like a wolf or a coyote under the ideal windows. See his red eyes in the dark? This is the self who is coming into his own. [SCAL 9]

If the voices of our education prompt us, like the speaker in "Snake" (CP 349–51), to throw a stick at the phallic serpent of instinct that crawls "[f]rom out of the dark door of the secret earth" (line 40) of the unconscious, seeking the "hospitality" of our civilized consciousness to satisfy a need as basic as thirst, the problem is not with this innermost beast, who comes "[l]ike a king in exile, uncrowned in the underworld" (line 69), but with the internalized voices of our education. In their judgmental demands that the speaker prove his manhood by killing the snake, these voices derive from an imbalance that badly distorts his view of what it means to be a man. Although he gives in to them and throws the stick, he recognizes his behavior as a "pettiness" (line 74).

In the fragmentary "Man is essentially a soul . . . ," Lawrence declares, "The soul is instinctive. Real education is the learning to recognise and obey the instincts of the soul" (RDP 389). As Lawrence expresses it in "Introduction to These Paintings":

Any creative art occupies the whole consciousness of a man. This is true of the great discoveries of science as well as of art.

The truly great discoveries of science and real works of art are
made by the whole consciousness of man working together in
unison and oneness: instinct, intuition, mind, intellect all
fused into one complete consciousness, and grasping what we
may call a complete truth, or a complete vision. . . . [P 573–74]

That wholeness is what the "trembling balance" encompasses organically in a dynamically shifting equilibrium but without any break in
the integrity. Education that emphasizes only one side of consciousness, on whatever level, contributes to the imbalance.

In Lawrence's view, both modern science and modern religion represent a decline from the wholeness of the ancients. In the vitalistic
science of the pre-Socratic cosmologists, he believes, there had been
no contradiction between scientific observation and intuition. Modern science, derived from logical positivism, has lost the faculty of
physiologically based intuition as a mode of knowing the material
world. In "The Two Principles," Lawrence says, "There certainly does
exist a subtle and complex sympathy, correspondence between the
plasm of the human body, which is identical with the primary human
psyche, and the material elements outside." Modern religion, similarly, has lost the faculty of spiritual intuition as a means of communication with the material world: "The religious systems of the pagan
world did what Christianity has never tried to do: they gave the true
correspondence between the material cosmos and the human soul. . . .
In them science and religion were in accord" (SM 160).[6]

In the psychological theory presented in his two essays on the
unconscious, Lawrence, as much as Freud, rooted the forces of developmental human psychology firmly in biology. He located the religious impulse, just as unequivocally, in the body. In his well-known
letter to Ernest Collings (17 January 1913), Lawrence declares: "My
great religion is a belief in the blood, the flesh, as being wiser than
the intellect. We can go wrong in our minds. But what our blood feels
and believes and says, is always true. . . . All I want is to answer to
my blood, direct, without fribbling intervention of mind, or moral, or
what not" (Letters 1:503).

The forces that Lawrence would answer to in "the blood" are fragments of feeling thrown up by the unconscious, conscious remnants
of instinctual processes, the visible portions of the iceberg of consciousness that are evidence of the vast, unconscious, biological processes that lie underneath. When Lawrence listens "to the voices of

6. See MacDonald, " 'The Two Principles,' " 132–55, for a detailed analysis of Lawrence's dualistic symbolic system in the essay.

the honorable beasts that call in the dark paths of the veins of our body, from the God in the heart" (*STH* 205), he does not expect to hear from such standard emotions as love or hate conceptualized as abstract principles, but from the instinctual remnants that reveal the self. These glimmerings of consciousness are identical to the "points of light, like the eyes of wild beasts, gleaming, penetrating, vanishing" (*R* 405), that Ursula is aware of as a source of knowledge in the outer darkness surrounding the known world of education.

Lawrence's homeostasis is profoundly humane. In his conception, there is a biological drive toward selfhood that, even if blocked by the idealizing consciousness or inhibited by conventional morality and education, emerges in instinctual fragments that are significantly "honorable" in themselves and with which one may honorably be in touch. Cannon, in describing "the wisdom of the body" in the regulation of supplies and processes in the maintenance of homeostatic conditions, dealt with the transport of ions across a biological membrane in the body. Lawrence, in seeking to strip back consciousness to reveal "the wisdom of the blood," deals with the emergence of instinctual fragments across the membrane of the biological self. The welling up of instinct in the form of specific, palpable, and finite fragments serves as a corrective to one's disconnection from the instincts in nebulous spirituality. If the ego strays so far into the abstract and spiritual that an imbalance occurs, the instinctual will come back in the calling of the "honorable beasts." The restoration of essential being proceeds similarly to Freud's principle of the return of the repressed. In a sense, the "fugitive self shut out and howling like a wolf or a coyote under the ideal windows" cries out in response to the deprivation experienced by the repressive self who sits like a "patient ass . . . in a tweed jacket" (*SCAL* 9). The snake who crawls "from a fissure in the earth-wall" (*CP* 349, line 7) of consciousness comes in response to the unmet needs of the punitive self who listens to the voices of his education and throws the stick. Homeostatically, the self blocked from drinking at the wells of sexuality and selfhood throws up "the lowing of the innermost beasts, the feelings, that roam in the forest of the blood" (*STH* 205), which by their lowing require that attention be paid to them.

Whatever problems of self and identity Lawrence may have confronted, one looks to him for his commitment to life and for the courage to respond to the instinctual voices and risk the processes of change that foster life. Claude Bernard, recognizing that internal constancy kept the organism free from external vicissitudes, wrote in *Les Phénomènes de la Vie* (1878): "It is the fixity of the '*milieu intérieur*' which is the condition of free and independent life," and "all the vital mechanisms, however varied they may be, have only one object, that of preserving constant the conditions of life in the internal environment."[7] The physiologist Charles Richet elaborated in 1900, "The living being is stable. It must be so in order not to be destroyed, dissolved, or disintegrated by the colossal forces, often adverse, which surround it. . . . In a sense it is stable because it is modifiable—the slight instability is the necessary condition for the true stability of the organism."[8] Similarly, Lawrence's emphasis on "the trembling instability of the balance" (*STH* 172), which is neither fixed nor inflexible but quick with life, allows for modification and change within the organism. Without this ability to risk creative change, the individual, in Heinz Kohut's self psychology, maintains a sense of psychic balance only by clinging to idealized external representations of archaic "self-objects" (that is, early internalized objects narcissistically invested and incompletely differentiated from the self) instead of developing inner values and ego ideals by which the superego functions "as a source of meaningful internal leadership, guidance, and exhilarating approval, providing benefits in the realm of ego integration and narcissistic homeostasis."[9]

In advocating the courage to break the safe but static balance of habitual ego rigidities and emerge into the vulnerable but dynamic balance of vital life, Lawrence calls upon the same psychological strength that the psychiatrist Frederic Flach describes in his psychological hypothesis of "resilience": "Resilience is the psychobiological strength that enables us to fall apart and reintegrate as required." Flach delineates three dimensions of resilience: psychological, environmental, and biological. The psychological qualities fostering resilience include "flexibility; insightfulness; the ability to form meaningful relationships; knowing how to restore self-esteem when it is diminished (as it always will be from time to time); being able to balance autonomy with a need for and involvement with others; a philosophy of life that provides meaning, even when things may seem hopeless; skill in thinking and acting creatively." Creativity, as a part of resilience, Flach says, "is nothing more or less than the ability to destroy one homeostasis in favor of a new and better one, to reassemble data to form new constructs, to forfeit one way of

---

7. Claude Bernard, quoted in Cannon, *The Wisdom of the Body*, 38.
8. Charles Richet. *Dictionnaire de physiologie*, vol. 4 [10 vols., 1895–1923], (Paris: Baillière et Cie, 1900), 721; quoted in Cannon, "Physiological Regulation of Normal States," 246.
9. Kohut, *The Analysis of the Self*, 299.

looking at or experiencing something for a new and more adaptive one, and to tolerate the ambiguities and distress that inevitably go along with such events." Flach's conception of the environmental aspect of resilience, a view that Lawrence would certainly share, is "that success in completing the stress-activated cycle of disruption and reintegration is greatly enhanced by having a group of supportive people in one's life, at least one of whom serves as confidant." Finally, the biological dimension of resilience can be observed in the correlation that Flach, like Lawrence, sees between psychological and physiological homeostasis. This correlation is not altogether metaphorical: Flach's studies of calcium metabolism in depression led to the discovery "that depressed patients lost calcium from their bodies while depressed and then reversed the trend, retaining calcium and transporting it back into the bone, as they recovered."[10]

For Lawrence, the process of change in the unfolding and enunciation of the self began with an inward journey. For all his travels in the wide world, he knew that the journey to life is not out but down:

If you will go down into yourself, under your surface personality
you will find you have a great desire to drink life direct
from the source. . . .
                    ["The Primal Passions," lines 1–3, *CP* 481]

The willingness to submit to the kind of change Lawrence calls for requires genuine moral courage:

Do you think it is easy to change?
Ah, it is very hard to change and be different.
It means passing through the waters of oblivion.
                    ["Change," lines 1–3, *CP* 727]

Elsewhere Lawrence suggests that change contains new life as well as terrors:

The breath of life is in the sharp winds of change
mingled with the breath of destruction.
                    ["The Breath of Life," lines 1–2, *CP* 698]

Finally, at the end of *Last Poems,* he puts the matter even more unequivocally:

10. Flach, "The Resilience Hypothesis," 5.

Are you willing to be sponged out, erased, cancelled,
made nothing?
Are you willing to be made nothing?
dipped into oblivion?

If not, you will never really change.
                    ["Phoenix," lines 1–5, CP 728]

Lawrence himself, at the time, knew that he was confronting his
own death, and he used this knowledge for continued growth. Even
the change now required of him became the metaphor for resilience
and creativity, in the sense that Frederic Flach defines, "the ability
to destroy one homeostasis in favor of a new and better one," and to
tolerate the ambiguities attendant upon such change.

This study begins the exploration of these themes by considering the
"trembling balance" on the highest level of abstraction in Lawrence's thought and art by relating his dualistic world view to the
two great cultural traditions that Nietzsche calls the Apollonian and
the Dionysian, the former an analytical, discriminatory process of
the conscious mind, developing in a linear, causal sequence toward a
reachable, objective truth; the latter a synthesizing, imaginative
process of the creative unconscious, developing in a cyclic movement
toward a truth not to be defined discursively but to be encompassed
in concrete imagery and presentational symbols. Lawrence's establishment of the theoretical opposition between the two traditions in
The Ladybird is examined in terms of the competition for the soul of
Lady Daphne, a figure for the divided modern self, between her
husband, Major Basil Apsley, a demotic modern variant of the Apollonian archetype, and Count Dionys Psanek, an advocate of return
to the Dionysian mystery of power and creative dissolution as means
toward regeneration.
    The study turns then to an exploration of Lawrence's view of the
artist and the function of the arts. The figure of the artist is examined
in examples of both the true artist and the false or failed artist in a
number of Lawrence's major novels from The White Peacock to Lady
Chatterley's Lover. Typically Lawrence's artist figures are defined in
relation to the male body as artistic subject, to physical being and
assertive individualism, and to a dynamic, "trembling balance" of
conscious and unconscious forces that is essential to both masculine
identity and artistic endeavor. Lawrence predicates his satire of the
false artist not only upon the destruction of psychological homeostasis in his characterological imbalance between instinct and mind but

also upon his harmfully exploiting the artificial but fatal split between blood consciousness and spiritual consciousness. One of Lawrence's chief examples of the true artist is Herman Melville, presented in *Studies in Classic American Literature* as a myth-maker whose work embodies Western man's conflict between mental consciousness and blood consciousness. The "marriage" of Ishmael and Queequeg in *Moby-Dick* was a possible means of reconciling Christian and pagan consciousness, Lawrence thought, had Ishmael not been caught up in Ahab's obsessive quest to destroy the last "blood-being of the white race," Moby Dick. The twentieth-century cinema is Lawrence's major example of a false art. In *The Lost Girl*, stage performances, even of variety acts, are associated with instinctual life and creativity, whereas the movies are associated with neurotic withdrawal into an antilife convention of projective fantasy. Lawrence's comments on film throughout his work, paralleling the early history of cinema, encompass his objections to the fixity and imbalance of the ostensibly moving pictures. The effects of this imbalance are seen in the immaturity of film heroines, the stereotypical standards of beauty and sexuality in the movies, the encouragement by film of the society's preference for the counterfeit to the real, and the mechanization of consciousness through the mechanical repetition of cinematic form, all of which exploit the divisions rather than contributing to the "trembling balance" of human consciousness.

The following three chapters consider Lawrence's treatment of creative change in the theme of the resurrection of the body. For Lawrence, both psychological resilience and renascence of physical being were to be sought in the profound, intuitive knowledge available to man through sensual awareness as a corrective to the imbalance on the side of mind and mental-spiritual knowledge that modern society, with its materialistic values, promoted. Lawrence's psychological myth of the body in *Psychoanalysis and the Unconscious* and *Fantasia of the Unconscious,* which has its roots in the nineteenth-century neurophysiology of Marie-François-Xavier Bichat, in James M. Pryse's occult theory of the chakras, and in the organic scientific concepts of the ancient world, presents a homeostatic theory of psychobiological functioning that becomes the basis for his largely Asclepian medical model of illness and healing. Lawrence's thematic use of his psychobiological theory of the unconscious may be seen in his treatment of touch, which derives its extraordinary power to effect an almost mystical and irrevocable bonding, as in "Hadrian" ("You Touched Me"), from the fact that it activates unconscious instinctual motives, not rationally conceived ideas, into consciousness, thus making both self-confrontation and encounter with the other possible.

From the critical perspective of his psychological writings and other essays, Lawrence's use of the motif of touch in key scenes throughout his fiction, often a metaphor for being "in touch," is examined in several additional categories: touch as the instrument of both identifying and transforming the original instinctual aim in the sublimation of homoerotic motives; touch that has a sometimes disastrously different meaning for the toucher and the touched; and touch as a means of communication in sexual expression. An example of psychological resilience is seen in "The Thorn in the Flesh," in which the protagonist's divided consciousness is healed and psychological homeostasis is partially restored by a combination of developmental change through sexual experience and an attitude of acceptance in the area most resistant to change. Bachmann's acrophobia, which at several points parallels the agoraphobia in Freud's case of little Hans, is an impediment that he learns to accept and live with. But Bachmann's psychosexual development, considered in Erik Erikson's terms, is manifested as his sexual relationship with Emilie enables him to master his overwhelming sense of shame and to gain a measure of autonomy.

An examination of the pattern of rebirth encompassed in Lawrence's use of the phoenix myth throughout his canon introduces a study of the symbolic functions of image, myth, and allusion in three late works of fiction. The phoenix, the emblem by which Lawrence sought to reconcile his antinomies and encompass the central metaphysical concerns of his life, recurs throughout his work in a way that recalls its function as the culminating image in the process of alchemical transformation, a pattern of rebirth through commitment to the flames of experience, the reduction from traditional wisdom to essential ash, and the emergence of new being through acceptance of creative change. A discussion of the affinities between Lawrence's thought and the religioscience of alchemy, especially as interpreted psychologically by Carl G. Jung, forms the basis for a study of alchemy and *The Plumed Serpent*, Lawrence's most occult novel, which parallels in its development the structural and thematic balance of the imagery and procedural stages of the alchemical opus. In *Lady Chatterley's Lover* and elsewhere, Lawrence employs scenes of the type that James Joyce calls "epiphany" and Lawrence calls "visionary experience" as catalysts of creative change. Although the two writers approach these scenes from opposing theoretical positions and arrive at different thematic insights, the epiphanic pattern in Lawrence is structurally consistent with that in Joyce. Such scenes as the Chatterleys' visit to the denuded knoll, Clifford's motorized wheelchair stalled in the wood, Connie's vision of Mellors bathing (which is comparable to the bathing-girl epiphany in Joyce's *Portrait of the Artist as a Young Man*), and the pheasant-chicks scene culminate in profound epiphanic insights that propel Connie from stagnation toward meaningful existential growth. Lawrence's ultimate myth of the resurrection of the body emerges in *The Escaped Cock* principally by means of demythologizing the Christian story by setting it in creative balance with the myth of Osiris and Isis and by altering the context of Biblical allusions from Protestant Christianity to the religion of the blood.

These varied, seemingly disparate areas of Lawrence's work, examined through the informing metaphor of the "trembling balance," reveal his conception as functioning on a ladder of experience ranging from the relatively abstract, theoretical plane of Lawrence's dualism, his critical tenets, and his psychological theories of the unconscious, to the concrete presentation of dynamic balance in his literary work, especially in the fiction. In Lawrence's conception, the dynamic experience of life's quickness necessarily involves giving up static equilibrium in the ebb and flow of human consciousness between self and other, bringing about a sequence of stability, instability, resilience, and creative change. A comparison of Lawrence and Freud places Lawrence's ideas in the context of their development in dialogue with the new science of psychoanalysis and, for all their differences, emphasizes the Asclepian qualities of healing to be found in both.

2

Lawrence's Dualism:
The Apollonian-Dionysian Polarity and
The Ladybird

Lawrence's conception of the "trembling balance" may be thought of as an organicist ladder encompassing various levels of abstraction, ranging from the concrete and particular presentation of shifting homeostatic forces, instinctual, emotional, or social, within the individual or in the relationship between the self and the other or others, to the dynamic polarity of abstract principles, considered not as disembodied mechanistic entities but as dynamic forces that affect individual attitudes, choices, and commitments to life. I begin by examining Lawrence's conception of this polarity at its highest level of abstraction, by considering his dualistic world view in relation to the two great cultural traditions that Nietzsche calls the Apollonian and the Dionysian.

The American novelist Henry Miller, in his fragment "Creative Death," describes D. H. Lawrence's work as "altogether one of symbol and metaphor," with a world view characterized by its dualism: "Phoenix, Crown, Rainbow, Plumed Serpent, all these symbols," Miller writes, "center about the same obsessive idea: *the resolution of two opposites in the form of a mystery.*"[1] Miller then proceeds

---

1. Miller, *The Wisdom of the Heart*, 5. The terms of Lawrence's dualism are set forth systematically in Daleski, *The Forked Flame*, 18–41.

briefly to relate Lawrence's dualism to Friedrich Nietzsche's concept of the dialectical processes of thought lying behind creative art, the opposing processes that Nietzsche denoted by the names of their classical prototypes as the Apollonian and the Dionysian. For the moment, passing over the many individual and idiosyncratic differences with which the work of any imaginative writer, such as Lawrence, is concerned, I should like to explore Lawrence's characteristic way of perceiving the world as opposing forces contained in a "trembling balance" by relating it more fully to those two broad intellectual and cultural traditions in Western thought.

In his youthful manifesto, *The Birth of Tragedy* (1872), Nietzsche writes: "A great deal will have been won for the science of aesthetics when we shall have succeeded in not merely recognizing intellectually, but directly and clearly seeing, that the development of art depends on the dual influence of Apollonian and Dionysian forces— as reproduction depends on the sexes, in their unrelenting conflict and only occasional—periodic—reconciliation."[2] Identifying the two Greek divinities of art as figures eloquently embodying the "great division, with respect to both source and aim, between the art of the sculptor, Apollonian art, and the non-pictorial art, music, of Dionysus," Nietzsche says: "The two impulses, different as they are, were carried along side by side, generally in open opposition, provoking each other to ever new, more mighty births through which to perpetuate the war of a pair of opposites that the shared word 'art' only apparently overbridges; until at last, through a metaphysical miracle of the Hellenic 'will,' the two were united, and in that pairing generated the art that was as Dionysian as Apollonian: Attic tragedy."[3]

In a subsequent figure, Nietzsche identifies these opposing forces with the separate physiological and aesthetic worlds of *dream*—in its pre-Freudian, Apollonian sense as a formal, pictorial given—and *intoxication,* in its Dionysian sense as inward, psychic experience. *Dream,* in Nietzsche's usage, is analogous to the outer world of concrete perceptions ordered by spatial aesthetic relationships. *Intoxication,* on the other hand, is analogous to the inner world of psychic phenomena involving temporal aesthetic relationships. The arts of

2. Friedrich Nietzsche, *Die Geburt der Tragödie,* in *Werke,* I, 19, as trans. and quoted in Campbell, *The Masks of God: Creative Mythology,* 334. Jessie Chambers, in *D. H. Lawrence: A Personal Record,* 120, says that Lawrence began reading Nietzsche in the library in Croydon. See also Humma, "D. H. Lawrence as Friedrich Nietzsche," 110–20; Schneider, *D. H. Lawrence: The Artist as Psychologist,* 45–57; and Colin Milton, *Lawrence and Nietzsche.*

3. Nietzsche, in Campbell, *The Masks of God: Creative Mythology,* 334.

Apollo, as lord of light, "the glorious divine image of the *principium individuationis* itself, in whose gesture and glances the whole delight and wisdom of the 'world illusion' speaks to us," Nietzsche designates as sculpture and epic poetry. The arts of Dionysus, as lord of darkness, the divine image of the Eleusinian mysteries, are music, the dance, and lyric poetry. If Apollonian forces are at work in the rational and pictorial qualities of these Dionysian arts, then Dionysian forces are to be found, for example, in "the author's craftsmanly concern for the musical effects of his prose, its rhythms, verbal tones, and spheres of emotional association," as in leitmotivs.[4]

The Apollonian principle of individuation in consciousness involves the rational faculty of logical reason. But what happens when, with horror, as Schopenhauer describes it, the individual "suddenly finds himself in error with respect to his interpretation of the forms of appearance"—that is, "when the logic of causality . . . seems to have been fractured by an exception"? Joseph Campbell has observed: "The transition then is from an aesthetic (Apollonian) to a properly religious dimension of experience (or, in Nietzsche's terminology, toward Dinoysian rapture); and the sense of awe, dread, or terror that is then experienced is something different altogether from any 'kinetic,' natural loathing or terror before an odious or dangerous object." What happens, in short, is "a break in the tissue of temporal-spatial-causal relationships," which results in the "chilling . . . sense of the immediacy of something . . . that is inconceivable," whether it be god, ghost, or void.[5]

The immediate effect of this transport upon the individual is, in other words, the sense of the *numinous*. Rudolf Otto, in his theological study *The Idea of the Holy*, identifies "this experience of awe, of dread, as reciprocal to the Kantian x, the source and prime ingredient of religion—all religion: an experience *sui generis*, which is lost, however, when identified with the Good, the True, Love, Mercy, the Law, this conceptualized deity or that." The sense of the numinous cannot be taught; it can only be experienced.[6]

The subsequent effect of this transport upon society is the sense of unity in a higher commonalty. As Nietzsche explains: "Under the magic of the Dionysian force, not only does the bond between man and man again close together, but alienated, hostile, or suppressed Nature celebrates her festival of reconciliation with her lost son, man. . . . With flowers and garlands is the car all strewn of Diony-

4. Campbell, *The Masks of God: Creative Mythology,* 333–34.
5. Ibid., 352.
6. Ibid., 353. See Otto, *The Idea of the Holy,* 5–7.

sus: in its span stride panther and tiger." Nietzsche gives Schiller's
"Paean to Joy" in Beethoven's Ninth Symphony as an example:
"Now each, in the Gospel of World Harmony, feels himself to be not
only united with his neighbor, reconciled and blended, but one—as
though the veil of *māyā* had been rent apart and now only fluttered
in shreds around the mysterious primordial One. Mankind, singing,
dancing, professes itself to be a member of a higher commonalty."[7]

Despite this celebration of man's universal brotherhood, however,
Nietzsche did not, as Walter Kaufmann observes, thereby endorse
the Dionysian per se, but only the synthesis of this passion with the
Apollonian "principle of individuation." The Dionysian alone, far
from being glorified, is pictured throughout as a "fever" that, left
unchecked, led to "sexual licentiousness." As Nietzsche puts it, "precisely the most savage beasts of nature were unfettered here, to the
point of that disgusting mixture of voluptuousness and cruelty
which always seemed to me the proper 'witches' brew." Only the
Apollonian principle of the Greeks could "control this destructive
disease, . . . harness the Dionysian flood, and . . . use it creatively."
Thus, Nietzsche is already moving toward that principle of synthesis
which, in his later works, would be called Dionysian. As Kaufmann
points out, the Dionysus who is the opposite of Apollo in Nietzsche's
first book is not the same as that of the "Dionysus versus the Crucified" of his last: "The later Dionysus is the synthesis of the two forces
which are represented by Dionysus and Apollo in *The Birth of Tragedy*."[8] As Norman O. Brown observes of the Dionysian artist, "Instead of negating, he affirms the dialectical unity of the great instinctual opposites: Dionysus reunites male and female, Self and Other,
life and death."[9]

In the earlier book, Nietzsche sets up two diametrically opposed
cultural traditions between which, at this point, it should be possible
to draw several generic distinctions.

The Apollonian tradition, concerned with exterior objects that oc-
cupy linear space or with externalized mental conceptions, elevates
as "real" that mode of perception characterized by the objectifying
intellect. The ideal of intellectual beauty becomes, then, the rational
faculty, making analytical discriminations in the conscious mind. In
this mode, the intellectual seeker detaches himself from the subjective to project himself in quest of the light of truth in the outer
world. This tradition assumes a linear development in a causal se-

7. Nietzsche, in Campbell: *The Masks of God: Creative Mythology*, 337–38.
8. Kaufmann, *Nietzsche: Philosopher, Psychologist, Antichrist*, 108–9.
9. Brown, *Life against Death*, 175.

quence to be described in discriminatory language—as in the terminology of the sciences, social sciences, and technology—with a fixed, definite, objective truth as a reachable end point.

The Dionysian tradition, on the contrary, concerned with interior perceptions, elevates as "real" that mode of perception characterized by the creative imagination. The ideal of intellectual beauty becomes, now, the intuitive faculty, making synthesizing comparisons in the creative unconscious. In this mode, the intellectual seeker incorporates elements of the outer world into the inner world, to seek the truth darkly by plunging into the cyclic night within the self. This tradition assumes a cyclic development in which the intuitive perception of truth can never be described in discriminatory language but only, as in the writings of mystics and madmen, in the concrete imagery of what Susanne K. Langer calls *presentational symbols*.[10]

Returning to Lawrence in the context of the opposing creative modes articulated by Nietzsche, one recognizes in his characteristic themes and forms a similar dualism. Simplistic reading tends to attribute to Lawrence a one-sided, exclusively Dionysian sexual ecstasy, primitive religiosity, and intellectual irrationalism. In Lawrence's view, it is true, the times demanded a reassertion of these Dionysian elements to correct the imbalance on the side of Apollonian forces in decadent form—the imbalance on the side of spiritual will, rationalized faith, and sterile reason—which had resulted from the unholy wedlock of the industrial revolution and Christian idealism: the one divorced from natural cycles, the other divorced from religious cycles, and both united in the service of the utilitarian ethic that defined creativity as production, and progress as the proliferation of technology. But Lawrence no more advocated an imbalance on the opposite side than Nietzsche did. In every area of his thought—historiography, theology, psychology, literary criticism—Lawrence makes his plea for a balanced polarity between the Apollonian and the Dionysian; and the effect of much of his fiction derives from the dialectical tension between the two.

In the short novel *The Ladybird* (1923), Lawrence established the theoretical opposition between the Apollonian and the Dionysian in fictional terms. The radical contrast that he sets up rather overtly in this strange story may be useful in illustrating a conflict that is worked out with greater subtlety, complexity, and ambiguity in Lawrence's major fiction. In the novella, the divine and the terrible, in the person of a mysterious stranger, make an incursion into the

10. Langer, *Philosophy in a New Key*, 236.

ordinary life of a young aristocratic British wife as a first step toward reasserting an ancient mythic power as a principle of charismatic leadership to regenerate the war-wasted modern world. If we
stand back from the complex surface of the story, in which myths
from several different cultures are merged syncretically and the
mythic and the actual modulate into each other in an atmosphere of
suspended time, what we may see is an abstract design, a Laurentian triad in which two male figures, the one of light, the other of
darkness, compete for the soul of modern woman.

Lady Daphne's prototype in Greek mythology is a nymph, the
daughter of a river (the Pēnēus or the Ladon) and the beloved of both
Apollo and the mortal Leucippus. When Leucippus, disguised as a
woman, wooed Daphne, he was discovered and slain by the nymphs.
Still pursued by Apollo, who tried to ravish her, Daphne appealed to
the goddess Hera, who changed her into the laurel tree, which remained sacred to Apollo. Although the myth is cited in Freudian
psychology "as symbolizing a girl's instinctive horror of the sexual
act," Robert Graves says that Daphne's name is "a contraction of
Daphoene, 'the bloody one," the goddess in orgiastic mood whose
priestesses, the Maenads, chewed laurel leaves as an intoxicant."[11]
The modern Lady Daphne, in Lawrence's story, has the same division within herself. From her father's "desperate race," she derives
her own wild energy of the blood; from her mother's upbringing she
learns "to admire only the good" (L 47). For Lawrence, this conflict
between blood and will would be etiology enough for almost any
malady. Her conscious will determines that she be gentle and benevo-
lent, "but her blood had its revenge on her." She is associated with
death and metaphysical illness: "Her husband was missing in the
East. Her baby had been born dead. Her two darling brothers were
dead. And she was ill, always ill." That her sickness is intended to be
generalized as that of the modern world is evident from the narrator's statement "[s]o it is with strong natures to-day: shattered from
the inside" (L 46–47). Living on bitter hope, which "had become
almost a curse to her," Daphne anticipates the apocalypse, almost as
if she perceives, though she cannot articulate it, that the old order
must be irrevocably ended before a new one can emerge: "Why could
it not all be just clean disaster, and have done with it? This dilly-
dallying with despair was worse than despair" (L 48).

Major Basil Apsley, Lady Daphne's husband, in his slightly sim-
pleminded humanism, resembles Apollo not so much as he does

---

11. See Harvey, ed., *Oxford Companion to Classical Literature*, 131, and Graves,
The Greek Myths, 1:18.

Leucippus, his war scar suggesting his symbolic slaying. As a fusion of the two figures, he represents what has become of the Apollonian impulse in the modern world: In the decline of its divine and shaping as well as its erotic and heroic functions, its conscious humanism and commitment to technology support a war machine. As "a commoner, son of one of the most famous politicians in England" (L 46),[12] Basil is associated with democratic egalitarian politics, the logical outcome of which, unforeseen by the respectable older generation of leaders like his father or Lady Daphne's father, Earl Beveridge, has been a debasement of culture and the reduction of all to the lowest common denominator in the hysteria of war: "the degrading spectacle of the so-called patriots who had been howling their mongrel indecency in the public face. These mongrels had held the Press and the British public in abeyance for almost two years. Their one aim was to degrade and humiliate anything that was proud or dignified remaining in England" (L 92). Yet the ordeal of war is, for Basil, a refining process through which he believes that he has arrived at "a higher state of consciousness, and therefore of life. And so, of course, at a higher plane of love. A surprisingly higher plane of love, that you had never suspected the existence of before" (L 85). That this "higher plane" is rather lower, in Lawrence's eyes, is made graphically clear as Basil, like the ancient druidic poets of Graves's *White Goddess* who worship Cynthia or Diana or "la belle dame sans merci," kneels before Daphne in a rapture of courtly love adoration that is really designed to keep her in her place on the pedestal of childlike chastity and out of his marriage bed: ". . . —you perfect child! But that is the beauty of a woman like you: you are so superb and beyond worship, and then such an exquisite naïve child. Who could help worshipping you and loving you: immortal and mortal together. . . . Ah, darling, you are more goddess than child, you long, limber Isis with sacred hands. White, white, and immortal! . . . I *can't* help kneeling before you, darling. I am no more than a sacrifice to you, an offering. I *wish* I could die in giving myself to you, give you all my blood on your altar, for ever" (L 81). Basil's ultimate renunciation of sex in favor of a "pure love" suggests the final abstraction of Apollo, Daphne's would-be ravisher, into pure spirit.

12. On one level, *The Ladybird* is a roman à clef in which Lady Cynthia Asquith figures as Lady Daphne; her husband, the Honorable Herbert Asquith, son of Herbert Henry Asquith (the prime minister from 1908 to 1916) who saw active service in France and Flanders (1914–18), figures as Major Basil Apsley; and Lawrence himself is imaginatively portrayed as Count Dionys.

The third member of the triad, Count Johann Dionys Psanek, has no counterpart in the original myth of Daphne and Apollo but is imported from another to supplant Apollo as Daphne's pursuer. His name, his appearance, his language underline his function in the story to reassert the Dionysian mystery. It is appropriate for Lawrence's figure of male dominance that his classical prototype, the son of Zeus and the mortal woman Semele, was called the "twice-born." His mother was struck by lightning from Zeus and perished, but Zeus took his son and carried him in his own body until he was ready for the world. Deriving from two realms, the mortal and the eternal, Dionysus remained the god of duality and paradox. He was a god of fertility, appearing in the spring to awaken the energy of life, bringing forth the vegetation of the season and evoking in his followers a divine madness in which they tore their victims apart and ate their flesh. According to Walter F. Otto, Dionysus brought no illusions or fantasies but "the elemental forms of everything that is creative, everything that is destructive" so that, in the divine madness he induced, not only human laws but "even the dimensions of time and space are no longer valid."[13]

Count Dionys's middle name is, of course, derived from the god's. His surname, Psanek, he says, means "outlaw" (L 59); it also contains anagrams of both "asp" and "snake," and, as John B. Humma points out, of "Pan" and "sane" as well.[14] Dionysus's epiphany at the winter solstice was as a serpent, and his followers wore serpent-wreathed crowns.[15] When Lady Daphne was seventeen, Count Dionys had given her a thimble ringed with a serpent. That he considers giving up his first two names and retaining only his last suggests which part of the Dionysian duality he wants to emphasize (L 53, 59).

Imagery and symbol associate Count Dionys throughout with the Dionysian nature religion and the rituals of its annual cycle. One of the major motifs on which the novella turns is that of death and rebirth. When Lady Beveridge discovers Count Dionys among the wounded prisoners in the hospital, the "yellowish swarthy paste of his flesh" seems drawn "on the face of one dead," but " his black eyes watched her from that terrible remoteness of death" (L 45). This condition, as much metaphysical as physical, makes him almost acquiesce in death, but images of life in the fecund darkness of the earth suggest that, however painful it may be, he will consent to

13. Otto, *Dionysus: Myth and Cult*, 95–96.
14. Humma, "Lawrence's 'The Ladybird' and the Enabling Image," 222.
15. Otto, *Dionysus: Myth and Cult*, 95–96. See, especially, plate 6, opposite p. 94, depicting a maenad in serpent-wreathed crown.

rebirth. When Lady Daphne visits him in the hospital, he tells her: "No, no! No, no! If I could be buried deep, very deep down, where everything is forgotten! But they draw me up, back to the surface. I would not mind if they buried me alive, if it were very deep, and dark, and the earth heavy above" (*L* 53). Dionys calls himself "a subject of the sun" and says, "I belong to the fire-worshippers" (*L* 57). But his is not the bright sun of Apollo but the dark sun of the underworld: "The true fire is invisible," he tells Lady Daphne. "Flame, and the red fire we see burning, has its back to us." It is here that Lawrence first elaborates the image that was to become a major symbol in *The Plumed Serpent:*

> Well, then, the yellowness of sunshine—light itself—that is only the glancing aside of the real original fire. You know that is true. There would be no light if there was no refraction, no bits of dust and stuff to turn the dark fire into visibility. You know that's a fact. And that being so, even the sun is dark. It is only his jacket of dust that makes him visible. You know that too. And the true sunbeams coming towards us flow darkly, a moving darkness of the genuine fire. The sun is dark, the sunshine flowing to us is dark. And light is only the inside-turning away of the sun's directness that was coming to us. [*L* 67]

The Apollonian-Dionysian polarity is clear: "The true living world of fire is dark, throbbing, darker than blood. Our luminous world that we go by is only the reverse of this" (*L* 67). Now he tells Lady Daphne, "The year has turned—the sun must shine at last, even in England" (*L* 56). Basil and Lady Daphne visit the Count at Vornich Hall at the winter solstice just before Christmas (*L* 83), and he visits them as Thoresway in the spring (*L* 93).

There is an element of Dionysian madness in Count Dionys. In one of his conversations with Lady Daphne he admits to talking absurdly (*L* 54), a suggestion that his speech derives from his inner perceptions of reality, not from the logic of the outer world. He tells her that "the Psaneks have had a ladybird in their bonnets for many hundred years," a reference to the family crest, and Lady Daphne replies, "Quite, quite mad" (*L* 61). Privately she thinks him "An impertinent little fellow! A little madman, really. A little outsider" (*L* 69), and she determines to keep her mind on her well-bred husband.

Dionys associates the course of his blood with the organic cycle of nature, with yellow chestnuts and chattering squirrels, but not with the world of man. Following the Dionysian cycle, he has already made his journey over the North Sea to "the Eskimo in Siberia, and across the Tundras" where "a white sea-hawk makes a nest on a high stone": "It is not only a world of men, Lady Daphne" (*L* 59). The count's swart, aboriginal appearance (*L* 45) and demonic visage (*L* 84) link him with the underworld, and the devil in his body (*L* 55) identifies him with Hades. He associates himself with the god of destruction:

> ". . . I found the God who pulls things down: especially the things that men have put up. Do they not say that life is a search after God, Lady Daphne? I have found my God."
> "The god of destruction," she said, blanching.
> "Yes—not the devil of destruction, but the god of destruction. The blessed god of destruction. . . . The god of anger, who throws down the steeples and the factory chimneys. Ah, Lady Daphne, he is a man's God. I have found my God, Lady Daphne." [*L* 73]

With the factories of industrial civilization out of the way, along with the steeples of the traditional Christian faith that supports the established Western world order, Dionys can establish a new faith on power rather than on love—or, more accurately, on an elision of power and love, not Christian, submissive love but "profane" love that is elemental and subversive. As if to propose a new creed, he hisses darkly, "his eyes dilated with a ring of fire," an incantation of power: "I believe in the power of my red, dark heart. God has put the hammer in my breast—the little eternal hammer. Hit—hit—hit! It hits on the world of man. It hits, it hits! And it hears the thin sound of cracking. The thin sound of cracking. Hark!" (*L* 47). As Daphne listens, he continues, a strange laugh on his face and a shivering, delicate crackling sound in the air: "You hear it? Yes? Oh, may I live long! May I live long, so that my hammer may strike and strike, and the cracks go deeper, deeper! Ah, the world of man! Ah, the joy, the passion in every heart-beat! Strike home, strike true, strike sure. Strike to destroy it. Strike! Strike! To destroy the world of man. Ah, God. Ah, God, prisoner of peace. Do I not know you, Lady Daphne? Do I not? Do I not?" (*L* 74–75).

I have quoted this passage at some length because I want to draw a parallel and a contrast with the incantation of negatives by which Roderick Usher impels the lady Madeline in Poe's story to fall upon him in an incestuous embrace of death that fissures the house of Usher so that it literally sinks beneath the surface of the tarn:

"Not hear it—yes, I hear it, and *have* heard it. Long—long—long—many minutes, many hours, many days, have I heard it—yet I dared not—oh, pity me, miserable wretch that I am!—I dared not—I *dared* not speak! *We have put her living in the tomb!* Said I not that my senses were acute? I *now* tell you that I heard her first feeble movements in the hollow coffin. I heard them—many, many days ago—yet I dared not—*I dared not speak!* And now—tonight—Ethelred—ha! ha!—the breaking of the hermit's door, and the death-cry of the dragon, and the clangor of the shield!—say, rather, the rending of her coffin, and the grating of the iron hinges of her prison, and her struggles within the coppered archway of the vault! Oh whither shall I fly? Will she not be here anon? Is she not hurrying to upbraid me for my haste? Have I not heard her footstep on the stair? Do I not distinguish that heavy and horrible beating of her heart? Madman!"—here he sprang furiously to his feet, and shrieked out his syllables, as if in the effort he were giving up his soul—*"Madman! I tell you that she now stands without the door!"*[16]

Lawrence's passage in *The Ladybird* employs, without improving on, Poe's technique of incantatory repetition and echoes certain of Poe's key words and phrases. Poe's "Not hear it" becomes Lawrence's "You hear it?" Poe's "long—long—long" becomes Lawrence's "hit—hit—hit." Poe's "clangor of the shield" and "grating of the iron hinges" are replaced by Lawrence's "thin sound of cracking." The prison of the "coppered archway" of Madeline's vault becomes the prison of peace that encompasses Lady Daphne. The incantation of negatives (the word *not* occurs eleven times in Poe's paragraph) is transmuted into the reiterated image of striking (the word *hit* occurs six times and the word *strike* eight times in the Lawrence passage) and is echoed in Count Dionys's "Do I not? Do I not?" with which the excerpt ends. The frenzied eye of the poet, the tone of madness in his voice, and the atmosphere of death that surrounds him are focal elements in both passages.

Yet in several significant respects the two selections are not equivalent. Both their heroes, Roderick Usher and Count Dionys Psanek, seem literally to incant their women from their premature

16. Poe, "The Fall of the House of Usher," 416.

burial in the tomb and to impel them to an embrace of death in an underworld rendezvous. But Usher dominates by sheer will, Dionys by charismatic power. The distinction is more than an academic subtlety, for the result is not, ultimately, the same. Lawrence comments in the essay on Poe in *Studies in Classic American Literature* (1923) that

> the rhythm of American art-activity is dual.
> 1. A disintegrating and sloughing of the old consciousness.
> 2. The forming of a new consciousness underneath.
>
> [*SCAL* 65]

As an examination of Lawrence's theoretical formulations in historiography, theology, and psychology shows, this dual rhythm of creation also characterizes his thinking in other areas. Moreover, Lawrence's personal emblem, the phoenix, incorporates the same principle in the cyclic pattern of destruction and resynthesis. As he interprets the myth in the third essay in "The Crown" (1915), the phoenix attains perfection in wisdom as natural aristocrat, but, rather than maintaining "her own tight ego," she commits herself to the flames of experience; thus, she is reduced to the essential ash from which a new phoenix emerges to rise toward the same zenith of perfection and to the same consummation in flame (*RDP* 270). In *The Ladybird,* the principle of creative evolution is associated with the ladybird of the Psanek family crest, which, Dionys says, "is a descendant of the Egyptian scarabaeus," connecting him with the pharaohs. In a discussion between Lord and Lady Beveridge, Basil and Daphne, and Count Dionys, Lord Beveridge observes "that the beetle rolling a little ball of dung before him . . . must have suggested to the Egyptians the First Principle that set the globe rolling. And so the scarab became the symbol of the creative principle—or something like that." Count Dionys suggests, "Perhaps they meant that it was the principle of decomposition which first set the ball rolling" (*L* 97). The count's reply reveals the scarab to be an emblem of the cycle of disintegration and renewal.

As Lawrence sees it, Poe is concerned with only one side of the duality. Whereas "Fenimore Cooper has the two vibrations going on together," Poe has only one, the disintegrative vibration. That makes him "rather a scientist than an artist" (*SCAL* 65). In terms of the dialectic with which this study is concerned, Lawrence's commitment is to the Dionysian cycle, which follows destruction with a new synthesis. Poe, on the other hand, offers an example of Apollonian rationalism in decadent form, analytic reduction by mechanistic will. He is concerned analytically with psychic processes—or, in Lawrence's words, "with the disintegration-processes of his own psyche"—in tales that are "a concatenation of cause and effect" (*SCAL* 65). Lawrence's is not, then, a hellish vision in the same sense that Poe's is: In Poe the dark forces only destroy, in Lawrence they are ultimately the source of rebirth as well.

To return to *The Ladybird* in this context, Count Dionys, as natural aristocrat, is a spokesman for charismatic power; and Basil, as democratic egalitarian, is a spokesman for Christian love. Dionys is the prophet, if not the agent, of a kind of leadership that Lawrence proposes as a possible means of regeneration for modern Europe, first by finishing the destruction of worn-out cultural traditions already begun in the reductive process of the war, then by resynthesizing civilization around the dynamic center of "the man whose soul is born single, able to be alone, to choose and to command," to whom the masses will turn "[b]ecause we see a light in your face, and a burning on your mouth" (*L* 89). To Lawrence's way of thinking, this is not fascism, which he characterizes as bullying by mechanical will, but charismatic leadership of the sort he speaks of in the last chapter of *Movements in European History:*

> [A] great united Europe of productive working people, all materially equal, will never be able to continue and remain firm unless it unites also round one great chosen figure, some hero who can lead a great war, as well as administer a wide peace. It all depends on the will of the people. But the will of the people must concentrate in one figure, who is also supreme over the will of the people. He must be chosen, but at the same time responsible to God alone. Here is a problem of which a stormy future will have to evolve a solution. [*MEH* 252]

Those who have lived through the "stormy future" that Lawrence foresaw are likely to find his leadership proposition rather less promising than he did. Lady Daphne, who has a feminist side, perceives immediately that, in a system where men cannot criticize their chosen leader, women will no longer be able to criticize their husbands (*L* 90). Significantly, it is Major Basil Apsley who recognizes that "there is really an allowable distinction between responsible power and bullying" and that Count Dionys means the former (*L* 91).

Count Dionys speaks for a quasi-religious relationship between the Dionysian leader and his followers. Lady Daphne's Apollonian consciousness, on the other hand, seems "to make a great gulf between her and the lower classes, the unconscious classes. . . . She could never meet in real contact anyone but a super-conscious, finished being like herself: or like her husband" (L 99). As Lawrence's representative of the British upper class, then, she must make her journey of initiation into the unconscious with Count Dionys as her guide. Unlike Roderick Usher, who impels the lady Madeline from the tomb by a litany of negatives, Dionys, "half-unconscious," calls Daphne to his room by crooning "in a small, high-pitched, squeezed voice . . . a curious noise: almost the sound of a man who is going to be executed" (L 99). The song Dionys sings in his native dialect is of "a woman who was a swan, and who loved a hunter by the marsh. So she became a woman and married and had three children. Then in the night one night the king of the swans called to her to come back, or else he would die. So slowly she turned into a swan again, and slowly she opened her wide, wide wings, and left her husband and her children" (L 102). This Dionysian parable—which has affinities with *Swan Lake*, with such ballads as "The Great Silkie of Sule Skerry" (Child, no. 113), as well as with fairy tales, such as "Beauty and the Beast"—serves to associate Count Dionys with the principle of divine destruction by comparing him to the swan, which Lawrence identifies in "The Crown" as "one of the symbols of divine corruption. With its reptile feet buried in the ooze and mud, its voluptuous form yielding and embracing the ooze of water, its beauty white and cold and terrifying, like the dead beauty of the moon, like the water-lily, the sacred lotus, its neck and head like the snake, it is for us a flame of the cold white fire of flux, the phosphorescence of corruption, the salt, cold burning of the sea which corrodes all it touches, coldly reduces every sun-built form to ash, to the original elements" (RDP 293).

In interpreting the significance of the sexual consummation between Daphne and Dionys, one should bear in mind Lawrence's statement in "The Crown" that "when a man seeks a woman, he seeks not a consummation in union, but a frictional reduction" (RDP 283). The reduction, however, should be followed by rebirth. The image of the dark sun, which is associated with the scarab symbolism of the Psanek family crest, is reinforced in the scene in which Lady Daphne visits the count's room. When her fingertips merely touched his arm, "a flame went over him that left him no more a man" but the figure of a deity: "He was something seated in flame, in flame unconscious, seated erect, like an Egyptian King-god in the statues" (L 103). The allusion is possibly to Khepri, who was identified with the rising sun and thus with the eternal renewal of life.[17]

17. Posenet, *A Dictionary of Egyptian Civilization*, 252.

Lady Daphne kneels involuntarily and presses her face and hands against his feet and ankles. The words of the song also associate Dionys with Zeus, "the king of the swans." Where Daphne is concerned, one may ask with Yeats, "Did she put on his knowledge with his power / Before the indifferent beak could let her drop?" ("Leda and the Swan," lines 14–15).[18]

Count Dionys's knowledge is what Lawrence calls "blood consciousness," the ancient, dark, mysterious power that Lawrence reasserts, not as the sole value, but as a corrective to the imbalance on the side of the modern, light, rational "mental consciousness." As Lawrence says in his essay "Nathaniel Hawthorne and *The Scarlet Letter*" in *Studies in Classic American Literature:*

> Blood-consciousness overwhelms, obliterates, and annuls mind-consciousness.
>
> Mind-consciousness extinguishes blood-consciousness, and consumes the blood.
>
> We are all of us conscious in both ways. And the two ways are antagonistic in us.
>
> They will always remain so.
>
> That is our cross. [*SCAL* 85]

There is a sense in which the mind-conscious Lady Daphne does "put on his knowledge with his power." Like such Laurentian heroines as Kate Leslie in *The Plumed Serpent* and Connie in *Lady Chatterley's Lover,* she is regenerated sexually and integrated psychologically by her contact with the destructive power of the blood-conscious male: "She was so still, like a virgin girl. And it was this quiet, intact quality of virginity in her which puzzled [her husband] most" (*L* 105), so that Basil renounces sexual relations with her in preference for a "pure love" reminiscent of medieval Mariolatry.

Count Dionys, employing an ancient metaphorical link between sexual orgasm and death, says to Daphne:

> "Now you are mine. In the dark you are mine. And when you die you are mine. . . . In the night, in the dark, and in death,

---

18. Millett, *The Vultures and the Phoenix,* 137–40, discusses Lawrence's use of the Leda myth in the paintings *Leda* and *Singing of Swans* in relation to the swan as a corruptive image in such poems as "Leda," "Swan," "Fight! O my Young Men," "Give Us Gods," and "Won't it be Strange—?" The two water color paintings are also reproduced in *Paintings of D. H. Lawrence,* ed. Levy; see *Leda,* color plate XVI, 77; and *Singing of Swans,* black and white plate no. 24, 97.

you are mine. And that is for ever. No matter if I must leave
you. I shall come again from time to time. In the dark you are
mine. But in the day I cannot claim you. I have no power in
the day, and no place. So remember. When darkness comes, I
shall always be in the darkness of you. . . . So don't forget—
you are the night wife of the ladybird, while you live and even
when you die." [L 104]

The metaphysical pun turns on the principle of reduction shared by
death and sex. As Lawrence puts it in "The Crown," "In sex, we have
plunged the quick of creation deep into the cold flux of reduction,
corruption, till the quick is extinguished" (RDP 290). Picking up the
swan image, he elaborates: "When the swan first rose out of the
marshes, it was a glory of creation. But when we turn back, we seek
its consummation again, it is a fearful flower of corruption" (RDP
293). The narrative song Dionys sings suggests just such a turning
back.

The principle that Henry Miller calls "creative death" has long
been recognized as a central Laurentian concept. One critic, Colin
Clarke, in River of Dissolution, has explored extensively the implications of Lawrence's related concepts of destruction, dissolution, decomposition, corruption, and reduction, concepts with which not all
Lawrence scholars are comfortable.[19] My purpose in introducing
these ideas here is to identify the "destructive element," to borrow
Stein's phrase in Conrad's Lord Jim, as a living element in which
Lawrence's most vital characters must, as Stein advises, immerse
themselves. As Clarke correctly perceives, "What is most in question . . . is the distinction between corruption that is creative and
corruption that is not."[20] Lawrence himself provides a partial answer to the question in "The Crown" in a passage cited briefly by
Clarke: "And corruption, like growth, is only divine when it is pure,
when all is given up to it. If it be experienced as a controlled activity
within an intact whole, this is vile. . . . When corruption goes on
within the living womb, this is unthinkable" (RDP 293). It has
seemed to some critics that Clarke blurs the distinction between the
two forms of corruption, the one leading to life, the other to death,[21]
in such passages as the following:

19. See, for example, Spilka, "Lawrence Up-tight," 252–67, and the replies by
Ford, Kermode, and Clarke in "Critical Exchange," 54–70.

20. Clarke, River of Dissolution, 70.

21. Rossman, for example, states this view in "Four Versions of D. H. Lawrence,"
55.

I have emphasized . . . that in Lawrence's best work the negative potentialities in dissolution are apt to be held in tension with the positive. . . . For degradation is not . . . a process that Birkin and Ursula altogether emerge from, renewed. Something like this is intimated at one level, certainly; but what is more pervasively suggested is that the two processes—renewal and dissolution, regeneration and the descent into corruption—can never in fact be dissociated; or more accurately, that there is after all only the one process, the ambivalent process of reduction. Accordingly, we find that every intimation that Birkin and Ursula are liberated, or "re-born," is undercut or obscurely qualified.[22]

As a statement about complexity of character in Lawrence's major works of fiction, this is a tenable view. Clarke rightly emphasizes an ambivalence of character even in "creative death," a tension arising out of persons' struggles to make viable moral choices in a world of moral ambiguity and flux. Their struggles are necessarily made without the certitude of those who accept the status quo, and the results to which their choices lead are not unmixed.

In the theories that underlie his fictional practice, Lawrence presents the two sides of the dialectical tension through a radical contrast and asserts that morality consists in establishing a balance in tension between the two. In the discourse that follows the passage Clarke cites from "The Crown," Lawrence draws a clear distinction between the two forms of corruption, forms that, in the context of the present discussion, may be designated the Apollonian and the Dionysian. To the Apollonian consciousness, corruption is an analytic or sensational function of a linear process under the control of the ego. To the Dionysian consciousness, corruption is a spontaneous function of a cyclic process in the creative unconscious. Lawrence declares:

We cannot subject a divine process to a static will, not without blasphemy and loathsomeness. The static will must be subject to the process of reduction, also. For the pure absolute, the Holy Ghost, lies also in the relationship which is made manifest by the departure, the departure *ad infinitum,* of the opposing elements.

   Corruption will at last break down for us the deadened forms, and release us into the infinity. But the static ego, with

22. Clarke, *River of Dissolution,* 129.

its will-to-persist, neutralises both life and death, and utterly defies the Holy Ghost. The unpardonable sin! [*RDP* 293]

Creative destruction is, of course, a vital process of nature. Moreover, the reductive activities of modern society—war, the disintegration of cultural institutions, the dissolution of older moral traditions, the fragmentation of society, and the compartmentalization of the individual—affect everyone. So the question is not whether to participate in destruction but in what spirit to do so. On the one hand, one may keep intact one's egoistic will as a static entity within which one seeks the sensation of reduction, whether in parlor games of analysis or in bedroom games of sexual manipulation. On the other hand, in Lawrence's radical conception of psychological resilience, one may submit one's whole self, including one's static will and one's "tight ego," to the cycle of destruction and regeneration: "We may give ourselves utterly to destruction. Then our conscious forms are destroyed along with us, and something new must arise. But we may not have corruption within ourselves as sensationalism, our skin and outer form intact. To destroy life for the preserving of a static, rigid form, a shell, a glassy envelope, this is the lugubrious activity of the men who fight to save democracy and to end all fighting" (*RDP* 294). Lawrence does not want to end all fighting, because that would mean that one side of the duality had finally won. Quoting the lines "The Lion and the Unicorn / Were fighting for the Crown," he says, "Thus we portray ourselves in the field of the royal arms. The whole history is the fight, the whole *raison d'être*." "This is a terrible position," he admits; "to have for a *raison d'être* a purpose which, if once fulfilled, would of necessity entail the cessation from existence of both opponents. They would both cease to be, if either of them really won in the fight which is their sole reason for existing" (*RDP* 254). "The lion and the unicorn are not fighting *for* the Crown. They are fighting beneath it," Lawrence says. "And the Crown is upon their fight" (*RDP* 259). Lawrence does not, in this contest, favor the Dionysian lion any more than he does the Apollonian unicorn. He speaks, rather, for a balanced opposition between the two, with the crown, here a figure for the Holy Ghost, as the principle of unity in opposition established in the "trembling balance" of all true art.

3

Lawrence and the
Figure of the Artist

If only the Holy Ghost can heal the dualistic breach in man's consciousness by serving as the "trembling centre of balance" (*STH* 173) about which the antinomies of existence sway and oscillate, then the question is how to get in touch with this principle and effect the reconciliation. Is the Holy Ghost in Lawrence's conception to be invoked, or does it descend, like the Holy Ghost of Milton's *De Doctrina Christiana,* as a gift of grace? Significantly, Lawrence suggests, one way of making contact with this principle of balance is through art. The novel is "the one bright book of life" (*STH* 195) precisely because, unlike other forms of art, it is so hard to falsify, hard to codify in ways that stabilize the equilibrium by reducing life to an abstraction. The novel, Lawrence says, can put us in touch with our real feelings by enabling us to "hear the cries far down in our own forests of dark veins" (*STH* 205). But if the novel is the form that best reveals "the highest complex of subtle inter-relatedness" (*STH* 172), other forms of art, by reflecting living experience rather than fixed ideals, can also reveal something of the same quality. The matter finally comes down to a choice between the quick and the dead. One way of posing Lawrence's critical question is to ask, is the work of art animated with the vitality of the "trembling balance" that arises out of the artist's genuine identity, or does it, in effect,

deny identity itself by denying the body and subjugating its instinctual impulses to abstract principles?

The quickness of D. H. Lawrence's own art emerges from its essentially experiential and exploratory nature. According to Maurice
Beebe, "Lawrence's insistence on art as experience, a corollary of
which is his likening of the artistic process to the sex act, puts him in
the tradition of those writers who feel that the richness of a work of
art may be measured by the completeness and intensity of the felt
life manifested in the work."[1] The "felt life" in a work of art is
directly related to its presentation of life as oppositional forces held
in the "trembling instability of the balance" (STH 172), as in the
homeostasis of the body itself. Other critics have commented from
different perspectives on Lawrence's thematic use of art, particularly the visual arts, in his fiction.[2] In this study, I propose to examine Lawrence's fictional presentation of the artist theme through the
figure of the artist, both the true artist and the false or failed artist,
whether in the musical, visual, or literary arts, whose experience,
revealed in numerous comments on art and the creative process,
serves to clarify Lawrence's view of the function of the artist in
maintaining the morality of the "trembling balance."

Throughout his work, Lawrence associates aesthetic beauty and
artistic creation with physical being, and especially with the male
body, which became for him the iconographic image by which he

1. In Beebe's view, "This conception of art places Lawrence outside the tradition
represented by such writers, as James, Flaubert, and Joyce, writers who held that the
artist must remain detached from life in order to see it clearly, and who produced
static works of art dealing often, it is true, with personal experience, but experience
sonehow finished, exhausted, and thus subject to the artist's deliberate control and
manipulation." See Maurice Beebe, "The Artist Theme in Sons and Lovers," in Ivory
Towers and Sacred Founts, reprinted in D. H. Lawrence: "Sons and Lovers," ed.
Salgādo, 177.

2. Among these critics are the following: Alldritt, in Visual Imagination of D. H.
Lawrence, 11, demonstrates the function of visual art in Lawrence's fiction in terms of
the social orders and historical periods of painting and "the evolving consciousness of
main characters" reflected in allusions to art; Torgovnick, in Visual Arts, Pictorialism, and the Novel, proposes that pictorial arts inform the novel in four interrelated ways: the decorative, the biographical, the ideological, and the perceptual and
hermaneutic; Meyers, in Painting and the Novel, 46–82, considers the iconography of
three particular paintings, Maurice Greiffenhagen's Idyll, Fra Angelico's Last Judgment, and Mark Gertler's Merry-Go-Round, as sources of thematic and structural
motifs in three respective novels, The White Peacock, The Rainbow, and Women in
Love. Stewart, in a series of essays, two of which are cited as notes 24 and 25 to this
chapter, focuses on the phenomenology of Lawrence's visual imagination as expressed
in the rhetoric of his fiction, in particular by means of color, space, rhythm, and bodily
sensation.

asserted the individuality of his own identity as a center around which the tremulous forces of life were held in balance. As early as *The White Peacock*, the narrator, Cyril Beardsall, contrasts George Saxton's figure with his own in terms of art. When Cyril first sees "reproductions of Aubrey Beardsley's 'Atalanta', and of the tail-piece to 'Salomé', and others,"[3] his "soul leaped out upon the new thing," and even George drawls, " 'Good Lord!' " (*WP* 159). Later, in the bathing scene, George, who is "well-proportioned, and naturally of handsome physique," laughs at Cyril, telling him he is "like one of Aubrey Beardsley's long, lean, ugly fellows." Cyril sees George aesthetically in a sculptural image:

> As I watched him, he stood in white relief against the mass of green. He polished his arm, holding it out straight and solid; he rubbed his hair into curls, while I watched the deep muscles of his shoulders, and the bands stand out in his neck as he held it firm. I remembered the story of Annable. [*WP* 222]

What Cyril remembers, of course, is the gamekeeper Frank Annable's account of provocatively drying himself on the bank after a swim to exhibit his body to Lady Chrystabel and later posing for her "in her bedroom while she drew Greek statues of me." Cyril is duly impressed by the hardness of Annable's arm muscle. "You don't know what it is to have the pride of a body like mine," Annable tells him (*WP* 150). Lady Chrystabel's fate is also spelled out in artistic allusions. According to Annable, "A poet got hold of her, and she began to affect" the "souly" attitude of a woman in a Burne-Jones or Waterhouse painting: "she was a lot like one of his women—'Lady of Shalott', I believe. At any rate, she got souly and I was her animal . . . " (*WP* 150–51). If the comparison to Beardsley's "long, lean, ugly fellows" betrays Lawrence's feelings about his own body, the artistic allusions that define Lady Chrystabel and Annable suggest his reservations about the one-sidedness of art that represents the imbalance toward either soul or body: the sentimentality of Sir Edward Burne-Jones and John William Waterhouse versus the heroic ideal of Greek statues of Hercules.

   The genesis of these two scenes, as Carl Baron points out, is also associated with pictorial art in an incident described by Lawrence's friend George Henry Neville. Lawrence had been obsessively copy-

---

3. Morrison, "Lawrence, Beardsley, Wilde," 241–48, relates the white-peacock image, the Beardsley drawings, and Oscar Wilde to the ambiguity in sexual identity that she thinks leads to George's destruction.

ing and recopying Maurice Greiffenhagen's picture *An Idyll* (1891) without being able to get the nude but partially concealed male figure right. Lawrence, unlike Neville, did not work out in the gymnasium or go for a swim with his friends. Surmising that he had been drawing the figure either from having seen his father's body or from trying to see his own in a mirror, Neville accused him of drawing "scarecrows" rather than "MEN." Determined to show him what a good male physique actually looks like, Neville locked the back door and began to strip:

> But as my bare limbs began to come into view his eyes began to shine and they positively glittered when at last I stood naked before him and said, "There now! For God's sake have a good look at a man with a decent shape while you have the chance. Here! See some *muscles*—not lengths of rope. . . ." I was expanding and contracting, flexing and putting in a certain amount of showmanship I had picked up at gymnasium and in training. . . .

Hearing no response, Neville turned to find Lawrence arrested, gazing at him with "an expression of perfectly rapt adoration." This "very strong expression," Neville says, is the only one adequate to his meaning: "Lawrence adored strength and beauty with a kind of envious adoration; and in the same way he adored practically all personal characteristics he did not himself possess."[4]

The epiphany that Neville describes entered Lawrence's imagination and reverberates throughout his work: in the naked bodies and locked door of the wrestling scene in "Gladiatorial" in *Women in Love;* in the rapt worship of Constance Chatterley's gaze when she unexpectedly comes upon Mellors bathing in the wood; and in the scenes of male nudity or partial nudity that recur throughout Lawrence's work as a motif of self-discovery in physical being for the artist or the leader.

Even Siegmund MacNair, the doomed violinist of *The Trespasser,* glimpses what such physical life might be. In an early walk on the first morning of his five-day tryst with Helena Verden on the Isle of Wight, he discovers a little pool in a secluded bay and goes for an invigorating swim, heaving and falling with the waves in a game

---

4. Neville, *A Memoir of D. H. Lawrence,* 78–79. The editor, Carl Baron also notes verbal connections between Neville's anecdote and the uncensored passage on Annable's posing (177).

with the sea. But his sacrifice is foreshadowed in his Adonis-like wound as in "the sudden cruelty of the sea," "he caught his thigh on a sharp, submerged point." Offering "his body to the morning, glowing with the sea's passion," he delights in the uniqueness of his physical being as a living "centre of balance" about which opposite forces, reflected in color imagery, are arrayed: "That is I, that creeping red, and this whiteness I pride myself on is I, and my black hair, and my blue eyes are I. It is a weird thing to be a person" (T 73–74). Proud that he is physically at his best and strongest, he feels that Helena should rejoice in his body; instead, "she rejects me as if I were a baboon, under my clothing" (T 74). Glancing "at his whole handsome maturity, the firm plating of his breasts, the full thighs, creatures, proud in themselves," he regrets only that his body is "marred by the long, raw scratch": "If I was giving her myself, I wouldn't want that blemish on me" (T 74).

In the actual case, Helena, a "dreaming woman" in whom passion exhausts itself "at the mouth," remains adamantly unawakened, sexually cold beneath a surface warmth. Obsessively in his suffering, Siegmund goes over and over the ground of his failed existence: his unsurprisingly disastrous marriage to Beatrice, the unexpected failure of his love for Helena. Even if he were free, he thinks, Helena would ultimately leave him: "She is young and vigorous: I am beginning to set." "Is that why I have failed?" he wonders. The question wrings from him a painful recognition: "I cannot compel anybody to follow me." Siegmund's failure is not sexual, at least not overtly so, but artistic, an inability to assert the virility and dominant leadership that Lawrence had already begun to see as the artist's role. A failed artist who can find no footing, he confesses:

> "So we are here. I am out of my depth. Like the bee, I was mad with the sight of so much joy, such a blue space, and now I shall find no footing to alight on. I have flown out into life beyond my strength to get back. What can I set my feet on when this is gone?" [T 147]

In this state of despair, Siegmund seeks the only consummation left to him by choosing literally, to his undoing, to submit his body to the sun:

> The sun grew stronger. Slower and more slowly went the hawks of Siegmund's mind, after the quarry of conclusion. He

lay bare-headed, looking out to sea. The sun was burning deeper into his face and head.

"I feel as if it were burning into me," thought Siegmund abstractedly. "It is certainly consuming some part of me. Perhaps it is making me ill."—Meanwhile, perversely, he gave his face and his hot black hair to the sun. [*T* 147]

Helena begs him to seek relief under the edge of the rocks—"The naked body of heat was dreadful"—and questions whether the sun is not bad for him; but Siegmund only laughs "stupidly": "He knew that the sun was burning through him, and doing him harm, but he wanted the intoxication" (*T* 147). Herbert Howarth comments that Siegmund

reaches for the sun as male, autocrat, King. Siegmund lacks assertive fire, and knows that he lacks it. He tries to suck it from the sun by stripping his body to the sudden hot drenching. But like learning, like growth, the change from aetiolation to sun-strength requires time. To plunge into a blazing trough of power is as deadly at the symbolic as at the naturalistic level. Siegmund has destroyed himself.[5]

Blasted by the same sun that so often serves as a source of healing and power for other Laurentian protagonists, Siegmund MacNair is unable to preserve either physiological or psychological homeostasis. Lacking any quality of resilience, he suffers a psychic disintegration as the prelude not to establishing a new and more adaptive psychological homeostasis but to the final tragedy of his suicide by hanging. Even as Siegmund continues obsessively retracing the steps of what might have been, Helena recognizes the truth of what will be:

"I *think* we should be able to keep together if"—he faltered— "if only I could have you a little longer. I have never had you." Some sound of failure, some tone telling her it was too late, some ring of despair in his quietness, made Helena cling to him wildly, with a savage little cry as if she were wounded. [*T* 147–48]

5. Howarth, "D. H. Lawrence from Island to Glacier," 221.

It is, of course, from Helen Corke's wound that *The Trespasser* derives, while a pattern of operatic allusions lends a quality of Wagnerian myth to the "florid prose poem."[6]

Sons and Lovers is, at one level, as both Maurice Beebe and Keith Alldritt suggest, a portrait of the artist, although there are few examples of Paul Morel's work and he articulates no fully developed aesthetic theory such as the one Stephen Dedalus elaborates in James Joyce's *Portrait of the Artist as a Young Man.* Whereas Alldritt calls the novel a *Künstlerroman* in that "it concerns the struggle of an artist to develop and hold true to his vision at a particular moment in time,"[7] the very title of *Sons and Lovers* suggests the dominant theme of psychosexual development to which the artist theme is subsidiary.[8] But both themes derive from Lawrence's own experience. When Paul wins first-prize awards in the winter exhibition at Nottingham Castle museum for both a still life in oil and a landscape in watercolor that sells for twenty guineas, Walter Morel's incredulous response—"But twenty guineas for a bit of a paintin' as he knocked off in an hour or two!" (*SL* 312)—parallels Arthur Lawrence's reaction to his son's fifty pounds' advance for *The White Peacock.* According to Lawrence, he "looked at me with shrewd eyes, as if I were a swindler. 'Fifty pounds! An' tha's niver done a day's work in thy life!' "[9]

Paul's statement in an earlier version of the novel, "A pine-trunk's not a tree-trunk, it's a bit of fire": "I can feel it burning just as the sun burns,"[10] suggests that he sees the landscape as an impressionist. Primarily, Paul is a figure painter who strives for luminosity within representational parameters; but despite his disavowal of impressionist form, that he paints from memory rather than from

6. Mansfield, "Introduction" to Lawrence, *The Trespasser,* 9–10, says that "the Wagnerian allusions," which "contribute to the atmosphere of tragic love," are random and occasionally inaccurate. Billy James Pace, "D. H. Lawrence's Use in His Novels of Germanic and Celtic Myth from the Music Dramas of Richard Wagner," 78, establishes the parallel between Siegmund's career and Wagner's treatment in *Siegfried* and *Götterdämmerung* of the three stages of Siegfried's birth, life, and death: "Basically, Siegmund gives up an old life style which he considers absurd, woos a woman in the context of the flaming bridal chamber, and then dies psychically— complete with flaming funeral pyre and the twilight of the gods."

7. Alldritt, 18.

8. Even so, Torgovnick's view that Paul's role as a painter is, in her sense of the term, "*decorative,*" in that his artistic "vocation has virtually no consequence or felt influence in the novel" (17) is an unwarranted dismissal of the artist theme.

9. Moore, *The Priest of Love,* 128.

10. Ibid., 58–59.

models suggests that he is concerned with rendering subjective experience more than with the object:

> He loved to paint large figures, full of light, but not merely made up of lights and cast shadows, like the impressionists; rather definite figures that had a certain luminous quality, like some of Michael Angelo's people. And these he fitted into a landscape, in what he thought true proportion. He worked a great deal from memory, using everybody he knew. He believed firmly in his work, that it was good and valuable. [*SL* 364]

Alldritt shows that this kind of painting is "the last of several stages in the development of Paul Morel's art," which suggests his parallel "development in perception and feeling." As Beebe points out, this passage describes the way Lawrence worked in both his fiction and his painting.[11]

Lawrence's memory of the body may have been, as Neville surmised, primarily of his father's body. In *Sons and Lovers,* Walter Morel dries himself before the fire after his bath: "He had still a wonderfully young body, muscular, without any fat. His skin was smooth and clear. It might have been the body of a man of twenty-eight, except that there were, perhaps, too many blue scars, like tattoo-marks, where the coal dust remained under the skin, and that his chest was too hairy." When Paul observes " 'I suppose . . . you had a good figure once,' " Mrs. Morel confirms, " 'He had,' " though her husband protests, " 'Me! . . . I wor niver much more n'r a skeleton' " (*SL* 250).

The principal models for Paul's image of the body, however, are Clara and Baxter Dawes. In psychoanalytic terms, he projects upon this couple the introjected imagoes of his parents in his internal world. In aesthetic terms, he appropriates their assertive physical being for the iconographic images of male and female bodies in his art. From the beginning, when Paul responds most to Clara's defiant manner and her sensual mouth, he sees her as an artist does. When Miriam asks what he likes about Mrs. Dawes, Paul stammers: "I don't know—her skin and the texture of her—and her—I don't know—there's a sort of fierceness in her. I appreciate her as an artist, that's all" (*SL* 240). Later in their affair when they bathe at the seaside, Paul watches Clara with both the vision of a lover and the observation of an artist:

11. Alldritt, 17–18; Beebe, 180.

She was white and velvet skinned, with heavy shoulders. A
little wind, coming from the sea, blew across her body and
ruffled her hair.

The morning was of a lovely limpid gold colour. Veils of
shadow seemed to be drifting away on the north and the
south. Clara stood shrinking slightly from the touch of the
wind, twisting her hair. The sea-grass rose behind the white
stripped woman. She glanced at the sea, then looked at him.
He was watching her with dark eyes which she loved and
could not understand. She hugged her breasts between her
arms, cringing, laughing. [SL 424–25]

As if in answer to a series of questions that come unbidden to his
mind—"Why does she absorb me?," "What is she, after all?," "What
does she mean to me, after all?"—Paul becomes aware that it is not
Clara herself that he cares for but something she represents, as "a
bubble of foam represents the sea" (SL 425–26). Watching her laughing face as she dries herself and her swaying breasts that seem
frightening to him as he unconciously associates her with his
mother, Paul sees Clara as one of those "large figures full of light"
(SL 364) that he likes to paint: "But she is magnificent, and even
bigger than the morning and the sea. Is she—is she—?" (SL 426).
She has entered his imagination as an aesthetic image, and he stammers at the recognition.

A similar process occurs in Paul's relation to Clara's husband:

The smith was a man of thirty-one or thirty-two . . . —a big,
well-set man, also striking to look at, and handsome. There
was a peculiar similarity between himself and his wife. He
had the same white skin, with a clear golden tinge. His hair
was of soft brown, his moustache was golden. And he had a
similar defiance in his bearing and manner. [SL 238]

But Baxter Dawes, with his "sensual mouth" and his lidded, protrud-
ing, "quick-shifting," "dissolute" eyes, hates Paul from the first with
both a husband's jealousy and the resentment of one who feels himself objectified: "Finding the lad's impersonal, deliberate gaze of an
artist on his face, he got into a fury": " 'What are yer lookin' at?' he
sneered, bullying" (SL 238).

The exchange establishes the pattern in their encounters of Paul's
aesthetically objectifying gaze and Dawes's snarling rage. When the
two men eventually fight, Paul's knowledge of Baxter's body is

taken with the same instinctual tension building to a climax as his knowledge of Clara's body is taken in the sex act:

> He was a pure instinct, without reason or feeling. His body, hard and wonderful in itself, cleaved against the struggling body of the other man; not a muscle in him relaxed. . . . He lay pressed hard against his adversary, . . . feeling the struggles of the other body become wilder and more frenzied. Tighter and tighter grew his body, like a screw that is gradually increasing in pressure, till something breaks.
>   Then suddenly he relaxed, full of wonder and misgiving. . . . [*SL* 434]

Paul's response of oedipal guilt, transferred from Walter Morel to Dawes, emerges here in such misgivings about his death wishes for the father that he pulls back from the possibility of killing the father figure and allows himself to be beaten badly, as if in atonement.[12] But his sense of wonder in response to the man's physical body, including an unconscious homoerotic component that is also oedipal in origin, will become an important source of his art.

At their next meeting, when Paul goes to see Baxter in Sheffield Hospital, "The two men were afraid of the naked selves they had been" (*SL* 449). The scene prefigures the episode in which Lilly nurses Aaron Sisson back to health in *Aaron's Rod,* but with the difference that Paul views Baxter out of a highly ambivalent constellation of hate, guilt, love, and pity: "The sick man was gaunt and handsome again. Paul was sorry for him because his eyes looked so tired" (*SL* 450). "The strong emotion that Dawes aroused in him, repressed, made him shiver" (*SL* 451). With the repression comes sublimation. Baxter Dawes, like Clara, has entered Paul's imagination as an aesthetic image, and he shivers at the recognition.

Beebe, who sees Paul's mother and Miriam as rival patronesses and the latter as a kind of muse, perceptively links Paul's aesthetics with his psychology: "If Gertrude Morel suggests Hamlet's mother, so Paul is like Hamlet in that he stages a drama, with Clara and Baxter as player-queen and player-king, that represents his own

---

12. Weiss, *Oedipus in Nottingham,* 32, comments that "Paul commits just the right degree of parricide, recoils, and offers himself in atonement for the crime." In Weiss's Freudian interpretation, Dawes becomes the idealized father figure with whom Paul later acts out a fantasy of rescue and, in returning Clara to him, finally both squares the account and closes the parental arch over his own head in the synthetic family situation (31–37).

internal conflict."[13] Identifying himself with the outsider position of the father is essential to his evolution as an artist. Paul's aesthetic manipulation of both Clara and Baxter, whom he does not finally need as themselves but only as the images of the internal objects they have come to represent, is carried to the logical conclusion of artistic control in his reuniting his mistress with her husband. Where his parents' marriage is concerned, Paul cannot effect such a reparation. He can do so by proxy with the Dawes couple only because their iconographic status makes it possible for him to manipulate them aesthetically in reestablishing the homeostatic balance of the family unit that his oedipal relationship with his parents had helped to destabilize.

Observing that "Will Brangwen represents a more mature and extended account of the artist's situation" than Paul Morel, Alldritt says that "common to the description of both artists is the suggestion of the continuity between sexuality, feeling, perception and the art that is created."[14] Will Brangwen's first recorded wood-carving in *The Rainbow,* the phoenix butter mold he gives to Anna at the beginning of their courtship (R 108), encompasses all four of these in an image that is at once ordinary and mythic. Later, after the timeless still point of their early sexual relationship (R 135) has declined into occasional passion between their competitive power struggles centering in the question of Will's religious beliefs, he carves an uncompleted board panel of Adam and Eve, the traditional design and representation of which points up the division within Will and between Will and Anna.[15] Anna jeers at the carving as a piece of masculine presumption: "She is like a little marionette. Why is she so small? You've made Adam as big as God, and Eve is like a doll" (R 162). If the wood-carving expresses Will's sense of frustrated manhood, Anna's response to it expresses her frustrated womanhood: "It is impudence to say that Woman was made out of Man's body," she continues, "when every man is born of woman. What impudence men have, what arrogance!" (R 162). Will can win only a Pyrrhic

13. Beebe, 187.
14. Alldritt, 74.
15. The iconography of this carving seems to be traditional. See, for example, a bronze sculpture, *Adam and Eve* (1936, cast in 1978) by the German sculptor Max Beckmann, which shows Adam seated, open-mouthed, holding a tiny Eve in the palm of his hand while the serpent curls from the right leg of his stool at ground level upward through the fork of his legs at the genitals around his left side and up his back to rest its head on Adam's right shoulder. The statue is in the permanent exhibit of the Hirschhorn Museum in Washington, D.C.

victory by chopping up the panel and burning it, so that Anna, "much chastened in spirit," weeps for a whole day. The flame of love that comes out of the ashes of this painful experience results in Anna's first pregnancy.

Stimulated by Ruskin "to a pleasure in the mediæval forms" (R 105), Will Brangwen is interested most in the art of church architecture:

> . . . as he spoke of church after church, of nave and chancel and transept, of rood-screen and font, of hatchet-carving and moulding and tracery, speaking always with close passion of particular things, particular places, there gathered in her heart a pregnant hush of churches, a mystery, a ponderous significance of bowed stone, a dim coloured light through which something took place obscurely, passing into darkness: a high, delighted framework of the mystic screen, and beyond, in the furthest beyond, the altar. [R 106]

As Will talks of "Gothic and Renaissance and Perpendicular, and Early English and Norman" architecture, Anna is "carried away. And the land seemed to be covered with a vast, mystic church, reserved in gloom, thrilled with an unknown Presence" (R 106).[16]

Will Brangwen does have a strong sense of his physical being, but primarily as a sensualist. It is in physical, sexual relationship that he and Anna, early in their marriage, feel themselves "at the very centre of all the slow wheeling of space and the rapid agitation of life": "They found themselves there, and they lay still, in each other's arms; for their moment they were at the heart of eternity, whilst time roared far off, forever far off, towards the rim" (R 135). But as Gerald J. Butler points out, Will takes a feminine attitude toward Anna, who assumes the dominant role and uses him sexually as the instrument of her own satisfaction and her self-absorption in child-bearing.[17]

Will's sense of his physical body is evident also in the scenes in which he swims with Ursula, leaping from the canal bridge into the water far below, with the naked child clinging to his shoulders. The sense of daring physicality she absorbs in this childhood experience influences Ursula's awareness of the body in her own psychosexual

---

16. Miko, *Toward "Women in Love"*, 137, suggests that Will's Ruskinizing does not bring unconscious motives into consciousness and that Anna responds to it because it extends her "religious sensibility" without threatening her self-centeredness.

17. Butler, *This Is Carbon*, 78, 80.

development: "She was used to his nakedness, and to her mother's nakedness, ever since she was born" (*R* 209).

But Will's inability to relate his deeper sensibility to experience in the daylight world prevents its informing his art.[18] He can reconcile his sense of the body neither to his artistic work nor to his love for the church, which pleases his aesthetic sense even while it leaves his soul unsatisfied. Hence, his art becomes mostly restoration and sculptural copy work, and his religious devotion is to the external forms of the church, of which its architecture is the metaphor:

> It was the church *building* he cared for; and yet his soul was passionate for something. He laboured cleaning the stonework, repairing the wood-work, restoring the organ, and making the singing as perfect as possible. To keep the church fabric and the church-ritual intact was his business; to have the intimate, sacred building utterly in his own hands, and to make the form of service complete. There was a little bright anguish and tension on his face, and in his intent movements. He was like a lover who knows he is betrayed, but who still loves, whose love is only the more tense. The church was false, but he served it the more attentively. [*R* 193]

The artist theme in *Women in Love* is presented through two artist characters, several others who make critical judgments of art, and still others who affect arty pretensions. It would be a mistake to assume that any single character in the novel exclusively represents the authorial voice. Lawrence presents a world in which art matters, and his own position emerges essentially out of the dialectic between opposing positions in a dialogue on art.

In the opening scene in "Sisters" (chap. 1), Ursula Brangwen stitches "a piece of brightly-coloured embroidery," while Gudrun draws on a board held on her knee. As if in reaction to Ursula's suggestion that marriage is "likely to be the end of experience," Gudrun angrily rubs out part of her drawing (*WL* 7). Gudrun's statement, "*Nothing materialises!* Everything withers in the bud" (*WL* 8), is the verbal equivalent of this action. The countryside seems to her "like a country in an underworld" and its inhabitants the ghoulish replicants of the real world (*WL* 11). In such a world art become more real than life.

In "Class-Room" (chap. 3), when Rupert Birkin, as school inspec-

---

18. Miko, 142–43.

tor, finds Ursula's class "doing catkins," he suggests that the botany lesson be taught by means of art:

> "Give them some crayons, won't you?" he said, "so that they can make the gynaecious flowers red and the androgynous yellow. I'd chalk them in plain, chalk in nothing else, merely the red and yellow. Outline scarcely matters in this case. There is just one fact to emphasise." [*WL* 36]

The real subject is, of course, sexual reproduction, more specifically, sexual desire and gender differences. Birkin continues:

> "It's the fact you want to emphasise, not a subjective impression to record. What's the fact?—red little spiky stigmas of the female flower, dangling yellow male catkin, yellow pollen flying from one to the other. Make a pictorial record of the fact, as a child does when drawing a face—two eyes, one nose, mouth with teeth—so—" [*WL* 36]

Hermione Roddice's question, "Do you really think the children are better for being roused to consciousness?" (*WL* 39), derives from an opposing view of education and art, one that renders only a generalized subjective impression of the whole and does not disturb the viewer with new or specific knowledge: "Isn't it better that they should remain unconscious of the hazel, isn't it better that they should see as a whole, without all this pulling to pieces, all this knowledge?" she asks. Birkin's reply confronts Hermione—and the reader—with the important function of both science and art to present a truthful record of existence, including sexuality: "Would you rather, for yourself, know or not know, that the little red flowers are there, putting out for the pollen?" (*WL* 40).

Actually, both Hermione and Gudrun have what Leo Bersani calls an "obsessive lust for knowledge"; but the two women seek finality of knowledge in two opposing, equally destructive modes: Gudrun's lust is for ultimate sensual knowledge, as Hermione's is for mental knowledge. As Bersani observes, Gudrun disposes of people by placing them, "sealed and stamped and finished with"; the same kind of perfected knowledge characterizes her art, and "final knowledge about anything is deathlike."[19] In "Sketch-Book" (chap. 10), Gudrun sits "staring fixedly at the water-plants that rose succulent from the mud of the low shores. . . . But she could feel their turgid fleshy structure as in a sensuous vision, she *knew* how they rose out of the mud, she

19. Bersani, *A Future for Astyanax,* 177.

knew how they thrust out from themselves, how they stood stiff and succulent against the air" (*WL* 119). Hermione, after looking at Gudrun's sketches, "accidentally" drops them into Willey Water. The narrator implies that the accident is unconsciously determined by her recoil from Gerald Crich, to whom she is reluctantly handing the sketchbook (*WL* 121). But it is equally purposive in attacking Gudrun's drawings as a factual record of her sensual mode of knowing, in a "stupor of apprehension" of the phallic forms of "the rigid, naked, succulent stems," "surging" out of the corruptive mud (*WL* 119).

The central art symbols in *Women in Love*, however, are the contrasting aesthetic metaphors of the West African statuary, which Lawrence introduces in "Crême de Menthe" (chap. 6) and elaborates in "Fetish" (chap. 7) and "Moony" (chap. 19), and Loerke's sculpture of the girl on the horse, in "Continental" (chap. 29). These contrasting images, I argue, represent two opposing reductive aesthetics, reduction to an art of absolute, kinetic sensationalism and reduction to an art of absolute, static formalism. Thus, neither can embody the integration of the "trembling balance" of art by which Lawrence seeks to reconcile the antinomies of life.

In "Crême de Menthe," Gerald Crich discovers the black African sculpture in Halliday's otherwise nondescript London flat:

> . . . there were several negro statues, wood-carvings from West Africa, strange and disturbing, the carved negroes looked almost like the foetus of a human being. One was of a woman sitting naked in a strange posture, and looking tortured, her abdomen stuck out. The young Russian explained that she was sitting in childbirth, clutching the ends of the band that hung from her neck, one in each hand, so that she could bear down, and help labour. The strange, transfixed, rudimentary face of the woman again reminded Gerald of a foetus, it was also rather wonderful, conveying the suggestion of the extreme of physical sensation, beyond the limits of mental consciousness. (*WL* 74]

It is appropriate that Gerald Crich, who, with his blond, Nordic, industrial consciousness, represents the direct opposite of the West African figures, is the first to notice them.[20] In "Fetish" (chap. 7),

20. Morris, "African Sculpture Symbols in *Women in Love*," 28. See also Moody, "African Sculpture Symbols in a Novel by D. H. Lawrence," 73–77. For a discussion of the African and Nordic symbolism as antithetical ways to destruction, see Chamberlain, "Pussum, Minette, and the Africo-Nordic Symbol in Lawrence's *Women in Love*," 407–16.

Gerald's response is conditioned by the setting as the naked men in Halliday's flat, their white bodies in striking contrast to the ebony statues, draw near to look. In both, Gerald finds the extreme of sensation. He is moved by Halliday's "rather heavy, slack, broken beauty, . . . like a Christ in a Pietà," but repelled, somehow shamed, by the healthy animality of Maxim Libidnikov's "suave, golden coloured body with black hair growing fine and freely, like tendrils, and his limbs like smooth plant-stems" (*WL* 78).

Looking at the statue, Gerald sees in the "terrible face, void, peaked, abstracted almost into meaninglessness by the weight of sensation beneath," the same reduction in sensation that he finds in Pussum (*WL* 79). Unable to recognize a difference between the organic sensationalism represented in the primitive statue and the world-weary perversity of modern Bohemian sensationalism, Gerald cannot see the figure as art:

> "Why is it art?" Gerald asked, shocked, resentful.
>
> "It conveys a complete truth," said Birkin. "It contains the whole truth of that state, whatever you feel about it."
>
> "But you can't call it *high* art," said Gerald.
>
> "High! There are centuries and hundreds of centuries of development in a straight line, behind that carving; it is an awful pitch of culture, of a definite sort."
>
> "What culture?" Gerald asked, in opposition. He hated the sheer African thing.
>
> "Pure culture in sensation, culture in the physical consciousness, really *ultimate* physical consciousness, mindless, utterly sensual. It is so sensual as to be final, supreme." [*WL* 79]

Gerald's response almost parodies Roger Fry's argument, in a review of a London exhibition of African sculpture in 1920, that "[c]omplete plastic freedom with us seems only to come at the end of a long period, when the art has attained a high degree of representational skill," but that, because it does not derive from a "culture in our sense of the word," which requires not only "artistic creativity" but "critical appreciation" as well, the African statuary shows "no trace of this process."[21] Lawrence, on the other hand, attempts to place the

---

21. Roger Fry, "Negro Sculpture," in *Vision and Design*, 66–68. In Fry's view, "It is for want of a conscious critical sense and the intellectual powers of comparison and classification that the negro has failed to create one of the great cultures of the world, and not from any lack of the creative aesthetic impulse, nor from lack of the most exquisite sensibility and the finest taste" (68). See also Heywood, "African Art and

African sculpture in its own tradition and so learn how to *see* it. He comments in "Art and Morality," "Design, in art, is a recognition of the relation between various things, various elements in the creative flux." Rather than being invented and imposed mentally, this design must be recognized "with your blood and your bones, even more than with your eyes." "The dim eye-vision and the powerful blood-feeling of the negro African, even today, gives us strange images, which our eyes can hardly see, but which we know are surpassing. . . . The African fetish-statues have no movement, visually represented. Yet one little motionless wooden figure stirs more than all the Parthenon frieze" (*STH* 167–68). Birkin's response to Gerald Crich corrects Fry's view by placing the African statuary in the aesthetic tradition of extreme physical sensation rather than the intellectual cultural tradition required for critical appreciation.

Birkin himself is not an artist, but throughout the novel his encounters with art are essential to the process of his self-definition. In "Breadalby" (chap. 8), still struggling with the question of extremes raised by the African statuary, he copies a Chinese drawing of geese. To Hermione, the drawing is only an exquisite object given to her by the Chinese ambassador. To Birkin, copying the drawing is a means of understanding Chinese consciousness: "I know what centres they live from—what they perceive and feel—the hot, stinging centrality of a goose in the flux of cold water and mud—the curious bitter stinging heat of a goose's blood, entering their own blood like an inoculation of corruptive fire—fire of the cold-burning mud—the lotus mystery" (*WL* 89). In copying the drawing, in other words, Birkin gains an insight, through the example of Chinese integration of opposites (cold and heat, mud and blood), into how to incorporate the process of corruption without being destroyed.

In "Moony," Rupert Birkin, long after the scene in Halliday's flat, vividly recalls the African fetishes. But rather than the fertility figure that had both fascinated and repelled Gerald, Birkin reflects particularly on the statuette of a standing female,

> . . . a tall, slim, elegant figure from West Africa, in dark wood, glossy and suave. It was a woman, with hair dressed high, like a melon-shaped dome. He remembered her vividly: she was one of his soul's intimates. Her body was long and ele-

---

the Work of Roger Fry and D. H. Lawrence," 102–13. Heywood finds in the work of Fry and Lawrence the most significant instances of partial assimilation of African art.

gant, her face was crushed tiny like a beetle's, she had rows of round heavy collars, like a column of quoits, on her neck. He remembered her: her astonishing cultured elegance, her diminished, beetle face, the astounding long elegant body, on short, ugly legs, with such protuberant buttocks, so weighty and unexpected below her slim long loins. [*WL* 253]

Marianna Torgovnick argues that the African statuary indirectly encodes the taboo: "Birkin and Gerald approach, but do not discuss, extremes of 'physical sensation': they are interested in a complex of attitudes toward sado-masochistic, homosexual, and other unconventional sexual practices, and toward cultures whose art and mores could encompass such practices." The "protuberant buttocks" and beetle face of the standing figure encode Birkin's response of repulsion and attraction to anal intercourse and, recalling Lawrence's recurrent "dream of beetles" (*Letters* 2:319, 321, 323) after meeting the Bloomsbury homosexuals, to homosexuality.[22] Against Horace Gregory's interpretation of the African figures as a positive representation of life, George H. Ford argues convincingly that "the African statues signify for Birkin a whole process of decline and fall,"[23] a process of disintegration to which Birkin is strongly attracted but one associated with sexual perversion and culminating (like Kurtz's "The horror! the horror!" in Conrad's *Heart of Darkness*) in death itself. Birkin reflects that "[s]he knew what he himself did not know": the lapse of her race from integrated consciousness in the death of spiritual knowledge and thousands of years since then of "purely sensual, purely unspiritual knowledge" (*WL* 253). As Jack F. Stewart observes, "To Lawrence, the distortions of primitive art suggest subtle affinities between primitive and civilized forms of degeneration."[24] Birkin realizes that the same process, "imminent in himself," could lead to a similar loss of integration in modern man. The horror is that even this death of the soul would not be the end:

There is a long way we can travel, after the death-break: after that point when the soul in intense suffering breaks, breaks away from its organic hold like a leaf that falls. We fall from the connection with life and hope, we lapse from pure integral being, from creation and liberty, and we fall into the long,

22. Torgovnick, 194, 196.
23. Ford, *Double Measure,* 192. For the full discussions, see Ford, 188–94; and Gregory, *D. H. Lawrence: Pilgrim of the Apocalypse,* 45–47.
24. Stewart, "Lawrence and Gauguin," 386.

long African process of purely sensual understanding, knowledge in the mystery of dissolution. [*WL* 253]

There is no question of Lawrence's ambivalence about both culture and primitivism. As Stewart comments, "Culture, for Birkin . . . is a search for homeostasis in a constantly shifting world."[25] According to Michael Bell, "Primitivism . . . is born of the interplay between the civilized self and the desire to reject or transform it."[26] Readers who think Lawrence unilaterally rejects mind consciousness and advocates blood consciousness, however, have been misled by the culture and elegance of the figure into assuming that the African statuary offers a viable alternative for modern man. What Lawrence recognizes, on the contrary, is that the extremes of sensual consciousness, like the extremes of mental consciousness, lead to the same sorry end, the lapse from integral being. The epiphany for Birkin is a glimpse into the abyss.

Set in contrast to the African statuary is a photogravure reproduction of a green bronze statuette by Loerke in "Continental":

> The statuette was of a naked girl, small, finely made, sitting on a great naked horse. The girl was young and tender, a mere bud. She was sitting sideways on the horse, her face in her hands, as if in shame and grief, in a little abandon. Her hair, which was short and must be flaxen, fell forward, divided, half covering her hands.
>
> Her limbs were young and tender. Her legs, scarcely formed yet, the legs of a maiden just passing towards cruel womanhood, dangled childishly over the side of the powerful horse, pathetically, the small feet folded one over the other, as if to hide. But there was no hiding. There she was exposed naked on the naked flank of the horse.
>
> The horse stood stock still, stretched in a kind of start. It was a massive, magnificent stallion, rigid with pent-up power. Its neck was arched and terrible, like a sickle, its flanks were pressed back, rigid with power. [*WL* 429]

In the dialogue that follows, Loerke, with support from Gudrun, debates aesthetic theory with Ursula. Basically Ursula's objection to the sculpture is on the ground of its infidelity to nature, while Loerke's defense is on the ground of "Significant Form." Ursula ques-

25. Stewart, "Primitivism in *Women in Love*," 49.
26. Bell, *Primitivism*, 80.

tions, almost in parody of Laurentian doctrine, why Loerke made the horse so stiff: *"Look* how stock and stupid and brutal it is. Horses are sensitive, quite delicate and sensitive, really." Loerke replies condescendingly, in an echo of formalist theories of art, "that horse is a certain *form,* part of a whole form. . . . It is not a picture of a friendly horse to which you give a lump of sugar, do you see—it is part of a work of art, it has no relation to anything outside that work of art" *(WL* 430). Ursula calls it "his idea. I know it is a picture of himself, really—" *(WL* 430). In connection with Loerke's reply, "It is a work of art, it is a picture of nothing, of absolutely nothing" *(WL* 430), Joyce Carol Oates quotes Flaubert's remark that his idea of beauty is "a book about nothing, a book dependent on nothing external. . . ."[27]

Equally relevant are the formalist theories of Oscar Wilde, James MacNeill Whistler, and Clive Bell. Vivian's first two aesthetic dicta in Wilde's dialogue "The Decay of Lying" are "Art never expresses anything but itself" and "All bad art comes from returning to Life and Nature, and elevating them into ideals."[28] Loerke's view of the autonomy of art (like his homosexuality) may allude obliquely to Wilde's. It echoes even more directly Whistler's decorative aesthetic, which holds that the quality of a painting depends on the arrangement of form and color, not on the subject matter: "Art should be independent of all clap-trap—should stand alone, and appeal to the artistic sense of eye and ear, without confounding this with emotions entirely foreign to it, as devotion, pity, love, patriotism, and the like." That is why Whistler calls his works "arrangements" and "harmonies," as in the familiar portrait exhibited at the Royal Academy as *Arrangement in Grey and Black:* "To me it is interesting as a picture of my mother; but what can or ought the public to care about the identity of the portrait?"[29] This view of the relation between art and life, even with its characteristic hyperbole, becomes the Bloomsbury position, as articulated by Clive Bell, who says that while "a realistic form may be as significant, in its place as part of the design, as an abstract," its value "is as form, not as representation." Loerke's reply to Ursula has behind it such statements as the following:

> Before a work of art people who feel little or no emotion for pure form find themselves at a loss. . . . And so they read into the forms of the work those facts and ideas for which they are

27. Oates, "Lawrence's Götterdämmerung: The Apocalyptic Vision of *Women in Love,"* 164.

28. Wilde, "The Decay of Lying," in *The Artist as Critic,* 319.

29. Whistler, *The Gentle Art of Making Enemies,* 126–28.

capable of feeling emotion, and feel for them the emotions that they can feel—the ordinary emotions of life. When confronted by a picture, instinctively they refer back its forms to the world from which they came. They treat created form as though it were imitated form, a picture as though it were a photograph.[30]

Despite Ursula's objections, Loerke's aesthetic ideas are neither unusual nor, in his frame of reference, unreasonable. In fact, as Oates says, "He expresses a view of art that all artists share, to some extent."[31]

Thematically, if the African statuary suggests "the extreme of physical sensation, beyond the limits of mental consciousness" (*WL* 74), Loerke's sculpture, as an example of his theory in practice, represents the extreme of mental sensation, beyond the limits of sensual consciousness. Like the African statuary of the opposite extreme, Loerke's statue encodes unconventional homosexual and sadomasochistic sex practices. Loerke had sadistically slapped Annette von Weck, his model for the short-haired, boyish young girl, to make her keep still (*WL* 433). Regarding the Venus of Milo as a "bourgeoise," Loerke has no use for mature women after twenty, though he thinks men "good at all ages": "A man should be big and powerful—whether he is old or young is of no account, so he has the size, something of massiveness and stupid form" (*WL* 434).

Will Brangwen's art serves the antiquarian form of the once vital Church. Loerke's view that "[a]rt should *interpret* industry, as art once interpreted religion" (*WL* 424) represents the next stage in cultural disintegration. His great frieze for the factory in Cologne, as several critics have noted,[32] recalls the iconography of Mark Gertler's *Merry-Go-Round:*

> It was a representation of a fair, with peasants and artizans in an orgy of enjoyment, drunk and absurd in their modern dress, whirling ridiculously in roundabouts, gaping at shows, kissing and staggering and rolling in knots, swinging in

30. Bell, *Art*, 25.

31. Oates, 164.

32. In addition to Alldritt, 196, and Torgovnick, 193–94, see, for example, Moore, 269; and Meyers, *Painting and the Novel*, 73–78. *The Merry-Go-Round* is reproduced in color in *British Art in the 20th Century*, ed. Compton, plate 74; and in black and white, with a quotation from Lawrence's letter of 9 October 1916, in Shone, *The Century of Change*, plate 50.

swing-boats and firing down shooting galleries, a frenzy of
chaotic motion. [*WL* 423]

Lawrence had seen a photograph of *The Merry-Go-Round,* which, in
a letter to Gertler (9 October 1916), he pronounced "the best *modern*
picture I have seen" but "horrible and terrifying" (*Letters* 2:660). In
another letter, Lawrence tells Gertler, "In my novel there is a man—
not you, I reassure you—who does a great granite frieze for the top of
a factory, and the frieze is a fair, of which your whirligig, for example, is part.—(We knew a man, a german [*sic*], who did these big
reliefs for great, fine factories in Cologne)" (*Letters* 3:46). As the
editors of the Cambridge Edition of *Women in Love* note, the German
model has not been identified, but Lawrence's original description of
Loerke's frieze as "a village attacked by wolves, great naked men,
ten feet high, fighting with . . . [a] horde of wolves, and women running, falling, and a rush of wolves sweeping all . . . across the whole
frieze" (*WL* 578) was altered in mid-November after he had seen the
photograph of Gertler's painting. For Lawrence, the painting was
obscene:

> But then, since obscenity is the truth of our passion today, it is
> the only stuff of art—or almost the only stuff. . . . But I *do*
> think that in this combination of blaze, and violent mechani-
> cal rotation and complex involution, and ghastly, utterly
> mindless human intensity of sensational extremity, you have
> made a real and ultimate revelation. [*Letters* 2:660]

Celia McLean relates Loerke's two contradictory theories of art—
socialist realism serving industry and absolute aestheticism—to his
incorporation of will and passion in "his entropic internal being":
"Loerke perversely binds the two opposites so that they negate rather
than complement each other." In "this inverse equilibrium . . . the
mind and the senses are brought together, not . . . in a creative, dynamic balance, but in an unconscious, stagnant coexistence."[33]
Loerke's simultaneous commitment to the "dark Satanic mills" and
antinatural abstraction confirms that his direction of mental sensation leads as inexorably as the African way of physical sensation and
mindlessness to the ultimate dissolution of integrated consciousness.
The qualitative difference, Torgovnick suggests, lies in the "good

33. McLean, "The Entropic Artist: Loerke's Theories of Art," 277.

artists—but villainous characters—like Gudrun and Loerke, who willingly advance cultural dissolution."[34]

The corollary between the artistic process and the sex act echoes throughout Lawrence's work in analogies between the artistic instrument and the penis. In *Aaron's Rod,* the sexual double entendre by which the flute becomes the metaphorical equivalent of both the phallus and the sacred instrument of divine creation, Aaron's rod in Exodus, resonates in references to the flute throughout the novel, as in Lilly's comments when Aaron tentatively plays the flute for the first time since his severe illness:

> ". . . Aaron's rod is putting forth again." . . .
> "What rod?"
> "Your flute, for the moment." [*AR* 108]

Aaron Sisson, who prefers a simple melody[35] on the flute to chords and harmony (*AR* 136), says, in an implied analogy between flute and pen that clearly applies to Lawrence's aesthetics in this novel, "I don't think about it." "I'm sure you don't. You wouldn't be so good if you did," Lady Artemis Hooper replies, adding: "You're awfully lucky, you know, to be able to pour yourself down your flute" (*AR* 129). As Maurice Beebe notes, Aaron's phallic flute "is not only the means of his art, but also a symbol of his aloneness. It is significant that Lawrence represents art by means of a strongly masculine symbol," which incorporates his thesis "that a man's work, his art, is something that can never be fully shared with women."[36]

The implications for his music may be seen in Aaron's admiration, in a discussion with Lady Franks, for composers like Bach, Beethoven, and Chopin, of whom he says, "I find them all quite as modern as I am" (*AR* 167), in preference to contemporary composers, of whom Lady Franks says: "I can appreciate Strauss and Stravinsky, as well, some things. But my old things—ah, I don't think the moderns are so fine. They are not so deep. They haven't fathomed life so

34. Torgovnick, 194.

35. Compare Aaron's preference in music for simple melodic line to Ivy Low Litvinoff's account of her visit to the Lawrences in Italy, "A Visit to D. H. Lawrence," 411–18 (reprinted in Nehls, ed., *D. H. Lawrence: A Composite Biography,* 1:215–22. As Mme. Litvinoff recalls, Lawrence observed "that I was somehow *unmusically* musical, that I chose pieces that really had no music in them, not because I liked them—nobody could have!—but because I was suspicious of simple melody. 'Cultivated people' . . . had to say they liked Bach, but they didn't really" (Nehls 1:219).

36. Beebe, 10.

deeply" (*AR* 167). Lady Franks's view that the great masters "have such faith" (*AR* 168) that they inspire faith in one's personal destiny, while the moderns "haven't the capacity" for "depths" (*AR* 167), represents a critical judgment that Lawrence himself also makes with reference to much of modern music, painting, and literature.[37]

In the sculpture of Florence, Aaron finds, in Marguerite Beede Howe's words, "the self . . . objectified in the body of man": "in *Aaron's Rod* male supremacy is self-supremacy, for the male body represents the self that stands alone."[38] For Aaron, "the great naked David" of Michaelangelo and "the heavy naked men of Bandinelli" in the Piazza della Signoria convey the physicality of a masculine presence: "the David, . . . standing forward stripped and exposed and eternally half-shrinking, half-wishing to expose himself, he is the genius of Florence. The adolescent, the white, self-conscious, physical adolescent" (*AR* 211). But Lawrence emphasizes as well a version of the male body that is realistic rather than idealized: "And behind, the big, lumpy Bandinelli men are in keeping too. They may be ugly—but . . . they have their own lumpy reality . . . , representing the undaunted physical nature of the heavier Florentines" (*AR* 211–12). In contrast, the bronze Perseus of Benvenuto Cellini looks female, "with his plump hips and his waist, female and rather insignificant: graceful, and rather vulgar. The clownish Bandinellis were somehow more to the point" (*AR* 212).[39]

Paul G. Baker comments, "The close connection here between Aaron, hesitant and newly tumbled out of the chestnut burr of his former self, and Michaelangelo's David, shrinking and exposed, is obvious." Howe observes that in the marble of "the physically flawless young male body" of the statue, "Aaron sees his ideal self."[40] During the last few days of November 1919,[41] with the writing of *Aaron's Rod* still in progress, Lawrence composed a short poetic essay on Michaelangelo's *David* as "the presiding genius of Florence":

---

37. For a more detailed discussion of music in the novel, see Paul G. Baker, "The First Wild Natural Thing: A Study of Music in *Aaron's Rod*," in Baker, *A Reassessment of D. H. Lawrence's "Aaron's Rod,"* 61–91.

38. Howe, *The Art of the Self in D. H. Lawrence,* 89.

39. Lawrence, who would have been familiar with Benvenuto Cellini's presentation of Baccio Bandinelli, in his *Autobiography,* as an untalented artist in the court of Cosimo I de' Medici, refers to Bandinelli's statue of Hercules and Cacus in the Piazza della Signoria.

40. Baker, 131; Howe, 89.

41. Sagar, *D. H. Lawrence: A Calendar of His Works,* 98. Baker, 200 n. 18, discusses the problems in dating the essay.

So young: sixteen, they say. So big: and stark-naked. Revealed. Too big, too naked, too exposed. Livid, under today's
sky. The Florentine! The Tuscan pose—half self-conscious all
the time. Adolescent. Waiting. The tense look. No escape. The
Lily. Lily or iris, what does it matter? Whitman's Calamus,
too. [P 61]

What is exposed, "revealed," is the arrested moment of adolescence,
between childhood and adulthood, still uncommitted to either north
or south, or, as the allusion to Whitman's Calamus poems suggests, to
either heterosexual or homosexual identity, but containing the potential of these opposities in balanced harmony. The true genius of Michaelangelo's *David*, like that of Attic tragedy in Nietzsche's *Birth of
Tragedy*, is its perfect union of Apollonian and Dionysian elements.
More precisely, the statue is the "Dionysus and Christ of Florence,"
perfectly embodying, like the figure of Dionysus in Nietzsche's *"Dionysus versus the Crucified"* (in *Ecce Homo*), the dynamic, "trembling
balance" of opposites: "For one moment Dionysus touched the hand of
the Crucified . . ." (P 63).

In *Aaron's Rod,* the Florentine sculptures have a direct bearing on
the renascence of unapologetic maleness, which Lilly sees as essential to masculine identity and which Aaron must incorporate in his
role as artist:

Aaron felt a new self, a new life-urge rising inside himself.
Florence seemed to start a new man in him. It was a town of
men. . . . The dangerous, subtle, never-dying fearlessness,
and the acrid unbelief. But men! Men! A town of men, in spite
of everything. The one manly quality, undying, acrid fearlessness. The eternal challenge of the unquenched human soul.
Perhaps too acrid and challenging today, when there is nothing left to challenge. But men—who existed without apology
and without justification. Men who would neither justify
themselves nor apologise for themselves. Just men. The rarest thing left in our sweet Christendom. [AR 212–13]

No such men are left in the world of *St. Mawr.* The young Lou Witt, a
New Orleans girl educated in Europe, has the "quaint air of playing
at being well-bred, in a sort of charade game" (*St. M* 21); and Rico
Carrington, the Australian heir to an English baronetcy, affects the
behavior of a young artist "in a most floridly elegant fashion" (*St. M*
22). Married when both are twenty-four, Rico and Lou settle into a
Platonic, sexless marriage in Westminster society, where Rico in-

dulges in nonsexual flirtations with young society women like Flora Manby. Lou and her mother, the acerbic Mrs. Witt, join the Hyde Park riding set, while Rico, who had earlier gone to Paris under the inspiration of Cézanne and Renoir, is now "becoming an almost fashionable portrait painter" (*St. M* 23).

Rico, an unrealistic, contrived character in the opinion of critics like Graham Hough and Eliseo Vivas, becomes for Kingsley Widmer "the living symbol of emasculation used by Lawrence for harsh satire of modern sophisticated men."[42] As "canny and shrewd and sensible as any young poser could be" (*St. M* 22), Rico assumes a kind of Wildean aesthetic pose without the wit to carry it off. He arrays himself in flamboyantly antinatural dress, on one occasion "appearing all handsome and in the picture, in white flannels with an apricot silk shirt" (*St. M* 47), on another donning "white riding-breeches and a shirt of purple silk crape, with a flowing black tie, spotted red like a ladybird, and black riding-boots. Then he took a *chic* little white hat with a black band" (*St. M* 49). Rico, like the fop of Restoration comedy, is a target of satire because his social ascendancy is proportionate to the social decline of the kind of man whose values the author finds to be more worthy, the phallic male. Albeit a "spiritual castrato,"[43] Rico is dangerous because, as a false artist, he is a false prophet, exploiting the very fragmentation and self-division that the true artist seeks to reconcile into wholeness.

One index to Rico's state of being is his preference for the mechanical to the organic. "Lou dearest," he says, "*don't* spend a fortune on a horse for me, which I *don't* want. Honestly, I prefer a car" (*St. M* 32). Lawrence prefigures his identification of Sir Clifford Chatterley with the motorized wheelchair in *Lady Chatterley's Lover* in Mrs. Witt's judgment of modern manhood in general from a view of her son-in-law as a kind of human Model-T: "Like little male motor-cars. Give him a little gas, and start him on the low gear, and away he goes: all his male gear rattling, like a cheap motor-car" (*St. M* 97).

If in *Aaron's Rod* the phallic male is "The rarest thing left in our sweet Christendom" (*AR* 213), in *St. Mawr* the state of masculinity has further declined in "[o]ur whole eunuch civilisation, nastyminded as eunuchs are, with their kind of sneaking, sterilising cruelty" (*St. M* 96). Mrs. Witt, determined to save the last embodiment of male divinity mythically personified in the stallion St. Mawr from threatened gelding by Rico and Flora Manby, urges Lou to say:

---

42. Hough, *The Dark Sun*, 182; Vivas, *D. H. Lawrence: The Failure and the Triumph of Art*, 155; and Widmer, *The Art of Perversity*, 71.
43. Vivas, 151.

"Miss Manby, you may have my husband, but not my horse. My husband won't need emasculating, and my horse I won't have you meddle with. I'll preserve one last male thing in the museum of this world, if I can" (*St. M* 97).

In *Lady Chatterley's Lover,* Lawrence presents three examples of the false artist: Sir Clifford Chatterley, Michaelis, and Duncan Forbes, all of them modeled in part on artists Lawrence knew, but at the same time incorporating Lawrence's own self-criticism. I argue that in all three the independent, assertive masculine identity that Lawrence in *Aaron's Rod* sets forth as essential to the male artist is severely attenuated. Unable to present either themselves or their art as a "trembling balance" that reconciles opposites, they exploit the divisions in an art of surface form and inner fragmentation.

Sir Clifford Chatterley's stories are described in this way:

> He had taken to writing stories; curious, very personal stories about people he had known. Clever, rather spiteful, and yet, in some mysterious way, meaningless. The observation was extraordinary and peculiar. But there was no touch, no actual contact. It was as if the whole thing took place in a vacuum. And since the field of life is largely an artificially-lighted stage to-day, the stories were curiously true to modern life, to the modern psychology, that is. [*LCL* 15]

When these stories appear in modern magazines, Clifford wants everyone to think them the *"ne plus ultra"* and is "morbidly sensitive" to any negative criticism; but in response to her father, Sir Malcolm's judgment that the stories were inconsequential and wouldn't last, Connie reflects: "Why should there be anything in them, why should they last? Sufficient unto the day is the evil thereof. Sufficient unto the moment is the *appearance* of reality" (*LCL* 18).

The narrator says nothing more about the subject matter or style of Clifford's fiction but provides several clues to his literary preferences. Dennis Jackson observes that Clifford, more than other characters in *Lady Chatterley's Lover,* "is characterized by allusions, which serve to enhance the ironies of his character and to associate him with what Lawrence regarded as the twin evils of modern life— the 'mental life' and scientific materialism." Clifford likes metaphorical conceits, such as Shakespeare's "Sweeter than the lids of Juno's eyes" (*The Winter's Tale,* 4.4.121), which Connie sees as a false metaphor unrelated to the "actual violets" (*LCL* 105); and

Keats's "Thou still unravished bride of quietness" ("Ode on a Gre-cian Urn," line 1), which reflects Clifford's assumption of Connie's chastity but provokes her response, "How she hated words, always coming between her and life: they did the ravishing, if anything did: ready-made words and phrases, sucking all the life-sap out of living things" (*LCL* 108).

Clifford is in favor of "classic control": "one gets all one wants out of Racine. Emotions that are ordered and given shape are more important than disorderly emotions" (*LCL* 108). Jackson delineates the ironic subtext: "Clifford reads Racine to Connie soon after her third sexual encounter with Mellors," while she, hearing not a word, "is fulfilled by the ecstatic 'after-humming' of her own disorderly emotions. . . ."[44] While Proust bores Connie—"He doesn't have feel-ings, he only has streams of words about feelings"—Clifford admires him: "I like Proust's subtlety and his well-bred anarchy" (*LCL* 233). But as Jackson points out, "Lady Chatterley's criticism of Proust is leveled at not only Clifford's reading tastes but his attitudes as well," and her exclamation, "I'm tired of self-important mentalities" (*LCL* 233) applies equally to Clifford.[45]

Both John Pearson and Derek Britton argue persuasively that many of the personal and literary mannerisms attributed to the char-acter in the third version of the novel have their source in Osbert Sitwell, who, with his sister Edith, made a two-hour visit to Lawrence and Frieda at the Villa Mirenda in May 1927.[46] In a letter to S. S. Koteliansky (27 May 1927), Lawrence describes Osbert and Edith Sitwell as nice and unaffected, but comments: "I never in my life saw such a strong, strange *family* complex: as if they were marooned on a desert island, & nobody in the world but their lost selves. Queer!" (*QR* 314). He writes to Richard Aldington (24 May 1927) that he and Frieda liked the Sitwells better than they had expected, but adds that Osbert upset and worried him: "I want to ask: But what ails thee, then? Tha's got nowt amiss as much as a' that!" (*CL* 978). Frieda confirms that the Lawrences were strangely moved and disturbed by the Sitwells: "They seemed so oversensitive, as if something had hurt them too much, as if they had to keep up a brave front to the world, to pretend they didn't care and yet they only cared much too much." But

44. Jackson, "Literary Allusions in *Lady Chatterley's Lover*," 172–73, 171.
45. Ibid., 182. Jackson also discusses allusions to Plato, Benvenuto Cellini, the Marquis de Sade, Edgar Allan Poe, Walt Whitman, Alfred North Whitehead, and others.
46. The fullest discussions of the Sitwells as a source for the novel are in John Pearson, *The Sitwells*, 222–32; and in Britton, *"Lady Chatterley": The Making of the Novel*, chap. 8.

she declares, inaccurately, that *Lady Chatterley's Lover,* "written and finished before Lawrence ever set eyes on any Sitwell," had nothing to do with them.[47] While Sir Osbert Sitwell was not the original source for Sir Clifford Chatterley in *The First Lady Chatterley,* Lawrence, as Derek Britton has shown, modeled Clifford's Aunt Eva and her butler Collingwood in *John Thomas and Lady Jane* on Osbert's mother, Lady Ida Sitwell, and her butler Henry Moat.[48] The family situation of the Chatterleys, in other respects, reflects that of the Sitwells: "The Chatterleys, two brothers and a sister, had lived curiously isolated, shut in with one another at Wragby, . . . cut off from those industrial Midlands in which they passed their lives" (*LCL* 10).

The withering tone of Edith Sitwell's description of the visit, in contrast to the friendly tone of Osbert's account,[49] may derive in part from Lawrence's unmistakable portrait of her as Clifford's sister Emma, the muse for his smart but curiously empty stories:

> Miss Chatterley came sometimes, with her aristocratic thin face, and triumphed, finding nothing altered. She would never forgive Connie for ousting her from her union in consciousness with her brother. It was she, Emma, who should be bringing forth these stories, these books, with him; the Chatterley stories, something new in the world, that *they,* the Chatterleys, had put there. There was no other standard. There was no organic connection with the thought and expression that had gone before. Only something new in the world: the Chatterley books, entirely personal. [*LCL* 16]

Pearson attributes Edith's scathing account mainly to her belief that Lawrence "had based the character of Chatterley on that of her own beloved Osbert—who, like Sir Clifford, was a baronet, a famous writer and a soldier from the war. Worse still, she was convinced that Lawrence had intentionally written to attack Osbert on two forbidden grounds—that of class and, more distressing still, of sex." But the attributes of social status and sexual impotence were already evident in the main outline of Clifford's character in the first two drafts. The visit that so affected Lawrence occurred well before

47. Frieda Lawrence, *"Not I, But the Wind . . .",* 195–96.

48. Britton, "Henry Moat, Lady Ida Sitwell, and *John Thomas and Lady Jane,"* 69–76.

49. See Edith Sitwell, *Taken Care Of: The Autobiography of Edith Sitwell,* 122–27; and Osbert Sitwell, "A Visit with D. H. L.," *New York Herald Tribune,* 20 December 1960. See also Osbert Sitwell, "Portrait of Lawrence," *Weekend Review,* 7 February 1931, reprinted in *Penny Foolish,* 293–97.

he began the third version of the novel in late November, or no later than 3 December 1927.[50] Pearson, who contends that the additional details of Clifford's character found in the third version "almost without exception, have been drawn from Osbert," notes, in particular, Lawrence's acute observation of the sense of uneasiness and fear underlying Clifford's rage and vulnerability, his bold and frightened eyes reflecting his ambivalent combination of superciliousness and self-effacement, assurance and uncertainty.[51]

Michaelis, a "Dublin mongrel" who pines "to be where he didn't belong . . . among the English upper classes" (LCL 22), has an instinct for making money as a writer of popular plays. Although Sir Clifford Chatterley is contemptuous of him as an outsider, he invites the playwright for a weekend at Wragby Hall, where Michaelis plays on Connie Chatterley's sympathies sufficiently to get her into bed. Michaelis's superficiality as both man and artist is emphasized. As the affair progresses, he and Connie fall into a sexual pattern characterized by his ejaculating quickly, then remaining "firm inside her," while she is "wildly, passionately active, coming to her own crisis" (LCL 31), as Leo Bersani puts it, "by working herself up and down on Mick's penis after he had had his orgasm." Bersani points out the marked distinction between the frictional "pleasures of rubbing and rubbed skin" and the "deepening whirlpools of sensation" in "liquefying" orgasm to which Mellors introduces Connie.[52] As Britton suggests, Michaelis's "active mental sexuality" delineates by antithesis a clear definition of the keeper's phallic sexuality.[53] Michaelis takes the same curious pride in Connie's "achieving her own orgasmic satisfaction from his hard, erect passivity" (LCL 31) that he takes in the superficial thrills induced by his plays.

Although Clifford knows nothing of the affair, he considers Michaelis a "bounder beneath his veneer" and thinks Connie mistakes his "unscrupulousness for generosity" (LCL 29). Clifford is flattered, however, when Michaelis seizes upon him as the central figure for a

50. The exact date is debatable. Sagar, D. H. Lawrence: A Calendar of His Works, 168, notes that "[t]he beginning of the MS . . . bears this date." Squires, Creation of "Lady Chatterley's Lover," 7, says "it is more likely that be began rewriting the novel a few days after his chance meeting with Michael Arlen on 17 November" and that the date on the flyleaf, written in a different ink from the first manuscript notebook but in the same ink as the second manuscript notebook, "likely refers to the date on which he continued writing the novel in the second notebook." Derek Britton agrees; see his "Lady Chatterley," 247.

51. Pearson, The Sitwells, 223, 229–31.

52. Bersani, 161.

53. Britton, "Lady Chatterley," 246.

play. Arriving for another weekend at Wragby, he brings Act One and sketches in the rest of the plot for Clifford and Connie, who are duly "thrilled." In a metaphor that curiously recalls the West African statuary of *Women in Love,* in both image and meaning, Connie sees in Michaelis "that ancient motionlessness of a race that can't be disillusioned anymore": "On the far side of his supreme prostitution to the bitch-goddess he seemed pure, pure as an African ivory mask that dreams impurity into purity, in its ivory curves and planes" (*LCL* 58). Connie praises the play "rapturously": "Yet all the while, at the bottom of her soul, she knew it was nothing" (*LCL* 59).

The addition of Michaelis as a new character in the third version was probably prompted by Lawrence's chance encounter with the popular Mayfair novelist Michael Arlen (pseudonym of Dikrān Kouyoumdjian) on the Lungarno in Florence, 17 November 1927. Lawrence's response to Kouyoumdjian, on the evidence of his letters, was not unsympathetic. In fact, Michael Squires ventures the conjecture that Connie's attraction to Michaelis reflects Lawrence's own personal feelings: "Presumably (though one must not press the point) Lawrence was attracted to Michael Arlen, was stung with guilt for his intense feeling, and so allowed Connie to act out his ambivalent response of attraction and repulsion."[54] While Michaelis's thematic functions in the novel do not invariably reflect Lawrence's views of the model, Squires draws an illuminating parallel between Lawrence's comments on Kouyoumdjian in letters to Aldington and Koteliansky (18 and 22 November 1927, *CL* 1023–24) as an outcast, "sad dog" that people throw stones at and kick and his description of Michaelis in the third version as a "sad dog" with a "slightly tail-between-the-legs look."[55]

The third, artist, Duncan Forbes, the painter, arrives at the Villa Esmeralda to visit Connie and her sister Hilda during their stay in Venice. Forbes, like another "mental lifer," Tommy Dukes, sometimes speaks in Laurentian language. When Connie confides in him an account of the gamekeeper's history, he tells her: "It's the one thing they won't let you be, straight and open in your sex. You can be as dirty as you like. In fact the more dirt you do on sex, the better they like it. But if you believe in your own sex, and won't have it done dirt to: they'll down you" (*LCL* 319).

When Connie proposes that Forbes pose as the father of her unborn child and allow himself to be named as corespondent in Clifford's divorce proceedings, he insists first on meeting Mellors. On a

---

54. Squires, *Creation of "Lady Chatterley's Lover,"* 61.
55. Ibid., 228 n. 6.

visit to Forbes's studio, Mellors responds negatively to both the artist and his painting: "His art was all tubes and valves and spirals and strange colors, ultra modern, yet with a certain power, even a certain purity of form and tone: only Mellors thought it cruel and repellent." At first reluctant to venture a comment on what he recognizes as Forbes's "personal religion," the gamekeeper at length turns art critic and denounces the pictures: "It is like a pure bit of murder" (*LCL* 345). When Hilda contemptuously demands, "And who is murdered?" Mellors replies, "Me! It murders all the bowels of compassion in a man" (*LCL* 346). As a condition to the proposed arrangement, Forbes stipulates that Connie pose as an artist's model for him. "But he'll only shit on you on canvas," Mellors tells her, to which she replies, "He'll only be painting his own feelings for me . . ." (*LCL* 347). Her letter to Clifford informing him that she is staying in Duncan Forbes's flat misleadingly implies without directly saying that he is the lover for whom she is leaving Wragby (*LCL* 350).

David Garnett identifies the source of the scene in Forbes's studio as a visit Lawrence made to Bloomsbury artist Duncan Grant's studio (22 January 1915) in company with Garnett and E. M. Forster. By Garnett's account, while Frieda, in deference to Grant's feelings, made consolatory protestations to the contrary, Lawrence savagely denounced one picture after another: "It was not simply that the pictures themselves were bad—hopelessly bad—but they were worthless because Duncan was full of the wrong ideas."[56] In a letter to Lady Ottoline Morrell (27 January 1915), Lawrence was critical of both Grant's sexual proclivities and his painting. Referring to a series of abstract shapes painted on a long cotton band exhibited in motion between two winding rollers, Lawrence urges Lady Ottoline, "Tell him not to make silly experiments in the futuristic line, with bits of color on a moving paper." Alluding to three huge puppets eight feet tall that Grant painted and cut out of cardboard for a performance of the last scene from Racine's *Bérénice* at a Bloomsbury party,[57] Lawrence adds, "Neither to bother making marionettes—even titanic ones. But to seek out the terms in which he shall state his whole." Garnett remarks that although Lawrence's "spate of verbiage" suggests that he is "refuting ideas that Duncan had put forward," he is actually "belabouring a figment of his imagination, as well as pouring out a lot of non-

56. David Garnett, *The Flowers of the Forest*, 34–35.
57. Holroyd, *Lytton Strachey*, 2:136.

sense."[58] But Lawrence praises Grant's search, like Fra Angelico's, for "a whole conception of the existence of Man—creation, good, evil, life, death, resurrection, the separating of the stream of good and evil, and its return to the eternal source. It is an Absolute we are all after. . . ." As Paul Delany recognizes, Lawrence, albeit dogmatically, proposes a valid critique of Grant's art: that the Absolute cannot be built up from such "ready stated" geometric figures as a triangle or circle, but only from "the 'concrete Units' that precede the abstraction."[59] This is the basis for Lawrence's conclusion: "Painting is *not* architecture." Hence, he rejects as "puerile" Grant's Futuristic experiments in conveying the third dimension by means of "lines of force" and suggests that the architectonics of painting consist only in "some conception which conveys . . . the whole universe" (*Letters* 2:263). As Emile Delavenay comments on this passage: "He has worked out his own position, accepting the futurists' criticism of the abstract and analytical aspect of cubism, but rejecting Boccioni's plea . . . that painting and sculpture must be architectural."[60]

Italian painting provides a clue to why Lawrence recalled the visit twelve years later and used it as a basis for the scene in *Lady Chatterley*. As both Squires and Britton suggest, Lawrence was also drawing on the much more recent visit he and Earl Brewster made in January 1927 to the studio of Florentine abstract painter Alberto Magnelli, whom Lawrence describes, in a letter to Dorothy Brett (20 January 1927), as "very self-important and arch-priesty, . . . very 'my work'—Very clever work, quite lovely new colour and design, and inside it all, nothing—emptiness, ashes, an old bone. All that labour and immense self-conscious effort, and real technical achievement, over the cremated ashes of an inspiration!" (*Letters* 5:629). As Britton suggests, "the paintings and the artist's high-priestly conception of his art are Magnelli's, and the hostility between the two men was true only of the mutual dislike that arose between Lawrence and the Italian."[61]

A third model, the writer and painter Wyndham Lewis, has been proposed by Jeffrey Meyers, chiefly on the ground that Duncan Forbes's "ultra modern" paintings, with their violently abstract "tubes and valves and spirals and strange colours," bear no resem-

---

58. Garnett, *The Flowers of the Forest*, 36.
59. Delany, *D. H. Lawrence's Nightmare*, 49–50.
60. Delavenay, "Lawrence and the Futurists," 155.
61. Britton, *"Lady Chatterley,"* 189. A similar view is expressed in Squires, *Creation of "Lady Chatterley's Lover,"* 229 n. 14.

blance to "Grant's tepid Post-Impressionist pictures" but "resemble those of Lewis' Vorticist period." Meyers recounts Lewis's several attacks on Lawrence, but provides no evidence that Lawrence had actually seen Lewis's paintings and responded to them, as Mellors does to Forbes's, as "cruel and repellent," hardly the kind of reaction Lawrence was likely to keep to himself.[62]

Lawrence's work reveals a world in which art is essential, not decorative. His criticism supports his presentation of the figure of the artist in his fiction by stating several principles that distinguish the true artist from the false artist.

As myth-maker, Lawrence suggests in "The Spirit of Place," the artist presents paradigms of living reality that establish a myth meaning, not necessarily a literal or rational meaning but an essential truth presented as art speech. For this reason, the real meaning of the work of art may remain unconscious; it may even be in conflict with the artist's conscious didactic intention. Because the passion that his conscious purpose masks and censors emerges in the symbolic wish fulfillment of the work, the true artist, nevertheless, functions as a channel for the myth meaning expressed indirectly through the "subterfuge" of "art-speech."[63] It is in this sense that the artist may be a "damned liar," setting out "to point a moral and adorn a tale," while "the tale points the other way": "Two blankly opposing morals, the artist's and the tale's." The principle leads to Lawrence's central critical dictum: "Never trust the artist. Trust the tale" (SCAL 2).

In portraying character, Lawrence suggests in his familiar letter to Edward Garnett (5 June 1914), he is concerned not with the external, social ego of the personality in "a certain moral scheme" but with "another ego," the elemental basis of character that is, in Lawrence's analogy, neither diamond nor coal but carbon (Letters 2:182–83). This letter, which Keith Cushman calls "the key statement in the articulation of Lawrence's mature aesthetic," formulates in quasi-scientific terms Lawrence's idea of "the great impersonal." "In focusing on man as a representative of 'some greater, inhuman will,' " Cushman says, "Lawrence seeks to understand him at his lowest common denominator: in terms of the basic, elemental laws of matter and energy that govern the universe."[64]

Finally, the true artist reconciles opposites not by proliferating

62. Meyers, The Enemy, 144–45.
63. See Ragussis, The Subterfuge of Art, 1–5.
64. Cushman, " 'I am going through a transition stage,' " 181.

mechanistic systems that become substitutes for life but by holding the antinomies of existence in a dynamic, "trembling balance" of "true and vivid relationships" (*STH* 172–74). This does not mean, of course, that good art, whether narrative or pictorial, is necessarily naturalistic, or that it cannot encompass various levels of representation, as Lawrence's art does. It does mean that the true artist, in the presentation of natural forms, maintains a fidelity to nature that presents it neither as the wholly subjective impression of the artist's nor as something to be known only as finished, dead, or fragmentary particles to be manipulated, formalized, and objectified as "Significant Form" in his art. As Lawrence puts it in "Introduction to These Paintings," "Cézanne's apples are a real attempt to let the apple exist in its own separate entity, without transfusing it with personal emotion" (*P* 567). Cézanne's intuitive leap was to grasp the real existence of the body, the denial of which has been the preoccupation of Platonism, Christianity, and much of Western thought.[65] In the view of John Adkins Richardson and John I. Ades, Lawrence's profound critical insight in penetrating to the heart of Cézanne's artistic struggle for resolution emerges from an empathic leap that suggests "a far deeper alliance between an artist and his critic than is generally recognized."[66] Lawrence's criticism of Cézanne, in other words, emerges from precisely the kind of imaginative empathy with the artist that I have advocated in the Introduction to this book:

> He was dominated by his old mental consciousness, but he wanted terribly to escape the domination. . . . He terribly wanted to paint the real existence of the body, to make it artistically palpable. . . . The man of flesh has been slowly destroyed through centuries, to give place to the man of spirit, the mental man, the ego, the self-conscious I. And in his artistic soul Cézanne knew it, and wanted to rise in the flesh. He couldn't do it, and it embittered him. Yet, with his apple, he did shove the stone from the door of the tomb. [*P* 568]

Cézanne, in doing so, did not produce mere mental or photographic representation; he rendered the elemental, "carbon" reality of the object. Works of true art, like genuine scientific discoveries, "are made by the whole consciousness of man working together in unison

65. This principle is set forth as a critical tenet of "contextualism" in Burns, "The Panzaic Principle," in *Towards a Contextualist Aesthetic of the Novel*, 121–23.
66. Richardson and Ades, "D. H. Lawrence on Cézanne," 441–53.

and oneness: instinct, intuition, mind, intellect all fused into one complete consciousness" (*P* 574).

Lawrence sees the true artist as a myth-maker who re-creates in his art the "trembling balance" of living existence and in so doing establishes the connection between the elemental "carbon" substratum of the object and the cosmos. The false artist, on the other hand, functions in none of these ways. Rather than drawing on a deeper consciousness to forge new myths, he conveys a surface reality, often expressing a conventional morality that comfortably supports the societal status quo. Hence, his presentation of character is superficial and social, not elemental. Far from reconciling opposites or establishing a connection with the elemental cosmos, the false artist exploits the fragmentation. In these terms, artists like Cooper and Whitman, almost in spite of their conscious intentions, and especially Melville, with whom Lawrence had a number of affinities, were true artists.

4

The Artist as Myth-Maker:
D. H. Lawrence and Herman Melville

Lawrence sees Herman Melville as a true artist who, by tapping the unconscious instinctual energy of his own deepest dreams and wishes, was able to establish a correspondence between his deeper self and the external world. Because it emanates from the unconscious, the "art-speech" of the true artist embodies a symbolic truth that transcends, and may even be at variance with, the artist's conscious, didactic intentions. But the artist thereby becomes a myth-maker who recreates in his art the "trembling balance" of living existence and reveals the connection between the elemental "carbon" substratum of the self and the cosmos.

What makes Lawrence's criticism of Melville central to these issues is Lawrence's manifestly identifying himself with Melville in the two essays on *Typee* and *Omoo* and on *Moby-Dick,* published as chapters 10 and 11 of *Studies in Classic American Literature.* Lawrence's criticism of Melville is informed by a profoundly subjective response, which is not reducible to projective identification. That is, Lawrence does not appear to split off parts of his nuclear self and project them unknowingly into Melville in an unconscious defense mechanism by which the objects of his inner world can be manipulated and controlled. Rather, he seems, through imaginative empathy, to employ his own subjective response critically in a method comparable to what he does in fiction in his shifting narrative identification with first one character and then another, not so much with their technical point of view as with their subjective position. That is, Lawrence makes his own psychic apparatus available, as it were, to the full impact of Melville's experience and feelings in an identification that is, for the most part, concordant. His critical insights are then presented in a form that is close to imaginative art. In examining Lawrence's criticism of Melville with reference to the core critical principles by which, Lawrence believes, the artist functions as myth-maker, I want to focus on two themes, both of them versions of the "trembling balance," which Lawrence shares with Melville—the relation of males to other males in blood brotherhood and the relation of the self to the cosmos through the elemental image of the sea.

Lawrence sees authentic literary creation as the imaginative articulation of "myth-meaning." As David J. Gordon comments, "Lawrence suggests that art in the modern world is the 'fallen' state of myth. And one can observe in his own art an effort to recapture the mythic consciousness."[1] Seeing Melville as a myth-maker like himself, Lawrence says that Melville "wrote from a sort of dream-self, so that events which he relates as actual fact have indeed a far deeper reference to his own soul, his own inner life" (*SCAL* 134), ultimately embodying the ill-fated saga of the American soul. Lawrence's insight on the unconscious sources of Melville's art perhaps derives from his recognition of similar sources of his own art, so that in writing of Melville he evokes many themes of his own life. Sickened by "the horror of the cracked church bell" of modern Western consciousness, Lawrence turns back imaginatively with Melville to the unconscious life of the Pacific peoples: "for how many thousands of years has the true Pacific been dreaming, turning over in its sleep and dreaming again: idylls: nightmares" (*SCAL* 132–33). "[M]ad with hatred of the world," Melville, he says, "was looking for paradise." When Lawrence describes Melville's "entry into the valley of the dread cannibals of Nukuheva," he sets forth his own personal myth of a nightmare of birth into what should have been a paradise but turned out to be a childhood society in which family members devoured each other: "Down this narrow, steep, horrible dark gorge he slides and struggles as we struggle in a dream, or in the act of birth, to emerge in the green Eden of the Golden Age, the valley of the cannibal savages" (*SCAL* 134). In both Melville and Lawrence, the psychic structure of the unconscious nuclear self becomes the source of a creative mythology.

1. Gordon, *D. H. Lawrence as a Literary Critic*, 58–59.

Lawrence's function as critic of Melville, correlatively, was to slice through the "high sententiousness" of Melville's style to reveal the psychic myths that encapsulated the essential truth of his artistic vision: "The artist was so *much* greater than the man" (*SCAL* 146). Thus, despite the many carefully chosen quotations, especially from *Moby-Dick,* Lawrence's essays concentrate on larger mythic themes rather than on details of technique. He does not explicate; he prophesies.

Melville fits conveniently into Lawrence's own dualistic Weltanschauung—his urge to see the world as a conflict between Apollonian and Dionysian forces: light and dark, fair northern peoples and dark southern peoples, mental consciousness and "blood consciousness," abstract intellectuality that "murders to dissect" and imaginative empathy that synthesizes experience. It was the artist's function to reconcile opposites not by merging but by holding the dualities in the "trembling balance" of art. Melville's work, for Lawrence, defines the terms in which the conflict was fought out in nineteenth-century American literature to the unfortunate victory of the first term in each dichotomy. "He was a modern Viking," Lawrence says, an elemental figure of the great northern, Atlantic civilization that "has almost completed its round," returning "to the oldest of all the oceans, to the Pacific" (*SCAL* 131, 132), the cradle of a pre-Christian civilization of sensual consciousness, where pagan rituals embody directly values that the Christian world only parodies palely. Lawrence finds even the savage "sacrament" of cannibalism "as awe-inspiring as the one Jesus substituted" (*SCAL* 135).[2]

One of the means by which Lawrence sought to establish the "trembling balance" between the spiritual and the sensual components of the self and a "nourishing creative flow" between the self and the

---

2. Lawrence's liberal view of the "cannibal sacrament" may have been influenced by his reading of Frazer. See Sir James George Frazer, *The Golden Bough,* 3d ed., 2:117–18:

> Indeed the evidence which I have just adduced suggests that the intention of forming a blood-covenant with the dead may have been a common motive for the cannibalism which has so often been practised by savage victors on the bodies of their victims. If that was so, it would to some extent mitigate the horror with which such a practice is naturally viewed by civilised observers; since it would reveal the cannibal feast, no longer in the lurid light of a brutal outburst of blind rage and hatred against the vanquished, but in the milder aspect of a solemn rite designed to wipe out the memory of past hostilities and to establish a permanent relation of friendship and good fellowship with the dead.

other was the concept of Blutbrüderschaft. In his reading of *Moby-Dick,* Lawrence sees Ishmael and Queequeg's "marriage" as a potential reconciliation of pagan and Christian consciousness, which is needed to open in Ishmael "the flood-gates of love and human connexion." In view of the pervasiveness of the theme in Lawrence's work, one should perhaps speak of his affinity for, rather than the influence of, Melville's treatment of this kind of male bonding. Before reading *Moby-Dick,* Lawrence had, of course, already tentatively explored the theme in *The White Peacock* and *Sons and Lovers.* But the reconciliation of spiritual and sensual modes of consciousness through male bonding was to become a dominant theme in *Women in Love, Aaron's Rod, Kangaroo,* and *The Plumed Serpent,* all written after Lawrence had read *Moby-Dick.* In his later works, Lawrence's treatment of the theme proposed direct confirmation of Blutbrüderschaft in conscious rituals on the order of Ishmael and Queequeg's "marriage" in "A Bosom Friend" (chap. 10) in *Moby-Dick.* Sacramental though the action may be in Cyril and George's bathing scene in *The White Peacock,* the ritual is that of pastoral romance, not the open invitation to vows of blood brotherhood that Rupert Birkin offers to Gerald Crich in *Women in Love,* as "the old German knights" had sworn a "Blutbrüderschaft" by making a little wound in their arms" and rubbing "each other's blood into the cut," swearing "to be true to each other, of one blood, all their lives.—That is what we ought to do. No wounds, that is obsolete.—But we ought to swear to love each other, you and I, implicitly and perfectly, finally, without any possibility of going back on it" (*WL* 206–7).

Such passages in Lawrence, except for the notable absence of Melville's saving humor, are not so very far from the suggestive imagery of "The Counterpane" (chap. 4) in *Moby-Dick,* in which Ishmael awakens in the Spouter Inn to find "Queequeg's arm thrown over me in the most loving and affectionate manner. You had thought I had been his wife" (*MD* 25).[3] The "bridegroom clasp" is correlated with the tomahawk at Queequeg's side, the phallic threat of which is attenuated while its sexual meaning is completed by the simile that likens it to "a hatchet-faced baby" (*MD* 26, 27). After their day's business, the "cosy, loving pair" exchange confidences in bed, with "Queequeg now and then affectionately throwing his brown tattooed legs over mine, and then drawing them back" (*MD* 52, 53). As Ishmael describes their rite of friendship in "A Bosom Friend" (chap. 10), "He seemed to take to me quite as naturally and unbiddenly as I

---

3. Melville, *Moby-Dick, or The Whale.* Hereafter, cited parenthetically in the text by abbreviated title and page number.

to him; and when our smoke was over, he pressed his forehead against mine, clasped me round the waist, and said that henceforth we were married; meaning, in his country's phrase, that we were bosom friends; he would gladly die for me, if need should be" (*MD* 51). Lawrence's description of the yet undeclared friendship between Birkin and Gerald Crich in the canceled "Prologue" to *Women in Love* is almost identical: "They knew they loved each other, that each would die for the other" (*WL* 490).

It is hardly surprising that Gerald Crich, presented with a proposal that converts the strong bond between men into something like male marriage, is as bewildered as Ishmael at the Spouter Inn. What is surprising is that Lawrence thinks Ishmael's response to "the moment's heart's-brother, Queequeg" (*SCAL* 147) is essentially the same as Gerald's. For Ishmael, who has already decided, "Better sleep with a sober cannibal than a drunken Christian" (*MD* 24), assents to the union, unlike Gerald Crich in Lawrence's parallel scene. In Lawrence's view, which contrasts sharply with that of most Melville critics,[4] Ishmael is caught up in Ahab's monomaniacal obsession and regards Queequeg as someone to be "known," then forgotten "like yesterday's newspaper." Richard Swigg makes the point that in the final cataclysm, as Ahab encircles Moby Dick vowing to " 'dismember my dismemberer,' " "Ishmael stops short of the full destructive intent, extracting vague love from the fragments. . . ."[5] Lawrence's interpretation of Ishmael's relationship with Queequeg, though refuted by later Melville criticism, parallels Birkin's attributing Gerald Crich's destruction in *Women in Love* to his refusal of Birkin's life-giving offer of Blutbrüderschaft. The difference, which Lawrence failed to recognize, is that Ishmael does not refuse. Accepting Queequeg's unspoken view, "It's a mutual, joint-stock world in all meridians. We cannibals must help these Christians" (*MD* 62), Ishmael is, in fact, saved by the relationship, surviving by clinging to Queequeg's coffin.

Pleased but wary, and probably unaware that what Birkin is offering is not overt homosexuality but the sublimation of desire into blood brotherhood through sacramental ritual, Gerald, unlike Ishmael, responds ambivalently: "We'll leave it till I understand it better" (*WL* 207).

When the two men join in the nude wrestling scene in "Gladiatorial," "It was as if Birkin's whole physical intelligence interpenetrated into Gerald's body, as if his fine, sublimated energy entered

4. See, for example, Arvin, *Herman Melville*, 181–82.
5. Swigg, *Lawrence, Hardy, and American Literature*, 239.

into the flesh of the fuller man, like some potency, . . . through the muscles into the very depths of Gerald's physical being" (*WL* 270). Lawrence's description does make the union sound something like Iago's "beast with two backs" in *Othello* (1.1.118): "the swift, tight limbs, the solid white backs, the physical junction of two bodies clinched into a oneness" (*WL* 270). The psychological sensation of an altered state of consciousness is marked by "the strange tilting and sliding of the world" (*WL* 271) into darkness. The language is certainly sexual, but as the word "sublimated" suggests, the "potency" that is being "interpenetrated" into Gerald's "physical being" is metaphorically, not literally, phallic, as homoeroticism is transformed into the heroic ideal of blood brotherhood with its noble values of male commitment and loyalty. When the two men discuss the experience afterward, Birkin says, "We are mentally, spiritually intimate, therefore we should be more or less physically intimate too—it is more whole" (*WL* 272). But as the narrator comments, "There were long spaces of silence between their words. The wrestling had some deep meaning to them—an unfinished meaning" (*WL* 272).

Elsewhere I argue that this unfinished meaning lies in the idea that Birkin's homoerotic feeling, both in his attraction to men in the "Prologue" and as sublimated in his theory of Blutbrüderschaft, is to be understood as deriving not from an object-instinctive drive but from a psychic mechanism thrown up recurrently by the ego during a disturbing transitional period of his life to defend against the dissolution of the self, especially against the threat of the self's being swallowed up by spiritually possessive women.[6] Judith Ruderman, who identifies the twin poles of "[t]he longing for merger and the fear of merger" in Lawrence, observes astutely that "this psychic conflict is rooted in the author's earliest experiences with his caretaker mother. The blood brotherhood . . . —a relation of men—allows Lawrence the security of merger without the threat of annihilation that he associates with woman."[7] The wish for blood brotherhood is not disguised homoeroticism; indeed, Birkin's homoerotic fantasies are not disguised at all in the "Prologue" and scarcely so in the novel. It is, rather, a disguised defense against the dissolution of the self that Birkin fears in the "Prologue" (*WL* 500–501), especially being appropriated by the female as Magna Mater. Even so, the poignant dia-

6. Unpublished paper: "Blutbrüderschaft and Self Psychology in *Women in Love*."
7. Ruderman, *D. H. Lawrence and the Devouring Mother*, 148. The originality of Ruderman's study lies in her recognition that many of Lawrence's conflicts are preoedipal rather than oedipal in origin.

logue between Birkin and Ursula in equally balanced polarity after Gerald's death at the end of *Women in Love* suggests that Birkin's wish, because it is still largely in the service of pleasure gain rather than the reality principle, is doomed to tragic failure and disappointment. In addition to his marriage to Ursula, Birkin says, "I wanted eternal union with a man too: another kind of love." In her view, "It's an obstinacy, a theory, a perversity." "You can't have two kinds of love. Why should you!" Birkin reiterates, "Yet I wanted it." Ursula's final comment, "You can't have it, because it's false, impossible," and his intransigent reply, "I don't believe that" (*WL* 481), suggest her recognition and his failure of insight on why he is prevented from having what he wants: because he will not, or cannot, accept the realistic limits of such a relationship.

Lawrence's return to the same themes of cannibalism and male marriage in "Herman Melville's *Typee* and *Omoo*" and "Herman Melville's *Moby-Dick*" suggests that these essays be read as much as a revisionist dialogue with Lawrence's own earlier position as a criticism of Melville's works. Not surprisingly, Lawrence finds in Melville the same early objects that condition his own yearnings: "He even pined for Home and Mother, the two things he had run away from. . . . The two things that were his damnation" (*SCAL* 136). Like Lawrence himself in his dream of Rananim, Herman Melville, pinned by the "paradisal ideal," had sought for paradise but found a cannibal society. His own voracious needs, like Lawrence's, end in deprivation and longing. Making his escape, Melville comes home to face a demonstrably Laurentian series of disillusionments:

> He married and had an ecstasy of a courtship and fifty years of disillusion.
>
> He had just furnished his home with disillusions. No more Typees. No more paradises. No more Fayaways. A mother: a gorgon. A home: a torture box. A wife: a thing with clay feet. Life: a sort of disgrace. Fame: another disgrace, being patronized by common snobs who just know how to read. [*SCAL* 141]

Most disillusioning of all is the outcome of Melville's turning, like Lawrence, to the hopeless quest for blood brotherhood:

> From the "perfect woman lover," he passed on to the "perfect friend". He looked and looked for the perfect man friend.
> Couldn't find him.
> Marriage was a ghastly disillusion to him, because he looked for perfect marriage. . . .

Yet to the end he pined for this: a perfect relationship; perfect mating; perfect mutual understanding. A perfect friend.
Right to the end he could never accept the fact that *perfect*
relationships cannot be. Each soul is alone, and the aloneness
of each soul is a double barrier to perfect relationship between
two beings. [*SCAL* 142]

This criticism of Melville, asserted with an insight derived from
hindsight, represents, I suggest, Lawrence's tentative revision of his
own earlier position, though the vexing problem of how to achieve
male bonding without being destroyed remained and the dialogue
continued.

If his human relationships ended in failure, Melville, Lawrence suggests, "did have one great experience, getting away from humanity:
the experience of the sea," uniting self and cosmos in a universal
"trembling balance": "The South Sea Islands were not his great
experience. They were a glamorous world outside New England.
Outside. But it was the sea that was both outside and inside: the
universal experience" (*SCAL* 140).

Like Melville, Lawrence recognized a need to establish a connection between modern man's material consciousness and the elemental consciousness that the sea, among other images, embodied for
him. In "The Two Principles," the eighth essay in the first version of
the *Studies*, intended as an introduction to the essays on Dana and
Melville but omitted in the published third version, Lawrence
writes: "We need to find some terms to express such elemental connections as between the ocean and the human soul. We need to put
off our personality, even our individuality, and enter the region of
the elements" (*SM* 159–60).

Lawrence admires Melville as "[t]he greatest seer and poet of the
sea" (*SCAL* 131), a distinction that it would be surprising to find
attributed to Lawrence himself. Yet Lawrence wrote some of his
finest passages of both prose and poetry under the impression of
Melville's sea imagery. Lawrence also shared with Melville the
habit of seeing in nature, particularly in those animals that he employs as archetypal symbols, the numinous quality that he could not
find in established religion.

In *Kangaroo*, sea imagery of sharks and whales, reappearing now
and again, suggest man's need to reestablish the lost connection
with natural wildness. Repeatedly seen from Harriet Somers's point
of view, this imagery presents the "trembling balance" as that of

elemental male and female instinct. The thunderous Pacific, "roaring at one's feet" at Coo-ee (*K* 78), suggests the primitive female force as powerfully as the sharks suggest the primitive phallic force. When a shark is "caught in the heave of a breaker" and hurled toward the shore, Harriet sees "the quick flurry of his tail as he flung himself back. The land to him was horror—as to her the sea, beyond that wall of ice-blue foam" (*K* 99). Lawrence insists on the inviolable separateness of the two worlds, the human and the elemental, but yearns still for the means of reconciling the two in a "trembling balance" between man and nature and within man's self.

Such passages are reminiscent of "The Grand Armada" (chap. 87) in *Moby-Dick,* which Lawrence singles out for special admiration and echoes in "Whales Weep Not!"[8] In the flood of unconscious being in which the whales move, theirs is "the hottest blood of all, and the wildest, the most urgent" (line 2), and in their instinctual sexuality, as Sandra M. Gilbert aptly puts it, they "incarnate the demiurge."[9]

In the fragment "The Flying Fish" (1925), Lawrence blends his memories of Melville and Coleridge, of "The Grand Armada" and the Ancient Mariner's blessing of the sea creatures, in an imaginative fusion with his own recent experience on the return passage to England in 1925 following his nearly fatal illness in Mexico the preceding winter. Gethin Day, the autobiographical persona, gazes into the sea for hours, "curled in the wonder of this gulf of creation," trying to fathom the mysteries of flying fish and porpoises. The flying fish, in their momentary surge into air, are a figure for mutability, suggesting the perfect correlation of the wonder of life with its transitoriness. The dolphins, as elsewhere in Lawrence's work, are a more complex symbol. In the poem "Blueness," they embody the quickness of life in the midst of mysterious darkness, which "Breaks into dazzle of living, as dolphins leap from the sea / Of midnight and shake it to fire, till the flame of the shadow we see" (lines 15–16, *CP* 136). In *Etruscan Places,* Lawrence explains the mysterious image of the dolphin's leap in phallic terms: "Out he leaps; then, with a head-dive, back again he plunges into the sea. He is so much alive, he is like the phallus carrying the fiery spark of procreation down into the wet darkness of the womb" (*EP* 53). In "The Flying Fish," consistent with his earlier use of the image, Lawrence employs the dolphins to evoke the spontaneous source of vivid life and creativity:

8. Pinto and Roberts, eds., "Notes to Poems," *Complete Poems of D. H. Lawrence,* 1019.

9. Gilbert, *Acts of Attention,* 282–83.

They moved in a little cloud, and with the most wonderful sport they were above, they were below, they were to the fore, yet all the time the same one speed, the same one speed, and the last fish just touching with his tail-flukes the iron cutwater of the ship. Some would be down in the blue, shadowy, but horizontally motionless in the same speed. Then with a strange revolution, these would be up in pale green water, and others would be down. Even the toucher, who touched the ship, would in a twinkling be changed. [*P* 794]

If the ship encompasses the forward thrust of consciousness for the thought adventurer, the porpoises, in their joyous accompaniment, are a figure for creative change through instinctual sexuality deriving from the unconscious, which in Lawrence's psychology is not the repository of repressed material but the source of almost prelapsarian harmony and joy.

How to understand and incorporate the prelapsarian consciousness, with its unity and integration, into the modern antinomian consciousness, with its division and fragmentation, became for Lawrence, as it had been for Melville, a major question. Although the "sleep-forgotten past magnificence of human history" (*SM* 202), which Wordsworth only hints at in the "Intimations of Immortality" ode, but which Melville describes in *Typee*, suggests a way out of civilization's present impasse, Western man cannot reclaim the prelapsarian state merely by adopting primitivist modes. "We can't go back to the savages," Lawrence says. Though beautiful, generous, and childlike, "They are far off, and in their eyes is an easy darkness of the soft, uncreate past." They are "centuries and centuries behind us in the life-struggle, the consciousness-struggle, the struggle of the soul into fulness." We can, however, in Lawrence's anterior view of the future, "take a great curve in their direction, onwards" (*SCAL* 136, 137). This curious image, describing again in the archetypal curve that Lawrence employed as a symbol of reconciliation in *The Rainbow*, evokes the "trembling balance" of a new, whole consciousness, incorporating the feelings manifested "within the aboriginal jungle of us" (*STH* 203), those vital components of self, wildness, and instinct that Western man had rejected as "uncivilized."

Melville, in Lawrence's view, was unable finally to make that incorporation. Determined to find his paradise in Typee, naked with Fayaway but pinned by his own fixed ideals, Melville was disillusioned by "[t]hree little quibbles: morality, cannibal sacrament, and stone axes" (*SCAL* 135). When in *Omoo* he encountered in Doctor

Long Ghost "a white man really 'gone savage,'. . . with a blue shark tattooed over his brow" (*SCAL* 141), Melville retreated from the renegade life to reenlist in civilization, ironically aboard the American man-of-war depicted in *White-Jacket*. Nevertheless, Lawrence places Melville among those writers, including Poe, Hawthorne, and Whitman, who served, sometimes unconsciously, to destroy the old moral forms of the established Christian culture.

"The greatest seer and poet of the sea for me," Lawrence says at the outset, "is Melville" (*SCAL* 131). Lawrence declared, quite early among critics of American literature, that *Moby-Dick* "is a great book" (*SCAL* 159). He recognized in Melville an artist like himself, whose work is attuned to the "trembling balance" between "[t]he sheer naked slidings of the elements" and "the human soul experiencing it all" (*SCAL* 146): "Melville was, at the core," he says, "a mystic and an idealist," whose "bodily knowledge moves naked, a living quick among the stark elements. For with sheer physical vibrational sensitiveness, like a marvellous wireless-station, he registers the effects of the outer world" (*SCAL* 143, 147). For Lawrence, Melville's greatness lay in his response to the outer world with fidelity to his own inner vision, which became in his work our "myth-meaning."

Organic "myth-meaning" was hard to come by in the forms of modern art, with its vision of life as a mechanistic assemblage of fragmented pieces, as in cubism, the stream-of-consciousness novel, or, most popularly with the public and objectionably to Lawrence, the movies.

5

Lawrence and the Movies: *The Lost Girl* and After

Why didn't D. H. Lawrence like the movies?

Why did he see the cinema not merely as a medium that attracted popular artists who catered to the tastes of a mass audience by exploiting the industrial system in the manufacture and distribution of commercial product, but as, by its very form, a false art?

The motion picture has perhaps a claim to being the major original art form of the twentieth century. It seems probable that, as we see Renaissance drama and the Victorian novel as the characteristic art forms of those eras, future generations will see the film as the art form that quintessentially defines the twentieth century. Almost from its inception, cinema emerged from two contrary impulses—toward reality and toward fantasy. From fin de siècle Paris emerged both the realistic documentation of ordinary life in the *cinématographe* of Louis Lumière and his brother, Auguste, in such short descriptive works as *L'Arrivée d'un Train en Gare* (1895) and *Le Déjeuner du chat,* and the conjuror's trick photography and the illusionist's artifice in the fantasies of Georges Méliès, such as *Le Voyage dans la lune* (1902). It would be hard to deny that cinema, with its combined elements of camera work, mise en scène, sound, and editing, is a better medium, in some respects, for creating both realism and fantasy than written language alone is. But in neither film realism nor film fantasy could Lawrence find the "trembling balance" of life. Lawrence's objections to film, expressed variously throughout his canon, fall into three interrelated categories: audience response, stereotypic film conventions, and mechanical form.

Lawrence's comments on cinema parallel the early history and development of film as a narrative medium and the concomitant decline of theatrical variety entertainment. When he began *The Insurrection of Miss Houghton* in January 1913, the narrative cinema, which had emerged as early as *The Great Train Robbery* by Edwin S. Porter in 1903, was on the verge of its most important artistic breakthrough since then. By the time Lawrence published the completed novel as *The Lost Girl* in 1920, the cinema had shown itself capable, at its best, of a high degree of narrative sophistication. The epic sweep of D. W. Griffith's *Birth of a Nation* (1915) was followed by the same director's analogical narrative intercutting with accelerating tempo of four separate stories in four different time frames in *Intolerance* (1916). The rise of film as a middle- and working-class art, comparable to the rise of the novel in the eighteenth century, was well established. But Lawrence's response to the emergence of cinema as a mass medium was almost entirely negative.

The cinematograph that James Houghton purchases in *The Lost Girl* is dedicated to fairly modest examples of the filmmaker's art on the same bill with relatively minor vaudeville acts. Woodhouse already has a more imposing cinema, the famous Empire, modeled on the Eastwood Empire, built in 1913 by F. G. Stubbs. George Hardy and Nathaniel Harris suggest that its existence persuaded George Henry Cullen, the model for James Houghton, "to try his luck outside Eastwood," in Langley Mill (Lumley in *The Lost Girl*), a village about a mile from Eastwood, where he erected his cinema. Parker's cinema in Eastwood, a temporary wooden structure, unlike the majestic Empire, was the source of Wright's Cinematograph and Variety Theatre, which Mr. May comes to Woodhouse to visit. According to G. W. Hardy, "the inspiration for Alvina Houghton" was Cullen's daughter, Flossie, who "played the piano accompaniment in a four piece band for the silent films at the Langley Mill cinema," and who "eventually married Mr. George Hodgkinson, who worked in the pay box of the same cinema."[1]

<hr/>

1. See George Hardy and Nathaniel Harris, "Fact into Fiction: *The Lost Girl*," *A D. H. Lawrence Album*, 67–77. Photographic plate no. 66 shows the Eastwood Empire, referrred to by name in *The Lost Girl*. No. 67 is a view of the center of town in Langley Mill. Nos. 58 and 65 are portraits of Flossie Cullen, and no. 69 shows her in a family portrait with her husband, George Hodgkinson, and her son William. See also G. W. Hardy, "Short Communication—'The Lost Girl.' " 23.

The cinema, even in the silent era, was, of course, never really silent. When the job of musical accompaniest is assigned to Alvina Houghton in *The Lost Girl,* she views the position with a certain irony:

> She just saw herself at that piano, banging off the *Merry Widow Waltz,* and, in tender moments, *The Rosary.* Time after time, *The Rosary.* While the pictures flickered and the audience gave shouts and some grubby boy called "Chot-let, penny a bar! Chot-let, penny a bar! Chot-let, penny a bar!"—away she banged at another tune. [*LG* 99]

According to Kevin Brownlow, in the silent-film era, "Theater musicians worked from a standard repertoire, unless the picture was a big special. . . . A regular picture would be issued with a cue sheet, sent out by the exchange as part of the promotional material," with the film's intertitles keyed to tempos and musical selections. There were, however, exceptions. Brownlow reports that D. W. Griffith's *Broken Blossoms* (1919) "was released with a largely original score by Louis F. Gottschalk."[2] At the opposite extreme, Witter Bynner records that at a showing of the silent film *The Passion of Christ,* which he and the Lawrences attended in Mexico City on Holy Saturday, 31 March 1923, the approach of Jesus, looming "nearer and larger, into the hearts of His audience," was accompanied by marimbas playing a gaily swinging tune that during the Crucifixion scene, became, incongruously, "Three O'Clock in the Morning."[3] Already in *The Lost Girl,* Lawrence's satiric description hardly encourages one to think of music at the movies as an experience of art.

Alvina and Miss Pinnegar, who is to sell the tickets, think Mr. Houghton's entire plan of housing the cinema in "an old wooden traveling theatre" a "disgrace." One can hear the authorial chuckle, and a sly comment on the briefly arousing but ultimately disappointing effect of film, in Mr. Houghton's defense of the "admirable scheme": " 'Of cauce,' he said, 'the erection will be a merely temporary one' " (*LG* 101). Mr. Houghton's use of "th' pews out of the old Primitive Chapel" (*LG* 106) for seating at the cinematograph demonstrates how easily the accoutrements of the old medium of Protestant Fundamentalism are adaptable to the requirements of the new medium, the cinema. As media of popular mass culture, both seem to Lawrence to dull

2. Brownlow, *The Parade's Gone By . . . ,* 384.
3. Bynner, *Journey with Genius,* 46. I am unable to identify the film with certainty, but possibly it was *La Vie et la Passion de Jesus Christ* (1902).

the capacity for genuine instinctual response. But as he observes ironically in *Twilight in Italy,* "since that triumph of the deaf and dumb, the cinematograph, has come to give us the nervous excitement of speed—grimace, agitation, and speed, as of flying atoms, chaos— many an old church in Italy has taken a new lease of life" (*TI* 70).

The program that Mr. May, the manager, books for the first week consists of *The Human Bird,* "which turned out to be a ski-ing film from Norway, purely descriptive," like the Lumières' realistic documentaries; *The Pancake,* a comedy; and the first chapter of a serial, *The Silent Grip,* a title suggesting a suspense thriller. (According to John Worthen, the three titles are invented by Lawrence [*LG* 376].) The vaudeville interlude features a skirt dancer, "Miss Poppy Traherne, a lady in innumerable petticoats, who could whirl herself into anything you like, from an arum lily in green stockings to a rainbow and a catherine wheel and a cup and saucer"; and a tumbling act, the "Baxter Brothers, who ran up and down each other's backs and up and down each other's fronts, and stood on each other's heads and on their own heads, and perched for a moment on each other's shoulders, as if each of them was a flight of stairs with a landing, and the three of them were three flights, three storeys up, the top flight continually running down and becoming the bottom flight, while the middle flight collapsed and became a horizontal corridor" (*LG* 107).

Alvina's piano numbers range from "Welcome All" at the beginning, to the "March of the Toreadors" for the opening curtain, to the "Dream Waltz" for the interval between films, to "God Save Our Gracious King" at the end, the better to bring the audience to its feet for the exit. Lawrence's description of "a comic drama, acted by two Baxter Bros. disguised as women, and Miss Poppy disguised as a man" (*LG* 110) hints at the sexual role confusion encouraged by popular entertainment. But for all his satirical thrusts, Lawrence's presentation shows great affection for the vaudeville troupes and directly links his nostalgia at their inevitable passing to his criticism of their supersession by the cinema in terms of the audience's different relationship to stage and film performers.

Lawrence's presentation of the issue through the differing views expressed by Alvina Houghton, Mr. May, Miss Pinnegar, and Madame Rochard suggests that the difference in the audience's relationship to the performers in stage and film derives from a difference in the media themselves. Stated simply, in terms of the informing argument of this study, it is the difference between empathic and projective response: Whereas the stage performance involves the audience's active interaction by means of imaginative empathy, the cinema encourages passive projection and projective identification. That is why, as Lawrence sees it, the theater can achieve the "trembling balance" of life that characterizes true art, and the cinema cannot.

When Alvina suggests that "common people" are jealous of the performing *artistes,* Mr. May protests, ". . . then why aren't they jealous of the extraordinary things which are done on the film?" Alvina replies, "Because they don't see the flesh-and-blood people. . . . And pictures don't have any feelings apart from their own feelings: . . . Pictures don't have any life except in the people who watch them." That is why the audience can "identify themselves with the heroes and heroines on the screen" but not with a living performer: "They're up against the performer himself" (*LG* 116).

Miss Pinnegar, who apparently speaks for the majority in Lawrence's sample of public opinion, is glad to see the end of vaudeville, which is "only men dressed up, for money." Film allows you to "*know* everything," she says, because "you see it all": "I like to go to the cinema once a week. It's instructive, you take it all in at a glance, all you need to know, and it lasts you for a week" (*LG* 142–43).

Madame Rochard correctly perceives that this shift in popular taste will mean the death of vaudeville. She tells Mr. May, "The pictures are driving us away. Perhaps we shall last for ten years more. And after that, we are finished." When Mr. May asks why, her reply is a purely Laurentian analysis: "The pictures are cheap, and they are easy, and they cost the audience nothing, no feeling of the heart, no appreciation of the spirit, cost them nothing of these. And so they like them, and they don't like us, because they must *feel* the things we do, from the heart, and appreciate them from the spirit" (*LG* 148–49).

The paradox was that the cinema, though it seemed more realistic than a live performance, insulated the audience from the reality presented. As Roger Fry observed in 1909, cinema "resembles actual life in almost every respect, except that . . . the conative part of our reaction to sensations, that is to say, the appropriate resultant action is cut off." The result, he says, citing the example of *The Arrival of a Train,* "is that in the first place we *see* the event much more clearly; see a number of quite interesting but irrelevant things, which in real life could not struggle into our consciousness. . . . In the second place, with regard to the visions of the cinematograph, one notices that whatever emotions are aroused by them, though they are likely to be weaker than those of ordinary life, are presented more clearly to the consciousness."[4]

4. Fry, "An Essay in Aesthetics," in *Vision and Design,* 12–13.

Lawrence shows in *The Lost Girl* and elsewhere that stage performances, even of popular variety acts, involve interaction between audience and performer in a spontaneous flow of human feeling between the self and the other that preserves the "trembling balance." Movies, on the other hand, evoke a neurotic response of projective fantasy that allows the audience to remain on the relatively safe, superficial level of narcissistic indulgence rather than risking the venture into deeper levels of "blood conscious" relationship.

Far from establishing "a trembling centre of balance" in the art form or the quickness of life in the relationship of audience to performer that might put the viewer in touch with his feelings and help him to integrate the antinomies of his own existence, the cinema, Lawrence suggests, depends on the separation and exploits the division. The superficial emotional response that audiences, in his opinion, make to film does not involve spontaneity or depth of feeling, any more than the strains of "The Rosary" evoke a response of spiritual depth. Sam Solecki correctly suggests that Miss Pinnegar's speech "points toward Lawrence's central objection to film as a medium: according to him, film—a primarily visual medium—makes an appeal only to the viewer's mental consciousness and in no way involves or relates to his vital, sensual unconscious self."[5]

In the psychological theory that Lawrence elaborates in *Fantasia of the Unconscious* (1922), although the "eyes have . . . their sensual root as well," the visual sense is primarily a function of the nerve-brain self, which is controlled by the upper, spiritual centers of consciousness. By the cardiac plexus, one goes "forth in the wonder of vision to dwell upon the beloved, or upon the wonder of the world"; by the thoracic ganglion, without sympathy or communication, one "stares outwards" in analytic objectivity and curiosity (*FU* 100–101). In the former mode, the cinema encourages viewers to "identify themselves with the heroes and heroines on the screen," not to respond to the otherness of either actors or characters but to incorporate their film personae so that "there isn't anything except themselves" (*LG* 116). In the latter mode, it satisfies curiosity and provides instruction, as in descriptive documentaries. The context of *The Lost Girl*, Solecki says, associates film "with that which is mechanical and those who are spiritually dead: in contrast, it is significant that those characters who are a force for life in the novel are all stage performers." Lawrence argues "that theatre, unlike film,

5. Solecki, "D. H. Lawrence's View of Film," 12.

makes its primary appeal to the senses and not to the mind."[6] This is because the spectator's response involves the blood-conscious self, which is asserted from the lower, sensual centers of consciousness, the solar plexus and the lumbar ganglion. Hence, a stage performance, even of a variety act, involves a subjective response to the otherness of the performer and depends on a vital interchange between actor and audience that is largely unconscious and instinctual, whereas film evokes only the passive response of fantasy. At its best, the live performance also synthesizes experience, enlarging the immediate response to what Madame Rochard calls "appreciation of the spirit."

In a forum on translating literary works into film, Arthur Miller and Edward Albee, whose plays were popularly so adapted, make similar points. Miller's view of the spectator's passivity supports Lawrence's: "Images are registered in a much more primitive part of the human mind. So you can go to the movies and relax . . . because you're a receiver; you're not being exercised. In a movie house you can be perfectly passive. That's the nature of the medium. . . . But it's a whole different ball game than the theater." Albee agrees that responses to cinematic images and language are basically different: "The word is the enemy of the film. Even though you see a play, you get most of it through the ear, through the dialogue." The reasons he elaborates for the audience's sense of emotional risks at a play and passive security at a film are similar to Lawrence's: "When you are at a play, it is a present-tense dangerous experience. It is something that is happening. And when you go to a film, you realize this is something that never has happened. It is an unreal experience which gives the opportunity for safe emotional response. Where a play is dangerous, a film is always safe."[7]

It is clear which side Lawrence is on. In *Fantasia of the Unconscious,* he says:

> . . . we live far, far too much from the *upper* sympathetic centre and voluntary centre, in an endless objective curiosity. Sight is the least sensual of all the senses. And we strain ourselves to see, see, see—everything, everything through the eye, in one mode of objective curiosity. There is nothing inside us, we stare endlessly at the outside. [*FU* 102]

6. Ibid., 13.
7. "Can Great Books Make Good Movies?," 38. Other writers in the forum are Jules Feiffer, John Irving, John Knowles, William Styron, and Kurt Vonnegut, Jr.

The thrills of the movies provide a vicarious knowledge heretofore unavailable to man, but the consequence is a dulling of immediate response, a loss of ability to know by means of direct experience. Instead, life itself imitates the cinema. In *Aaron's Rod*, at Sir William Franks's mansion in Novaro, Aaron is "allured," in a visual and verbal pun, by "two black-and-white chambermaids" and a footman, as if in a tracking shot, "down the corridor, and presented to the handsome, spacious bathroom, which was warm and creamy coloured and glittering with massive silver and mysterious with up-to-date conveniences" (*AR* 134). Lawrence is perhaps alluding to the extravagant mise en scène of such recent films as the series of modern comedies directed by Cecil B. De Mille, including *Male and Female* (1919), *For Better, for Worse* (1919), *Don't Change Your Husband* (1919), and *Why Change Your Wife?* (1920), which, as Arthur Knight says, "catered to the postwar trend toward higher living, heavier drinking and looser morals. Dwelling on both the fashions and the foibles of the fabulously rich, he opened up a whole new world for the films, a world that middle-class audiences . . . very much wanted to see." As De Mille's brother, William C. deMille, recalls in *Hollywood Saga:* "He made of the bathroom a delightful resort which undoubtedly had its effect upon bathrooms of the whole nation. The bath became a mystic shrine dedicated to Venus, or sometimes to Apollo, and the art of bathing was shown as a lovely ceremony rather than a merely sanitary duty."[8] Lawrence's narrator comments ironically on Aaron Sisson's confrontation with such hedonistic opulence:

He felt he ought to have his breath taken away. But alas, the cinema has taken our breath away so often, investing us in all the splendours of the splendidest American millionaire, or all the heroics and marvels of the Somme or the North Pole, that life has now no magnate richer than we, no hero nobler than we have been, on the film. *Connu! Connu!* Everything life has to offer is known to us, couldn't be known better, from the film. [*AR* 134–35]

On their voyage from Sydney to San Francisco aboard the HMS *Tahiti* (10 August–4 September 1922), the Lawrences encountered members of a Hollywood motion-picture company, who boarded the ship at Tahiti, where they had been on location filming a melodrama under the working title "Captain Blackbird," later released as *Lost and Found on a South Sea Island* (1923), directed by Raoul Walsh.

8. Knight, *The Liveliest Art*, 118.

The cast included House Peters (Captain Blackbird), Pauline Stark, Antonio Moreno, Rosemary Theby, and George Siegmann (the villain).[9] Lawrence was both socially and morally offended by the "cinema people": He found the women "rather like successful shop-girls, and the men like any sort of men at the sea-side. Utterly undistinguished" (*Letters* 4:287). Later he wrote, "We picked up a cinema crowd at Papeete, all of them hating one another like poison, several of them drunk all the trip" (*Letters* 4:303). According to Mabel Dodge Luhan,

> Their unrestraint and their wild, care-free love-making amazed and at the same time infuriated him. He became acquainted with some of them. They were like a new species of creature he had never seen before. He watched and registered every move—not like a scientist, with coolness and interest—not like a poet— . . . for he was so angry, so incensed when he told us about them. And evidently he had not got away without an antagonistic scene on board—for in the end he had a scene with some of them, and they, angered too—"jeered at him". . . . [10]

Knud Merrild says Frieda told Lawrence, "It's the school teacher in you; but the naughty, adult children just jeer at you. Many times I have suffered when they drew you out, just to see 'your goods,' and then they jeer, and you, too, suffer. You must not do it, Lorenzo."[11]

Lawrence's response to major film productions was sometimes warmer than might be expected from his negative comments on the cinema and cinema people. When Lawrence, on his return to London in 1923 after a year in New Mexico and Mexico, went with S. S. Koteliansky, Mark Gertler, John Middleton Murry, and Dorothy Brett to see *The Covered Wagon* (1923), directed and produced by James Cruze, he responded at first with the predictable distinction between film and life. The stereotypic screen cowboy good guy (J. Warren Kerrigan), "in his white shirt, white pants, black cowboy boots and big white Stetson," irritated Lawrence, who felt "sure he has never sat on a horse." But when seven real "Red Indians" appeared on stage before the movie began, Lawrence, watching as a "man, wrapped in a blanket, with his hair in a nob at the back of his head," walked on, whispered to Brett, "he is real," and sighed deeply,

---

9. Film, director, and cast are identified by the editors of the Cambridge edition of *The Letters of D. H. Lawrence*, 4:287 n. 1.

10. Luhan, *Lorenzo in Taos*, 47.

11. Merrild, *With D. H. Lawrence in New Mexico*, 11.

as if homesick for New Mexico. With the western mood established, the film worked its magic even on Lawrence, who, as the lights faded, watched as if he were part of it himself: "How like it is, how like it is," he kept saying (though the phrase itself also calls attention to the real difference), and softly hummed the film's keynote song, "Oh, Susannah!"[12] When the Lawrences and Brett saw Douglas Fairbanks in *The Thief of Baghdad* (1924), at the opera house in Oaxaca the following year, Lawrence seems not to have remembered the director, Raoul Walsh, as the director of the film whose players had so offended him on board the *Tahiti*. In Brett's account, the film was all Fairbanks: "He thrills us: you enjoy it just as much as Frieda and I do."[13]

Lawrence suggests repeatedly that movies present a conventionalized and artificial world that promotes mental stereotypes rather than putting one in touch with real feelings. The convention of childlike immaturity for film heroines was an idealization in fantasy of the presexual state, and the conception of beauty for both women and men, based on regularity of features rather than fineness of sensibility, promoted a superficial and stereotypic view of real human beings. Such conventions inevitably engendered counterfeit emotion and sentimentalism, rather than the discovery and expression of genuine feelings such as the novel evoked.

Lawrence objects in "The Crown" to the convention of immaturity to which film heroines of the day were often made to conform: "In the movies, the heroine is becoming more and more childish, and touched with infantile idiocy. We cannot bear honest maturity. We want to reduce ourselves back, back to the *corruptive* state of childishness." Lawrence relates this "pornographically reaching out for child-gratifications" to "the prevalent love of boys" (*RDP* 285). Since he does not elaborate, it would be difficult to say which film heroines he has in mind, but several of D. W. Griffith's young actresses fit the description. According to Lillian Gish, she and her sister Dorothy, at sixteen and fourteen in 1912, "were in a transitional stage when we came to Mr. Griffith—no longer children and not yet young women."

12. Brett, *Lawrence and Brett: A Friendship*, 26–27. Lawrence's response has been borne out in the film's critical reputation. Although charged by William S. Hart with inaccuracies in the western mise en scène and slow in action by today's standards, *The Covered Wagon*, by its impressive location photography, semidocumentary style, and deliberate pacing, created an impression of authenticity that led to the resurgence of the western film genre.

13. Ibid., 189. Parmenter, *Lawrence in Oaxaca*, 177, gives the date as 7 December 1924.

Uncomfortable with adult female sexuality, Griffith insulated himself with a "dreamlike idealization" of women in a series of figures that Lillian Gish teasingly referred to as "gaga babies."[14] She was, Richard Schickel says, "a master of those fluttery, childlike gestures that Griffith required of his heroines when he wanted them to suggest—as he often did—a virginal condition."[15] Lillian Gish understood, however, as Lawrence could not have known, that there was also a practical reason for Griffith's surrounding himself with youthful players. As Eric Rhode explains, his cinematographer "Billy Bitzer's mutoscope camera harshly exposed lines and wrinkles, and Griffith had to cast his heroines from girls in early adolescence." While she "photographed young," Miss Gish says, "sometimes the harsh cameras made a fourteen-year-old seem an old hag. Children of fourteen and fifteen often played parts far beyond their experience or understanding."[16] In addition to the Gish sisters, Griffith established the careers of Carol Dempster, Mary Pickford, Blanche Sweet, Bessie Love, and Mae Marsh. Even such a hostile critic as Eric Rhode is forced to admit that "no one has equalled his ability to draw performances of such quicksilver grace and spontaneity out of young women."[17]

The most obvious example of the kind of heroine Lawrence refers to is Mary Pickford, whose long reign as queen of the box office was based on producer Carl Laemmle's, as well as her own and her mother's, shrewd exploitation of her public persona as "America's Sweetheart." According to Rhode:

> She was confined for most of her acting life—until well into her thirties—to child roles, and these of the most unattractive sort: good little girls who spread sweetness and light about them and who, like some of Dickens's heroines, become through death, or quasi-death, redeemers of stony-hearted mothers and aunts.[18]

For Miss Pickford herself, however, "the little girl" was an artistically individualized, never standardized, persona. Believing that Charles Chaplin's artistry had been destroyed "when he discarded the little tramp," she left the screen when she could no longer por-

14. Gish, with Pinchot, *The Movies, Mr. Griffith and Me*, 88–89.
15. Schickel, *D. W. Griffith: An American Life*, 217.
16. Gish, 89.
17. Rhode, *A History of the Cinema*, 48.
18. Ibid., 65.

tray her character. "The little girl made me," she declared. "I wasn't waiting for the little girl to kill me."[19] Kevin Brownlow, for whom Miss Pickford's "naturalistic" performances remain vital and undated, says, "She had legions of imitators, but no rivals."[20]

One of her imitators, or counterparts, F. Scott Fitzgerald's character Rosemary Hoyt as *Daddy's Girl* in *Tender Is the Night,* though based on another film actress, Lois Moran, is described in terms that tally perfectly with the Pickford persona[21] and support Lawrence's reading of the type:

> There she was—the school girl of a year ago, hair down her back and rippling out stiffly like the solid hair of a tanagra figure; there she was—*so* young and innocent—the product of her mother's loving care; there she was—embodying all the immaturity of the race, cutting a new cardboard paper doll to pass before its empty harlot's mind. . . .
>
> Daddy's girl. Was it a 'itty-bitty bravekins and did it suffer? Ooo-ooo-tweet, de tweetest thing, wasn't she dest too tweet? Before her tiny fist the forces of lust and corruption rolled away; nay, the very march of destiny stopped, inevitably became evitable; syllogism, dialectic, all rationality fell away.[22]

Lawrence's observation that "honest maturity" has given way in the popular culture to the impulse "to reduce ourselves back, back to the *corruptive* state of childishness" is borne out in the trend, continuing into the thirties, of inverting the roles of parent and child in the idealization of the child as a creature of innocent and natural, if precocious, wisdom that enables it to become the mentor of the adult in such films as *The Champ,* directed by King Vidor (1931). Lawrence's death in 1930 spared him, among other things, the ascendancy of Shirley Temple, who, as "Daddy's little girl," set Daddy's affairs in order in film after film, and became, from 1935 to 1938, "the top box-office star in both the United States and Great Britain."[23]

Another problem with film characterization, which emphasized

19. Brownlow, 155.

20. Ibid., 138.

21. See Mizener, *The Far Side of Paradise,* 203–5. Fitzgerald's model for Rosemary Hoyt was the movie actress Lois Moran, whom he met in Hollywood, where he had been asked by John Considine of United Artists to write a college flapper comedy for Constance Talmadge. Fitzgerald was invited to lunch at Pickfair with Mary Pickford and became friends with Lillian Gish, but it was Lois Moran who fascinated him.

22. Fitzgerald, *Tender Is the Night,* 130.

23. Rhode, 343.

types rather than individuals, was the stereotyping of the concept of beauty. As Lawrence comments in "Sex versus Loveliness," "We try to pretend it is a fixed arrangement: straight nose, large eyes, etc. We think a lovely woman must look like Lilian [*sic*] Gish, a handsome man must look like Rudolph Valentino." We wrongly use the word *beautiful* to describe a set of "stereotyped attributes": "Beauty is an *experience,* nothing else. It is not a fixed pattern or an arrangement of features. It is something *felt,* a glow or a communicated sense of fineness." The statement compares with Alexander Walker's description of Valentino: "The glossy hair emphasizes the extraordinary regularity of his features placed in perfect arrangement on the oval face." In *The Sheik,* "his eyelids look suspiciously as if they've been gummed back to expose more of the passionate 'whites,' though this occasionally produces an unfortunate 'pop-eyed' effect."[24] For Lawrence, "there is a greater essential beauty in Charlie Chaplin's odd face than there ever was in Valentino's. There is a bit of true beauty in Chaplin's brows and eyes, a gleam of something pure." But because "our sense of beauty is so bruised and blunted," "[w]e can only see the blatantly obvious, like the so-called beauty of Rudolph Valentino, which only pleases because it satisfies some ready-made notion of handsomeness" (*P II* 528–29). Lawrence's discussion, however casual, asserts the irregularity of beauty as an aesthetic principle comparable to the modernist aesthetic that Virginia Woolf opposes to the tyranny of the well-made novel's preconceived patterns.[25]

The cinema's sexual stereotypes appealed directly to what Lawrence refers to in "Pornography and Obscenity" as the "great pornographical class," the common men and women, whose "grey disease of sex-hatred, coupled with the yellow disease of dirt-lust" places them ostensibly "always on the side of the angels": "They insist that a film-heroine shall be a neuter, a sexless thing of washed-out purity. They insist that real sex-feeling shall only be shown by the villain or villainess, low lust" (*P* 176). Lawrence's point may be illustrated by Griffith's *Birth of a Nation,* in which sexuality is largely confined to liberated Negroes: The sexual liaison between the Abolitionist Senator Austin Stoneman and his villainous mulatto housekeeper is made responsible for the divisive corruption of the Reconstruction period. Michael Paul Rogin argues that the threatening female sexuality that Blanche Sweet had shown in Griffith's *Judith of Bethulia* (1913) in the symbolic castration scene in which she beheads the passive Holofernes (Henry B. Walthall) is now transferred to liberated Ne-

24. Walker, *Rudolph Valentino,* 27, 50.
25. Woolf, "Modern Fiction," in *The Common Reader,* 153–155.

groes, whose threat of rape against white women is invented and projected as a displacement not only of the sexual desires of white males but more importantly of the more threatening sexual desires of white women in a psychologically racist political maneuver designed to keep the liberated New Woman in line. That the blacks were played by white actors in blackface, Rogin says, suggests their function as masks for the repressed portion of the gentlemanly *auteur* director's own sexual inclinations toward his youthful female performers.[26] In *The Birth of a Nation*, Gus, a renegade freed slave (Walter Long), tries to rape the white "gaga baby" Flora, "The Little Dear One" (Mae Marsh), who, by leaping from a cliff, chooses death before dishonor. The heroine, Elsie Stoneman (Lillian Gish), fights off the advances of Silas Lynch, the mulatto Abolitionist (George Siegmann), leading to the climactic heroic ride of the Ku Klux Klan, to the accompaniment of strains borrowed from Wagner's "Ride of the Valkyries," to restore a white-supremacist "Christian" order. The same people who acclaim such sexual stereotypes in films, Lawrence observes with justifiable irony, "find a Titian or a Renoir really indecent, and they don't want their wives and daughters to see it" (*P* 176).

The trouble with the stereotyped conception of beauty promoted by the cinema is that it deadens our capacity to respond to reality in the flesh. In Lawrence's poem "Film Passion," Rudolph Valentino is again the example:

If all those females who so passionately loved
the film face of Rudolf Valentino
had had to take him for one night only, in the flesh,
how they'd have hated him!

Hated him just because he was a man
and flesh of a man.
For the luscious filmy imagination loathes the male substance
with deadly loathing.

All the women who adored the shadow of the man on the screen
helped to kill him in the flesh.
Such adoration pierces the loins and perishes the man
worse than the evil eye.

[*CP* 538]

Lawrence may be responding to the darker components of Valentino's persona, which were only confirmed after his death. This per-

26. Rogin, *"Ronald Reagan", the Movie*, 205–9.

sona had emphasized both sadoerotic "menace" (*The Sheik*) and masochistic suffering and sacrificial death (*The Four Horsemen of the Apocalypse, Blood and Sand*). The motives of misogyny, revenge, and torture in Valentino's last film, *The Son of the Sheik,* Walker comments, carried "the concept of the 'Latin Lover' to a perverse extreme." He argues that Valentino "was a romantic star who could be killed off at the end of the film without disenchanting the fans" because "[t]hey felt that his romantic pact was with death, not with some competitive" female. This "deliberate calculation of where the fans' gratification was to be found" led ultimately to the conscious exploitation of "the necrophilia that followed him to the grave."[27] Small wonder that Lawrence finds the preference for glamour to reality, shadow to substance, film to flesh to be ultimately perverse and destructive.

Another Laurentian comment on the subject may be seen in his oil painting *Close-Up (Kiss)*. Kissing scenes had been standard fare in films at least as far back as the notorious short film the *May Irwin–John C. Rice Kiss* (1896). While there had been nothing scandalous about the full-length play *The Widow Jones* from which the action was taken, the kiss, framed in close-up, became provocatively "realistic." According to Knight, "Its few moments of magnified osculation resulted in the first scandalized attempt at film censorship."[28] Lawrence's painting, though framed as a film close-up, presents, like the *May Irwin–John C. Rice Kiss,* a full-fleshed couple in a manner that emphasizes their fleshly rather than their cinematically romantic qualities.

Lawrence suggests again and again that the preference for film to reality leads to a wholesale societal substitution of the counterfeit for life. In another poem, "When I Went to the Film," he attributes the counterfeiting process to the abstracting and distancing effect of black-and-white film. Projected upon a two-dimensional screen, the human image is reduced to pure personality without instinctual depth:

When I went to the film, and saw all the black-and-white feelings
    that nobody felt,
and heard the audience sighing and sobbing with all the emotions
    they none of them felt,
and saw them cuddling with rising passions they none of them for a
    moment felt,

27. Walker, 112.
28. Knight, 14.

and caught them moaning from close-up kisses, black-and-white
    kisses that could not be felt,
It was like being in heaven, which I am sure has a white
    atmosphere
upon which shadows of people, pure personalities
are cast in black and white, and move
in flat ecstasy, supremely unfelt,
and heavenly.

[*CP* 443–44]

"Sentimentalism," Lawrence's major critical charge against John
Galsworthy, is defined in similar terms:

> Sentimentalism is the working off on yourself of feelings you
> haven't really got. We all *want* to have certain feelings: feel-
> ings of love, of passionate sex, of kindliness, and so forth. Very
> few people really feel love, or sex passion, or kindliness, or
> anything else that goes at all deep. So the mass just fake these
> feelings inside themselves. Faked feelings! The world is all
> gummy with them. They are better than real feelings, be-
> cause you can spit them out when you brush your teeth; and
> then tomorrow you can fake them afresh. [*STH* 215]

"Sentimentalism," he thought, characterized the female fans' response to Rudolph Valentino, who is compared unfavorably to the
toreador Cuesta in "None of That": "Women went mad, once they felt
him. It was not like Rudolf [*sic*] Valentino, sentimental. It was madness, like cats in the night which howl . . ." (*CSS* 3:704).
    Lawrence returns to the theme of counterfeit emotion in the popu-
lar media in *A Propos of "Lady Chatterley's Lover"*:

> Never was an age more sentimental, more devoid of real feel-
> ing, more exaggerated in false feeling, than our own. . . . The
> radio and the film are mere counterfeit emotion all the time,
> the current press and literature the same. People wallow in
> emotion: counterfeit emotion. They lap it up: they live in it
> and on it. They ooze with it. [*P II* 493]

He elaborates with examples of counterfeit life in "The Real Thing":

> Everything is counterfeit: counterfeit complexion, counterfeit
> jewels, counterfeit elegance, counterfeit charm, counterfeit en-
> dearment, counterfeit passion, counterfeit culture, counter-

feit love of Blake, or of *The Bridge of San Luis Rey,* or Picasso, or the latest film-star. Counterfeit sorrows and counterfeit delights, counterfeit woes and moans, counterfeit ecstasies, and, under all, a hard, hard realization that we live by money, and money alone: and a terrible lurking fear of nervous collapse, collapse. [*P* 201]

Lawrence's idea of the Fall was as a fall into consciousness in which man begins "to live from a picture of himself." The inevitable effect is the projection of the counterfeit image, the animation of shadows in which the real instinctual self has no part at all. As Lawrence says in *Etruscan Places,* "There is plenty of pawing and laying hold, but no real touch. In pictures especially, the people may be in contact, embracing or laying hands on one another. But there is no soft flow of touch" (*EP* 46). The pictures that most consistently served as his examples of contemporary decadence were motion pictures, as when he says of the corrupted consciousness of the Texas cowboys in *St. Mawr,* "inwardly they were self-conscious film heroes":

It was like life enacted in a mirror. Visually, it was wildly vital. But there was nothing behind it. Or like a cinematograph: flat shapes, exactly like men, but without any substance of reality, rapidly rattling away with talk, emotions, activity, all in the flat, nothing behind it. No deeper consciousness at all. [*St. M* 131]

In *Lady Chatterley's Lover,* the narrator posits two opposing "groups of dogs wrangling for the bitch-goddess": "the flatterers, those who offered her amusement, stories, films, plays: and the other, much less showy, much more savage breed, those who gave her meat, the real substance of money" (*LCL* 125). Success in either of these terms has a hardening effect that undercuts "the trembling instability of the balance" (*STH* 172). In her relationship with Mellors, Connie discovers that "[s]omewhere she was tender, tender with a tenderness of the growing hyacinths, something that has gone out of the celluloid women of today" (*LCL* 140), that is, out of those who live only from a celluloid film model of womanhood. Hence, coincident with the development of the love affair, Connie develops an aversion to "the plaster-and-gilt horror of the cinema with its wet picture announcements, 'A Woman's Love'!" (*LCL* 180).

Lawrence finds in the analytic quality of film form a commitment to mechanistic structure that runs counter to organic homeostasis and other organicist values. The machine method of film reproduction led to meaningless, mechanical repetition, as opposed to the organic repetition in memory that was characteristic, for example, of Lawrence's own literary style.

Film form, of course, is basically analytical: Montage, in Sergei Eisenstein's theory, represents the dialectical approach to film composition.[29] The aesthetic of film editing, then, is the artistic triumph of the analytic mind. Film form, according to the film historian Eric Rhode, is inextricably allied with "Cubism and with the many kinds of assemblage that resulted from Cubism," but Edwin S. Porter and other pioneers of the medium went beyond that: "Art traditionally has consisted of cult objects offered up for contemplation. Cinematic narrative . . . escapes this reverential gaze. It assaults the audience with impressions; it raises and casts off metaphors so rapidly that the consciousness may barely perceive them; it affects us like some agile yet penetrating notation."[30] It is only in this subliminal sense that, in Miss Pinnegar's words, "you take it all in at a glance." The commercial failure of D. W. Griffith's *Intolerance* (1916), "a drama of comparisons," which intercut four separate stories in four different time frames, after the popular and critical success of *The Birth of a Nation* (1915), which employed a more straightforward narrative form and appealed more directly to prejudicial stereotypes, is attributable, in Eisenstein's opinion, not to the audience's inability to process the information but to a basic failure in Griffith's understanding and mastery of montage: "the effect didn't come off. For again it turned out to be a combination of *four different stories,* rather than *a fusion of four phenomena* in *a single imagist generalization.*"[31]

The means of artistic composition by editing together separate photographic images and the means of artistic reproduction by mechanical projection of these images upon a blank screen, Lawrence suggests, determines that the aesthetic of film will be mechanistic, not organic. He says in "Art and Morality":

> As for us, we have our kodak-vision, all in bits that group or jig. Like the movies, that jerk but never move. An endless shifting and rattling together of isolated images, "snaps," miles of them, all of them jigging, but each one utterly incapable of movement or change, in itself. A kaleidoscope of inert images, mechanically shaken. [*STH* 168]

29. See Eisenstein, "A Dialectic Approach to Film Form," in *Film Form,* 45–63.
30. Rhode, 41.
31. Eisenstein, "Dickens, Griffith, and the Film Today," in *Film Form,* 243.

As might be expected, Lawrence also emphasizes the mechanical quality of the cinema in his fiction and poetry. When James Houghton announces his purchase of the cinematograph building, he adds, "We are negotiating for the machinery now: the dynamo and so on" (*LG* 114). The mechanism of cinematic means extended to the movies' effect on the audience as well. In "But I Say Unto You: Love One Another," a poem from *Pansies*, Lawrence writes:

> Oh I have loved the working class
> where I was born,
> and lived to see them spawn into machine-robots
> in the hot-beds of the board-schools and the film.
>   [lines 4–7, *CP* 644]

Derek Britton has called attention to the similar view of England in the early 1920s presented by Lawrence's contemporary, the historian C. F. G. Masterman, in his book *England after the War:* "The public had become 'like a child which escapes from a drab reality into the fairyland of pantomime' or into the celluloid fantasies of 'the ever multiplying cinema.' "[32]

"Ever multiplying," in Masterman's phrase, refers, of course, to proliferation. It also means pointless repetition, a characteristic of mechanical duplication as opposed to organic repetition in memory. Jacques Derrida's discussion of the principle with reference to the invention of writing illuminates Lawrence's point in regard to film:

> *Hupomnēsis,* which is here what forecasts and shapes the thought about writing, not only does not coincide with memory, but can only be constructed as a thing dependent on memory. . . . It is thus from the start stripped of all its own attributes or path-breaking powers. Its path-breaking force is cut not by repetition but by the ills of repetition, by that which within repetition is doubled, redoubled, that which repeats repetition and in so doing, cut off from "good" repetition (which presents and gathers being within living memory), can always, left to itself, stop repeating itself. Writing would be pure repetition, dead repetition that might always be repeating nothing, or be unable *spontaneously* to repeat itself, which also means unable to repeat anything *but* itself: a hollow, cast-off repetition.[33]

32. Masterman, *England after the War,* 19; quoted in Britton, *"Lady Chatterley,"* 163.
33. Derrida, "Plato's Pharmacy," in *Dissemination,* 135.

Derrida's discussion brings up the question of whether Lawrence's indictment of film as a medium indicates a failure to consider that his own medium of writing can be as mechanically and meaninglessly repetitive as film. But Lawrence's many strictures against substitution of the logos for flesh and being, as in the "Foreword to Sons and Lovers" (Letters, ed. Huxley, 98–99), suggest otherwise. Lawrence, like Whitman, attempted to erase the distinction between book and man. Thus, his books as acts of memory were examples of organic repetition as he thought films could never be.

Lawrence's conception of the cinema was primarily industrial. He admired Chaplin, and according to David Garnett, "There was more than a little of Charlie Chaplin in his acting: but bitterer, less sentimental."[34] Even so, he mildly satirizes Chaplin's industrial productivity in a send-up of Whitman's democratic theme of "One Identity":

> He was not able to assume one identity with Charlie Chaplin, for example, because Walt didn't know Charlie. What a pity! He'd have done poems, pæans and what not, Chants, Songs of Cinematernity.
> "Oh, Charlie, my Charlie, another film is done————"
> [SCAL 166]

Although Chaplin wrote, directed, and acted in his own films, Lawrence had no conception of the film director as auteur, nothing corresponding to the "One man, one film" principle by which Frank Capra challenged the prevailing power structure of executive control to demand total artistic responsibility for his films.[35] Largely oblivious to the art of even the best filmmakers of his own day, Lawrence never saw the work of later masters of organic form in the cinema such as Ingmar Bergman or Federico Fellini. Hence, for Lawrence, the cinema remained a mechanistic medium without organic qualities—a false art reflecting and furthering the false society that engendered it.

34. David Garnett, The Golden Echo, 244; quoted in Nehls, ed., D. H. Lawrence: A Composite Biography, 1:177.
35. Capra, The Name above the Title, 185–86.

6

Lawrence's Myth of the Body:
The "Biological Psyche" in
Illness and Healing

"I believe in the resurrection of the body!" Lady Constance Chatterley says (*LCL* 98), and she means it rather literally in the here and
now. D. H. Lawrence uses the Christian mystery of resurrection as a
profound symbol for the emergence into the "trembling balance" of
organic life in full sensuality. He wanted to see humanity arise in
his time from the torpor, indeed the death and putrefaction, of an
overintellectualized established religion that supported the economic and social status quo of an industrial society. For it was not
only the body politic of the society that was sick. Because the system
exploited an imbalance that turned people of flesh and blood into
machines, the body, more specifically the psychic body, was ill. On an
individual level, the process could be reversed only by finding new
models of healing and transformation that restored the "trembling
balance" by marshaling the homeostatic forces that promoted recov-
ery from physical disease and the psychological resilience that made
creative change possible.

Mythically speaking, Lawrence, in "Sun in Me," as Stephen
Spender points out, reverses the process of projecting man's torpor
upon the natural environment and internalizes nature itself as a
resurrective principle:[1]

1. Spender, *D. H. Lawrence* (audiotape).

A sun will rise in me,
I shall slowly resurrect,
already the whiteness of false dawn is on my inner ocean.
[lines 1–3, *CP* 513]

A familiar image in Lawrence, the sun recurs, especially in late works like "Sun" and *The Escaped Cock,* as a life-giving, health-restoring force in the ancient tradition of Asclepian medicine.[2] According to C. Kerényi, "The rising sun was the great nature symbol of that mysterious divine principle that the Asklepiads of Kos revered. . . ." In the morning song incised on a marble tablet in the Asclepieion at Athens, Asclepius, the divine physician and son of Apollo, is evoked in relation to the sunrise: "Awaken, Paieon Asklepios. . . . Awaken and hear thy hymn!"[3] Lawrence's poem "Sun in Me" has a similar purpose, as a hymn to the solar epiphany, in calling forth the healing power of the sun.

Throughout Lawrence's canon, particularly in his later work, resurrection is a paradigm for a resurgence of the flesh and the deep, intuitive knowledge available to man through sensual awareness as equal in value to the mind and the mental-spiritual knowledge elevated by the Protestant-capitalist-materialist ethos of modern industrial society. If the emphasis in Western culture upon rational, objective knowledge validated in the laboratory may be seen as the masculine thrust of spirit (the externalization of Idea in the technological penetration, control, and exploitation of nature, from the smallest organism to the moon and solar system, in the quest for immutable scientific law), then Lawrence's reaffirmation of intuitive, subjective knowledge validated experientially in the body is an attempt to redeem the feminine, the inward, the mutable as a significant mode of knowing lost to whole generations immured in scientism.

In *Etruscan Places,* Lawrence envisions ancient Etruria as a civilization whose knowledge emerged from integrated physical, intellectual, and emotional being rather than from compartmentalization of both knowledge and being into so many intersecting surfaces and manipulatable fragments:

It must have been a wonderful world, that old world where everything appeared alive and shining in the dusk of contact

2. For a discussion of the themes and imagery of Asclepian medicine in *The Escaped Cock,* see Hinz and Teunissen, "Savior and Cock," 279–96.
3. Kerényi, *Asklepios,* 59–60.

with all things, not merely an isolated individual thing played upon by daylight; where each thing had a clear outline, visually, but in its very clarity was related emotionally or vitally to strange other things, one thing springing from another, things mentally contradictory fusing together emotionally. . . . [*EP* 68]

This vitalistic philosophy was rooted in a nonanthropomorphic religion whose gods "were not *beings*, but symbols of elemental powers": "The undivided Godhead, if we can call it such, was symbolized by the *mundum*, the plasm-cell with its nucleus: that which is the very beginning; instead of, as with us, by a personal god, a person being the very end of all creation or evolution" (*EP* 66).

The *mundum* as plasm-cell is the central metaphor for man in the psychological system that Lawrence, more as myth-maker than as scientist, sets forth in *Psychoanalysis and the Unconscious* and elaborates in *Fantasia of the Unconscious*[4] as a theory of the structure and dynamics of the psyche as a physiologically based "trembling balance." In Lawrence's mythic histology, "[T]he original nucleus, formed from the two parent nuclei at our conception, remains always primal and central, and is always the original fount and home of the first and supreme knowledge that *I am I*" (*FU* 75). As the first of four dynamic psychic centers in what Lawrence calls "the first field of consciousness," this center remains "within the solar plexus" as the medium of a sympathetic, positive mode of knowing by incorporating the outer world into the self. Through this medium, in vital polarity with the mother's solar plexus, the infant maintains a pure, effluent, preverbal communication with her. Individuation occurs as the original nucleus divides (though paradoxically Lawrence suggests, in contradiction to the principle of cell division, that it remains in the solar plexus): "This second nucleus, the nucleus born of recoil, is the nuclear origin of all the great nuclei of the voluntary system, which are the nuclei of assertive individualism" (*FU* 75). In the adult, this second center remains in what Lawrence calls "the lumbar ganglion" as a subjective medium of differentiation and negativity: "*I am myself, and these others are not as I am*" (*FU* 79). The third and fourth centers emerge as the first two divide horizontally. Whereas the centers of the lower dynamic plane are subjective,

---

4. Differences between the two books in scale, tone, and method are emphasized by Hinz, "The Beginning and the End: D. H. Lawrence's *Psychoanalysis* and *Fantasia*," 251–65; and Ellis, "Poetry and Science in the Psychology Books," in Ellis and Mills, *D. H. Lawrence's Non-Fiction*, 67–97.

those of the upper dynamic plane are objective, and upper and lower are supposed to complement each other (*FU* 34). The cardiac plexus has the same relation to the thoracic ganglion that the solar plexus has to the lumbar ganglion. Like the solar plexus, the cardiac plexus is positive and sympathetic, but rather than incorporating the other into the self, it sees in the other an object of adoration in which to lose the self: "The wonder is without me. . . . The other being is now the great positive reality, I myself am as nothing" (*FU* 78). The thoracic ganglion, like the lumbar ganglion, is negative in polarity, but whereas the lumbar ganglion functions instinctually, for example in expressing rage, the thoracic ganglion is the seat of the spiritual will whereby one manipulates others. In harmonious balance with the lower centers, the upper centers serve useful functions. The thoracic ganglion becomes the source of "eager curiosity, of the delightful desire to pick things to pieces, and the desire to put them together again, the desire to 'find out,' and the desire to invent . . ." (*FU* 80). In *Fantasia* the "biological psyche," as it is now called, acquires four new psychic centers. At puberty, on the lower plane the sympathetic center, the hypogastric plexus in the "deeper abdomen," and the voluntary center, the sacral ganglion in "the loins," awaken as "deeper centres of consciousness and function," marking the emergence of genital sexuality. On the upper plane, the cervical plexuses and cervical ganglia emerge as corresponding sympathetic and voluntary poles (*FU* 138–39).[5]

In Lawrence's system, the brain has an instrumental rather than a creative role:

> The brain is, if we may use the word, the terminal instrument of the dynamic consciousness. It transmutes what is a creative flux into a certain fixed cipher. It prints off, like a telegraph instrument, the glyphs and graphic representations which we call percepts, concepts, ideas. It produces a new reality—the ideal. The idea is another static entity, . . . thrown off from life, as leaves are shed from a tree, . . . dry, unliving, insentient. . . . The mind is the instrument of instruments; it is not a creative reality. [*FU* 46–47]

For the same reason, the mind is also not the primary means by which one relates to the other.

In the integrated individual, Lawrence suggests, not only do the

---

5. Dervin, *A "Strange Sapience,"* 81, presents a useful table of "D. H. Lawrence's 'Pollyanalytics.'"

eight dynamic psychic centers function harmoniously together, but they also function in balanced polarity with the psychic centers of the other in a human relationship (*FU* 46). As N. Katherine Hayles explains it,

> His "subjective science" is an attempt to define a field of inter-action that includes both subject and object. For Lawrence, the "field" is always identified with a breakthrough into what he calls the "unconscious." In order to reach the "uncon-scious," from which the "field" originates, the body centers of one person engage those of another in a fierce dialectic that ends when the two "polarities" come together in mystical union.[6]

These concerns are reflected in Lawrence's epistolary relation-ship with Trigant Burrow, a psychoanalyst who broke with the orthodox Freudian position to pioneer group therapy as a method of psychoanalysis. On 13 July 1927, Lawrence writes, "What ails me is the absolute frustration of my primeval societal instinct. . . . There is no repression of the sexual individual comparable to the repression of the societal man in me, by the individual ego, my own and everybody else's" (*CL* 989–90). By the time he returned from New Mexico in 1925, Lawrence had given up his long-cherished dream of establishing Rananim as a colony of like-minded people. But the same yearnings for group relationship attracted him to Dr. Burrow's ideas, and he fantasized participating in one of his thera-peutic groups. Three weeks later, on 3 August 1927, Lawrence ten-tatively proposes the idea of attending one of these sessions: "I wish I saw a little clearer how you get over the cut-offness. I must come and be present at your group-analysis work one day, if I may. My-self, I suffer badly from being so cut off. But what is one to do?" (*CL* 993). Dr. Burrow answers this letter on 9 September 1927: "—but really it is not you who are cut off, but the image *you* have of 'you.' . . . If it is not your organism that is cut off—your organism with its feelings and instincts and its unending joy of life—but some purely artificial image, superstitiously sponsored under the traditional mood-protectorate of a primitive fear-ridden society, what avails it to look to the organism for one's mending?"[7] The two men never met, but in their correspondence they developed a warm relationship of mutual respect. Dr. Burrow, a clinician who held

6. Hayles, *The Cosmic Web*, 86.
7. Burrow, *A Search for Man's Sanity*, 186.

both the M.D. and Ph.D. degrees, sent Lawrence several reprints of his articles. Lawrence, though he had reservations about Freudian psychoanalysis, was sympathetic to Burrow's dissident position in developing his group method of analysis. In his review of Burrow's book *The Social Basis of Consciousness*, Lawrence says: "[T]he cure would consist in bringing about a state of honesty and a certain trust among a *group* of people. . . . So long as men are inwardly dominated by their own isolation, their own absoluteness, which after all is but a picture or an idea, nothing is possible but insanity more or less pronounced" (*P* 382).

On 7 May 1918, Lawrence wrote to Edith Eder, the wife of David Eder and the sister of Barbara Low, both of them London psychoanalysts,[8] asking her to lend him "a book which describes the human nervous system, and gives a sort of map of the nerves of the human body. . . . Ask [Ernest] Jones or somebody" (*Letters* 3:243). Three weeks later (28 May 1918), he writes to thank her and return the book: "I got the pages of the medical book—many thanks. Certain things I was able to find from it: but it was repulsive with diagnoses, and not very plain for me—I wanted of course a book of physiology rather than medicine. But it managed" (*Letters* 3:245).

The book is not identified, although Lawrence's implication that it concentrated on diagnoses suggests a pathology text. If Edith Eder had referred Lawrence to a standard anatomy text such as Gray's *Anatomy of the Human Body*, then available in the 20th edition revised, edited by Warren H. Lewis,[9] he would have found a scientific exposition of the two broad divisions of the human nervous system: the central nervous system, composed of the brain and spinal cord; and the peripheral nervous system, composed of the voluntary nervous system, which mediates voluntary movements, and the

8. In the year before, M. D. Eder, M.D., had published two psychoanalytic studies, *War Shock: The Psycho-Neuroses in War, Psychology and Treatment* and, with Edith Eder, *The Conflicts in the Unconscious of the Child* (both 1917). Two years later, Barbara Low, a lay analyst, published *Psycho-Analysis*. The attack on Freud in Lawrence's *Psychoanalysis and the Unconscious,* which appeared in the following year (1921), should be read in the context of the Freudian intellectual ferment in the British Psycho-Analytical Society, of which Ernest Jones, who later became the author of a three-volume biography of Freud, was president and Low a training college lecturer. Real differences between Lawrence and Freud, however, are noted by Hoffman in "Lawrence's Quarrel with Freud," in *Freudianism and the Literary Mind*, 151–76, and by Rieff in "The Therapeutic as Mythmaker: Lawrence's True Christian Philosophy," in *The Triumph of the Therapeutic*, 189–231. Lawrence and Freud are considered further in chapter 13.

9. Gray, *Anatomy of the Human Body*, 20th ed. rev., ed. Lewis, 701–21.

autonomic or, as it is called in Lewis's edition of Gray's *Anatomy*, the sympathetic nervous system, which mediates involuntary physiological functions of the glands, blood vessels, and the like.[10]

Christopher Heywood argues persuasively that one source of Lawrence's conception of the nervous system is the ganglionic theory of Marie-François-Xavier Bichat, the nineteenth-century physiologist, who "envisaged an absolute division" between what he termed the "organic" functions of the autonomic, or sympathetic, nervous system and its ganglia, and the "animal" functions of the cerebrum:

> To the latter he assigned the functions of sensation and the rational, voluntary, wakeful, exploratory, aesthetic and perfectible, but also destructive and predatory functions of man. . . .
> To [the former] . . . system he assigned the beneficent, synthesising, vegetative, creative and positive functions of restoring tissue destroyed by the depradations of the wakeful, predatory, 'animal' system.

The ganglionic system, in modern terminology, contributes the homeostatic agents that preserve homeostasis against the onslaught of imbalancing abuses from the voluntary system. As Heywood explains Bichat's dramatic ensemble, "the voluntary, will-dominated, active cerebrum . . . drives the organism towards dissolution and death," while the synthesizing, restorative powers of "the ganglia and plexuses of the 'sympathetic' nervous system" "resist the onrush of destruction."[11]

Lawrence, while sometimes claiming scientific validity and sometimes admitting to scientific inexactitude, "particularly in terminology" (*FU* 36), makes no claim to objective scientific knowledge based on the principles of logical positivism, which limits science to what can be deduced by rigorous logic from the observation and classification of factual data and sensory phenomena. Rather he posits a "subjective science," as he calls it, like that of the theosophists, though he wants to translate it into acceptable physiological terms. While developing his theory, Lawrence writes to ask Dr. David Eder (24 August 1917), with reference to Mme. Helena P. Blavatsky's

10. See Cannon, "The General Functions of the Two Grand Divisions of the Nervous System," in *The Wisdom of the Body*, 244–62, for a scientific exposition of the function of these systems in the maintenance of physiological homeostasis.

11. Heywood, " 'Blood-Consciousness,' " 108. Heywood also discusses Lawrence's use of the reflex-arc theory of the Nottingham-born physiologist Marshall Hall, which, by mid-nineteenth century, had largely superseded Bichat's "ganglionic" theory.

Secret Doctrine and James M. Pryse's *Apocalypse Unsealed,* "Do you
know the physical—physiological—interpretations of the esoteric
doctrine?—the *chakras* and dualism in experience?" (*Letters* 3:150).
Pryse, too, divides the nervous system into two separate components, a cerebrospinal structure and a sympathetic, or ganglionic,
structure, and identifies as chakras, or life centers, seven ganglia
grouped at four places in the body: in the genital area, the sacral and
the prostatic chakras; in the navel area, the epigastric chakra; in the
heart area, the cardiac chakra; and in the area of the head, the
pharyngeal, the cavernous, and the conarium chakras (the last being the pineal gland, identified as the "third eye" of the seer).[12] This
occult philosophy enlarges the understanding, Lawrence says, but
not of "the physiological interpretations," possibly because the oc-
cultists don't understand these themselves but probably because
"they do—and won't tell" (*Letters* 3:150). Even so, one may detect in
Lawrence's conception of the plexuses and ganglia as psychic energy
centers, which he at one point calls "chakras" (*PU* 35), a source in
Pryse's "gnostic chart" of the seven chakras at least equivalent in
importance to the medical book Edith Eder lent him.

Lawrence's own experience as a patient with an incurable, chronic
disease, tuberculosis, is discussed authoritatively by a physician,
Noah D. Fabricant,[13] in the light of available evidence of Lawrence's
contact as a patient with medical practitioners. Maitland Radford,
English medical officer of health, who, at the request of his mother,
the poet Dollie Radford, visited and examined Lawrence in Porth-
cothan, St. Merryn, North Cornwall, in January 1916, told him that
his "nerves" were "the root of the trouble" and that he "must lie and
rest" (*Letters* 2:516). Dr. Fabricant says that Dr. Radford's medical

12. Lawrence's use of the occult doctrine of the chakras was noted by Tindall, *D. H.
Lawrence and Susan His Cow,* 50–61. Dervin, 83–89, discusses Lawrence's use of the
chakras in his structural theory of the unconscious. Delavenay, *D. H. Lawrence: The
Man and His Work,* 408, discusses Pryse's chakra theory in relation to *Women in Love.*
Pryse's two diagrams of the chakras, reproduced by Dervin on pp. 84–85 and by
Delavenay in fig. 28, facing p. 161, may be instructively compared to Cannon's scientific "Diagram of the general arrangement of the autonomic nervous system," in
Wisdom of the Body, fig. 34, p. 251.
13. Fabricant, "Lingering Cough of D. H. Lawrence," in *Thirteen Famous Patients,*
102–12. For a discussion of Lawrence's health between 1914 and 1919, see Delavenay,
216–22. See also Ober, "Lady Chatterley's What?," in *Boswell's Clap and Other Essays,* 89–117, for a discussion of the impact of Lawrence's "pulmonary tuberculosis,
an organic disorder, and his psychosexual problems, a complex set of functional disorders," on a "novel written during its author's last illness" (89).

advice was standard at the time for tubercular patients. Nine years later, Sidney Ulfelder, an American physician and surgeon who, called in by Luis Quintinilla, examined and attended Lawrence at the Imperial Hotel in Mexico City in March 1925, told Frieda in Lawrence's presence, "Mr. Lawrence has tuberculosis."[14] At the Villa Mirenda, when Lawrence coughed up blood, Frieda called in a medical professor whom Lawrence refers to as "the best doctor in Florence—Prof. Giglioli—head of the Medical Profession for Tuscany," whose treatment by administering coagulin did not stop the hemorrhages, but who told Lawrence that a sanitorium was unnecessary (CL 991–92).

Both Max Mohr, a German physician and dramatist, and Hans Carossa, a Bavarian physician and poet, examined Lawrence in Germany in the fall of 1927. Dr. Mohr, who met Lawrence in Irschenhausen in August 1927, visited him at Les Diablerets in February 1928, saw him again when Lawrence stayed at Angermeir, Rottach-am-Tegernsee, Bavaria, near Mohr's farm home in Wulfsgrube, and in Bandol in September and October 1929, wrote an obituary of Lawrence and published a selection of his letters in Shanghai.[15] Dr. Carossa, a specialist in tuberculosis, told Franz Schoenberner, the German writer and editor, that Lawrence's deteriorated lungs would have killed the average man already but that nothing could really save him now.[16] Andrew John Morland, an English medical practitioner, later Fellow of the Royal College of Physicians, visited and examined Lawrence in Bandol at Mark Gertler's request on 20 January 1930. Dr. Morland, who as a resident physician at Mundesley sanitorium was associated with S. Vere Pearson, an early specialist in the treatment of tuberculosis, was himself the author of Pulmonary Tuberculosis in General Practice and was later Head of the Department of Chest Diseases, University College Hospital, London.[17] Dr. Morland followed with interest Lawrence's treatment by Dr. Medinier and other physicians at Ad Astra sanitorium in Vence,

14. Parmenter, Lawrence in Oaxaca, 354, note 6, has thus identified the "Dr. Uhlfelder" in Frieda Lawrence's account of this medical visit in "Not I, But the Wind . . . ," 151.

15. Dr. Mohr's obituary article was published in German as "David Herbert Lawrence," Vossische Zeitung (Berlin), 21 March 1930. See Arnold, "D. H. Lawrence and Max Mohr," 126–39. See also Owen, "D. H. Lawrence and Max Mohr," 137–56, which includes brief synopses of Lawrence's letters to Mohr in an appendix.

16. Schoenberner, "More about My Collaborators," 284–90.

17. Dr. Morland's account of his visit with Lawrence is published in Nehls, ed., D. H. Lawrence: A Composite Biography, 3:423–25. See also Zytaruk, ed., "Last Days of D. H. Lawrence," 44–50.

where Lawrence died at the Villa Robermond on 2 March 1930, the day after leaving the sanatorium.

Lawrence's conception of his illness, as presented in three poems in *Pansies,* may be instructively juxtaposed with the nearly contemporaneous responses of medical readers to his medical, psychological, and sexual theories, as presented in three early essays on Lawrence by physicians. One of the most savage attacks on Lawrence in his lifetime was Joseph Collins's chapter "Even Yet it Can't Be Told—the Whole Truth about D. H. Lawrence" in *The Doctor Looks at Literature: Psychological Studies of Life and Letters* (1923). Two years after Lawrence's death, two more moderate but less than favorable medical articles on him appeared: S. Vere Pearson's "The Psychology of the Consumptive" (1932) and W. Langdon Brown's "The Return to Aesculapius" (1932).

Lawrence had little confidence in modern medicine. In one poem, "The Scientific Doctor," he senses a "lust" in the physician "to wreak his so-called science on me / and reduce me to the level of a thing." Resistant to accepting medical advice or orders from any spokesman for mechanistic science, he concludes: "So I said: Good-morning! and left him" (lines 2–4, *CP* 620).

It would be difficult to see Dr. Joseph Collins as the epitome of "the scientific doctor," but his first objection to Lawrence is that *Psychoanalysis and the Unconscious* is riddled with misinformation and biological inaccuracies:

> Mr. Lawrence has mapped out a plan of the sympathetic nervous system and has manipulated what biologists call the tropisms in such a way as to convince himself that he has laid the scientific foundations for his work, but as there is scarcely a page or paragraph in his little book that does not contain statements which are at variance with scientific facts, it is unnecessary to say that his science will not assist him in his propaganda nearly so much as his fiction.[18]

It soon becomes apparent, however, that the veneer of objective science masks Dr. Collins's real objection, which is the familiar one of sex.

What disturbs Dr. Collins most about Lawrence's fiction is what he takes to be the advocacy of various sexual perversions: Lettie Beardsall as "the *anlage* for all his female characters, their im-

18. Collins, *The Doctor Looks at Literature,* 269.

moralities and bestialities"; Helena Verden's abnormal "genetic instincts" for the deliberate "biologic aberration" for which "the Lord slew Onan"[19] without thereby eliminating the aberration, which "even today gives more concern to parents and pedagogues than any other instinct deviation"; Tom Brangwen's "marital lust" in a "great debauch" through which he feels that God has made himself known to the married couple; Will Brangwen's "extrauxorial," "revolting scene with a grisette" that leads to "wild lubricity" with his wife; the "indecent and disgusting" gathering of men around the African wood carvings in Halliday's flat "in a state of complete nudity"; Birkin and Gerald's "so-called wrestling scene" ("the most obscene narrative that I have encountered in the English language"); Hermione Roddice's sadistic pleasure in inflicting injury on Birkin, who then satisfies his "masochistic lust" by rolling naked among the pine needles ("And this is the man who Mr. Lawrence would have us believe was Inspector of Schools in England in the beginning of the Twentieth Century!"); Birkin and Ursula's practice in "Excurse" of a "supercorporeal contact that beggars description"; and Lilly's "inverted genesic instinct."[20]

Dr. Collins, inferring Lawrence's affinities with Otto Weininger's misogyny, Walt Whitman's exaltation of the body, and the offense of an unnamed poet (Oscar Wilde) "whom the English public found necessary to put in the Reading Gaol," objects most to the advocacy, in *Aaron's Rod* and elsewhere, "of the enigmatic aberration whose doctrines Mr. Lawrence is trying to foist upon an unsuspecting English-reading public," that is, homosexuality. Presumably, this is what "Even Yet . . . Can't Be Told"; but it can be suggested by pointed innuendo, as when Collins follows Lawrence's statement, "And the polarity is between man and man," with the comment: "That sentence contains to him who can read it aright the whole truth of Mr. D. H. Lawrence." Far from being objective or scientific, Dr. Collins's language throughout is loaded and his tone is vitriolic, moralistic, and judgmental in the extreme. All must travel "the road leading from Original Sin to the street called Straight," he says, but "those who have morbid sex-consciousness in one form or another, inadequate or deviate genetic endowment, are unable to finish the

19. Dr. Collins refers to masturbation, for which "onanism" had become a popular euphemism; however, Genesis 38:9 clearly describes coitus interruptus. Onan's "sin" was not the sexual act per se but disobedience to his father's order and patriarchal tradition in refusing to act as surrogate in providing the semen to preserve his brother's line of familial descent.

20. Collins, 263, 264–65, 271, 272–73, 278, 278, 279–80, 282, 284, 285.

journey at all." It's a pity, he concludes, that the British "do not annihilate every trace" of D. H. Lawrence.[21]

In another poem, "Sick," Lawrence suggests that the etiology of his illness lies in having given too much of his life energy away to other people, who, being emotionally dead, treated life as carrion: "so they pecked a shred of my life, and flew off with a croak / of sneaking exultance." He declares:

> I am trying now to learn never
> to give of my life to the dead,
> never, not the tiniest shred.
> [lines 4–5, 7–9, *CP* 500]

This is basically what Lawrence says in a contemporaneous letter to Lady Ottoline Morrell (24 May 1928), in which he attributes illness to a deficiency in appropriately selfish self-preservation so that "these microbes, which are the pure incarnation of invisible selfishness, pounce" and one is wasted with pure "chagrin": "The hurts, and the bitterness sink in, however much one may reject them with one's spirit," he says. "One ought to be tough and selfish: and one is never tough enough, and never selfish in the proper self-preserving way. Then one is laid low" (*CL* 1063).

The same assumption underlies the fear of infection that pervades *Aaron's Rod*, a novel in which, Marguerite Beede Howe says, "both self and body are diseased by sex."[22] Aaron Sisson's bout with flu is actually with a viral infection transmitted by casual contact rather than sexually, but he attributes his feeling of enervation to a loss of physical energy resulting from his having "given in" to Josephine Ford in the sex act: " 'I felt, the minute I was loving her, I'd done myself. And I had,' " he tells Rawdon Lilly. " 'I felt it—I felt it go, inside me, the minute I gave in to her. It's perhaps killed me' " (*AR* 89–90). As Judith Ruderman notes, although Aaron's attributing his inactive liver to his "giving in" to Josephine does not explain the nature of his illness, the diagnosis may be traced to Lawrence's psychological theory that "[a]ny excess in the sympathetic dynamism tends to accelerate the action of the liver, to cause fever and constipation" (*FU* 96). For Ruderman, "Lawrence's frequent images of 'anal retention' or constipation suggest that humankind's service to the love ideal has caused sickness to be endemic in this modern

---

21. Ibid., 273, 284, 270, 258, 287.
22. Howe, *The Art of the Self in D. H. Lawrence*, 83.

age."[23] Since Lawrence usually associates passion with vital renewal, obviously more is involved in Aaron's enervation than the
simple connection of loss of vital energy with loss of semen. What
leaves Aaron so savagely depressed is his sense that his acquies-
cence in Josephine's seduction has reduced him to "nothing but a
piece of carrion" (*AR* 93), an image implying a view of the sexually
aggressive woman as vulture. Lilly's treatment of Aaron in this
depressed state by therapeutic massage is discussed in chapter 7,
"Lawrence and Touch."

S. Vere Pearson, a pioneer in the treatment of tuberculosis, noting
that "stimulating powers to genius" have been "frequently ascribed
to the toxins of tuberculosis," says that, except for "restless agitation" and "apprehension lest life should be shortened," this stimulus
has been "over-emphasized." The more important influences on the
individual psyche are those of early childhood, including the Freudian "sexual factor" and especially the Adlerian "will to power." Since
"the flight to illness" is made as often to pulmonary tuberculosis as
to other diseases, "the abnormal psychological state present must be
looked upon as a cause rather than as a consequence of consumption." Examination of the biographies and letters of five tubercular
writers—Robert Louis Stevenson, D. H. Lawrence, Anton Chekov,
Elizabeth Barrett Browning, and John Keats—reveals that none
received "proper treatment for their malady," partly because appropriate medical instruction was not given them, partly because of
their own temperamental resistance to doctor's orders.[24]

Pearson, who as a senior physician at Mundesley sanitorium
greatly influenced Dr. Andrew Morland during his seven years as a
resident physician there, traces the major psychological and social
influences on Lawrence—his working-class background, his "hard-
drinking, rather uncouth" father and refined, intelligent mother, his
marriage to a German woman several years his senior, his simultaneous political and censorship difficulties during the War years.
Lawrence received very little competent medical treatment for his
chronic disease, Dr. Pearson says, apparently drawing on Dr. Morland's experience in the case. Though he was urged by relatives and
artist friends to enter a sanatorium, in his "desire for dominance" he
resisted placing himself under such a regimen. Dr. Pearson attributes Lawrence's struggles not to his having allowed his reserves of
vitality to be pecked away by others like scavenger birds but to a

23. Ruderman, *D. H. Lawrence and the Devouring Mother*, 97–98.
24. Pearson, "The Psychology of the Consumptive," 477, 478, 479.

"divided personality": "His body and brain was harassed by his split-ting up of love too much into the physical and psychical components, due originally largely to his mother-fixation."[25]

Unlike other medical readers, Dr. Pearson notes that "D. H. Law-rence, of all modern writers, shows an appreciation of the connection between mental contentment or perturbation and the onset of illness or, when illness has become established, the progress towards recov-ery or death." Pearson is struck by Lawrence's "comprehension of mental upsets being a causal factor in producing ill-health," as in the case of Lady Daphne in *The Ladybird*. Pearson concludes: "Much of the peculiarities of the writings of Lawrence are erroneously as-cribed to his being a sufferer from pulmonary tuberculosis: whereas they ought to be ascribed to the other influences indicated."[26]

In a third poem, "Healing," Lawrence makes clear that what he rejects is not the need for healing but the reductive, mechanistic assumptions of the present biomedical model:

I am not a mechanism, an assembly of various sections.
And it is not because the mechanism is working wrongly, that I am
    ill.
I am ill because of wounds to the soul, to the deep emotional self
and the wounds to the soul take a long, long time, only time can
    help
and patience, and a certain difficult repentance
long, difficult repentance, realisation of life's mistake, and the
    freeing oneself
from the endless repetition of the mistake
which mankind at large has chosen to sanctify.

[*CP* 620]

As Lawrence writes in the letter to Lady Ottoline on illness: "If only one could have two lives: the first, in which to make one's mistakes, which seem as if they *had* to be made; and the second in which to profit by them" (*CL* 1063).

Lawrence's attributing the origin of his illness to "life's mistake," the unbalanced elevation of the love ideal, sanctified by mankind as a whole, sounds at first like the moral interpretation of disease common to the Bible and other ancient authorities, not like the rational interpretation of disease of whatever modern medical model. Moreover, Lawrence had already satirized the mechanical-

25. Ibid., 480, 482.
26. Ibid., 483, 484.

structural model that is explicitly rejected in the first two lines, by the strategy of reducing his own theory to the extended simile of the bicycle in *Fantasia:*

> Well, well—my body is my bicycle: the whole middle of me is the saddle where sits the rider of my soul. And my front wheel is the cardiac plane, and my back wheel is the solar plexus. And the brakes are the voluntary ganglia. And the steering gear is my head. And the right and left pedals are the right and left dynamics of the body, in some way corresponding to the sympathetic and voluntary division. [*FU* 96]

The mechanical-structural model, though it of course continued to serve as a basis for such specialties as surgery and orthopedics, had largely been superseded in internal medicine (by the 1870s) by the invasion model of disease, the conception of the body's being invaded from the outside by germs. The invasion model led to the doctrine of a specific etiology for each disease, an idea implicitly rejected in Lawrence's poetic reference to "wounds to the soul" and his comment that the medical book Edith Eder lent him was "repulsive with diagnoses."

Lawrence's disease, tuberculosis, had been identified three years before his birth as having its etiology in the tubercle bacillus. But in *Fantasia of the Unconscious,* Lawrence bases his psychosomatic theory of heart and lung disease on his conception of neurophysiology:

> Thence, since we live terribly and exhaustively from the upper centres, there is a tendency now towards pthisis and neurasthenia of the heart. The great sympathetic centre of the breast becomes exhausted, the lungs, burnt by the over-insistence of one way of life, become diseased, the heart, strained in one mode of dilation, retaliates. . . . So, weak-chested, round-shouldered, we stoop hollowly forward on ourselves. It is the result of the all-famous love and charity ideal, an ideal now quite dead in its sympathetic activity, but still fixed and determined in its voluntary action. [*FU* 90–91]

The etiology of tuberculosis, he believes, lies in the unnatural forcing of the love ideal:

> On the upper plane, the lungs and heart are controlled from the cardiac plane and the thoracic ganglion. Any excess in the sympathetic mode from the upper centres tends to burn the

lungs with oxygen, weaken them with stress, and cause consumption. So it is just criminal to make a child too loving. No child should be induced to love too much. It means derangement and death at last. [*FU* 97]

W. Langdon Brown comments on Lawrence and the etiology of his illness in the context of his thesis that a "striking feature of twentieth century medicine has been a return to the cult of Aesculapius; cleanliness, fresh air, suggestion, dream analysis and psychological explanation." The physician should take account of the patient's total homeostatic functioning, both physiologically and psychologically: "medicine is a department of biology and unless we consider the patient as a whole, as a living organism, reacting to changes in either the external or the internal environment, we shall miss an essential part of his case." Committed to the principles of psychosomatic medicine, Dr. Brown sees pitfalls in emphasizing exclusively either body or mind: "Ordinary materialistic medicine is apt to forget the fact that the patient's emotional and mental outlook will inevitably influence and be influenced by disease; the psychotherapist is apt to forget that the patient has a body which may be suffering from some physical distress." "It is by this combined attack on the physical and psychological side that medicine in the future will make advance and still further aid human suffering."[27] Tracing the history of organic medicine from the Temple of Aesculapius (he uses the Latin form of the Greek name), Brown then briefly reviews modern medical research on the central nervous system by Rivers, Head, Gordon Holmes, Hughlings Jackson, Gaskell, Langley, and Cushing.

In this context, "to illustrate some of the features of psychoneuroses," he turns to the life and work of D. H. Lawrence, especially as interpreted by John Middleton Murry in *Son of Woman* (1931), which Dr. Brown fails to recognize as a less than objective account with its own hidden agenda.[28] Accepting Murry's view that the homosexuality implicit in earlier novels becomes explicit in *Aaron's Rod,* where Lilly, Lawrence's "scarcely disguised" autobiographical persona, "wants a homo-sexual relation with Aaron to complete his incomplete hetero-sexual relation with his wife," Dr. Brown comments:

27. Langdon Brown, "The Return to Aesculapius," 11, 14, 14–15, 15.
28. T. S. Eliot found his biases confirmed by Murry. See " 'The victim and the sacrificial knife,' " 241–47. Dr. Brown is not, of course, a literary scholar, but a more alert psychiatrist's sensitivity to the vested interests of a former friend of the subject would prevent his taking such a person's report unquestioningly at face value.

Naturally when a man reaches a stage like this he has to try and construct a philosophy to rationalize his abnormal cravings. Hopelessly divided between his sexual appetites and his spiritual love for his mother's memory, while yet knowing how it has destroyed him, he portrays growth as duality, i.e., an increasing cleavage between the senses and the spirit. A tragic if laughable misinterpretation of decay for growth.[29]

In Dr. Brown's view of the situation (seen through the distorting lens of Murry's failed friendship), out of Lawrence's frustration in relationships with both men and women, his "power motive grows to fantastic dimensions" and he seeks "release in mindless sensuality . . . among pre-mental primitive people." For Lawrence, unable to achieve leadership in "the complete submission of others" and "completely divided between love and hatred," "death loomed almost as an escape":[30]

For his physical frame was by now exhausted by the hopeless struggle of his divided personality. It is a story as inevitable as Greek Drama—mother-fixation—the splitting of love into physical and psychical components—impotence—and an attempted compensation for it in a fantastic power motive which became completely asocial, and so destroyed itself. His writing is exhibitionism, but also an attempt to explain himself to himself. Mingled with his turgid philosophy and preposterous physiology there are passages of really lovely comprehension of external nature, and flashes of self-knowledge. . . .[31]

Despite his misunderstanding of Lawrence's philosophical dualism and his reductive view of Lawrence's personal psychology, Dr. Brown would apparently share Lawrence's view that modern man must make a "curve" of return to reclaim something valuable in the lost knowledge of the ancients. Brown envisions modern medicine's coming full circle to treat the divided consciousness of modern man. As in "the Temple of Aesculapius at Cos, where Hippocrates, the founder of scientific medicine, taught and practised, the work of healing was carried on in a delightful setting, designed to help the whole man," so in "a not-impossible hospital of the future, . . . everything in its environment and equipment shall tend not only to bodily

29. Brown, "The Return to Aesculapius," 24.
30. Ibid., 24, 26.
31. Ibid., 26.

welfare, but to a quiet mind, to ensure 'A sleep full of quiet dreams, and health and quiet breathing.' "[32]

Lawrence's model for the body, both in illness and in healing, arises from his theory of neurophysiology. David Ellis asserts that "[b]oth the psychology books challenge their readers to distinguish the metaphorical from what is meant to be taken literally."[33] The intimate connection that Lawrence, like Freud, sees between biological and psychological being is not in question. What is increasingly apparent from a reading of the texts, however, is that very little in Lawrence's conception of neuroanatomy can be taken, or is even intended, as empirically validated scientific fact. The medical text Edith Eder sent him must have served, if nothing else, to confirm to Lawrence that his theory is not consistent with contemporary medical models arising out of a science of logical positivism. His eight dynamic centers are all parts of the autonomic nervous system, transmitting impulses and mediating involuntary functions, not as he hypothesizes the great integrative centers, which modern neurophysiology locates in the central nervous system, of such complex functions as integration, origination of impulses, and consciousness. Although Lawrence adduces from his own experience and creative work evidence that, loosely speaking, may be called clinical, the system he proposes is based on the evidence of neither laboratory experimentation nor clinical observation. His theory is supported, for example, neither by the microscopic examination of tissue in slide sections such as Bichat dissected in the laboratory nor by clinical material such as the information that Freud elicited from patients in his consulting room. The hypothesis that the first four "nuclei are centres of spontaneous consciousness," Lawrence asserts, "is obvious, demonstrable scientific fact, to be verified under the microscope and within the human psyche, subjectively and objectively, both"; however, he cites no empirical validation but appeals only to the experiential verification of the reader's "bowels of comprehension" (PU 43). Lawrence, in fact, directly disclaims both scholarly method (FU 54) and scientific authority: "We profess no scientific exactitude, particularly in terminology. We merely wish intelligibly to open a way" (PU 36).

That Lawrence's conceptions of neurophysiology is based on anatomical inaccuracies does not invalidate his psychological theory. At

32. Ibid., 27.

33. Ellis, "Lawrence and the Biological Psyche," 104. Ellis, who recognizes that Lawrence's psychobiology is factually inaccurate but thinks he intends it literally, takes issue with my comment, in D. H. Lawrence's American Journey, 20, that Lawrence reifies metaphor into literal fact, burdening "his four dynamic centers with more than these peripheral circuits can actually bear."

least one mental-health professional, Malcolm Brown, accepts Lawrence's psychological theories of male and female psychology and child development and employs his concept of localizing psychic energy in four specific areas of the body in his practice as a neo-Reichian psychotherapist. One of Dr. Brown's methods, placing his hands firmly and undemandingly on his patient's body at the four primal centers, in repeated therapeutic encounters over a period of time, has the effect, he says, of freeing the rigidity blocking the flow of psychic energy at these centers.[34]

If Lawrence's texts cannot be taken literally as modern scientific treatises, they may nevertheless be taken seriously as works of the literary imagination. Lawrence's statement that the theory is derived from the novels and poems (*FU* 57), that is, from literary constructs, points to its origins in metaphor, one of the strategies of which is to insist on its concreteness. When a poet elaborates a large-scale metaphorical system encompassing a world view for understanding inward experience or a poetic myth for ordering the insights of the literary imagination, as in Blake's *Four Zoas,* Yeats's *Vision,* or Graves's *White Goddess,* surely it may be more usefully considered as metaphor than as fact. I submit that "intelligibly to open a way" is a legitimate purpose for a literary artist.

Lawrence's theory is a grand synthesis of meanings derived from multiple sources, ancient and modern, presented in the form of a psychobiological myth of the human body. Lawrence's "subjective science," he repeatedly makes clear, arises from a pre-Socratic cosmology identified with the mythic lost continent Atlantis but surviving in symbolic forms among the "Druids or Etruscans or Chaldeans or Amerindians or Chinese" (*FU* 55). Lawrence asserts: "I honestly think that the great pagan world of which Egypt and Greece were the last living terms, the great pagan world which preceded our own era, once had a vast and perhaps perfect science of its own, a science in terms of life."

Modern science, in contrast, "is a science of the dead world" (*FU* 54). Treating "mechanistic functioning" rather than life, modern medicine, for Lawrence, promotes no such healing of body and transformation of spirit as that evoked in the words of Tommy Dukes: "I believe in the resurrection of Man, and the Son of Man, and that is a great comfort to me. . . . Somehow, I shall always be part of mankind. That's what I feel. So that if men can rise up again, with new flesh on their spirits, and new feelings in their flesh, and a new fire to erect their phallus—that is immortality to me" (*JTLJ* 63).

34. Malcolm Brown, *Psychological Genius of D. H. Lawrence* (Audiotape).

Lawrence's attempt to revive the esoteric science, once "invested in a large priesthood" who practiced and taught, he believes, throughout the ancient world, places his science with that of the Asclepians of Cos, where Hippocrates, according to legend, was crowned with a golden wreath, which "represents rays and symbolizes the sunlike." Like Malcolm Brown's use of touch in psychotherapeutic practice, Lawrence's own conception of the restorative power of touch, which is discussed in chapter 7, was rooted in the "intuitive science" of his myth of the body. Lawrence's statement "I proceed by intuition" (*FU* 54) evokes "the special nature of the Asklepiad, the true physician," whose "special gift," Kerényi says, "is neither a religious nor a philosophical knowledge" but "a spark of intuitive knowledge about the possibilities of rising from the depths, a spark which by observation, practice, and training can be fanned into a high art and science: into a true art of healing."[35]

35. Kerényi, 67–69.

7

Lawrence and Touch

Of all the senses available as means of integration and of communication with others, touch had the most profound significance for
D. H. Lawrence. In keeping with Joseph Conrad's declaration in the
preface to *The Nigger of the "Narcissus"* that his task in fiction is "to
make you hear, to make you feel—it is, before all, to make you *see*,"[1]
modern critics have tended to place greater emphasis on the visual
than on any other sensory element. As important as visual images
are in Lawrence's fiction,[2] however, both in conveying the substance
of reality and in embodying visionary experience, sight, for him, "is
the least sensual of all the senses" (*FU* 102). Lawrence's criticism
suggests that morality in the novel is not a matter of intellectual
understanding but of relationship. His task in fiction is not to make
the reader *see* or *see into* but to put him *in touch* with his own being,
with others, with nature and the world. The novel would function, so
to speak, as a homeostatic agent that by putting the reader in touch
with his own feelings, would serve to correct the imbalance between
spiritual aspirations and instinctual needs and so help prepare him

1. Conrad, "Preface" to *The Nigger of the "Narcissus,"* xl.
2. Alldritt, *Visual Imagination of D. H. Lawrence,* explores in impressive detail
Lawrence's use of the visual element by means of art allusions.

to establish the "trembling balance" of a living relationship with the other. In this chapter, I argue that Lawrence presents the greater moral significance of "true relatedness" through the medium of human touch, the function of which he grounded in his theory of the psychobiology of the unconscious and illustrated in numerous scenes of touch variously involving unconscious motivation and insight, nurturance, bonding, intrusiveness, ritual, and sexuality.

As Lawrence says in "Morality and the Novel," "morality is that delicate, forever trembling and changing *balance* between me and my circumambient universe, which precedes and accompanies a true relatedness" (*STH* 172). In isolation from human relationships, Lawrence suggests in his review of *The Social Basis of Consciousness* by Trigant Burrow, one can live only from a mental image of reality, not from life itself. He elaborates: "Men must get back into *touch*. And to do so they must forfeit the vanity and the *noli me tangere* of their own *absoluteness*: . . . and fall again into true relatedness" (*P* 382). In "Why the Novel Matters," the human body becomes the metaphor for the "trembling balance" of life, and the sense of touch becomes the metaphor for being "in touch." Rejecting the mind-body dichotomy, Lawrence says: "My hand is alive, it flickers with a life of its own. It meets all the strange universe, in touch, and learns a vast number of things, and knows a vast number of things. My hand . . . is just as much *me* as is my brain, my mind, or my soul" (*STH* 193).

This view accords with Lawrence's theory of the psychophysiology of the senses in *Fantasia of the Unconscious:* "Of the five senses, four have their functioning in the face-region. The fifth, the sense of touch, is distributed all over the body. But all have their roots in the four great primary centres of consciousness" (*FU* 97); that is, on the lower, sensual plane, the solar plexus and the lumbar ganglion, and on the upper, spiritual plane, the cardiac plexus and the thoracic ganglion.

In Lawrence's theory, "the body is planned out in areas," with each of the "primary centres" controlling sensory responses in its designated zone. The two voluntary centers, the lumbar and thoracic ganglia, have the function of resistance, while the two sympathetic centers, the solar and cardiac plexuses, have the function of reception. Hence, "On the back the sense of touch is not acute. . . . But in the front of the body, the breast is one great field of sympathetic touch, the belly is another." Because the cardiac plexus functions spiritually whereas the solar plexus functions sensually, "On these two fields the stimulus of touch . . . has a quite different psychic quality and psychic result. The breast-touch is the fine alertness of quivering curiosity, the belly-touch is a deep thrill of delight and avidity." This difference extends to the limbs and instruments of touch in the corresponding areas of the body: "the hands and arms are instruments of superb delicate curiosity, and deliberate execution," whereas "the legs and feet are instruments of unfathomable gratifications and repudiations. The thighs, the knees, the feet are intensely alive with love-desire, darkly and superbly drinking in the love-contact, blindly. Or they are the great centres of resistance, kicking, repudiating" (*FU* 97–98).

Lawrence concludes: "Thus the fields of touch are four, two sympathetic fields in front of the body from the throat to the feet, two resistant fields behind from the neck to the heels." There are, however, two exceptions, "two fields of touch . . . where the distribution is not so simple: the face and the buttocks. Neither in the face nor in the buttocks is there one single mode of sense communication" (*FU* 98). The theory of touch presented in *Fantasia of the Unconscious* is, like the psychological theory of which it is a part, a poetic metaphor to which Lawrence returns again and again for his major thematic imagery.

As Lawrence sets forth in a poetic sequence in *Pansies,* modern society, with its mechanistic conception of people not as selves belonging to an organic whole but as so many separate "personalities," inevitably uses touch to reflect the fragmentation. "For if, cerebrally, we force ourselves into touch," he says in "Touch," the contact is not a means of communication but a violation of self and other (*CP* 468). One of Lawrence's basic tenets is that sensory or sensual experience should not be dominated by mental ideas or spiritual ideals. This is why he denounces "sex in the head" and cries, in "Noli Me Tangere": "O you with mental fingers, O never put your hand on me!" (*CP* 468). Thus, in "Chastity," Lawrence calls for "Chastity, beloved chastity," to keep one "clean from mental fingering" and "the cold copulation of the will" in "this mind-mischievous age" (*CP* 469–70). The alternative he offers, in "Touch Comes," is the regeneration, "when the white mind sleeps," of touch that is "of the blood" (*CP* 470–71).

In *Etruscan Places,* Lawrence imagines ancient Etruria, in contrast to modern society, to be a kind of Rananim of true relatedness where the whole of life is integrated through the medium of touch. His description of a banquet scene in a wall painting, in which a bearded man is softly touching a woman, is the exemplar for the function of touch as Lawrence would have it:

> Rather gentle and lovely is the way he touches the woman under the chin, with a delicate caress. That again is one of the

charms of the Etruscan paintings: they really have the sense
of touch; the people and the creatures are all really in touch.
It is one of the rarest qualities, in life as well as in art. There
is plenty of pawing and laying hold, but no real touch. In
pictures especially, the people may be in contact, embracing
or laying hands on one another. But there is no soft flow of
touch. The touch does not come from the middle of the human being. It is merely a contact of surfaces, and a jux-
taposition of objects. . . . Here, in this faded Etruscan painting, there is a quiet flow of touch that unites the man and
the woman on the couch, the timid boy behind, the dog that
lifts his nose, even the very garlands that hang from the
wall. [*EP* 45–46]

Del Ivan Janik, for whom "*Etruscan Places* is less concerned with
the analysis of a fully developed ancient civilization than with the
projection of a possible future one," comments that "genuine touch"
as the means of overcoming ego isolation stands at the thematic
center of Lawrence's late works.[3] Thus, in *John Thomas and Lady
Jane,* Tommy Dukes, who often speaks in a Laurentian voice, declares: "We're not civilised enough even now, to be able to touch one
another." "The next civilisation," he prophesies, will be "based on
the mystery of touch, and all that that means; a field of consciousness which hasn't yet opened into existence. *We're* too much afraid of
it—. . . . We paw things—but probably we've never *truly* touched
anybody in all our lives, nor any living thing—Oh, there'll be a
democracy—the democracy of touch. . . . We're only an experiment
in mechanisation, that will be properly *used* in the next phase"
(*JTLJ* 58).

Lawrence's conception includes self-touch as a means to self-
knowledge. In a letter to Blanche Jennings in summer 1908, he
remarks that in rubbing himself down after a bath, "as I passed my
hands over my sides where the muscles lie suave and secret, I did
love myself. I am thin, but well skimmed over with muscle; my skin
is very white and unblemished; soft, and dull with a fine pubescent
bloom, not shiny like my friend's" (*Letters* 1:65). What is remarkable
in this account, besides its being sent to Miss Jennings, is the way
the experience that, in a man of different sensibility, would have

3. Janik, *The Curve of Return,* 80 and 88–89. As Janik notes, "Being in touch
meant for Lawrence not only personal connection with other individuals but a larger
connection, which he believed the Etruscans had experienced, with the universe as a
whole."

been overtly masturbatory has, for Lawrence, the wonder of "an almost religious imagining."[4]

Because its motivations are largely unconscious, touch has extraordinary power to bind relationships and to bring into consciousness hidden forces at work in them. "Hadrian" ["You Touched Me"] is a fable about the power of a single touch to be irrevocably binding. In the tale, Matilda Rockley, anxious about her father, goes somnambulantly by moonlight to his room:

> "Are you asleep?" she repeated gently, as she stood at the side of the bed. And she reached her hand in the darkness to touch his forehead. Delicately, her fingers met the nose and the eyebrows, she laid her fine, delicate hand on his brow. It seemed fresh and smooth—very fresh and smooth. A sort of surprise stirred her, in her entranced state. But it could not waken her. Gently, she leaned over the bed and stirred her fingers over the low-growing hair on his brow. [*EME* 99]

But it is Hadrian, once a Cockney foundling her father had adopted, now a soldier who is visiting them after an absence of five years, whom she has touched. Awakened by his voice, Matilda remembers that her father is downstairs and that Hadrian is sleeping in his room. The next day she tries to pass the incident off as a mistake, but Lawrence keeps the reader aware of its unconscious determinants, which are so potent that the touch functions as a kind of demonic fate.

Hadrian, aroused, slyly gets Mr. Rockley to tell Matilda to marry him, an order that the dying man reinforces economically by threatening to cut Matilda and her sister out of his will, although Hadrian insists that his offer of marriage was not based on the money. The difference between speech and touch as means of communicating emotional truth is made clear in an exchange between Matilda and Hadrian:

> "I don't want to speak to you," she said, averting her face.
> "You put your hand on me, though," he said. "You shouldn't have done that, and then I should never have thought of it. You shouldn't have touched me."
> "If you were anything decent, you'd know that was a mistake, and forget it," she said.

---

4. The phrase is from Black, *D. H. Lawrence: The Early Fiction,* 65. Black relates this "central text" to the bathing scene in *The White Peacock,* discussed below.

"I know it was a mistake—but I shan't forget it. If you wake a man up, he can't go to sleep again because he's told to." [*EME* 106]

Matilda, who is eleven years older than Hadrian, consciously recognizes the "indecency" of the proposal but unconsciously responds to it. "I'm old enough to be your mother," she says. "Doesn't matter," Hadrian replies, as if to defend against the obvious psychological interpretation while accepting the compulsion of the aroused instinct. "You've been no mother to me" (*EME* 106).

In "You Touched Me," the touch opens a kind of two-way oedipal street whereby Hadrian attains sexual conquest of his quondam "mother," and whereby Matilda, by her father's collusion in what she recognizes as a socially inappropriate match, gains sexual access to her father through Hadrian, a younger version of himself in his own working-class origins, whom the father has chosen as his successor.

Touch not only proceeds from unconscious motives but also activates them into consciousness, where they can become the source of self-knowledge and understanding of others. In "Odour of Chrysanthemums," the sight of her husband lying dead precipitates Elizabeth Bates's tragic recognition of the gulf that had lain between them in life, and her touching of his naked corpse becomes for her a means of incorporating the reality that this distance is made permanent and impassable by death: "She was almost ashamed to handle him; what right had she or anyone to lay hands on him; but her touch was humble on his body" (*PO* 199).

In the play adapted from this story, *The Widowing of Mrs. Holroyd*, Lizzie Holroyd, in the laying out and bathing of her dead husband, achieves tragic insight, in her address to the body, as touch precipitates self-confrontation on her part that makes conscious the needs and truths of the relationship that have been denied on both sides, including the narrowness of her own former perspective, but that does so after it is too late to use these insights to heal the relationship:

> My dear, my dear—oh, my dear! I can't bear it, my dear—you shouldn't have done it. You shouldn't have done it. Oh—I can't bear it, for you. Why couldn't I do anything for you? The children's father—my dear—I wasn't good to you. But you shouldn't have done this to me. Oh, dear, oh dear! Did it hurt you?—oh, my dear, it hurt you—oh, I can't bear it. No, things aren't fair—we went wrong, my dear. I never loved you enough—I never did. What a shame for you! It was a shame.

But you didn't—you didn't try. I *would* have loved you—I
tried hard. What a shame for you! It was so cruel for you. You
couldn't help it—my dear, my dear. You couldn't help it. And I
can't do anything for you, and it hurt you so! [*WMH* 58–59]

What lifts the disaster in the mine to tragedy is the "supreme
struggle" (*P II* 291) by which Mrs. Holroyd achieves insight, its
heightening through irony assuring that Lawrence's emphasis, not
on meaningless disaster but on the meaning of mutability in human relationships in time, will not be lost on the audience.

Unconscious instinctual energy may be deflected by sublimation
from its original sexual or aggressive aim into such a higher cultural goal as idealistic, humanitarian, religious, intellectual, or artistic pursuits. Freud cites Leonardo da Vinci's madonnas as the
sublimation of the artist's longing for his mother, from whom he had
been separated in early childhood. Lawrence, of course, opposed idealism and, according to Earl H. Brewster, inveighed "against what
he called the attempt to overcome the tiger, whose being in us is
real, he maintained, and not to be suppressed or sublimated." It is
difficult to know how precisely Lawrence used these psychological
terms, but they are linked here in such a way as to imply an equa-
tion between the two in his mind. What is clear is his "desire for an
environment where his contact with people would be more vital" and
unimpeded by mental processes.[5] Lawrence's writing, nevertheless,
emerges from insight, not from acting out; and insight, to the extent
that it is different from doing, necessarily involves sublimation. Sublimation, as the outcome of a successful renunciation of an instinctual aim, differs from neurotic defense mechanisms in that while the
source and aim of the instinctual energy remain the same, the instinct is partially satisfied by means that are acceptable to both the
individual and the society rather than being totally repressed only
to emerge in a neurotic or destructive form. In three major scenes in
Lawrence's work, in which homoerotic yearnings are sublimated
into idealized friendship, nurturance, and religious ritual, touch becomes the instrument of both identifying and transforming the original instinctual aim.

In "A Poem of Friendship" in *The White Peacock*, the bathing
scene in which George Saxton rubs Cyril Beardsall dry with a towel
expresses an idealized homoeroticism that marks one stage of adolescent development as, in Cyril's words, "the sweetness of the touch of

5. Brewster, in Nehls, ed., *D. H. Lawrence: A Composite Biography*, 2:60.

our naked bodies one against the other was superb. It satisfied in some measure the vague, indecipherable yearning of my soul; . . . and our love was perfect for a moment, more perfect than any love I have known since, either for man or woman" (*WP* 222–23). Meyers, who thinks that "[t]he 'rubbing' is explicitly homosexual," compares Cyril's posture to that "of the limp, passive figure [of the female] pressed against the powerful male in [Maurice Greiffenhagen's] *An Idyll*."[6] As an expression of homosexual conflict, the "yearning" of Cyril's soul is not "indecipherable," but it is as simplistic to reduce the experience to this single motive as it would be disingenuous to deny the feeling, which, strictly speaking, does not express a sexual need per se but uses the sexual impulse as a screen for the dependency needs that Cyril actually brings to George. Lionel Ovesey, who sees both dependency needs and power strivings as in reality "pseudohomosexual" motives in ostensibly homosexual conflict, observes, "The resort to dependency represents the seeking of magical solutions to the failures in assertion. . . ."[7] Cyril's yearning is for gratification of his longing for the father. George, in his easy grace, nobility of body, and generous spirit, is the embodiment for Cyril of ideals he has not yet successfully internalized. As such, he is the precursor of the ego ideal, which, according to Freud, is formed at the resolution of the Oedipus complex and "answers to everything that is expected of the higher nature of man. As a substitute for a longing for the father, it contains the germ from which all religions have evolved. The self-judgment which declares that the ego falls short of its ideal produces the religious sense of humility to which the believer appeals in his longing."[8] Cyril's response, which encom-

6. Meyers, *Homosexuality and Literature*, 139. Meyers points out that several male friendships with homoerotic overtones in Lawrence's work are modeled on the biblical friendship of David and Jonathan (131–32). Cyril's phrasing certainly echoes that of David's lament for Jonathan: "I am distressed for thee, my brother Jonathan: very pleasant hast thou been unto me: thy love to me was wonderful, passing the love of women" (2 Samuel 1:26). Further examples include the reference in the "Prologue" to *Women in Love* to Birkin's "old friends . . . to whom he had been attached passionately, like David to Jonathan" (*WL* 503); and Somers's response in *Kangaroo* to Jack Callcott's "sensitive delicacy really finer than a woman's": "All his life he had cherished a beloved ideal of friendship—David and Jonathan" (*K* 104).

7. Ovesey, *Homosexuality and Pseudohomosexuality*, 61. Dr. Ovesey argues that the homosexual conflict in either homosexuals or heterosexuals "can be broken down into three component parts: sexual, dependency, and power. Only the first is truly sexual in its motivation. The other two are not sexual at all, although they make use of the sexual apparatus to achieve their ends. They are in reality *pseudohomosexual* components of the homosexual conflict" (28).

8. Sigmund Freud, *The Ego and the Id, Standard Edition*, 19:37.

passes his perception of George's godlike form and fatherly affection,[9] may be seen as a quasi-religious sublimation.[10] The satisfaction that Cyril feels is not sexual, at least not in the orgastic sense, but the gratification of a universal adolescent male need for identification through masculine contact, here symbolized by nonthreatening physical touch, in which the erotic component is sublimated into idealized friendship.

Lawrence imagines the healing touch to be nurturant. In a scene in "Low-Water Mark" in *Aaron's Rod,* Rawdon Lilly takes a very ill Aaron Sisson into his rooms and looks after him during a severe bout with flu. The doctor, who prescribes appropriate medications but thinks that Aaron's life is threatened chiefly by depression and the lack of a will to live, says to Lilly: "Can't you rouse his spirit?" (*AR* 95). Lilly decides to rub Aaron's body with oil "as mothers do their babies whose bowels don't work" (*AR* 96):

> Quickly he uncovered the blond lower body of his patient, and began to rub the abdomen with oil, using a slow, rhythmic, circulating motion, a sort of massage. For a long time he rubbed finely and steadily, then went over the whole of the lower body, mindless, as if in a sort of incantation. He rubbed every speck of the man's lower body—the abdomen, the buttocks, the thighs and knees, down to his feet, rubbed it all warm and glowing with camphorated oil, every bit of it, chafing the toes swiftly, till he was almost exhausted. Then Aaron was covered up again, and Lilly sat down in fatigue to look at his patient. [*AR* 96]

Since so many distinguished critics have speculated on the homosexual overtones of the scene,[11] one could perhaps consider the ques-

9. Black, *D. H. Lawrence: The Early Fiction,* 65, while rejecting the interpretation of "latent homosexuality" as "too simple," comments that "Cyril is taken with the nobility of George's body, and George, like a father, holds Cyril to him and rubs him dry": "George looks like a god and acts like a father, and Cyril's attitude to him is reverence without overtones of simple desire."

10. This view is supported by Gajdusek's argument, in "A Reading of 'A Poem of Friendship,' " 56, that "the significance of such a sacramental action culminating in such communion is the translation of desire to spirit and the resolution of spirit in form."

11. Although Spilka, *Love Ethic of D. H. Lawrence,* 157, views the scene as a uniquely binding, nonsexual rite of communion between men, other critics have tiptoed gingerly around the question of homoeroticism. Hough, *The Dark Sun,* 97–98, relates Lilly's "womanly ministrations" in tending Aaron to Rupert Birkin's expressed need for "eternal union with a man, too; another kind of love" (*WL* 473), as

tion settled: The massage is a homoerotic pledge confirming male bonding in a leader-follower relationship after the failure in each man's experience of a male-female relationship. But there is more in the scene than that. The limitation is not in identifying the implicit (some would say overt) homoeroticism inherent in Lilly's sensual massage but in failing to note the sublimation of the erotic into healing nurturance. Alone among critics, Sandra Barry recognizes the function of this quasi-biblical anointing of the sick with oil to restore the principle of love to reestablish the equilibrium between Law and Love in the kind of "trembling balance" I have attempted to describe.[12] Most critics are curiously silent on the question of Aaron's healing, which forms the main action of the chapter, and on Lilly's therapeutic massage, which is the focus of this scene.[13] While the touch may represent the transformation of homoerotic energy, Lilly is literally following the doctor's suggestion in trying to rouse Aaron's spirit, not his penis. The situation itself, with Aaron's severe viral infection and symptoms of bowel obstruction, high fever, and low depression, rendering him nonambulatory, is hardly conducive to overt sexual behavior. While it may be conducive to authoritarian control, I do not think, despite Lilly's later pronouncements on power and leadership, that this is the primary motive here. The mother and baby analogy has far less to do with authoritarian power (see Daleski, 203) than with nurturance, a role that gender stereotypes would deny to men but that Lawrence did not. In Lawrence's psychological terms, Lilly massages Aaron's lower body to activate the healing forces of the "primary centres" of consciousness that control psychic functioning on the sensual plane: the solar plexus (identification and a healthy sense of self) and the lumbar ganglion (spinal resistance and bowel elimination).

In a scene in "The Living Huitzilopochtli" in *The Plumed Serpent*, ritual touch is used in a liturgical, if private, ordination ceremony by which Cipriano Viedma assumes the godhead of "the red Huitzilo-

---

the men search for "a substitute for marriage rather than a solution to its problems." Cavitch, *D. H. Lawrence and the New World*, 113, suggests that Lilly "transfers his vitality" into the body of Aaron, who, "by submitting to the authority of the greater male soul," seeks to extricate himself from woman and come into self possession. Meyers, *Homosexuality and Literature*, 149–55, treats "the nursing episode" as overt sexual behavior in a homosexual novel.

12. Barry, "Singularity of Two," 38.

13. Spilka, *Love Ethic of D. H. Lawrence*, 159, says, almost in passing, that "Aaron recovers, of course"; and Daleski, *The Forked Flame*, 203, while noting that Lilly is "directly motivated by concern for Aaron's health," thinks the rubbing an indirect assertion of dominance.

pochtli" (*PS* 367). Closing his hand in succession over Cipriano's eyes, his naked breast, his navel, his loins, his knees, and his ankles, Ramón Carrasco pronounces a series of incantatory questions in a voice that sounds "far off," eliciting a series of hypnotic responses from Cipriano, who progressively loses ego consciousness as he descends further and further into the darkness of the creative unconscious. After each question and answer, Ramón binds the designated body center with a strip of black fur.

As Ramón presses Cipriano's navel and the small of his back, Cipriano feels "as if his mind, his head were melting away in the darkness, like a pearl in black wine," and he becomes "a man without a head, moving like a dark wind over the face of the dark waters." When Ramón closes "with his hands the secret places," Cipriano can no longer answer his ritual questions: "The last circle was sweeping round, and the breath upon the waters was sinking into the waters, there was no more utterance." Ramón binds the loins and completes the ritual in silence; then he lays Cipriano, in a deep sleep, on the skin of a mountain lion and lies "down at his feet, holding Cipriano's feet to his own abdomen" (*PS* 368–69), a position suggesting that Cipriano is figuratively growing out of Ramón's solar plexus.

Critical response has again centered on the homoerotic subtext of the scene.[14] I have no problem with Ruderman's idea of Ramón's sexual ambiguity as charismatic leader, reconciling opposing male and female principles within the self, or, for that matter, with his sublimation through touch of an unconscious homoeroticism; but before one accepts the interpretation of *overt* homosexual behavior, one should at least review the facts as Lawrence presents them. First, Ramón does not sexually arouse Cipriano by genital manipulation, as Meyers implies, but the very opposite: he puts this center of Cipriano's consciousness to sleep as he had done with eyes, breast, and navel. Second, there is no identifiable orgasmic phase marked

---

14. Clark, *Dark Night of the Body*, 96, comments that this initiation rite is "easily misinterpreted . . . as latent homosexuality." Meyers, *Homosexuality and Literature*, 159, finding nothing "latent" in the scene, declares that the passage "has the familiar, though heightened characteristics of Lawrence's homosexual scenes: the powerful rhythm and highly charged abstract language, the biblical allusion to the mysterious beginning of Genesis, the fondling (or masturbation) of the genitals, and the mindless, swooning, orgasmic finale." Ruderman, *D. H. Lawrence and the Devouring Mother*, 151–52, for whom "*The Plumed Serpent* provides a textbook case for the study of charismatic leadership and political interdependencies," is perhaps closer to the mark in her view that Don Ramón has the characteristic sexual ambiguity of the charismatic leader, the mystery of whose resolution of masculine and feminine opposites "adds to his sacredness, and hence to his power."

by either literal or figurative ejaculation, and the conclusion resembles hypnotic trance far more closely than it does the coital resolution phase or postorgasmic sleep.[15] Third, all of the action is ritual action, which, of course, does not preclude its also being sexual in motivation but which, by establishing a religious context, again suggests the sublimation of erotic aims into transpersonal values.

Ramón is for Cipriano, as George is for Cyril, the embodiment of the ego ideal. Moreover, Ramón does not violate the trust that Cipriano places in him as the religious leader who offers the means to emerge from fragmentation into wholeness in a context in which individuality is paradoxically developed and expressed through the greater religious movement. Jung, who departs from Freud in placing sublimation in the service of the individuation process and the transcendent function and in seeing the formation of religion as integral to ego growth rather than as an illusion, observes:

> Since the making of a religion or the formation of symbols is just as important an interest of the primitive mind as the satisfaction of an instinct, the way to further development is logically given: escape from the state of reduction lies in evolving a religion of an individual character. One's true individuality then emerges from behind the veil of the collective personality. . . .[16]

In the ordination scene, the ceremonial nature of the occasion, the strong rhythms of the language, the repetitions of the question-and-response formula, the psychic function in Lawrence's psychobiology of the centers of the body that are touched and bound, and the ritualistic impersonality of each touch and gesture—all establish that Lawrence is presenting nothing of the human spontaneity that he evokes in scenes of sexual behavior but a Laurentian version of ecclesiastical liturgy in which words and gestures are rubrical.

The scene in *The Escaped Cock* in which the priestess of Isis anoints the risen man's scars "with oil and tender healing" (*EC* 54) combines nurturant, ritual, and sexual touch in a single image of sexual healing:

---

15. Parmenter, *Lawrence in Oaxaca,* 304, points out that in the counterpart of this scene in the typescript, p. 278, written before Lawrence greatly elaborated the scene in Oaxaca, "Ramón merely hypnotizes Cipriano to bring him into consciousness of 'his divine self.' "

16. Jung, *Structure and Dynamics of the Psyche, Collected Works,* 8:58.

Having chafed all of his lower body with oil, his belly, his buttocks, even the slain penis and the sad stones, having worked with her slow intensity of a priestess, . . . she pressed him to her, in a power of living warmth, like the folds of a river. And . . . there was stillness and darkness in his soul, unbroken dark stillness, wholeness. [*EC* 56]

The structural parallels with the rubbing action of body drying in *The White Peacock*, therapeutic massage in *Aaron's Rod*, and ritual initiation in *The Plumed Serpent* are obvious. In all four scenes, the primary instinctual drive is, in some sense, transformed sacramentally by sensual touch, but there is a marked difference in culmination in *The Escaped Cock:* Whereas both Aaron and Cipriano fall into deep sleep, the man who had died

. . . felt the blaze of his manhood and his power rise up in his loins, magnificent.
"I am risen!"
Magnificent, blazing indomitable in the depths of his loins, his own sun dawned, and sent its fire running along his limbs, so that his face shone unconsciously. [*EC* 57]

Lawrence should be credited with understanding the subtle differences in instinctual expression, whether the instinct is partially transformed or consummated sexually, and with knowing how to employ the varieties of instinctual response according to his thematic purpose.

The motif of touch points in two directions: back toward the original primitive instinctual aim and forward towards its transformation or consummation. Critics who find homoerotic feeling in scenes involving sensual touch between men are not wrong in identifying this sexual component of the motivation, although the root aim is often otherwise, deriving from narcissistic needs of the self rather than from object-instinctive drives. On the other hand, critics who emphasize the techniques and themes by which Lawrence renders the literary product of the transformation are also correct in identifying the issue as something other and more profound than simple homosexual desire. But there are pitfalls to be avoided in both positions. To see only the primitive instinctual root of a complex psychodynamic process is regressive and reductive. To deny its existence and to see only the final development of the process is to ignore the dynamic energy that gives such a scene its vitality. Whether touch functions in the sublimation or direct consummation of the primary instinctual drive, Lawrence's literary work is never reductive but always moves in a forward, evolutionary direction. If criticism is sometimes, like psychoanalysis, a reductionist process that strips a manifest thought or behavior back to its primitive instinctual root, the critic should not make the further reduction of seeing the final product of a psychodynamic process as nothing more than the original primitive instinctual drive. As Jung puts it, "It is obvious that the spirit of the *reductio ad causam* or *reductio in primam figuram* can never do justice to the idea of final development, of such paramount importance in psychology, because each change in the condition is seen as nothing but a 'sublimation' of the basic substance and therefore as a masked expression of the same old thing."[17]

Touch does not necessarily have the same meaning for the toucher as for the touched. In three major scenes touch is either personally meaningful or routinely or aggressively professional on the part of the toucher, but the response it arouses in the one who is touched is so unsettling that he is unable to incorporate or channel his feelings constructively and, in one instance, neurotically suppresses them so that they are converted into destructive ends.

The scene in "The Blind Man" in which Maurice Pervin touches Bertie Reid's head and face and insists on Reid's touching Pervin's own scarred face provides an ironic example of divergent responses:

> Then he laid his hand on Bertie Reid's head, closing the dome of the skull in a soft, firm grasp, gathering it, as it were; then, shifting his grasp and softly closing again, with a fine, close pressure, till he had covered the skull and the face of the smaller man, tracing the brows, and touching the full, closed eyes, touching the small nose and the nostrils, the rough, short moustache, the mouth, the rather strong chin. [*EME* 62]

Seeming "to take him, in the soft, travelling grasp," Pervin offers similar knowledge of himself by pressing Reid's fingers to his disfigured brow and scarred eye-sockets, which metonymically encapsulate his basic identity. But the two men respond to the experience with ironically disparate feelings of horror and ecstasy. Reid, having been forced into contact, feels violated; he has "an unreasonable fear, lest the other man should suddenly destroy him. Whereas Mau-

17. Ibid., 8:22.

rice was actually filled with hot, poignant love, the passion of friendship" (*EME* 62).

As an exclusive mode of knowing, touch has limitations, which the story acknowledges. "We've become friends," Pervin tells Isabel happily, unaware of either Reid's recoil or any destructive motive on his own part. For relying solely on intuitive touch in the subjective darkness, without the objective controls of sight or intellectual understanding, he never guesses that Reid has been left "a mollusc whose shell is broken" (*EME* 63). The story turns on the irony that the blind man, to whom the touch represents meaningful sensual knowledge, is unable to sense that his sighted companion experiences it as intrusive and shattering.[18]

In "The Prussian Officer," touch, unconsciously on the part of the toucher, contributes to awakening in the other a homoerotic desire, the denial of which leads inevitably to the double catastrophe of the ending. This most obvious and purposive psychological level of the theme correlates with Lawrence's literary treatment of the dualistic conflict between opposing forces, which critics have defined variously:[19] Satan and Adam (Amon); inorganic rigidity and organic wholeness (Spilka); masculine aggression and feminine self-surrender and passivity (Weiss); the "unhappy conscious man" and the man of "simple, satisfied nature" (Ford, by way of Frieda Lawrence); and the ethnic representatives of the blond, aristocratic, Prussian militarist class and the swarthy, artistic, Bavarian peasant class (Scott).[20]

The orderly, Schöner, having to rub his captain down, "admired the amazing riding-muscles of his loins"; otherwise, he "scarcely

---

18. Abolin, "Lawrence's 'The Blind Man,' " 220, calls attention to Lawrence's definition of the three characters by means of touch: "The physical reality of touch itself becomes a central factor in the story, and we are shown in a number of ways precisely how each character operates in relation to this sensory experience." Wheeler, "Intimacy and Irony in 'The Blind Man,' " 246, extends the ironic meaning to include the reader's participating in the story's cruelty.

19. See Amon, "D. H. Lawrence and the Short Story," 226; Spilka, *Love Ethic of D. H. Lawrence,* 172; Weiss, *Oedipus in Nottingham,* 70–71; Ford, *Double Measure,* 77; and Scott, "D. H. Lawrence's *Germania,*" 145–46.

20. Remarkably, some critics deny the homoerotic element in the story. Spilka, *Love Ethic of D. H. Lawrence,* 172, declares flatly: "there is nothing homosexual about this relationship." Black, *D. H. Lawrence: The Early Fiction,* 223, while agreeing that "the captain's cruelty to the orderly may have a sexual origin," rejects the explanation of "suppressed homosexuality" as a simplification and sees the dynamics of the relationship as a conflict between the captain's repressive discipline and the orderly's naturally free vitality, which makes him enviable, desirable—and "a natural prey" (215–16).

noticed the officer any more than he noticed himself." The officer, "at first cold and just and indifferent" to the enlisted man, gradually develops an acute awareness, which becomes an unwilling obsession with "his servant's young, vigorous, unconscious presence." The significance of the touch for the officer is made clear in a pointed metaphor: "He did not choose to be touched into life by his servant" (*PO* 2–3). Angrily suppressing his passion, the officer, in a "mockery of pleasure," tries unsuccessfully to substitute a brief sexual connection with a woman he does not want. His homoeroticism, until it is "touched into life" by his orderly, has been, with moderate success, repressed and channeled into an undistinguished military career. His awakened homosexual desire is neither acknowledged directly nor transformed into other goals but emerges in his increasingly sadistic treatment of the orderly. Schöner's innocence, his almost prelapsarian quality of animal grace, in the fallen modern world becomes destructive. His instinctive killing of the captain also separates Schöner forever from his sweetheart, his self, and the natural integrity of his former life.

In another instance, touch is ostensibly neutral and professionally motivated on the part of the physicians who are touching but is experienced by the one who is touched as intrusive or invasive. D. H. Lawrence's opinion of medical doctors, as he told Dorothy Brett, was not high.[21] In a passage in "The Nightmare" in *Kangaroo*, Lawrence's persona Richard Lovat Somers's reaction to his preinduction physical examination at a late stage in the First World War is so filled with rage that it borders on the irrational. On his first examination, early in the war, Somers is treated with gentlemanly courtesy, but he experiences the later examination as willful humiliation:

> The elderly fellow then proceeded to listen to his heart and lungs with a stethoscope, jabbing the end of the instrument against the flesh as if he wished to make a pattern on it. Somers kept a set face. He knew what he was out against, and he just hated and despised them all.
>
> The fellow at length threw the stethoscope aside as if he were throwing Somers aside, and . . . strolled over to the great judgment table. [*K* 259]

In the next section "a young puppy, like a chemist's assistant," comes

---

21. Brett, *Lawrence and Brett*, 139–40.

forward close to him, right till their bodies almost touched, the one in a navy blue serge, holding back a little as if from the contagion of the naked one. He put his hand between Somers' legs, and pressed it upwards, under the genitals. Somers felt his eyes going black.

"Cough," said the puppy. He coughed. [K 259]

Somers is ordered to turn around and "Bend forward—further—further—" so that the medical man can look at his anus (K 260).

To most men who have undergone similar examinations without any lasting sense of humiliation, Somers's response is bound to seem paranoid:

Never would he be touched again. And because they had handled his private parts, and looked into them, their eyes should burst and their hands should wither and their hearts should rot. So he cursed them in his blood. . . . [K 261]

This may be the most extreme reaction to a hernia and rectal examination on record. But leaving aside (though not discounting) Lawrence's possibly homophobic motives and his residual working-class prudery, Somers is responding, more than anything else, to the manner in which he is touched, as a thing to be objectified and known, rather than as human and subject, a person to be treated with sensitivity and consideration.[22] Paul Delany comments astutely: "For Lawrence, to touch another person is a gesture of recognition—and one that creates a mutual responsibility if it is accepted. But when the doctor lays his hand on Somers he wants only to humiliate him, to show him that even the secret recesses of his body are at the disposal of the authorities."[23] Somers finds the touch intrusive and the examination dehumanizing. His rage derives in large part from his perception that his humiliation is intentional and politically motivated.[24] The faceless

22. Of the conscription examination on which this scene is based, Lawrence wrote to Lady Cynthia Asquith (26 September 1918): "It kills me with speechless fury to be, pawed by them. They shall *not* touch me again—such filth." A letter of the same date to Catherine Carswell echoes the same sentiments (*Letters* 3:287, 288).

23. Delany, *D. H. Lawrence's Nightmare,* 376.

24. Lawrence is not alone in being sensitive to this kind of humiliation. A psychiatrist, Peter Kramer, in "What Hurts," 33, recounts his own humiliation at being strip-searched by police at the airport on arrival in the Dominican Republic during a politically unsettled time: "They poked and prodded, on the pretext of looking for drugs, I was in a rage, red from head to foot with poorly suppressed anger. I felt capable of anything, of making a mistake which would land me in a Latin prison."

bureaucracy, the "naked civilised men" herded about with a "grue-some" loss of "life-meaning," the instrument that inscribes its pat-terns on the flesh, the final judgment table—all are part of the larger "nightmare" of the war, a surrealistic phantasmagoria reminiscent of Franz Kafka.

In these three examples, touch, whatever its conscious meaning, proves to be destructive. A significant element in both "The Blind Man" and "The Prussian Officer" is the destructive innocence of the toucher, who, though unconscious of ulterior motive, nevertheless effects the destruction of the one he touches. In *Kangaroo,* the cloak of professionalism does not prevent the intrusion into the examina-tion of the doctors' resentment of able-bodied men who are not al-ready in uniform.

The significance of touch in sexual expression, not only as foreplay but also, more importantly for Lawrence's fiction, as a medium for communicating empathy, compassion, and tenderness, is clearly pre-sented in the sexual relationship between Connie and Mellors in *Lady Chatterley's Lover.* Touch is precisely what is lacking in Con-nie's relationship with Clifford. Lawrence's characterization of the maimed, partially paralyzed baronet suggests, through the incre-mental repetition of the word *touch,* that, detached from its uncon-scious motivating source in sexual being, touch loses its vital func-tion in all human contact. Connie recognizes "how little connection" Clifford has with people: "He was remotely interested; but like a man looking down a microscope, or up a telescope. He was not in touch." Beyond the tradition of Wragby and "the close bond of family defense" with his sister Emma, "nothing really touched him": "Con-nie felt that she herself didn't really, not really touch him; perhaps there was nothing to get at ultimately; just a negation of human contact" (*LCL* 14–15).

In the sexual relation, in contrast, "The great river of male blood touches to its depths the great river of female blood—yet neither breaks its bounds. It is the deepest of all communions . . ." (*P II* 505). Mark Spilka argues that Lawrence recognizes touch as "a continuum, sensual rather than sexual, which runs through all close relations; but he does not see that touch, as the medium for tender feelings, originates with the mother who usurped his selfhood and manhood." Thus, in *Lady Chatterley's Lover,* Lawrence can see "only Clifford's infantile dependence on nurturing love; he cannot see that Mellors' strength converts the same conditions into masculine warmth, by which a man may offer nurturing love without losing male identity; nor can he see finally, that tenderness, founded in touch, is the true maternal heritage by which . . . we claim the deepest love and release the highest feelings."[25]

In the eight sexual scenes between Connie and Mellors, the word *touch* is used both to denote the physical gesture and to connote an understanding more profound than the casual sex that Lawrence generally despised. The relationship begins as Connie weeps forlornly over the pheasant chick and Mellors reaches out in compassion and strokes her back and "the curve of her crouching loins . . . in the blind instinctive caress" (*LCL* 136) that leads to their first sexual encounter in the hut. In their next meeting, despite Connie's assuming a spectator role in their lovemaking, Mellors says, "I could die for the touch of a woman like thee" (*LCL* 150). In their third encounter, Mellors bares "the front part of his body and she felt his naked flesh against her as he came into her" (*LCL* 157). The frontal body touch evokes the response of the two "primary centres" of the sympathetic mode—the cardiac plexus (the "quivering curiosity" of "the breast-touch") and the solar plexus (the "delight and avidity" of "the belly-touch") (*FU* 98)—as, for the first time, Mellors brings Connie to resplendent simultaneous orgasm and "another self" comes "alive in her" (*LCL* 159). On her next visit, Connie for the first time asserts her own desire "to touch you like you touch me" (*LCL* 202). Although sexually the experience is largely unsatisfactory, touch proves to be the means of restoring sexual communication as "with that marvellous swoon-like caress of his hand in pure soft desire, softly he stroked the silky slope of her loins, down, down between her soft warm buttocks, coming nearer and nearer to the very quick of her" (*LCL* 207). After Connie stays the night in Mellors's bed, she reverences his risen phallus by touching the glans with her breast and taking the preejaculatory emission a moment before his sense of urgency at approaching "ejaculatory inevitability" leads him to proceed with haste.[26] After the lovers decorate their bodies with flowers and dance naked in the rain, Mellors touches "the two secret openings to her body, time after time, with a soft little brush of fire," and threads forget-me-nots in her pubic hair (*LCL* 267–68). The much debated "night of sensual passion" emphasizes not the softness of touch but the intrusive "phallic hunt of the

25. Spilka, "Lawrence's Quarrel with Tenderness," 236.

26. Masters and Johnson, *Human Sexual Response,* 211, in an objective discussion of "The Male Orgasm (Ejaculation)" based on empirical observation, describe the "preejaculatory secretion" of "mucoid material," the source of which has been attributed to Cowper's glands, as well as the sensation of "ejaculatory inevitability" and the physiological process of ejaculation.

man," in what I think has been critically established as consensual anal intercourse (*LCL* 297–98).[27]

Mellors's conscious philosophizing during intercourse, after Connie's return from Venice, may not be credibly realistic, but his statement succinctly summarizes the significance for Lawrence of sexual touch and tenderness:

> "I stand for the touch of bodily awareness between human beings," he said to himself, "and the touch of tenderness. And she is my mate. And it is a battle against the money, and the machine, and the insentient ideal monkeyishness of the world. . . . Thank God I've got a woman who is with me, and tender and aware of me. Thank God she's not a bully, nor a fool. Thank God she's a tender, aware woman." And as his seed sprang in her, his soul sprang towards her too, in the creative act that is far more than procreative. [*LCL* 336]

There has been a significant evolution through touch to reach this point in *Lady Chatterley's Lover*, progressing from the spontaneity of the first touch of consolation and compassion in the pheasant chicks scene, through the ecstatic "swoon-like caress" accompanying fully orgasmic sex and the intrusive, if accepted, touch of the "phallic hunt," to the finest flowering of the lovers' relationship in the touch of tenderness.

Touch is so pervasive in Lawrence's work that it is not difficult to multiply instances of its use as a powerful symbol in presenting significant statements on the human struggle, throughout the life cycle from adolescence to maturity, with the problems of friendship, sexuality, religion, and loss and tragic insight. Considered individually, there may be as many different kinds of touch in Lawrence's fiction as there are instances of it. Even the categories that I have considered are overlapping rather than mutually exclusive: unconsciously motivated touch that is irrevocably binding or that precipitates moral or psychological insights; touch that functions in the sublimation of unconscious motives, especially homoeroticism, into such suprapersonal goals as friendship, nurturance, or ritual; touch that is not the same experience for the toucher and the touched, who

---

27. From 1961 to 1963, in the wake of the English censorship trial of *Lady Chatterley's Lover* (Regina v. Penguin Books Ltd.), this scene was at the center of a critical controversy, debated mainly in the pages of *Essays in Criticism* and *Encounter*, on whether "the night of sensual passion" involved anal intercourse.

may find it intrusive, invasive, or even shattering; and sensual or sexual touch.

Touch in Lawrence's work is never neutral but always affectively charged, either negatively or positively. When the affect is negative, the touch is to be shunned at all costs; when it is positive, the touch establishes an almost mystical and irrevocable bonding. The extraordinary potency of touch derives in part from the fact that it is unconsciously driven. Touch has the power to activate unconscious, instinctual motives—not mentally derived ideas—into consciousness, thus making self-confrontation and relationship with a significant other possible. In this way touch functions both in restoring psychological homeostasis and in establishing a dynamic, "trembling balance" between the self and the other.

8

Phobia and Psychological Development in "The Thorn in the Flesh"

D. H. Lawrence wanted, of course, to correct psychological imbalances by restoring "the trembling instability of the balance" between opposing forces in the self, especially the antinomies of mind and body, or spiritual and instinctual being. Restoring dynamic balance did not mean to him, however, that one could assert conscious control over basic personality traits or that one should attempt to tame the feelings. In "The Novel and the Feelings," Lawrence says:

> Man is the only creature who has deliberately tried to tame himself. . . . Tameness is an effect of control. But the tamed thing loses the power of control, in itself. It must be controlled from without. Man has pretty well tamed himself, and he calls his tameness civilisation. True civilisation would be something very different. . . . Man has tamed himself, and so has lost his power for command, the power to give himself direction. He has no choice in himself. [*STH* 203]

That is the situation in which Bachmann finds himself in "The Thorn in the Flesh." Tamed to the point of phobia, he has lost his autonomy. This "is precisely man's predicament": "he is shut up within all his barb-wire fences." But Lawrence says, "It is nonsense to pretend we can un-tame ourselves in five minutes. That, too, is a slow and strange process, that has to be undertaken seriously. It is nonsense to pretend we can break the fences and dash out into the wilds" (*STH* 204). In the meanwhile, some personality traits, like some physical traits, had to be simply accepted and lived with. But that acceptance of oneself as one is, including limitations, constituted a beginning and was in itself a kind of "trembling balance."

In the story, Bachmann, a young German soldier, is unable, during an attack of anxiety, to write his weekly postcard to his mother. The soldier, who suffers from an almost incapacitating fear of heights, is confronted in a training exercise with the task of scaling a high rampart. Groping his way up the swaying ladder, he is so sick with fear that he cannot control his bladder. Feeling himself violated by his sergeant's enraged face, aggressive jaw, and shouted orders, Bachmann involuntarily strikes the noncommissioned officer, knocking him over the fortifications into the moat below. Running away from the barracks to his sweetheart, Emilie, who works as a maidservant in the house of a baron, Bachmann plans, with the help of Emilie and her friend Ida Hesse, the governess, to desert and go to America. In Emilie's bedroom, the sweethearts make love, and Bachmann feels restored and now resolves to accept his phobic affliction and live with it. Traced to the baron's house by the postcard to his mother, which Emilie has mailed for him, the soldier is taken into custody by the military authorities. Although the baron tells Emilie that Bachmann is "done for now," the youth departs confident in the knowledge of what he has shared with the girl: "They knew each other. They were themselves" (*PO* 38).[1]

The romantic art of the story, the way Lawrence carefully develops his theme, opposing the mechanistic, uniformitarian values of the military with the organicist, instinctual values of individual differences and young love, is admirably contained in the symmetry of its structure. The story turns, however, on a single imbalance of character, Bachmann's acrophobia, which I should like to consider in the light of a brief review of several conceptions of phobia, with particular emphasis on Sigmund Freud's psychoanalytic theory, as a means toward understanding Lawrence's treatment of Bachmann's psychological development.

---

1. Quotations are from the collected version in *The Prussian Officer and Other Stories*, ed. Worthen, in the Cambridge Edition; but see also the originally published version of the story, "Vin Ordinaire," in the *English Review* 17 (June 1914): 298–325; and a detailed discussion of Lawrence's revisions by Keith Cushman, "D. H. Lawrence at Work: 'Vin Ordinaire' into 'The Thorn in the Flesh,' " 46–58.

The first recorded case history of a phobic patient is attributed to Hippocrates, and John Locke is credited with making one of the earliest attempts to deal with the phobic reaction systematically. According to Locke, " 'Antipathies' and fears . . . often arise from an association of ideas, and, if such 'antipathies' were acquired in childhood, their causes may later be forgotten."[2] This view anticipates the psychologically oriented theories of twentieth-century psychologists and psychoanalysts. In accord with Locke's associationist theory, the behaviorist John B. Watson held that such fears were acquired by conditioned response. Pierre Janet, who thought the fear response a secondary effect rather than a cause, related the phobic reaction to hysterical paralysis, in that both function to prevent the individual from doing something that he does not want to do anyway.[3]

It was Sigmund Freud, however, who originated the first truly dynamic conception of phobia as a part of anxiety neurosis. In the first of his classic papers on the subject, "Obsessions and Phobias: Their Psychical Mechanism and Their Aetiology" (1895), he divides phobias

> into two groups according to the nature of the object feared: (1) common phobias, an exaggerated fear of things that everyone detests or fears to some extent: such as night, solitude, death, illnesses, dangers in general, snakes, etc.; (2) contingent phobias, the fear of special conditions that inspire no fear in the normal man; for example, agoraphobia and the other phobias of locomotion.[4]

At that time, Freud thought obsessions and phobias "entirely different" in mechanism. Substitution was a predominant feature in obsessions, but what the phobic individual actually fears, Freud thought, is neither the object of his phobia in itself nor the incompatible ideas that the object represents, but simply the occurrence of an anxiety attack "under the special conditions in which he believes he cannot escape it."[5]

By the time he wrote the second of his classic papers on phobia, "Analysis of a Phobia in a Five-Year-Old Boy" (1909), Freud had

2. Friedman, "The Phobias," 1:293.
3. Ibid., 1:293–94.
4. Freud, "Obsessions and Phobias: Their Psychical Mechanism and Their Aetiology," in *Early Psycho-Analytic Publications, Standard Edition* 3:30.
5. Ibid., 3:31.

revised his theory to include substitution, the replacement of incompatible ideas with an object that is feared because it represents those ideas. The patient, little Hans, is afraid to go out because, as he tells his mother, "*I was afraid a horse would bite me.*" Son of the musicologist Max Graf, who was long an adherent of psychoanalysis and a member of Freud's Wednesday-night group, the phobic child grew up to become the well-known producer and director of operas Herbert Graf.[6] The case history of the analysis, with the boy's father acting as intermediary analyst under Freud's direction, is an engrossing story followed by Freud's critical analysis. Piece by piece, the basic information is unfolded. One learns that little Hans is afraid of big animals that have big "widdlers," that is, penises (10:33–34); that he is afraid of white horses because he knows one that bites; that Hans's mother had once threatened to "have his widdler cut off if he went on playing with it" (10:35); that he is "most afraid of horses" with "something black on their mouths" (10:49), like a dray horse's thick harness; that he is particularly afraid that a dray horse may fall down and make "*a row with its feet*" (10:50), as he had seen a horse drawing a furniture van do; that he fantasizes that his little sister Hanna lived and traveled about before birth in a "stork-box" (10:76); and that he associates the falling dray horse with Hanna's arrival and rivalry with him. Analysis reveals that both the biting horse and the falling horse represent Hans's father, whose naked white skin and black mustache Hans associates with the white horse and the dray harness. As Freud analyzes it, "Behind . . . the fear of a horse biting him" was the "more deeply seated fear . . . of horses falling down," and both were "his father, who was going to punish him for the evil wishes he was nourishing against him" (10:126). Hans is "afraid of busses and luggage carts . . . when they're loaded up" (10:91), an image that analysis shows to be associated with his mother's pregnancy. Hence, the image of the falling dray horse is "over-determined," since it represents "not only his dying father but

6. Freud, "Analysis of a Phobia of a Five-Year-Old Boy," in *Two Case Histories, Standard Edition*, 10:24. Hereafter, cited parenthetically in the text by volume and page numbers. For a brief biographical background to the case, see Gay, *Freud: A Life for Our Time*, 255–61. Jack Schmertz, in *A Reinterpretation of "A Phobia in a Five Year Old Boy*," reanalyzes Hans's biting-horse phobia as the fear of being possessed and overwhelmed by his own phallic aggressive drives rather than the fear of castration in punishment for oedipal wishes (19–26). Dodge Fernald, in *The Hans Legacy: A Story of Science*, draws an analogy between Freud's case of Little Hans and the contemporaneous scientific study by Oskar Pfungst, which demonstrated that the celebrated horse Clever Hans did not do sums and spell but tapped out answers in response to cues from his questioners (64–78).

also his mother in childbirth" (10:128). His father correctly interprets his wish, despite his jealousy, for his mother to have another
baby: "You'd like to be Daddy and married to Mummy; you'd like to
be as big as me and have a moustache; and you'd like Mummy to
have a baby" (10:92). Hans's phobia lasted for about five months.
When he is at last able to go out for a walk with his father in the
Stadtpark, he points out a bus with wary humor: "Look! A stork-box
cart!" (10:97).[7]

To return to "The Thorn in the Flesh" in this context, as the story
opens Bachmann sits trying to write his weekly postcard to his
mother, but he breaks off at the line " 'We are just off to drill on the
fortifications—.' " The very thought calls up his paralyzing fear of
what is to come, and he sits "suspended, oblivious of everything,
held in some definite suspense" that remains unbroken because
what lies behind it remains repressed, resistant to consciousness,
and therefore unverbalized: "Out of the knot of his consciousness no
word would come" (PO 22).

The relation of speech and silence to anxiety invites a comparison
between the story situation in "The Thorn in the Flesh" and Herman
Melville's Billy Budd, Sailor, though of course Lawrence was not
influenced by that novella, since it was not published until 1924.[8]
Melville's "Handsome Sailor" has "a lingering adolescent expression
in the as yet smooth face all but feminine in purity and natural
complexion but where, thanks to his seagoing, the lily was quite
suppressed and the rose had some ado visibly to flush through the
tan."[9] Similarly, Lawrence's young soldier is "almost girlish in his
good looks and his grace. . . . There was also a trace of youthful
swagger and dare-devilry about his mouth and his limber body, but
this was in suppression now" (PO 22–23). Billy Budd's master-at-
arms, John Claggart, is described as "a man about five-and-thirty,
somewhat spare and tall" in figure with small, shapely hands and a
"notable" face, "the features all except the chin cleanly cut as those
of a Greek medallion; yet the chin, beardless as Tecumseh's, had

7. Coincidentally, in Fantasia of the Unconscious, Lawrence comments that a
child's mode of vision, unlike an adult's, is not registered as an accurate optical image
on the retina, but as a vital perception from the breast and abdomen deriving from his
"dynamic rapport" with external objects: "When a boy of eight sees a horse, he doesn't
see the correct biological object we intend him to see. . . . His consciousness is filled
with a strong, dark, vague presience of a powerful presence, a two-eyed, four-legged,
long-maned presence looming imminent" (FU 125–26).

8. See Humma, "Melville's Billy Budd and Lawrence's 'The Prussian Officer,' "
83–88.

9. Melville, Billy Budd, Sailor, 50.

something of strange protuberant broadness in its make. . . . It
served Claggart in his office that his eye could cast a tutoring
glance."[10] In contrast, Sergeant Huber is "a strongly built, rather
heavy man of forty . . . [with] head . . . thrust forward, sunk a little
between his powerful shoulders, and the strong jaw . . . pushed out
aggressively. But the eyes were smouldering, the face hung slack
and sodden with drink" (*PO* 23), an image almost certainly associated with Lawrence's view of his father as a drunkard. The sergeant's apelike physiognomy reveals nothing of Claggart's effete
cruelty, but the same oral aggression. At the crucial point in the
conflict in the two stories, both Billy Budd and Bachmann are unable to express in speech their anxiety, which derives for Billy from a
sense of outraged justice, for Bachmann from a sense of overwhelming shame. Both communicate their feelings with their fists, involuntarily striking their petty officers, thus placing themselves at the
mercy of the military justice system, though with direr results in
Budd's case than in Bachmann's.

Bachmann, at the beginning of the march, is "bound in a very
dark enclosure of anxiety within himself" (*PO* 23). Experiencing
dissociation, he feels his consciousness separated from his body. Later, as the soldiers go through the exercises, Bachmann watches,
"small and isolated" (*PO* 24) like a child, as another man, looking
insectlike and mechanical, climbs the rampart, and his own bowels
turn to water. When his turn comes, Bachmann places the ladder on
the rampart and determines to climb. But "at every hitch a great,
sick, melting feeling took hold of him . . . the blind gush of white-hot
fear, that came with great force whenever the ladder swerved, and
which almost melted his belly and all his joints, and left him power-
less" (*PO* 25). This feeling of powerlessness is manifested in a regressive symptom as Bachmann, unable to maintain urethral control,
clings to the ladder with his urine running down his leg and "the
echo of the sergeant's voice thundering from below." Lawrence emphasizes Bachmann's overwhelming sense of shame: "He waited, in
depths of shame beginning to recover himself. He had been shamed
so deeply. Then he could go on, for his fear for himself was conquered. His shame was known and published. He must go on" (*PO*
25). But even that victory is denied him as the sergeant takes his
wrists from above and drags him up over the edge of the earthworks.

"[G]rovelling in the grass to recover command of himself," Bachmann is overwhelmed by a sense of worthlessness: "Shame, blind,
deep shame and ignominy overthrew his spirit and left it writhing.

10. Ibid., 61.

He stood there shrunk over himself, trying to obliterate himself"
(*PO* 25); the voice of the sergeant comes "down on his veins like a
fierce whip" (*PO* 26). The psychological meaning of this image for
Lawrence is apparent if one recalls its use in the poem "Discord in
Childhood," in which the shrieking, slashing violence of the storm
battering the ash tree outside the house is the metaphor for the
family violence within. The first stanza, beginning:

> Outside the house an ash-tree hung its terrible whips
> [*CP* 36, line 1],

is paralleled with the second:

> Within the house two voices arose, a slender lash
> Whistling she-delirious rage, and the dreadful sound
> Of a male thong booming and bruising, until it had drowned
> The other voice in a silence of blood, 'neath the noise of the ash.
> [*CP* 36, lines 5–8]

In the story, the voice of Sergeant Huber is that of the punitive
father threatening violence to the frightened child. The noncommissioned officer appears to Bachmann with the same sense of large
animal violence that little Hans sensed in the falling horse, and the
threat of castration at the hands of a primordial father figure that
little Hans had feared in the biting horse is implicit to Bachmann in
the sergeant's lacerating voice and teeth:

> The brutal, hanging face of the officer violated the youth. He
> hardened himself with all his might from seeing it. The tear-
> ing noise of the sergeant's voice continued to lacerate his
> body.
>   . . . The face had suddenly thrust itself close, all distorted
> and showing the teeth, the eyes smouldering into him. The
> breath of the barking words was on his nose and mouth. He
> stepped aside in revulsion. With a scream the face was upon
> him again. [*PO* 26]

Raising his arm defensively, Bachmann involuntarily strikes the
sergeant, knocking him backward over the ramparts and into the
water of the moat below.
    Feeling "deep within him . . . the steady burning of shame in the
flesh," Bachmann is unable to "take the responsibility of himself"
and decides that "he must give himself up to someone." In this des-

perate need for mothering, he becomes "obsessed" with the thought of his sweetheart, Emilie: "He would make himself her responsibility" (*PO* 27). But Emilie "was virgin, and shy, and needed to be in subjection" (*PO* 32) herself. She acquiesces, somewhat reluctantly, in hiding Bachmann, with the aid of Ida Hesse, the governess, and lies to the soldiers who come looking for him: "she had wanted him as a distant sweetheart, not close, like this, casting her out of her world" (*PO* 33).

After Bachmann, as a result of severe tension and anxiety, has slept, Emilie comes to his bedside, waiting "as if in a spell." The description, from Bachmann's angle of vision, with her "standing motionless and looming there, [as] he sat rather crouching on the side of the bed," suggests the attitudes of mother and child. On one level Emilie appears as a mother surrogate, but Bachmann becomes aware of sexual needs beyond his need for nurturance. As he draws her to him, "[a] second will in him was powerful and dominating" (*PO* 34). Burying his face in her apron, "[h]e had forgotten. Shame and memory were gone in a whole, furious flame of passion." Afterward, "she lay translated in the peace of satisfaction":

> And he was restored and completed, close to her. That little, twitching, momentary clasp of acknowledgement that she gave him in her satisfaction, roused his pride unconquerable. They loved each other, and all was whole. [*PO* 34]

Bachmann's successful sexual experience provides him with clear evidence that, despite the castration fears brought to the fore by the imagery of tearing and whipping associated with the sergeant's oral aggression, his genitals, like the "widdler" that little Hans feared would be cut off, are still intact and not really threatened: "She loved his body that was proud and blond and able to take command" (*PO* 36).

Filled with plans to escape to France on a bicycle that Ida Hesse will borrow from her lover, Bachmann suddenly remembers the postcard to his mother and gives it to Emilie to post. The sweethearts sleep together again that night. The next day, when the lieutenant and his men arrive, having traced Bachmann to the baron's house by the postcard, the military no longer has the power to violate him. Impassively he joins the mechanical file: "There Emilie stood with her face uplifted, motionless and expressionless. Bachmann did not look at her. They knew each other. They were themselves" (*PO* 38).

This does not mean, however, that Bachmann's acrophobia has left him. Lawrence seems to reject the conscious uncovering and confrontation of unconscious motives employed in psychoanalytic therapy in the restructuring of personality. Earlier, with reference to Bachmann's shame (*PO* 30), he wrote in the page proofs, "Yet he dared not touch it, probe it, draw out the thorn, and bear the hurt to its depth" (*PO* 251 n. 30.31). Lawrence advocates, instead, self-acceptance and tolerance of what he sees as a basic personality trait and opening up creative alternatives to shame in the personal growth to be experienced in sexuality. Having conquered his shame, Bachmann decides that he can live with his phobia as a "thorn in the flesh":

> "If I'm made that way, that heights melt me and make me let go my water"—it was torture for him to pluck at this truth— "if I'm made like that, I shall have to abide by it, that's all. It isn't all of me." He thought of Emilie, and was satisfied. "What I am, I am; and let it be enough." [*PO* 35–36]

Little Hans, by a combination of psychoanalytic understanding and gradual desensitization by repetition of the feared action in company with an admired, powerful other is relieved of his agoraphobia. Bachmann's solution of accepting his acrophobia as a realistic limitation, his "thorn in the flesh," and getting on with his life is more ambiguous but perhaps more easily realized for an adult whose patterns of response are already well established but who has not necessarily ceased developing. The nodal insight that Bachmann gains through the successful sexual experience is a turning point, a developmental beginning that frees his formerly blocked potential for psychological growth. The allusion to St. Paul's "thorn in the flesh" (2 Corinthians 12:7) suggests obliquely that this solution reflects the compromise with perceived psychological limitations by Lawrence himself, whose autobiographical persona, named Paul in both *Sons and Lovers* and "The Rocking-Horse Winner," was caught in the same oedipal struggle that underlies Bachmann's phobia.

On the evidence of Bachmann's inhibition about writing his weekly postcard to his mother and his wish to have Emilie take maternal responsibility for him, one may infer that his phobia has its pathogenesis in an oedipal conflict. His acrophobia is, I think, more than a simple fear of heights, in that it is associated with mounting and with swaying motion, as in sexual intercourse, and with crossing a barrier, as in the stages of psychosexual development. His anger, the concomitant of his fear, is directed toward his sergeant, who stands as a father surrogate who can tell him what to do and punish him for not doing it. Bachmann expresses this hostility first in his failure to control his bladder, a regressive symptom, then in involuntarily striking the officer. If the sergeant, with his bared teeth and tearing voice, threatens castration, like little Hans's biting horse, he falls, like little Hans's falling horse, a symbolically slain father. Bachmann runs to Emilie, like a child to his mother, to be taken care of.

But if Bachmann's phobia is rooted in oedipal conflict of the phallic stage of psychosexual development, his sense of shame derives from the preoedipal anal stage, the basic problem of which, according to Erik Erikson, centers on the issue of control. The task one confronts in this phase is a resolution of the conflict between the alternatives of autonomy, on the one hand, and shame and doubt, on the other.[11] Bachmann's difficulties are all in the area of control. He suffers anxiety before the training exercise because he fears the loss of self-control that he later manifests in his failure to climb the ladder, his inability to maintain urethral control, and his striking the sergeant. His response is a deep sense of shame and humiliation. It is significant that at this point Bachmann feels shame, not guilt: shame results from a sense that one's perfectionistic self-image has been violated, guilt from a sense that one has violated oedipal prohibitions.

Lawrence's conclusion is a tentatively positive one that does not overstate the hard-won development that Bachmann achieves. Psychologically, his transformation is from the anal to the phallic stage. The question to be answered in the anal stage is "Is my whole being loathsome? Or is it all right for me to *be* as a person?" Bachmann has answered that question. The new question of the phallic stage is "Is it all right for me to *be* as a *sexual* person?" In Erik Erikson's terms, the new polar alternatives to be confronted in answering this question are *initiative* versus *guilt*.[12] Bachmann has achieved *autonomy*, the task of the anal stage: Through ego growth he has, both consciously and emotionally, asserted his own values and separated himself from the outside values of societal expectations. In the context of the story, however, his oedipal guilts remain unresolved, and he has not achieved *initiative*. After his sexual relations with Emilie, Bachmann is reminded—significantly, at the sound of retreat from the nearby army post—to send his postcard to his mother. Whether purposive in intent or not, this action is deterministic in effect, assuring his capture. Moreover, his stoical acceptance of both

11. Erikson, *Identity and the Life Cycle*, 65–74. See also Erikson, *Childhood and Society*, 251–54.

12. Erikson, *Identity and the Life Cycle*, 74–82. See also Erikson, *Childhood and Society*, 255–58.

his phobic affliction and his return to military authority suggest obedient resignation to deserved punishment. Although evidence of oedipal conflict remains, the autonomy that Bachmann has achieved represents a potential for further growth. In a scene paralleling the confrontation between Bachmann and the sergeant, the baron confronts Bachmann in Emilie's room. As master of the house and Emilie's solicitous employer, this aristocrat also stands as a father surrogate to Bachmann, just as the model for the character, Lawrence's father-in-law, Baron Friedrich von Richthofen, stood in relation to Lawrence. Bachmann confronts the fictional baron with autonomy rather than with the castration anxiety he had evinced in response to the sergeant. He feels no shame, for neither the baron nor the military world can have any hold on Bachmann's essential being now.

9

Lawrence's Phoenix

Lawrence was concerned with the theme of creative change, of death and rebirth, in both the psychological and cultural sense, long before 1914, but it was not until sometime after he read Katherine L. Jenner's *Christian Symbolism* in that year that he adopted the phoenix as his personal emblem for the theme. He wrote to Gordon Campbell (20 December 1914) that he liked the book "*very* much, because it puts me more into order" (*Letters* 2:250). The rest of the letter shows clearly his need to make the Christian symbols relevant to his own experience rather than merely accepting them as the icons of a tradition that he already regarded as outworn:

> It is very dangerous to use these old terms lest they sound like Cant. But if only one can grasp and know again as a new truth, true for ones own history, the great vision, the great, satisfying conceptions of the worlds greatest periods, it is enough. Because so it is made new. [*Letters* 2:249]

Although Lawrence does not mention the phoenix in the letter, his comments on the crucifixion and the resurrection reveal his interest in the implications of the religious themes embodied in the image. In the phoenix Lawrence found the mythic representation of creative change through resilience, the destruction of one's established psychological homeostasis in order to create a better one, that he would evoke, in whole or in part, throughout his canon. From this point on, the phoenix was so important to Lawrence, as both emblem and process, that it is instructive to examine his use of the two-thousand-year-old tradition. In this discussion, I should like to recall some representative examples of Lawrence's use of the phoenix as emblem and to suggest the range of his concern with the phoenix as process.

I am somewhat uncomfortable with the term *symbol* for a public device as consciously determined and as definite as Lawrence's phoenix, preferring instead to use Hawthorne's term *emblem,* as Lawrence does in *The Rainbow* (*R* 109). I mean to suggest that the phoenix was not one of Lawrence's original symbolic utterances arising out of the play of his creative imagination upon his artistic materials. It was, rather, a design consciously chosen as the heraldic device by which Lawrence could encompass the central metaphysical concerns of his life. Many of Lawrence's major symbols—plumed serpent, dolphin, flying fish, dark sun, phallus, gamecock—are manifestations of one current or another of the creative energy of which the phoenix is the archetypal image.

Lawrence presents the image as theoretical pattern in "The Crown" and *The Rainbow*. In the third essay of "The Crown" (1915), he contrasts the phoenix with the domestic ringdove:

> The unique phoenix of the desert grew up to maturity and wisdom. Sitting upon her tree, she was the only one of her kind in all creation, supreme, the zenith, the perfect aristocrat. She attained to perfection, eagle-like she rose in her nest and lifted her wings, surpassing the zenith of mortality; so she was translated into the flame of eternity, she became one with the fiery Origin.
>
> It was not for her to sit tight, and assert her own tight ego. She was gone as she came.
>
> In the nest was a little ash, a little flocculent grey dust wavering upon a blue-red, dying coal. The red coal stirred and gathered strength, gradually it grew white with heat, it shot forth sharp gold flames. It was the young phoenix within the nest, with curved beak growing hard and crystal, like a scimitar, and talons hardening into pure jewels.
>
> Wherein, however, is the immortality, in the constant occupation of the nest, the widow's cruse, or in the surpassing of the phoenix? She goes gadding off into flame, into her consum-

mation. In the flame she is timeless. But the ash within the
nest lies in the restless hollow of time, shaken on the tall tree
of the desert. It will rise to the same consummation, become
absolute in flame. [*RDP* 270–71]

This mythic image became the paradigm for a number of Lawrence's
major themes: the retreat to the desert of solitary selfhood, the creative center of the world tree, the natural aristocracy of the unique
individual, the achievement of the eternal through commitment to
the flames of experience, the reduction from traditional wisdom to
essential ash, the emergence of new being through the resilience
that engenders meaningful change.

   Lawrence's description of the new phoenix, arising from the red
coal "with curved beak growing hard and crystal, like a scimitar,
and talons hardening into pure jewels," prefigures Yeats's choice of
immortality, in "Sailing to Byzantium," in

> . . . such a form as Grecian goldsmiths make
> Of hammered gold and gold enamelling.
> [lines 27–28]

Lawrence's jeweled bird, like Yeats's, would live in art to keep more
than "a drowsy Emperor awake" and to sing to a wider audience
than

> . . . lords and ladies of Byzantium
> Of what is past, or passing, or to come.
> [lines 31–32]

   In *The Rainbow,* the first wood-carving that Will Brangwen makes
for Anna before their marriage is a butter-stamper carved in the
design of "a phœnix, something like an eagle, rising on symmetrical
wings, from a circle of very beautiful flickering flames that rose upwards from the rim of the cup" (*R* 108). Although Anna thinks little of
the gift at first, the next morning she is excited to discover that the
new mold, which replaces the old design of oak leaves and acorns, is a
template that reproduces the archetypal image again and again:

> Strange, the uncouth bird moulded there, in the cup-like hol-
> low, with curious, thick waverings running inwards from a
> smooth rim. She pressed another mould. Strange, to lift the
> stamp and see that eagle-beaked bird raising its breast to her.

> She loved creating it over and over again. And every time she
> looked, it seemed a new thing come to life. Every piece of
> butter became this strange, vital emblem. [*R* 109]

Although the customers who buy the butter echo Tom Brangwen's
puzzled question by asking, "What sort of a bird do you call *that,* as
you've got on th' butter?" (*R* 109), the scene in the dairy that follows
reiterates the phoenix imagery in the context of the growing love of
Will and Anna:

> He had kissed her once. Again his eye rested on the round
> blocks of butter, where the emblematic bird lifted its breast
> from the shadow cast by the candle flame. What was restrain-
> ing him? Her breast was near him; his head lifted like an
> eagle's. She did not move. Suddenly, with an incredibly quick,
> delicate movement, he put his arms round her and drew her to
> him. It was quick, cleanly done, like a bird that swoops and
> sinks close, closer.
> He was kissing her throat. She turned and looked at him.
> Her eyes were dark and flowing with fire. His eyes were hard
> and bright with a fierce purpose and gladness, like a hawk's.
> She felt him flying into the dark space of her flames, like a
> brand, like a gleaming hawk. [*R* 109]

The phoenix, here translated into the eagle and hawk in the
flames of youthful passion, becomes, in the concluding chapter of
Aaron's Rod, a "self-form," resembling Jung's archetype of the self,
unfolding organically and individually from within. I am hesitant to
read all of Rawdon Lilly's pronouncements, some of them patroniz-
ing, many of them sexist, most of them authoritarian, as Lawrence's
final statement on leadership, which he was exploring at the time.
But if Lilly's genetic conception of the self is incomplete in omitting
the equally important Laurentian concept that the self develops
only in relation to others, his final "words" to Aaron Sisson represent the radically individualistic pole of Laurentian doctrine:

> "You've got an innermost, integral unique self, and since it's
> the only thing you have got or ever will have, don't go trying
> to lose it. You've got to develop it, from the egg into the
> chicken, and from the chicken into the one-and-only phoenix,
> of which there can be only one at a time in the universe. There
> can only be one of you at a time in the universe—and one of
> me. So don't forget it. Your own single oneness is your destiny.

Your destiny comes from within, from your own self-form. And you can't know it beforehand, neither your destiny nor your self-form. You can only develop it. You can only stick to your own very self, and *never* betray it. And by so sticking, you develop the one and only phoenix of your own self, and you unfold your own destiny, as a dandelion unfolds itself into a dandelion, and not into a stick of celery." [*AR* 295–96]

In the context of Lawrence's leadership novels, as Lilly's mentorship of Aaron shows, the phoenix becomes an emblem of masculine renascence in a patriarchal revival. This conception of the image is similar to that of J. J. Bachofen, who sees the sun form of the phoenix as "the exact image of the Heliopolitan Zeus":

In the phoenix, then, the luminous principle is developed in supreme incorporeality and identified with paternity. The maternal principle is surpassed. The young phoenix is born of fire alone, motherless, in the manner of Athene springing from the head of Zeus; he is . . . (born of fire) in a far purer sense than Dionysus. The maternal egg is no longer the principle of life; it is ruled by the fecundating power of the sun, whose nature it has assumed. In no myth has the triumph of the paternal solar principle over the maternal lunar principle been embodied with such purity as in this Indo-Egyptian conception of the great year of the Phoenix.[1]

Creating the self out of the self-form within is essential to further meaningful activity in the world, but appropriating the language of this individual task as a means of rationalizing the subjugation of others is hardly the same thing. In *Kangaroo,* Jack Callcott calls Ben Cooley, the Diggers' quasi-fascist leader, "as odd as any phœnix bird I've ever heard tell of. You couldn't mate him to anything in the heavens above or in the earth beneath or in the waters under the earth" (*K* 102). Cooley himself exploits the phoenix myth to rationalize pulling down the old political system to erect a new order on its ashes: " 'I tell you I *hate* permanency,' barked Kangaroo. 'The phœnix rises out of the ashes' " (*K* 131). The phoenix image recurs in the context of the question of male dominance. So much has been written about the male chauvinism into which Lawrence's masculine characters sometimes retreat that it is overlooked that Lawrence's female characters often provide a practical and realistic view that functions

---

1. Bachofen, *Myth, Religion, and Mother Right,* 150.

as a corrective to the men's flights of male-supremacist fantasy. In "Harriet and Lovat at Sea in Marriage," a wit contest that presents both points of view but that seems weighted on her side, Harriet Somers deflates with comic irony her husband Richard Lovat's pretensions to male superiority:

> He had nothing but her, absolutely. And that was why, pre-sumably, he wanted to establish this ascendancy over her, assume this arrogance. And so that he could refute her, deny her, and imagine himself a unique male. He *wanted* to be male and unique, like a freak of a phœnix. And then go prancing off into connections with men like Jack Callcott and Kangaroo, and saving the world. She could *not* stand these world saviours. And she, she must be safely there, as a nest for him, when he came home with his feathers pecked. That was it. So that he could imagine himself absolutely and arrogantly It, he would turn her into a nest, and sit on her and overlook her, like the one and only phœnix in the desert of the world, gurgling hymns of salvation. [*K* 177–78]

The point has not been made with better wit. The one and only phoenix of tradition, viewed as a psychological image, integrates both masculine and feminine components of the psyche, but Somers's one-sided phoenix is a freak. Richard Lovat Somers's masculine posturing measures his dependency. His self-form cannot be elaborated by the fraudulent means of subjugating women or playing fascist power politics but only by means of the power of the dark god within the self in the sense of *pouvoir:* "to be able to."[2]

> He did not yet submit to the fact which he *half* knew: that before mankind would accept any man for a king, and before Harriet would ever accept him, Richard Lovat, as a lord and master, he, this self-same Richard who was so strong on kingship, must open the doors of his soul and let in a dark Lord and Master for himself, the dark god he had sensed outside the door. [*K* 178]

While this passage still suggests the Miltonic formula that man knows God directly and woman knows him only through the man, the real struggle in Lovat's consciousness is not with Harriet but with his own deeper nature in creating a viable identity.

2. See Freeman, *D. H. Lawrence: A Basic Study of His Ideas,* 193.

The use of the phoenix as an emblem for the natural aristocrat is consistent with Lawrence's understanding of power not as arbitrary bullying but as *pouvoir:* "the power to cause, the power to create, the power to make, the power to do, the power to destroy" (*RDP* 325). The decline of such power in the modern world is suggested in the last two stanzas of "St. John," a poem in the "Evangelistic Beasts" section of *Birds, Beasts and Flowers:*

> Ah Phœnix, Phœnix,
> John's Eagle!
> You are only known to us now as the badge of an insurance
>   Company.[3]
>
> Phœnix, Phœnix,
> The nest is in flames,
> Feathers are singeing,
> Ash flutters flocculent, like down on a blue, wan fledgeling.
>   [*CP* 330]

In *St. Mawr,* Lawrence suggests the contemporary decline of natural aristocracy in his most curious use of the phoenix—as the name that Mrs. Witt in *St. Mawr* gives to that "odd piece of débris," Geronimo Trujillo (*St. M* 24). Son of a Mexican father and a Navajo mother from Phoenix, Arizona, Phoenix is the victim of both "shell-shock" and a high-school education that left him with "no place in life at all" (*St. M* 25). For all his once dark virility, he can do little more than stiffen in surly malevolence at the reprimand of the effete Rico Carrington, while Morgan Lewis, the other groom, emerges as the Druidic priest serving the syncretic divinity of St. Mawr. Although his usual tone with his employers is one of willful, "naive ignorance," like that of the Mexican Indians in *The Plumed Serpent,* at once gratifying and deceptive (*St. M* 54), Phoenix does act purposefully in warning Lou of Rico's and Flora Manby's plan to geld or shoot St. Mawr (*St. M* 95) and helps to spirit him across the Atlantic.

After Lou leaves St. Mawr on the Texas dude ranch and purchases Las Chivas, Phoenix considers making advances to her or even marrying her, "a pact between two aliens." But his motives are egoistic and economic, not sexual. He sees Lou as "one of these nervous white women with lots of money. . . . One of these white women who talk clever and know things like a man," not as a real squaw, the female

---

3. For the badge of the insurance company, Phoenix Assurance Company Ltd., see Poesch, "The Phoenix Portrayed," [222–23] (unnumbered pages), figs. 15, 16, and 17.

object of the "half-savage male." "Nevertheless he was ready to trade his sex, which, in his opinion, every white woman was secretly pining for, for the white woman's money and social privileges" (*St. M* 135–36).

Lawrence's portrait of Phoenix is highly ambivalent. In so far as he is phoenixlike at all, he reflects the modern world's reduction to ash rather than the rebirth for which Lou waits. Perhaps the fragmentation of his character can be accounted for as the effect of the white man's education, the white man's materialism, the white man's war. Nevertheless, there is nothing more "phallic" about a Mexican-Navajo gigolo (a "sexual rat" [*St. M* 137]) than there is about any other gigolo. Recognizing his rodent sexuality for what it is and "weary of the embrace of incompetent men," Lou turns to "the unseen gods, the unseen spirits, the hidden fire" and devotes herself only to the phallic wild spirit of place at Las Chivas (*St. M* 138–39).

When Lawrence was preparing the third version of *Lady Chatterley's Lover* to be printed privately in the first edition by Giuseppe ("Pino") Orioli in Florence, he wrote to his English publisher, Martin Secker (24 April 1928), "I've done rather more than half the proofs—and ordered the binding paper—and made my phoenix design for the cover, and the printer has already made a block of it." To the same letter he added a triumphant postscript: "The Phoenix rises from the nest in flames" (*Letters MS* 106). To Orioli he wrote (28 June 1928), ". . . I think my phoenix is just the right bird for the cover. Now let us hope she will find her way safely and quickly to all her destinations" (*CL* 1065). Subsequently, in *A Propos of "Lady Chatterley's Lover,"* Lawrence distinguished between the various piracies and the original first edition, "bound in hard covers, dullish mulberry-red paper with my phoenix (symbol of immortality, the bird rising new from the nest of flames) printed in black on the cover. . ." (*P II* 514).

Lady Chatterley's Lover, in the pattern of both plot and imagery, suggests the personal and metaphysical implications of the fable heralded in the device on the binding. Constance Chatterley, in the course of the novel, comes to believe in the resurrection of the body, which comes about sexually with Oliver Mellors. The imagery of the novel is the stronger for making buried allusions to various movements in the phoenix fable rather than relying on the emblem per se. One such allusion, in the scene in which Mellors gives Connie a newly hatched chick to hold, suggests the vulnerable yet courageous commitment to life of the newly risen phoenix, as it "lifted its handsome, clean-shaped little head boldly, and looked sharply round, and gave a little 'peep.' " Connie begins to weep forlornly, and Mellors feels the phoenixlike "flame shooting and leaping up in his loins" (*LCL* 135). (The scene is discussed in detail in chapter 11.) Another buried allusion is the description of Mellors's penis as a rising phoenix: "The sun through the low window sent a beam that lit up his thighs and slim belly, and the erect phallus rising darkish and hot-looking from the little cloud of vivid gold-red hair" (*LCL* 251). And a third allusion, in Mellors's letter to Connie at the end of the novel, is to the creative "forked flame" of their sexuality: "We fucked a flame into being," he writes. Although the industrial world threatens organic nature with mechanical power, their hope lies in the sacramental quality of their sexual commitment: "You can't insure against the future, except by really believing in the best bit of you, and in the power beyond it," he writes. "We really trust in the little flame, in the unnamed god that shields it from being blown out" (*LCL* 364, 365).

In the poem "Give Us Gods" in *Pansies,* Lawrence again evokes the unknown god of the unuttered name, a syncretic deity lying beyond and encompassing his most numinous symbols:

Give us gods
give us something else—

Beyond the great bull that bellowed through space, and got his
throat cut.
Beyond even that eagle, that phoenix, hanging over the gold egg of
all things,
further still, before the curled horns of the ram stepped forth
or the stout swart beetle rolled the globe of dung in which man
should hatch,
or even the sly gold serpent fatherly lifted his head off the earth to
think—

Give us gods before these—
Thou shalt have other gods before these.

[*CP* 437]

The poem, a stronger version of an early variant entitled "Religion" (*CP* 949), turns on the implications of Lawrence's statement in the cited letter to Campbell: "All religions I think have the same inner conception, with different expressions" (*Letters* 2:249).

In the final poem, "Phoenix," in the posthumous volume *Last Poems,* edited by Richard Aldington, Lawrence employs the phoenix as an emblem of creative change through conscious and willing acceptance of being "dipped into oblivion," without which "you will never really change" (lines 4–5), and relates it to his own approaching death and to his faith in the prospect of rebirth:

> The phoenix renews her youth
> only when she is burnt, burnt alive, burnt down
> to hot and flocculent ash.
> Then the small stirring of a new small bub in the nest
> with strands of down like floating ash
> shows that she is renewing her youth like the eagle,
> immortal bird.
>
> [lines 6–12, *CP* 728]

Carl G. Jung, drawing an analogy with the sun's progress, sees the individuation process as a parabolic movement, first upward toward maturity, then downward in an equally goal-directed curve toward death. In this dual progress, the second movement is as necessary as the first and holds as great a potential for psychic growth and fulfillment.[4] I want to suggest that the parabola that Jung describes is one aspect of the rainbow that stands on the earth at the end of *The Rainbow*, which Ursula reads as a cosmic emblem of the restoration of "trembling balance" through creative change: Ursula knows that even in the most alienated, "the rainbow was arched in their blood and would quiver to life in their spirit, that they would cast off their horny covering of disintegration, that new, clean, naked bodies would issue to a new germination, to a new growth . . ." (*R* 459). The willingness to be "dipped into oblivion" of which Lawrence speaks in "Phoenix" is not "the final merge" of death to which he refers in the essay on Whitman (*SCAL* 169). In Jungian terms, it is a giving up of the ego, not of the self. The ultimate wisdom of the self, acceptance of the dissolution of the ego, depends paradoxically on the prior acceptance of life. Having committed himself to life, Lawrence came finally to incorporate, as both literary metaphor and psychological task, the fact of his own death. His finest images, far from serving a merely decorative function, were the symbolic means of his transformation. If the rainbow, with its two feet planted in darkness and in light, in the flesh and in the spirit, in the unconscious and in the conscious mind, describes the parabola of the "trembling balance" of life, the ship of death provides the basic psychic needs of the final journey. Always an emblem for creative living, the phoenix, in Law-

---

4. See Jung, "The Stages of Life" and "The Soul and Death," in *Structure and Dynamics of the Psyche, Collected Works,* 387–403 and 404–15.

rence's *Last Poems,* defines the nature of the coming change, the quality of immortality.

Like any archetypal image, the phoenix is not only to be understood intellectually through the moral abstractions it signifies in a particular context but also, more importantly, to be apprehended intuitively through the myth-meaning underlying its concrete imagery. For this reason, the phoenix is not to be identified merely as a static allegorical equivalent of resurrection. Rather, its archetypal dimensions must be grasped dynamically in terms of the imagistic motif of which it is a part. In Jung's alchemical studies, the phoenix emerges as the culminating image in a pattern of death, marriage of opposites, and rebirth that becomes the paradigm for the work of the alchemist, a pattern that Lawrence evokes in the imagistic structure of *The Plumed Serpent.*

10

Alchemy and *The Plumed Serpent*

From the dawn of the Christian era and throughout the Middle Ages, alchemy, a religioscience that sought the answers to questions about the properties of matter and the nature of moral philosophy, flourished alongside traditional Christianity as a heretical alternative to the dogma of the Church. According to Wayne Shumaker, there were two distinct traditions, experimental and philosophical or meditative: "The former were proto-chemists, the latter, in part, at least, mystics."[1] The Church established the orthodoxy of the Holy Trinity, not only excluding the powers of darkness from godhead but also relegating the feminine to a position outside that purely masculine divinity, where it could be venerated, separately and paradoxically, as virgin and mother. This orthodoxy, among other things, forced the Christian man to locate both evil and the feminine outside himself by the defense mechanisms of splitting and projective identification (as discussed in the Introduction). Projected upon the outer world, both the permanent and the temporal, these split off parts of man's consciousness, rather than an organic "trembling balance," characterized his perceptions of both universal truth and immediate experience. Hence, the division between lady and

1. Shumaker, *Occult Sciences in the Renaissance,* 170.

witch, mother and whore, has been an underlying assumption of Western art from the medieval romance to the films of twentieth-century popular culture.

A case in point is the split between angel and devil that D. H. Lawrence presents in the "Cathedral" chapter of *The Rainbow,* in which Will and Anna Brangwen respond in diametrically opposed ways to the sly little gargoyle faces that peep out of the "grand tide" of Lincoln Cathedral, mocking man's illusion that the cathedral is absolute, "giving suggestion of the many things that had been left out of the great concept of the church." In Anna's perception, what has been omitted is the feminine. She taunts Will with her own sly malice: "He knew her, the man who carved her. . . . I'm sure she was his wife" (*R* 189). Speaking from the position of traditional Christianity, Will insists, "It's a man's face, no woman's at all—a monk's—clean shaven." But Anna defeats him with a "Pouf!" of mocking, Mephistophelean laughter. Bitterly angry at her "for having destroyed another of his vital illusions" (*R* 190), Will recognizes, reluctantly, "There was life outside the church. There was much that the church did not include" (*R* 191).

To the alchemist, as much the priest of a counterreligion as the practitioner of a pseudoscience, the *prima materia,* the chaos preceding creation, necessarily included all, and in an effort to incorporate all that orthodoxy had split off from the self, he substituted an alchemical quaternity for the Church's Trinity. As Carl G. Jung defines it,

> Alchemy . . . describes a process of chemical transformation and gives numberless directions for its accomplishment. . . . Four stages are distinguished . . . , characterized by the original colours mentioned in Heraclitus: *melanosis* (blackening), *leukosis* (whitening), *xanthosis* (yellowing), and *iosis* (reddening).[2]

The tetrameria of the alchemical process was equivalent to the four elements of Empedocles: earth, air, fire, and water, to the four qualities: hot, cold, dry, and moist; to the four humours of medieval psychology: black bile, phlegm, yellow bile (lymph), and blood; and hence to the four types of character: melancholic, phlegmatic, choleric, and sanguine.

Because these four elements can be apprehended directly through

---

2. Jung, *Psychology and Alchemy,* in *Collected Works,* 12:218. Hereafter cited parenthetically in the text by volume and page numbers.

the senses without the intervention of analytical processes, Lawrence celebrates them in his poem "The Four" as

> . . . the elements of life, of poetry, and of perception,
> the four Great Ones, the Four Roots, the First Four
> of Fire and the Wet, Earth and the wide Air of the world.
> [lines 3–5, *CP* 706]

Lawrence, whose discussions of the Book of Revelation with the occultist Frederick Carter in the light of astrology and alchemy emerged in his last book, *Apocalypse,* places himself, in chapter 18, firmly on the side of quaternity:

> Three is the number of things divine, and four is the number of creation. The world is four-square, divided into four quarters which are ruled by four great creatures, the four winged creatures that surround the throne of the Almighty. These four creatures make up the sum of mighty space, both dark and light, and their wings are the quivering of this space, that trembles all the time with thunderous praise of the Creator. . . . [*A* 133]

Following this allusion to a cosmic level of the "trembling balance," Lawrence relates the four creatures to the four cosmic natures personified in the Archangels, the four Evangelists, the Four Elements, and "the Four Ages based on the four metals: gold, silver, bronze, and iron" (*A* 135).

Lawrence's interest in the occult sciences dates from his reading in occultism as early as April 1918 (*Letters* 3:239), but it was most intense during his association with Frederick Carter at the time he was writing *The Plumed Serpent.* The two began a correspondence in December 1922, and on 15 June 1923 Lawrence received and read, in Chapala, Mexico, Carter's manuscript "The Dragon of the Apocalypse," an astrological interpretation of the Book of Revelation. On his return visit to England in 1923–24, Lawrence stayed with Carter in Shropshire, 3–5 January 1924. A truncated and revised version of Carter's book was published as *The Dragon of the Alchemists* in 1926. In 1929, Carter sent Lawrence portions of the reconstructed original version, asking him to write an introduction. He also visited Lawrence in November 1929. Lawrence wrote the introduction that fall for the planned Mandrake Press edition, which fell through with the dissolution of the press. Ultimately, Lawrence's introduction appeared posthumously in the *London Mercury* (July

1930), and Carter's book was published as *The Dragon of Revelation* (1931).[3] According to Leonora Woodman, both versions of Carter's book "attempt to revive and explain a pagan spiritual vision that had relied on secret but nonetheless powerful knowledge to effect human godhead; and both focus on myth and symbol, regarded as psychic phenomena pointing to man's deepest spiritual needs."[4]

Lawrence remained not fully convinced by Carter's interpretation. "I'm not sure even now if the 'Apocalypse' is primarily Zodiacal," he writes to Carter. "It's a revelation of Initiation experience, and the clue is in the microcosm, in the human body itself . . ." (*Letters* 4:460). For Lawrence, Carter's acceptance of such occult systems as astrology and alchemy was perhaps too literal, and he instinctively returned to his original metaphor for the "trembling instability of the balance" that allowed for creative change, the human body. Recognizing that "[w]hen man changes his state of being, he needs an entirely different description of the universe, and so the universe changes its nature to him entirely" (*A* 53), Lawrence declares in his introduction to Carter's book, "We can never recover an old vision, once it has been supplanted. But what we can do is to discover a new vision in harmony with the memories of old, far-off, far, far-off experience that live within us" (*A* 54). Because Lawrence accepted the idea of a golden age, which he usually thought of as pre-Socratic, in which man had had a more direct, intuitive knowledge of the cosmos, he thought these memories of ancient modes valuable as metaphorical statements of human experience.

According to Carter, Lawrence "urged for some work that would give the significance of the entire scheme" of alchemy and hermetic philosophy, but he was exasperated that Carter's theory "depended on the exposition of a canonical work," and preferred "something outside—heterodox at least or heretic or pagan, a challenger, an outlaw to deliver onslaught."[5] T. S. Eliot's repeated charge against Lawrence of "ignorance" referred not to his "education" but to his failure "to develop a wise and large capacity for orthodoxy, to preserve the individual from the solely centrifugal impulse of heresy."[6] Whatever one may think of that deficiency, Lawrence's "heresy" correlates with his interest in myth and the occult, which emerged in the counterreligion of *The Plumed Serpent*. In 1918 Lawrence

3. For a fuller discussion, see Kalnins, "Introduction" to Lawrence, *Apocalypse,* 8–20.
4. Woodman, " 'The Big Old Pagan Vision,' " 40.
5. Carter, *D. H. Lawrence and the Body Mystical,* 60.
6. Eliot, " 'The victim and the sacrificial knife,' " 361.

read a book by Jung, which can be identified by the date as *Psychology of the Unconscious,* a work which relates the unconscious of modern man to ancient myths and symbols.[7] Lawrence might almost be echoing Jung in his statement in *Fantasia of the Unconscious:*

> And so it is that all the great symbols and myths which dominate the world when our history first begins, are very much the same in every country and every people; the great myths all relate to one another. And so it is that these myths now begin to hypnotize us again, our own impulse towards our own scientific way of understanding being almost spent. . . . [*FU* 55]

As Mara Kalnins expresses it, "Like Jung, Lawrence saw the human psyche poised between two worlds—the objective material universe, and the subjective inner world—with an equal need to relate to both, to integrate them for the enrichment and development of the psyche."[8] Although Lawrence could not have read Jung's later studies in psychology and alchemy, so that no direct influence from these studies is claimed, Jung's discussion of alchemy as the source of a number of these great archetypal symbols provides a useful context for understanding Lawrence's adoption of such alchemical imagery as the quaternity, the dark sun, the alchemical dragon, or *ouroboros,* and the alchemical process culminating in the emergence of the phoenix.

In alchemical tradition, according to Jung, the chthonic forces, rather than being regarded as abhorrent, were seen as necessary elements of the *prima materia* out of which the alchemist sought to distill a pure essence, symbolized on the material plane by the production of gold and on the spiritual plane by the quest for moral perfection.

---

7. First published in two parts in the *Jahrbuch für psychoanalytische und psychopathologische Forschungen* (Leipzig), vols. 3–4 (1911–12), and republished in book form as *Wandlungen und Symbole der Libido* (Leipzig and Vienna: Deuticke Verlag, 1912), Jung's book was published in English translation as *Psychology of the Unconscious: A Study of the Transformations and Symbolisms of the Libido; A Contribution to the History of the Evolution of Thought,* trans. with Introduction by Beatrice M. Hinkle (New York: Moffatt Yard and Co., 1916; London: Kegan Paul, 1917). The work was reissued, textually unaltered, in a 2d Swiss edition, 1924; again, with minor textual improvements, in a 3d Swiss edition, 1937; and finally, in extensively rewritten form, as *Symbole der Wandlung,* in a 4th Swiss edition (Zurich: Rascher Verlag, 1952). The fourth edition has become the standard version of the work under the title *Symbols of Transformation.*

8. Kalnins, "Introduction" to Lawrence, *Apocalypse,* 7.

As Jung explains the alchemical process, the beginning state is the *nigredo,* or blackness, which is either the original condition of the *prima materia* or a condition brought about by analysis of the elements, variously called the *solutio, separatio, divisio,* or *putrefactio.* If the *prima materia* is initially in a separated state, then the *nigredo* is brought about by first the uniting of the opposites, which are conceived as male and female elements, in a procedure called the *coniugium, matrimonium, coniunctio,* or *coitus,* then in the death of the product of that union in a procedure called the *mortificatio, calcinatio,* or *putrefactio,* resulting in the condition of *nigredo.* In the second stage, the washing, called the *ablutio* or *baptisma,* leads to the state of whitening, or *albedo,* in one of three ways: as a direct effect of the washing; as a result of the reunion of the soul, or *anima,* with the dead body, bringing about its resurrection; or as a consequence of the union of the many colors (*omnes colores*) or peacock's tail (*cauda pavonis*) in the one white color that contains all colors. This *albedo,* the first main goal of the process, is so highly valued by some alchemists that it is treated as an end in itself. For others, "[i]t is the silver or moon condition, which still has to be raised to the sun condition." The transition from dawn to sunrise, so to speak, is the third stage, the yellowing or *citrinitas,* although later alchemists tend to omit this part. The fourth stage, the reddening, or *rubedo,* is brought about by "raising the heat of the fire to its highest intensity. The red and white are King and Queen, who may also celebrate their 'chymical nuptials' at this stage" (12:219–21).

If the alchemical gold, taken literally, was a fraud satirized by such English authors as Chaucer (*The Canon Yeoman's Tale*) and Ben Jonson (*The Alchemist*), this gold, considered figuratively, was an emblem for moral perfection. Shorn of the stigma of either religious heresy or scientific fraudulence, alchemy may be seen as a metaphorical statement of the processes of the creative imagination (12:463). The alchemists themselves, of course, took their arcane laboratory procedure literally. If we cannot do so today, we may nonetheless, in Jung's view, take it seriously.

Jung sees in the alchemical symbols the archetypal language of the individuation process, the metamorphic growth through a series of psychic transformations to progressively higher levels of integration in the self. The alchemists were undertaking, in psychological terms, the progressive integration of conscious and unconscious forces in a new psychological synthesis, a concept that is itself a modern metaphor. But just as the philosopher's stone was never produced, Jung says, "so psychic wholeness will never be attained empirically, as consciousness is too narrow and too one-sided to comprehend the full inventory of the psyche."[9] Considered in this light, alchemy may be seen as an endeavor of the human mind, comparable to religious rite, to tap the energies of the unconscious for spiritual growth. The end point of the process, the distillation of pure essence out of the diversity of opposites, was marked by the emergence of the phoenix, the symbol par excellence of spiritual transformation.

Since the coming of the spirit was brought about by burning, variously called the *combustio, adustio, calcinatio, assatio, sublimatio,* or *incineratio,* the product "ash" is to be understood in the dual sense as the *scoriae* that remains after burning, a reminder of the chthonic nature of the sulphur, and as the bird of Hermes, the spirit that ascends. Thus, the *Rosarium* speaks of the ash as "sublime with fire," and Jung says, "the ash is the spirit that dwells in the glorified body" (14:194). If the alchemical process were successful, this incorruptible "glorified body" would be attained in the *albedo,* where the white substance of the ash denoted a purity no longer subject to decay. The ash was, then, identical with the "pure water" by which the soul was cleansed. The ash is sometimes identified with the *medicina* (12:189), the "spagyric," or secret substance, hidden within the human body. The threefold nature of this uncorrupted "aetheric substance," "metaphysical, physical, and moral" (12:256), makes it the best medicament for both body and mind. Such Christian mystics as St. Ambrose associated the *medicina* with the transformed bread of the Eucharist (12:297). Alchemists usually associated it with the *lapis philosophorum* or with Mercurius, who was the living stone (14:465).

Jung gives an account of the seventeenth-century alchemist Michael Maier, who made a mystic peregrination of Africa and the Near East in quest of Mercurius and the phoenix. While this fabulous bird is associated with Christ, whose advent was prophesied by the Erythraean Sibyl (14:213–16), Maier asked of that oracle not the way to Christ but the way to the Mercurius of alchemy, who paralleled Christ as universal man, Anthropos. With the rise of rationalist science in the Enlightenment, alchemy declined to the status of a "secret" "that has lost its vitality and can only be kept alive as an outward form," one to be guarded by secret societies such as the Rosicrucians, of which Michael Maier was a founder. The ages that followed, in their growing materialism, "dismissed alchemy as a huge disappointment and an absurd aberration" that produced only fool's gold. As Jung comments,

9. Jung, *Mysterium Coniunctionis,* in *Collected Works,* 14:533. Hereafter cited parenthetically in the text by volume and page numbers.

Michael Maier allows us a glimpse into this tragedy: at the end of his chef-d'œuvre he confesses that in the course of his grand *peregrinatio* he found neither Mercurius nor the phoenix, but only one phoenix feather—his pen! This is a delicate hint at his realization that the great adventure had led to nothing beyond his copious literary achievements. . . . [12:411]

So it is with D. H. Lawrence, whose peregrination took him in the opposite direction—to Mexico and his ultimate phoenix symbol, "the plumed serpent."

The structural balance of polarities in alchemy recommended it as a paradigm for Lawrence's vision of life as a "trembling centre of balance" about which opposites sway (*STH* 173). The quasi-religious and sexual imagery, progressive developmental stages, and transformation theme made alchemy a rich source of ritual and imagery for his "religion of the blood," which evokes mysterious, cosmic forces in an effort to tap unconscious sources of resilience to effect creative change. Lawrence, of course, did not take alchemy literally. But through his contact with Frederick Carter and his reading in occult writings in the early 1920s, alchemy became for him an important metaphor for the process of spiritual transformation and vital renewal.

From even a brief description, it is easy to recognize the alchemical source of much of the elaborate imagery of *The Plumed Serpent,* Lawrence's most occult novel. Alchemical processes are paralleled in the patterns he establishes on imagery of colors, elements, humours, and rituals, as well as in the alchemical meanings of such symbols as vessel, quaternity, dark sun, marriage, serpent, and phoenix. The secret of creation is recapitulated in the *opus alchymicum,* in which "Mercurius, a living and universal spirit, descends into the earth and mingles with the impure sulphurs, . . . is made captive and can be freed only by the art" (14:339). While it would be incorrect to claim that Lawrence's use of alchemy in *The Plumed Serpent* is mechanically systematic, a discernible pattern of alchemical imagery (see table 1) is operative in the progress which the novel describes of freeing the captive self by art.

The first movement, comprising chapters 1 through 4, presents the initial stage, the *melanosis* leading to the *nigredo.* The amphitheater of the bullring is a vessel containing, in microcosm, the *prima materia* of Mexico, the base elements that Ramón will have to work with if he is to effect a transformation of his people. The rite of this section is the bullfight, including the torment and killing of the bull

Table 1: Alchemical Patterns in *The Plumed Serpent*

	Stage 1	Stage 2	Stage 3	Stage 4
Chapters:	1–4	5–9	10–19	20–27
Process:	melanosis	leukosis	xanthosis	iosis
Condition:	nigredo	albedo	citrinitis	rubedo
Element:	earth	water	air	fire
Color:	black	white	yellow	red
Quality:	dry	moist	cold	hot
Humour:	[black bile]	[phlegm]	[yellow bile]	[blood]
Character:	melancholic	phlegmatic	choleric	sanguine
Rite:	slaying the dragon (bull-fight)	baptism	deconsecration/ consecration	marriage, communion, ordination
Process:	putrefaction	spiritual insemination	supersession	reconciliation
Mercurius:	corrupted body	spirit	soul	self
Aegis:	earth	moon	sun (Sol/Sol niger)	Morning Star
Theme:	death	potential for transformation	supersession	transformation

and the mutilation of the horses, a debased ritual corresponding to "slaying the dragon, the *mortificatio* of the first, dangerous, poisonous stage" of freeing Mercurius "from the imprisonment in the prima materia," that is, from the form of the corrupted body uninformed by spirit. According to Jung, "The idea that the dragon or Sol must die is an essential part of the mystery of transformation" (14:142). The corresponding process in the society is putrefaction. Far from promising, the life of the mass in the microcosm of the bullring seems filled with equal parts of thrill seeking and despair. Kate Leslie, who feels herself "going to prison" (*PS* 8), hates "common people" (*PS* 10) and is so revolted by the carnage in the bullring that she leaves early in a car provided by General Cipriano Viedma.

Mrs. Norris's tea party in Tlacolula is barely an improvement. The bullfight has shown Kate the loathsomeness of the human species

(*PS* 26). The tea party reveals the mean spiritedness of its ruling caste. The Aztec idols have "an expression of tomb-like mockery" (*PS* 33). Mexico as a whole strikes Kate as "evil" (*PS* 34): "It is so oppressive and gruesome," she says. "It *always* makes my heart sink" (*PS* 40). Don Ramón Carrasco tells her:

> "Whenever a Mexican cries *Viva!* he ends up with *Muera!* When he says *Viva!* he really means *Death for Somebody or Other!* If I think of all the Mexican revolutions, I see a skeleton walking ahead of a great number of people, waving a black banner with *Viva la Muerte!* written in large white letters. *Long live Death!* Not *Viva Cristo Rey!* but *Viva Muerte Rey! Vamos! Viva!*" [*PS* 40]

Kate feels that "the table was like a steel disc to which they were all, as victims, magnetised and bound" (*PS* 44), while to Judge Burlap, even the staircase is a "death-trap" (*PS* 45). Appropriately the basic color of the section is black, a point well-established in the discussion of the Aztec knives, which are of obsidian rather than jade (*PS* 45). Mrs. Norris wears a black shawl. In keeping with his emerging role as the adept who will direct the metaphorical work of alchemical transformation, Don Ramón appears "[s]tately in his black suit" (*PS* 41), and Cipriano is similarly dressed in black. The color is reiterated in the Mexican chauffeur's "black, dilated eyes of fathomless incomprehension" (*PS* 48).

Death and blackness are also the dominant motifs of Kate's fortieth birthday. She reflects, "Once, Mexico had had an elaborate ritual of death. Now it has death ragged, squalid, vulgar, without even the passion of its own mystery." Looking out over the parapet of her roof, Kate sees that "[t]he street beyond was like a black abyss" (*PS* 50):

> She was forty: the first half of her life was over. The bright page with its flowers and its love and its stations of the Cross ended with a grave. Now she must turn over, and the page was black, black and empty. [*PS* 50–51]

The question to be confronted is: "How could one write on a page as profoundly black?" (*PS* 51).

The socialist murals painted by Mexican artists on public buildings provide one answer, but they too are "ugly and vulgar. Strident caricatures of the Capitalist, and the Church, and of the Rich Woman, and of Mammon painted life-size and as violently as possible" (*PS* 53). "But," Kate says. "These caricatures are too intentional. They are like vulgar abuse, not art at all" (PS 53). Behind them is the impulse of hate, the desire to "kill all the capitalists" (PS 54). To Kate's mind, socialism is no answer at all.

Kate's question "To stay or not to stay" is debated with herself in the context of her sense of Mexico as a modern waste land characterized by "hopelessness" and "dauntlessness" (PS 76): "the dust of Mexico's infinite dryness, past broken walls, broken houses, broken haciendas, along the endless desolation left by past revolutions" (PS 75). She wonders if America is "the great death-continent" and "all the people who went there, Europeans, negroes, Japanese, Chinese, all the colours and the races, . . . the spent people, in whom the God impulse had collapsed" (PS 77–78). The first section closes with the words of Ramón: "The roots and the life are there. What else it needs is the word, for the forest to begin to rise again—And some man among men must speak the word" (PS 80).

The first four chapters are, if anything, the most realistic chapters of the novel, presented, in terms of scene, description, dialogue, action, and character development, with the verisimilitude appropriate to English realistic fiction. But if we stand back from the realistic surface to view the metaphorical pattern established in the imagery, the alchemical process of *melanosis* leading to the *nigredo* of the first stage is clear in a number of particulars: the element, earth; the color, black; the quality, dry; the character, melancholic; the ritual, bullfight (slaying the dragon); the process, putrefaction; the form of Mercurius, corrupted body without soul or life meaning; the prevailing theme, death. The carnage of the bullring, presented in apocalyptic detail, and its verbal counterpart in the tea party conversation in the following chapter begin the conflict, the breaking down of the *prima materia* out of which alchemical transformation can occur as the many races of the American continent (Negro, Caucasian, Asian, Native American) represent the alchemical colors—black, white, yellow, red, the *omnes colores* of the *cauda pavonis*. In alchemy, the many colors should meld into white, but at this point, they suggest the negative quality of fragmentation. As Lawrence writes to Earl and Achsah Brewster (15 May 1921): "All right, let white include all colours, if you like.—Only, white does *not* include all colours. It is only pure colourless light which includes all colours. And of even that I am doubtful. I doubt the exact sciences more than anything else . . ." (*Letters* 3:718). Ramón's suggestion that to effect the transformation from death to life "some man among men must speak the word" (PS 80) points, with deliberate evasiveness, to himself, for he has already assumed leadership of the Quetzalcoatl movement that will, in effect, cast him in the role of the alchemical adept who will officiate at the process.

The one fabular incident in the first section is reported only in a newspaper account in chapter 3, in which superstitious peasant women, washing their clothes on the shore of Lake Sayula, are "astonished to see a man of great stature rise naked from the lake" (*PS* 56), wade ashore, and take one of their garments. His body shining like gold, he proclaims, in an echo of the angel's words to Mary Magdalene at the risen Jesus' tomb (John 20:13):

> Why are you crying? Be quiet! It will be given back to you. . . . Quetzalcoatl and Tlaloc, the old gods, are minded to come back to you. Be quiet, don't let them find you crying and complaining. I have come from out of the lake to tell you, the gods are coming back to Mexico, they are ready to return to their own home— [*PS* 57]

This account presages the *leukosis* of the second stage of the alchemical process, the *albedo,* to be elaborated in the imagery of the second movement, comprising chapters 5 through 9. The risen man later appears to the husband of the woman from whom the garment was taken. To prepare him "for the return of the gods," this peasant is given a ritual baptism in a golden basin, with the words, "*This . . . is the bath of Quetzalcoatl. The bath of fire is yet to come.*" He is then given clean new clothes, a blanket decorated with flowers, and "two pieces of silver money" (*PS* 57). The "bath of Quetzalcoatl" from which the peasant emerges as the Laurentian natural aristocrat parallels the alchemical "bath of rebirth" from which the "Ethiopian" (the blackened product of the *nigredo*) emerges to take a new name, which the alchemist Nicholas Melchior says "the philosophers call the natural sulphur and their son" (12:385). The account is a mythic paradigm of the *ablutio* or *baptisma,* the washing leading to the *albedo.*

In chapter 5, when Kate moves to Sayula beside the lake, she first takes the train to Orilla. Images of dust and drought metaphorically define the moral waste land to be transformed: "The train drew out of the formless, dry, dust-smitten areas fringing the city" (*PS* 84). "The adobe was grey-black, of the lava dust, and depressing. Into the distance the fields spread dry . . ." (*PS* 85). As they near Ixlahuacan, "Dry country with mesquite bushes. . . . Parched slopes with ragged maize stubble . . ." (*PS* 87).

For the rest of the chapter the basic image is water—"an excellent symbol," Jung says, "for the living power of the psyche." The alchemists devised numerous synonyms for this water—"*aqua vitae, succus lunariae,* and so on, by which they meant a living being not devoid of substance, as opposed to the rigid immateriality of mind in the abstract" (12:71–72). In the town, Kate finds a crippled boatman to row her downriver to the lake. In an ironic reversal of classical tradition, this Charon rows the dead to the land of the living. Already the atmosphere of the lake environs effects a change in Kate's attitude from the contempt she felt in Mexico City to something like admiration: "There was a beauty in these men, a wistful beauty and a great physical strength. Why had she felt so bitterly about the country?" (*PS* 89). Kate notices "some men bathing, men whose wet skins flashed with the beautiful brown-rose colour. . . . Low against the water across-stream she watched the glitter of naked men, half-immersed in the river" (*PS* 90). (Jung reproduces an illustration of "Life-renewing influence of conjoined sun and moon on the bath," showing four standing nude male figures immersed to the loins in the alchemical bath [12:72, fig. 27].) A man in the water rises beside the boat to request that Kate "make a tribute to Quetzalcoatl, if you go on the lake" (*PS* 91). In Lawrence's reversal from death to life, the fee of an obol due to Charon becomes a tribute owed to the god.

The rite of this section is baptism, but the corresponding life process is not the death and resurrection of Christian sacrament but what may be called, alchemically, spiritual insemination. According to Nicholas Melchior, the "blessed gum" to be dissolved in the mercurial water, the red and white substance identified with Sol and Luna, who are to be married in the fourth stage of the alchemical *opus,* "is named the Sperm of the Philosophers," which impregnates the virgin bride with the metaphorical "child of good omen" (12:384). The boatman rows through "the frail-rippling, sperm-like water" (*PS* 93). At Sayula, Kate's symbolic baptism into the new life occurs as she bathes in it: "the great, lymphatic expanse of water, like a sea, trembling, trembling, trembling to a far distance, to the mountains of substantial nothingness" (*PS* 97). For it is the water that will mysteriously activate with life the *prima materia* of the dust. Kate involuntarily utters her prayer for renewal: "*Give me the mystery and let the world live again for me!* Kate cried to her own soul. *And deliver me from man's automatism*" (*PS* 105).

The second stage of the alchemical work is under the aegis of the moon, which is identified with the mercurial water and thus becomes mother of the Hydrolith, the water-stone. Jung quotes Zadith Senior (Zadith ben Hammuel): "The full moon is the philosophical water and the root of the science, for she is the mistress of moisture, the perfect round stone and the sea, wherefore I know that the moon is the root of this hidden science" (12:388). In *Apocalypse,* Lawrence gives the alchemical symbology of the moon a psychological interpretation: "It is she who would caress our nerves, smooth them with the silky hand of her glowing, soothe them into serenity again with her cool presence. For the moon is the mistress and mother of our watery bodies, the pale body of our nervous consciousness and our moist flesh" (*A* 77). In *The Plumed Serpent,* this alchemical association is not made explicit until later. Chapter 8, "Night in the House" is concerned with fear of bandit attack, which is subsequently projected in chapter 16, "Cipriano and Kate," in terms of a debate on the moon. "But the moon," Kate says, "isn't lovely and friendly as it is in England or Italy"; Cipriano replies, "It is the same planet." When Kate says that "the moonshine in America . . . doesn't make one feel glad as it does in Europe. One feels it would like to hurt one," he suggests, "Perhaps there is in you something European, which hurts our Mexican moon." To her insistence that she comes "in good faith," he replies pointedly with revolutionary logic, "European good faith. Perhaps it is not the same as Mexican" (*PS* 233).

Already, the generative, "earth-filmy," "water that was hardly like water at all" (*PS* 97) is linked with the second stage in alchemy, the whitening, an association carried out in the color imagery. In the plaza, young peons wear white blouses and a jaunty scarlet sarape over one shoulder (*PS* 115). As the men gradually form for the circle dance, the Indian drummer, "naked from the waist up, wore snow-white cotton drawers, very full, held round the waist by a red sash, and bound at the ankles with red cords" (*PS* 118). The linking of the mandala, the archetype by which opposites are integrated within the self, with the dominant color imagery of the passage foreshadows the alchemical union in the "marriage" of white and red. The half-naked men's "white sarapes, with borders of blue and earth-brown bars, and dark fringe" (*PS* 127) carry out the pattern in imagery of the union of earth and sky in the alchemical white. The spiritual regeneration to be effected by the symbolic process is signaled in Kate's clothes, as well as her inner experience, as she is led into the dance: "In her white dress and green straw hat, she felt a virgin again, a young virgin" (*PS* 130).

The action of the second section, unlike the first, often verges on the fabular. The imagery supports the sense of mystery and wonder. Again, beyond the surface of Lawrence's often highly lyrical prose, the pattern defined is the second stage of the alchemical process: the element, water; the color, white; the quality, moist; the character, phlegmatic; the rite, baptism; the process, spiritual insemination; the astral aegis, moon; the form of Mercurius, spirit as an informing principle in body; the prevailing theme, potential for transformation.

The agent of transformation, introduced in the second section but propelling the symbolic action forward, is the sun. The third section is under its aegis: both the bright sun and the dark sun (or, in alchemical terms, both *Sol* and *Sol niger*) are present in the man-dala design on the banner of Quetzalcoatl: "On the blue field of the banneret was the yellow sun with a black centre, and between the four greater yellow rays, four black rays emerging, so that the sun looked like a wheel spinning with a dazzling motion" (*PS* 120). Both sun and wheel are symbols of the creative process. Jung reproduces an illustration of "Mercurius turning the eight-spoked wheel which symbolizes the [alchemical] process" while "in one hand he holds the *telum passionis*," the erect phallus (12:156, fig. 80). Jung associates the yellow sun with the transitional stage of *citrinitis* in alchemy. In one of the dreams he interprets,

> *A yellow light like the sun looms through the fog, but it is murky. Eight rays go out from the centre. This is the point of penetration; the light ought to pierce through, but has not quite succeeded.* [12:180.]

Structurally, the image parallels Lawrence's description of the em-blem of Quetzalcoatl, but the difference in color patterns is signifi-cant. In the dream the murky yellow color, Jung says, suggests an incomplete understanding and the need for effort in penetrating to insight. In the creation myth that the speaker in the plaza recounts, the dark sun is the source of creation, as "from behind the bright sun the four dark arms of the greater sun shot out, and in the shadow men arose. They could see the four dark arms of the sun in the sky. And they started walking" (*PS* 123). The "Master-Sun, the dark one, of the unuttered name" is the source of the cycles of history in the death and rebirth of both humans and the gods. When Quetzalcoatl, in his previous incarnation, had grown old, the arm of the dark sun had lifted him into the sky and beckoned to white men, who came from the east "with a dead god on a cross, saying: Lo! This is the Son of God! He is dead, he is bone!" (*PS* 124).

Jung points out that in alchemy, the sun and gold share the same sign. "But just as the 'philosophical' gold is not the 'common' gold, so the sun is neither just the metallic gold nor the heavenly orb," but the possessor of an active red sulphur hidden in the gold or streaming, hot and dry, in the sun's "magically effective and transformative rays" (14:92). Understood symbolically, the alchemical meanings applied to the sun correlate closely with the meaning Lawrence attributed to the sun in such works as "Sun," *The Plumed Serpent, The Escaped Cock,* and *Apocalypse.* Behind the "miraculous power of the sun" in alchemical lore, Jung says, is the "primitive conception of a universal power of growth, healing, magic, and prestige, which is to be found as much in the sun as in men and plants, so that not only the sun but man too, and especially the enlightened man, the adept, can generate the gold by virtue of this universal power" (14:95). The sulphur as creative power is "a hot, daemonic principle of life, having the closest affinities with the sun in the earth, the 'central fire' or 'ignis gehennalis' (fire of hell). Hence there is also a *Sol niger,* a black sun, which coincides with the *nigredo* and *putrefactio,* the state of death" (14:94–95). As Jung explains, "The antinomian thinking of alchemy counters every position with a negation and vice versa" (14:98). Psychologically, Jung identifies the *Sol niger* with the feminine unconscious (14:181), which in men is the source of creativity.

Section three, comprising chapters 10 through 19, presents the process of *xanthosis* leading to the third stage, the *citrinitis.* In this section, the basic conflict between dark and light is defined and intensified as a battle for liberation of the soul. In religious terms, the conflict is between Christianity and the Quetzalcoatl movement. Doña Carlota, who emerges as the apologist for the traditional Christian values of charity and humility, charges her husband with heresy and thinks him motivated by power for its own sake, "horrible, wicked power" (*PS* 165). Verbal references associate Ramón's power with the demonic. But his appearance, "dressed in white, dazzling, in the costume of the *peones,* the white blouse jacket and the white, wide pantaloon trousers" (*PS* 167), in addition to associating him politically with the oppressed, identifies his power with his control of the metaphorical alchemy that has been seen in the whitening process.

The rites of this section, both private and public, are acts of consecration and deconsecration, and the corresponding life process is supersession, a casting off of the old life and an emergence into the new. Ramón is much concerned with defining the symbols and liturgy of the counterreligion. His prayer is a private act of consecration by muscular tension and will rather than language, an upright, physical prayer of pride, naked in the darkness: "I put off the world with my clothes. And standing nude and invisible in the centre of his room he thrust his clenched fist upwards, with all his might, feeling he would break the walls of his chest. And his left hand hung loose, the fingers softly curving downwards." After finding his own center, he encompasses in a single gesture the infinite beyond and the depths of his own unconscious, the realms of bird and serpent: "[H]e thrust up and reached down in the invisible dark, convulsed with passion. Till the black waves began to wash over his consciousness, over his mind, waves of darkness broke over his memory, over his being, like an incoming tide . . ." (PS 193).

Ramón's artisan constructs an iron emblem of the bird within the sun, made of triangular discs to form "a seven-pointed sun of the space inside" (PS 171). The phoenix, often synonymous with the raven, eagle, or vulture, depending on the stage of the alchemical process, is a widely known symbol in alchemy. The lapis philosophorum itself, the rebis or philosopher's stone, compounded of the two opposites as a hermaphroditic amalgam of Sol and Luna, is often represented with wings, suggesting intuition or spiritual potential. For Jung, this kind of pictorial image represents the consciousness-transcending totality of the self, "rather like a snapshot of an evolving process as it leads on to the next stage" (12:193).

In The Plumed Serpent, the process is defined in doctrinal hymns and sermons. When Ramón's followers, dressed in the ceremonial white of the peons' costume, drum and sing, "Who sleeps—shall wake! Who sleeps—shall wake! Who treads down the path of the snake shall arrive at the place; in the path of the dust shall arrive at the place and be dressed in the skin of the snake—" (PS 175), this overdetermined image evokes, among other meanings, the alchemical serpent, Mercurius, the fundamental substance to be transformed (12:241). Jung's statement that "[t]he transformation corresponds to the psychic process of assimilation and integration by means of the transcendent function," which unites the paired opposites (14:202–3), accords with Lawrence's meaning.

The snake imagery, with allusions to both the Hopi snake dances and the kundalini serpent, continues in Ramón's liturgical prayer stating one of the major principles of the Quetzalcoatl religion, the eternal present: "There is no Before and After, there is only Now" (PS 175). The imagery of the hymn, "The Lord of the Morning Star/ Stood between the day and the night" (PS 177), looks forward to the culmination of the process in which Ramón, as lord of two ways, seeks to reconcile night and day within the self. When Ramón declares in his sermon, "We will be masters among men, and lords among men. But lords of men, and masters of men we will not be" (PS 178), he advocates a sacramental rather than possessive attitude toward others, things, and nature (*PS* 179–80). The sermon suggests the moral purity out of which the adept must operate if he is to effect such a union of opposites.

This section also distinguishes between Ramón's religious movement and socialism. The socialist president Montes says: "I want to save my country from poverty and unenlightenment, he wants to save its soul" (*PS* 190). The emphasis on soul, which is characteristic of the third stage of alchemy, is, in Laurentian terms, an assertion of the principle that unites the opposites of body and spirit. Thus, in Lawrence's view, to focus on the masses' material and educational needs is to concentrate on the superficial when what is required is nothing less than rebirth. To state his position, Ramón develops the alchemical symbol of the egg into an epic simile:

> Mexico is like an old, old egg that the bird of Time laid long ago; and she has been sitting on it for centuries, till it looks foul in the nest of the world. But still, Cipriano, it is a good egg. It is not addled. Only the spark of fire has never gone into the middle of it, to start it.—Montes wants to clean the nest and wash the egg. But meanwhile, the egg will go cold and die. The more you save these people from poverty and ignorance, the quicker they will die; like a dirty egg that you take from under the hen-eagle, to wash it. While you wash the egg, it chills and dies. . . . And the old Dove of Europe will never hatch the egg of dark-skinned America. [*PS* 191]

Alchemy, in Jung's view, was an attempt to bring about creative transformation. (He reproduces a fifteenth-century illustration showing "The philosophical egg, whence the double eagle is hatched, wearing the spiritual and temporal crowns" [12:192, fig. 98].) As Jung puts it,

> In alchemy the egg stands for the chaos apprehended by the artifex, the *prima materia* containing the captive world-soul. Out of the egg—symbolized by the round cooking-vessel—will rise the eagle or phoenix, the liberated soul, which is ultimately identical with the Anthropos who was imprisoned in the embrace of Physis. . . . [12:193]

Ramón uses the same figure in explaining the goals of his movement: "I want to get inside the egg, right to the middle, to start it growing into a new bird" (*PS* 191).

The colors and images in the sarapes are carefully chosen for their occult and religious symbolism. Ramón's sarape is woven with the images of snake (around the shoulders) and bird (through which the head emerges), and its fringe is scarlet, foreshadowing the dominant red color of the last section. Cipriano's sarape, in keeping with his emerging role as "the red Huitzilopochtli" and his function in the *rubedo* stage, is "all scarlet and dark brown, a great scarlet sun at the centre, deep scarlet zig-zags at the borders and dark brown fringe at his knees" (*PS* 194). Kate's shawl, consistent with her function as the emergent soul, is yellow (*PS* 195).

As earth and water are the basic elements of the first two sections, the dominant element of the third section, thematically, is air. The work of alchemy itself is imagistically figured as both inspiriting and destructive wind in the gathering storm over the cauldron of the lake: "The lake was quite black, like a great pit. The wind suddenly blew with violence, with a strange ripping sound in the mango trees, as if some membrane in the air were being ripped" (*PS* 201). In a flash of lightning, the wind suddenly lifts Cipriano's blanket "straight up in the air," then drops it "in a scarlet flare over his head" (*PS* 201): "Down came the rain with a smash, as if some great vessel had broken" (*PS* 201–2).

Ramón's rebirth as the Anthropos means an inevitable break with his old life. He thinks of his two sons as the children of his "old body": "His new body had no children: would probably never have any" (*PS* 207). In a final rupture of his marriage, he tells Carlota: "Go away! I have smelt the smell of your spirit long enough" (*PS* 210). "The Written Hymns of Quetzalcoatl," correspondingly, concern the departure of Jesus and Mary from Mexico and the resurrection of Quetzalcoatl, whom the voice of the Unknown God summons to a new birth (*PS* 226).

As the form of Mercurius is body in the first stage and spirit in the second, so his form in the third stage is soul. Jung cites the seventeenth-century alchemist Michael Maier's interpretation of his Emblema XXI, "where the circle re-emerges from the triangle set in the square" (12:120):

> Similarly the philosophers maintain that the quadrangle is to be reduced to a triangle, that is, to body, spirit, and soul. These three appear in three colours which precede the redness: the body, or earth, in Saturnine blackness; the spirit in lunar whiteness, like water; and the soul, or air, in solar yellow. Then the triangle will be perfect, but in its turn it must change into a circle, that is into unchangeable redness. [12:120n]

Much of the imagery of this section is concerned with soul-making. When Kate declares that "Mexico *has* no soul," Cipriano replies that "the soul is also a thing you make, like a pattern in a blanket": "Mexico hasn't started to weave the pattern of her soul" (*PS* 234). John Keats suggests calling the world "[t]he vale of Soul-making." Lawrence's conception of that task is not far from Keats's:

> I say 'Soul making' Soul as distinguished from Intelligence— There may be intelligences or sparks of divinity in millions— but they are not Souls . . . till they acquire identities, till each one is personally itself. . . . —how then are Souls to be made? How then are these sparks which are God to have identity given them—so as ever to possess a bliss peculiar to each ones individual existence? How, but by the medium of a world like this?

Cipriano's metaphor of soul-weaving echoes Keats's statement "that almost any Man may like the Spider spin from his own inwards his own airy Citadel—. . . : man should be content with as few points to tip with the fine Webb of his soul and weave a tapestry empyrean— full of Symbols for his spiritual eye, of softness for his spiritual touch, of space for his wandering distinctness for Luxury."[10] James Hillman defines the task psychologically as the work of translating life events into soul through the crafting and articulation of images, as in the transformation of subjective experience into dreams or the conscious elaboration of imagination. He cites the example of Lawrence's building the "imaginal vessel" in "The Ship of Death."[11]

Cipriano invites Kate to "be the woman in the Quetzalcoatl pantheon," that is, to embody the archetype of the *anima*. His proposal of marriage, far from being conventionally romantic, seems motivated by religiopolitics: "Marry me, and help Ramón and me. We need a woman, Ramón says, to be with us. And you are the woman." Kate demurs that she has no "*impulse* to marry" Cipriano and that she does not want "horror in [her] soul" (*PS* 234–35).

After "The Attack on Jamiltepec," Kate looks at Ramón's naked, bandaged, inert body, and sees "vividly, how the body is the flame of the soul, leaping and sinking upon the invisible wick of the soul. And now the soul, like a wick, seemed spent, the body was a sinking, fading flame" (*PS* 300). As Ross Parmenter notes, this phrasing is a development beyond Lawrence's earlier conception as stated in a

10. Keats, *Letters of John Keats*, ed. Rollins, 2:102 and 1:231–32.
11. Hillman, *Archetypal Psychology*, 26–28.

letter to Ernest Collings (13 January 1913): "I conceive a man's body as a kind of flame . . . and the intellect is just the light that is shed on the things around" (*Letters* 1:503). The soul, unmentioned in the letter to Collings, has now become the flame, burning between the body and the spirit, in the triad of man's being.[12]

Lawrence's new conception is stated in a contemporaneous fragment, "Man is essentially a soul . . .":

> Man is essentially a soul. The soul is neither the body nor the spirit, but the central flame that burns between the two, as the flame of a lamp burns between the oil of the lamp and the oxygen of the air.
> The soul is to be obeyed, by the body, by the spirit, by the mind.
> The mind is the instrument of registering the soul in consciousness.
> The soul is instinctive. Real education is the learning to recognise and obey the instincts of the soul.

Lawrence's idea of a natural aristocracy of the soul is related, both in conception and by verbal echoes, to *The Plumed Serpent:*

> So men are really arranged in hierarchies of the soul, from the finest down to the dullest, in hierarchies of the soul.
> This is the new order of aristocracy, and it is a world-order. The finest soul in the world is the first man in the world, and the rest form themselves naturally into hierarchies.
> By the movement of the soul within himself, a man knows the soul within another man, and whether it be a purer, stronger flame, whether the man belong to a higher hierarchy or not. Man knows at first hand, *if he will. [RDP* 389]

The basic idea of this passage is already familiar, from *Twilight in Italy,* in the Laurentian version of the Christian Trinity, in which the Father represents the flesh, the Son represents the spirit, and the Holy Ghost is the principle of reconciliation between the two (*TI* 58–59). But here the concept is shifted from the theological ground to the human level. The lofty language and poetic conception prompt Parmenter to call it "a noble statement, summarizing many of Lawrence's chief ideas about man's nature in simpler, more comprehen-

12. Parmenter, *Lawrence in Oaxaca,* 236.

sive terms than in most previous tries."[13] But egalitarians and socialists will not find the doctrine of natural aristocracy and hierarchies of the soul noble, since it lends itself to the elitist position that some men are "Natural Aristocrats" (*PS* 248), who are innately superior to others *in basic human worth* and therefore, on the basis of instinctive response alone, have power of life and death over them. Parmenter is correct in saying that Lawrence opposed fascism, but doctrines like the foregoing have nevertheless left him open to the charge.

Ramón's (and Lawrence's) chief complaint against the Church is that it weakens rather than strengthens the believer's individual soul:

> Oh, if there is one thing men need to learn, but the Mexican Indians especially, it is to collect each man his own soul together deep inside him, and to abide by it. The Church, instead of helping men to this, pushes them more and more into a soft, emotional helplessness, with the unpleasant sensuous gratification of feeling themselves victims, victimised, victimised, but at the same time, with the lurking sardonic consciousness that in the end a victim is stronger than the victimiser. [*PS* 276]

The direct conflict between Christianity and the counterreligion intensifies throughout this section. Ramón wants "to be one of the Initiates of the Earth. One of the Initiators. Every country has its own Saviour," he tells Cipriano, and he wants to be Mexico's. Explaining his polytheistic theory of local gods, Ramón says he wants Mexicans "to speak with the tongues of their own blood" (*PS* 248): "the mystery is one mystery, but men must see it differently" (*PS* 249). When Ramón tells the Bishop of the West that he wants to establish the Quetzalcoatl religion in Mexico and asks for peace with the Church, the Bishop reminds him that he has invaded the churches, desecrated their altars, and burned the images of the Blessed Virgin. In view of the charge, Ramón's question, "Should there not be peace between the men who strive down their different ways, to the God-Mystery?" (*PS* 266), seems obtuse. Cipriano, who thinks the Jesuits want only power, advocates a response of power rather than conciliation.

In a ceremony in the plaza, Ramón stages an apparently orderly

13. Ibid.

transfer of ecclesiastical power. The priest, in a symbolic gesture repeating Christ's giving the Keys of the Kingdom to Peter, hands the keys of the church to Ramón. After distributing a leaflet hymn, "Jesus' Farewell," Ramón and his followers, bare to the waist, enter the church and remove the Roman Catholic images of the Blessed Virgin and the saints, leaving the church dark and bare. The images are taken by *canoa* to an island in the lake where they are arranged in a cluster on a grill and burned, as the priest also consigns his vestments to the flames. The unorthodox rite of deconsecration is presented as reverent, but there are disturbing reminders of the English Nonconformists' "purging" the churches of "popish" images and of the earlier burning of martyrs.

The rationalization for this expropriation of Church property comes in "The Attack on Jamiltepec," possibly the bloodiest, most violent scene in all of Lawrence's work, in which Kate helps Ramón in dispatching two attackers at his hacienda, Ramón by cutting one man's throat, Kate by shooting another through the head to prevent his killing Ramón. Afterward Ramón thanks Kate for his life, and his lieutenant tells her privately that the attackers were not bandits but Knights of Cortés men[14] (conservative Roman Catholics) who, but for Kate's intervention, would have succeeded in their purpose of murdering Ramón.

In section three, as in the first two sections, the action is both realistic and symbolic. The pattern delineated in the imagery is the third stage of the alchemical process: the element, air; the color, yellow; the quality, cold; the character, choleric; the ritual, deconsecration/consecration; the process, supersession; the astral aegis, sun (*Sol* and *Sol niger*); the form of Mercurius, soul; and the prevailing theme, supersession of the old order by the new.

The fourth section, comprising chapters 20 through 27, parallels the final stage of alchemy, the *iosis,* or reddening, leading to the *rubedo.* In alchemical terms, its subject is the projection of the *lapis philosophorum* in the emergence of Ramón as the Anthropos, the living stone who has the power of effecting transformation of base material into "gold." Throughout the section, however, there is an ironic discrepancy between the symbolism of the soul, which would transform

14. See Clark, ed., in Lawrence, *The Plumed Serpent,* 469 n. 247:8; and 471 n. 267:11. According to Clark, the Knights of Cortés are clearly, as Lawrence called them in an earlier manuscript, the Knights of Columbus, who in Mexico extended their original purpose of opposing the Masons to "resisting governmental control of the Church." The Catholic Dames were their female counterpart.

men into gods, and the actual world, which reveals their all too human limitations. Lawrence must be aware, since Kate certainly is, of the ambivalent interplay between the leaders' godlike aspirations and the occasional impression they give of being poseurs in a fantastic god-game. In retrospect, much of the poetry of the hymns and sermons by which the Quetzalcoatl myth is created may be seen as sublimity on the edge of bombast. In the last section, there is at times a stridency in the rhetoric, a forcing (sometimes even by extralegal, military action) of what is essentially inward and religious—to such an extent that the earlier religious insights are in danger of being lost or irreparably compromised.

As the leader of the Quetzalcoatl movement and the priest of a counterreligion, Ramón officiates at the rites of this section—marriage, dark communion, and ordination—and is master of the corresponding life process of transformation, although, characteristically of Lawrence's open form, it is still in progress as the novel ends.

Chapter 20, "Marriage by Quetzalcoatl," evokes the alchemical imagery of the marriage of red and white, Sol and Luna. Everything about the marriage emphasizes its impersonal, symbolic function. Cipriano presents the argument for marriage with unassailable logic: Ramón means "*more* than life" to him, Kate had saved Ramón's life, and this "meant that *therefore*—" (*PS* 309–10). Valued not for herself but for Ramón, Kate seems almost a substitute for Ramón, although this complex erotic motive is never made explicit or explored dramatically.

Cipriano refuses to woo Kate romantically but presents himself as the embodiment of "the ancient phallic mystery, the ancient god-devil of the male Pan." The marriage he proposes is, then, not personal but suprapersonal, a wedding of male and female principles, a union of archetypes like the "chymical nuptials" of Sol and Luna in the alchemical work:

> When the power of his blood rose in him, the dark aura streamed from him like a cloud pregnant with power, like thunder, and rose like a whirlwind that rises suddenly in the twilight and raises a great pliant column, swaying and leaning with power, clear between heaven and earth.
>
> Ah! and what a mystery of prone submission, on her part, this huge erection would imply! Submission absolute, like the earth under the sky. Beneath an over-arching absolute. [*PS* 311]

The problem with such absolutist language is that while it describes the uniting of male and female principles as impersonal forces, it involves two characters who have been presented as realistic human beings. If women understandably object to a conception of the female principle that defines the woman's sexual role as "Submission absolute" in a "prone" position,[15] the conception of the male principle defines the man's sexual role in equally restrictive terms. Producing the "great pliant column" of the "huge erection" towering to the sky is one of the more lurid male fantasies, but taken literally the conception reduces the man's humanity, no less than the woman's, by demanding that he too fulfill the impersonal role of an "overarching absolute" that leaves his individual humanity out of account.

Ramón discloses plans to assume quasi-divinity as "First Man of Quetzalcoatl," with Cipriano as "First Man of Huitzilopochtli." Since they need a goddess for the Mexican Olympus, Ramón nominates Kate and calls her "the bride of Huitzilopochtli." Kate, while at first resisting a legally binding marriage, agrees to a "Marriage by Quetzalcoatl." As in the alchemical emergence of the new Adam in a paradigm of the process of creation (14:421), Lawrence's imagery suggests the restoration of a prelapsarian state.

The wedding takes place in a twilight rain in Ramón's garden in ceremonial dress, with both bridegroom and officiant barefoot and naked to the waist and the bride wearing a white linen Indian chemise, embroidered with blue flowers and the bird of Quetzalcoatl. The marriage vows are rubrical, evoking the symbolic roles of man and woman, as conceived in the Quetzalcoatl movement: the woman takes the man as her "rain from heaven," and he takes her as his "earth." She kisses his feet and heels; he kisses her brow and breast. She prays him to meet her "in the heart of the night"; he prays her to receive him there in their "abiding place" (*PS* 329). If either shall betray the other as an individual, it shall be forgiven; "but if either betray the abiding place of the two, it shall not be forgiven." Ramón bids them to bathe: "And put oil on your bodies, which is the stillness of the Morning Star" (*PS* 330).

In the alchemical pattern, the wedding parallels the marriage of Sol and Luna. No wedding rings are exchanged, but necklaces with the Quetzalcoatl emblem of bird and serpent worked in alchemical colors, with white and yellow rendered as silver and gold (*PS* 331). This emblem is a form of the alchemical dragon, "a *monstrum*— . . .

---

15. Millett, *Sexual Politics*, 284, comments on this passage. See also Nixon, *Lawrence's Leadership Politics and the Turn Against Women*, 205. On the other hand, Apter, "Let's Hear What the Male Chauvinist is Saying," 164–67, argues that what Lawrence advocates is "positive passivity" and that the choice is Kate's, not one forced upon her by men.

combining the chthonic principle of the serpent and the aerial principle of the bird" (12:279–80). Ramón calls it "the symbol of Quetzalcoatl, the Morning Star" (*PS* 331).

The fourth section is under the aegis of the Morning Star, which is evoked not only in the marriage rite but also at the reconsecration of the church to Quetzalcoatl in chapter 21. In his poetic sermon, Ramón calls himself "the Son of the Morning Star," which becomes the symbolic equivalent of the soul: "midmost shines / Between night and day, my Soul-star in me" (*PS* 339). This unifying symbol enables him to reconcile opposing principles within the self, which becomes the form of Mercurius in this section:

> I am Quetzalcoatl of the eagle and the snake.
> The earth and air.
> Of the Morning Star.
> I am Lord of the Two Ways—
>
> [*PS* 341]

The rite of communion marking "The Opening of the Church" parallels, without employing the same set of correspondences, the alchemical paraphrase of the Mass whereby Nicholas Melchior of Hermannstadt "expounded the alchemical process in the form of a Mass" (12:380–89). Ramón emerges as the adept who controls the four colors and the four elements of alchemical tradition as liturgical colors and elements of the mass:

> Four men came to him. One put a blue crown with the bird on his brow, one put a red belt round his breast, another put a yellow belt round his middle, and the last fastened a white belt round his loins. Then the first one pressed a small glass bowl to Ramón's brow, and in the bowl was white liquid like bright water. The next touched a bowl to the breast, and the red shook in the bowl. At the navel the man touched a bowl with yellow fluid, and at the loins a bowl with something dark. They held them all to the light.
>
> Then one by one, they poured them into a silver mixing-bowl that Ramón held between his hands. [PS 341]

In addition to the red, yellow, and white belts of the vestments, Lawrence employs blue rather than black for the crown to suggest fidelity as well as the abstract intellectual or spiritual element of the quaternity, and represents the physical element of blackness by the dark liquid in the bowl held to the loins. The meaning of the rite in the counterreligion is made clear in the liturgy that Ramón then pronounces, which, in the second paragraph quoted below, curiously recalls Michael Maier's conception of the quadrangle reduced to the triangle from which the circle of self will emerge:

> "For save the Unknown God pours His Spirit over my head and His fire into my heart, and sends His power like a fountain of oil into my belly, and His lightning like a hot spring into my loins, I am not. I am nothing. I am a dead gourd.
> "And save I take the wine of my spirit and the red of my heart, the strength of my belly and the power of my loins, and mingle them all together, and kindle them to the Morning Star, I betray my body, I betray my soul, I betray my spirit and my God who is Unknown.
> "Fourfold is man. But the star is one star. And one man is but one star." [PS 341]

Circling the silver mixing-bowl to blend the four liquids, Ramón, in a ceremony recalling the Black Mass, then turns his back to the people and lifts the bowl upward, in an offertory to the image of Quetzalcoatl, and suddenly throws the contents of the bowl into the altar fire: "There was a soft puff of explosion, a blue flame leaped high into the air, followed by a yellow flame, and then a rose-red smoke. In three successive instants the faces of the men inside the chancel were lit bluish, then gold, then dusky red" (PS 342). The political implications of the scene are evident in the quasi-fascist form of the salute to Ramón. The religious implications for the established Christian order are made clear in the ensuing scene, in which Ramón's estranged wife, Carlota, interrupts the ritual, praying hysterically, "Almighty God, take his life from him, and save his soul," then dies herself in what seems to be intended as the shuddering death rattle of Christianity. "The Omnipotent," Ramón has told her, "is with me, and I serve Omnipotence!" (PS 343). The power of the Christian Trinity has been broken, and in its place stands a divinely sanctioned quaternity, which resolves itself first into the new trinity of body, spirit, and soul, then into the circle of the integrated self. The silver mixing bowl in Ramón's dark communion becomes, in effect, the retort or alchemical vessel out of which the "new bird" will emerge.

In chapter 22, Cipriano is initiated into godhead as "The Living Huitzilopochtli." Ramón has already asserted, in an open letter calling on the Roman Catholic clergy to join the Quetzalcoatl movement, "The final mystery is one mystery. But the manifestations are many." Hence, they will not be forsaking either their faith or God but embracing a larger catholicism in which different peoples approach God in response to his local manifestation, which in Mexico must be "in a blanket and in huaraches" *(PS* 360). Cipriano has prepared himself for the ordination by the religious discipline of primitive dancing, naked except for a black breechcloth and Indian body paint.

In the ordination ritual, Ramón successively closes with his hands the six dynamic centers of consciousness in Cipriano's body: eyes, breast, navel, loins, knees, and ankles. Each touch is correlated with formulaic question and response in liturgical dialogue—"Is it dark?" "Who lives?"—after which Ramón binds the designated center with black fur and moves ritualistically to the next. Cipriano remains motionless "in the dark, living warmth" as the darkness slowly moves over his consciousness, "to a centre that plunges into the bottomless depth, like sleep" *(PS* 367). (This scene is discussed in another context in chapter 7.) William York Tindall, who thinks this ceremony is modeled roughly on James M. Pryse's description of initiation rituals concerned with "the control of Kundalini, the serpent coiled at the base of the spine," comments superciliously that "the theosophist, knowing that Hindus and Aztecs are of one primitive faith, could not but be pleased with Lawrence's discovery."[16] If so, it is worth noting that the movement through the Laurentian equivalent of the chakras is not upward but downward, so that the stages through which Cipriano passes do not represent progressive enlightenment but progressive descent into the self in darkness.

A clue to Lawrence's meaning may be found in a statement in "Fenimore Cooper's Anglo-American Novels," written two years before *Psychoanalysis and the Unconscious* and a decade before *Apocalypse:*

> We can only begin to understand the initiation into the religious mysteries, such as the Eleusinian mysteries, when we can grasp the rise of pre-cerebral consciousness in the great plexuses, and the movement of passional or dynamic cognition from one centre to another, toward culmination in what we may call whole-experience, or whole-consciousness.
>
> It is quite certain that the pre-Christian priesthoods understood the processes of *dynamic* consciousness, which is pre-cerebral consciousness. It is certain that St. John gives us in the Apocalypse a cypher-account of the process of the con-

16. Tindall, *D. H. Lawrence and Susan His Cow,* 155–56.

quest of the lower or sensual dynamic centres by the upper or spiritual dynamic consciousness, a conquest affected centre by centre, towards a culmination in the *actual* experience of spiritual infinitude. This account is of scientific exactitude. [*SM* 69]

The ritual Ramón employs in the initiation of Cipriano is clearly intended to reverse the process that Lawrence thinks St. John describes.

On the evidence of chapter 23, "Huitzilopochtli's Night," the most immediate effect of godhead on Cipriano is to release his lust for the exercise of authoritarian power. The purity of motive by which Ramón dedicated his movement to being "masters among men," not "masters of men," deteriorates into Cipriano's considerably less noble proclamation, "The Lords of Life are the Masters of Death" (*PS* 380), which rationalizes his extralegal abrogation of life and death authority over others. Whatever the prisoners' guilt may be, their foreordained sentence of death is pronounced in the sadistic drama of a kangaroo court, not within the safeguards of due process in a legally constituted court. Cipriano's summary execution of five prisoners while releasing another on nothing more than the luck of the draw in the cruel leaf-drawing scene, far from extending the pardon of Malintzi as Cipriano pretends, only reinforces his autocratic power by demonstrating its functional basis in whim. On a signal from Cipriano, the guards garrot the two "grey dogs" who had conspired in the attack on Jamiltepec and consign their bodies to quicklime. In an updating of Aztec sacrifice, without the Aztecs' religious motive of replenishing the sun's energy, Cipriano stabs the other three to the heart and has their bodies laid at the foot of the Quetzalcoatl idol in the church. Ramón's acceptance of the bodies in an elaborate ritual to provide religious sanction for the murders reveals how far his own religious vision has declined.

Earlier in the novel, the narrator refers to the Mexican have-nots' "ever-recurring, fathomless lust of resentment, a demonish hatred of life itself," leading to sadistic killing as a preferred alternative to heterosexual sex: "Then, the instriking thud of a heavy knife, stabbing into a living body, this is the best. No lust of women can equal that lust. The clutching throb of gratification as the knife strikes in and the blood spurts out!" (*PS* 135). The passage echoes Jack Callcott's declaration in *Kangaroo* that "*nothing* bucks you up sometimes like killing a man—*nothing*": "Having a woman's something, isn't it? But it's a flea-bite, nothing, compared to killing your man when your blood comes up" (*K* 326). That this kind of sadistic, homoerotic displacement is relatively common in war does not lessen its perversity.

Lawrence's favorable presentation of the killing of the prisoners indicates the extent to which his own insights on sadistic human lust have been modified in the decade since he wrote to the pacifist Bertrand Russell, "What you want is to jab and strike, like the soldier with the bayonet, only you are sublimated into words. And you are like a soldier who might jab man after man with his bayonet, saying 'this is for ultimate peace'. . . . You are satisfying in an indirect, false way your lust to jab and strike" (*Letters* 2:392).

In chapter 24, "Malintzi," Kate observes: "When Cipriano said: *Man that is man is more than a man,* he seemed to be driving the male significance to its utmost, and beyond, into a sort of demonism. It seemed to her all terrible *will* . . ." (*PS* 387). Kate's ambivalence is marked: "spell-bound, but not utterly acquiescent," she recognizes that in the executions Cipriano and Ramón "did deliberately what they did" (*PS* 387). Lawrence's many strictures against will and instrumentality throughout his canon echo in her recognition of the meaning of their abrogation to themselves of "[t]he will of God": "At the centre of all things, a dark momentous Will sending out its terrific rays and vibrations, like some vast octopus. And at the other end of the vibration, men, created men, erect in the dark potency, answering Will with will, like gods or demons" (*PS* 387). Because this "terrible interchange" of potency with the deity leaves woman out of account except as "the soft lode-stone to magnetise his blade of steel" (*PS* 388), Kate knows that Cipriano will never recognize the "tiny star of her very self": "To him, she was but the answer to his call, the sheath for his blade, the cloud to his lightning, the earth to his rain, the fuel to his fire" (*PS* 388). Thus, the godhead offered to Kate, Malintzi, named for Malinche, the Aztec woman who became the mistress of Cortés and delivered her people to the conquistadors, can only confirm the halfness of her position as a subordinate in the strictly male hierarchy.

Cipriano's insistence that it takes a man and a woman to make one soul is related to Lawrence's conception of the soul as a flame that reconciles opposites. It also has the alchemical meaning of "[s]quaring . . . the circle to make the two sexes one whole." Jung quotes the *Rosarium:* " 'Out of man and woman make a round circle and extract the quadrangle from this and from the quadrangle the triangle. Make a round circle and you will have the philosophers' stone' " (12:122). In alchemical terms, the reason Ramón needs both a man and a woman for his pantheon is to personify his own bisexual attributes as Mercurius: Cipriano and Kate must fulfill their roles as Sol and Luna in the marriage of red and white. Insisting that he cannot be "the living Huitzilopochtli" without her to be Malintzi, Cipriano takes her to the darkened church, where their obeisance followed by sexual intercourse before the idol of Huitzilopochtli is presented as the performance of a suprapersonal ritual. Alchemically, the scene is the equivalent of the *coniunctio* or *coitus*. But the cost of assuming a mythic role is the degradation of individual character. Formerly, Kate has been presented as a morally and psychologically vital character, capable of independent thought and judgment, who is revolted by the carnage of the bullring and the brutality of the attack on Jamiltepec. Afterward, even in reference to Cipriano's killings, Kate shrugs: "Why should I judge him? He is of the gods" (*PS* 394).

When Ramón suddenly, two months after Carlota's death, takes a new wife, Teresa, the twenty-eight-year-old daughter of a neighboring *hacendado,* Kate sees her somewhat condescendingly as "the harem type." Although Kate is an independent woman of the world, she is made to learn her lessons from the smugly submissive Teresa, who thinks that Kate's Irish revolutionary husband had wanted to die because she had not given him her soul. When Kate says that Joachim had wanted her to have a soul of her own, Teresa replies with the smugness of the true believer: "Ah, yes, men are like that, when they are merely men" (*PS* 412). Kate still resists full commitment to the Quetzalcoatl movement. When Ramón wants to write the Song of Malintzi, she cries quickly, "Don't do that!" (*PS* 402). Later she asks Ramón if it is worth it to be "the living Quetzalcoatl," "if it isn't better to be just a man" (*PS* 407).

Whatever else the phrase may mean, "man that is more than a man" suggests that Ramón fills a larger-than-individual role. Uniting in himself the attributes of body, spirit, and soul (12:306n), he is both the Mercurius of alchemy and the artifex who effects the transformation. "The change has to be made," he tells Kate. "And some man has to make it" (*PS* 407). Jung's comments on the figure of Mercurius are instructive:

> Mercurius stands at the beginning and end of the work: he is the *prima materia,* the *caput corvi,* the *nigredo;* as dragon he devours himself and as dragon he dies, to rise again as the *lapis.* He is the play of colours in the *cauda pavonis* and the division into four elements. He is the hermaphrodite that was in the beginning, that splits into the traditional brother-sister duality and is reunited in the *coniunctio,* to appear once again at the end in the radiant form of the *lumen novum,* the stone. He is metallic yet liquid, matter yet spirit, cold yet fiery,

poison and yet healing draught—a symbol uniting all opposites. [12:281–82]

If Ramón's emergence as the living stone, reconciling within the self a series of fundamental antinomies, is arguable in view of the contradictions that remain, his ability to effect a similar transformation in others is even less clear. His original purpose, of course, was never to shape those around him to the mold of his own imposed will. "Quetzalcoatl is just a living word, for these people, no more," Ramón says. "All I want them to do is to find the beginnings of the way to their own manhood, their own womanhood" (*PS* 209). "Yet," as Graham Hough points out, "his ritual personifies Quetzalcoatl as a living, outward power."[17] The automatism of Ramón's followers, as in the ritualizing of the raised arm gesture of individual prayer into a collective salute to the leader, is as unthinking and automatic as the militarism of Cipriano's guards in ritualistically ratifying his killing of the prisoners. Other oppositions in Ramón's character finally appear not so much polarities held in "trembling balance" as direct contradictions of stated principles. Earlier Ramón, who fears that the Church will drive him closer to the socialists, who will only betray him, clearly recognizes the danger of allowing his movement "to acquire a political smell": "The surest way to kill it—and it can be killed, like any other living thing—is to get it connected with any political party" (*PS* 247). But after Ramón is excommunicated and makes common cause with the socialist government, President Montes declares "the old Church illegal in Mexico" and has a law passed establishing the Quetzalcoatl religion as the national religion (*PS* 420).

As the focal character of the novel, the "central intelligence" upon whose consciousness the development of the Quetzalcoatl movement is impressed, Kate intuitively understands the degree of will and abstraction behind the ostensibly instinctual religion. What is believable is not her commitment to the movement, which remains ambivalent and incomplete, but her involvement with Ramón and Cipriano, although this too is marked by contradictions: She is now "legally married to Cipriano" (*PS* 421), but continues to declare her intention to leave Mexico. Cipriano seems to her, in his naïve, boyish sexuality, "not a *will*" (*PS* 394); but she must acquiesce in his requirement that she forego the presumably clitoral orgasms that she had found so satisfying with her second husband, Joachim (*PS* 422). Aware of her own duality, Kate cannot "definitely commit herself,

17. Hough, *The Dark Sun*, 127.

either to the old way of life, or to the new": "The old was a prison. . . .
But in the new way she was not her own mistress at all . . ." (*PS*
429). She accuses Ramón of paralyzing her will to prevent her leaving, but he replies: "We must not do that" (*PS* 429). Even though, to
him, her going would represent a turning back, she must be left free
to arrive at her autonomous decision in her own good time. Her final
words, in the last line of the novel, reflect her continuing struggle:
"You won't let me go!" (*PS* 444).

How is this ambivalent ending to be understood? Horace Gregory
comments: "The half gods of Mexico cannot bring to full birth the
conversion of a single white woman."[18] L. D. Clark concludes that
"the final revision shows Kate staying on, magnetised by Cipriano
and Ramón, but still somewhat sceptical of their vision of the future."[19] Literally speaking, as the book ends, Kate neither goes nor
stays. The reader may speculate, but her decision lies outside the
novel. At the crucial point, Lawrence resists the temptation to stabilize the "trembling balance" by nailing it down. Lawrence's commitment to the open form of the novel determined that his ending
should be presented as part of an ongoing process that reflects the
final irresolution.

While the book is not framed as an allegory, the imagery has a
discernible alchemical pattern, which in this section parallels the
fourth stage of the alchemical process: the element, fire; the color,
red; the quality, hot; the character, sanguine; the rituals, marriage,
dark communion, and ordination; the process, reconciliation; the
form of Mercurius, self; the prevailing theme, transformation. The
alchemical opus theoretically culminates with "projection" in the
showing forth of the phoenix. But in the final chapters of *The
Plumed Serpent*, it is difficult to discern in Kate the transformation
of self that could be characterized as a phoenix epiphany. Even this
failure to reach projection ironically parallels the repeated failures
of the alchemical work. Observing that "in fact, all the attempts
were useless," Wayne Shumaker comments, "in so far as the occult
practices 'work' they do so only subjectively and therefore depend on
self-delusion."[20]

For Lawrence, the subjective, properly understood, led not to self-
delusion but to the insight that made resilience and change possible.
Lawrence's subsequent rejection of the heroic militaristic leadership
ideal of *The Plumed Serpent* (*CL* 1045) applies by extension to the

18. Gregory, *D. H. Lawrence: Pilgrim of the Apocalypse*, 73.
19. Clark, "Introduction" to Lawrence, *The Plumed Serpent*, xl.
20. Shumaker, 165, 198.

religious rituals that provide its propagandistic base. Significantly when genuine emergence occurs in his subsequent novels, it is not inculcated by occult rituals or metaphorical alchemy. It is brought about, as chapters 11 and 12 attempt to show, by inward visionary experience leading to personal growth and change in human sexual relationship in *Lady Chatterley's Lover* and by the demythologizing of traditional Christianity put in creative balance with the Osiris myth to define metaphorically Lawrence's religion of the blood in *The Escaped Cock*.

11

Lawrence, Joyce, and Epiphany in
Lady Chatterley's Lover

In immediate experiential terms, creative change in Lawrence's fiction is initiated more frequently by visionary experience than by ritual. While touch, because it is unconsciously driven, often has an irrevocably binding effect in Lawrence's writings, revelation and recognition, like Joyce's epiphanies, usually come with the impact of sudden, conscious, visual perception. In Lawrence's work, such revelations, even when framed as religious or aesthetic insights, occur as vital experiences in the immediate present rather than as static, timeless illuminations. Because they represent, in the terms of the central concept of this study, a dynamic "trembling balance" rather than an aesthetic or abstract stasis, they can foster resilience, enabling the character to give up an outmoded psychological homeostasis in order to create a new one that engenders growth and change.

D. H. Lawrence and James Joyce never met, but they read and despised each other's work. Their mutual dislike sprang in part from their commitment to contrasting theories of literary art. They represent opposing tendencies in modernism that are clearly visible in their differing treatments of the epiphanic scene.

For a writer who had experienced so many censorship problems himself, Lawrence was surprisingly uncritical in echoing the popular charge of obscenity against Joyce's *Ulysses*. Dorothy Brett reports a conversation in Taos in 1924 in which Frieda's calculated statement that *Ulysses* "is a wonderful book" provoked the predictable, vehement response from Lawrence: "The last part of it is the dirtiest, most indecent, obscene thing ever written. Yes it is, Frieda. . . . It is filthy."[1]

Lawrence had written to his American publisher, Thomas Seltzer (22 September 1922 and 7 October 1922), asking to borrow a copy of *Ulysses* (*Letters* 4:306 and 320). An acquaintance of Seltzer's, F. Wubbenhorst, sent the book to Lawrence, who returned it to him (14 November 1922) with a note admitting his inability to read *Ulysses* except in bits, but commenting that "in Europe they usually mention us together—James Joyce and D. H. Lawrence—and I feel I ought to know in what company I creep to immortality." Lawrence adds perceptively, "I guess Joyce would look as much askance on me as I on him. We make a choice of Paola and Francesca floating down the winds of hell" (*Letters* 4:340). Later he tells Seltzer (28 November 1922): "*Ulysses* wearied me: so like a schoolmaster with dirt and stuff in his head: sometimes good, though: but too mental" (*Letters* 4:345) But a few days later (5 December 1922), he writes to Seltzer: "Do you really want to publish my James Joyce remarks? No, I don't think it's quite fair to him" (*Letters* 4:355).

After Lawrence read a section of Joyce's *Work in Progress*,[2] he wrote to Aldous and Maria Huxley (15 August 1928): "My God, what a clumsy *olla putrida* James Joyce is! Nothing but old fags and cabbage-stumps of quotations from the Bible and the rest, stewed in the juice of deliberate, journalistic dirty-mindedness—what old and hard-worked staleness, masquerading as the all-new!" (*CL* 1075). He repeated the judgment in a letter to Earl Brewster on the same date (*CL* 1076). And he told Harry Crosby, whose Black Sun Press published both Lawrence's *Sun* (unexpurgated ed., 1926) and Joyce's *Tales Told of Shem and Shaun* (1928), "James Joyce bores me stiff— too terribly would-be and done-on-purpose, utterly without spontaneity or real life" (*CL* 1087). Lawrence thought Giovanni Verga a better writer. Although Verga's style "gives at first the sense of jumble and incoherence" in an effort to convey the "muddled" thought processes of the peasant mind, Lawrence says, "He is doing, as a great artist, what men like James Joyce do only out of contrariness and desire for sensation" (*P* 250). Lawrence's remark to Compton Mackenzie, "This *Ulysses* muck is more disgusting than Casanova. I

---

1. Brett, *Lawrence and Brett*, 81.
2. Lawrence read the section of Joyce's *Work in Progress* that became, with revisions, *Finnegans Wake*, III, ii, in *transition*, no. 13 (Summer 1928): 5–32.

must show that it can be done without muck," suggests that on one level *Lady Chatterley's Lover* may be read as a corrective to Joyce's book.[3]

The clue to Lawrence's dislike for Joyce is his repeated use of words like "would-be" and "sensation," terms that in Lawrence's criticism usually mean overconscious and deliberate, mechanical and inorganic. That is why he categorizes Joyce among the modern novelists whose "dominant note is the repulsiveness, intimate physical repulsiveness of human flesh" (*P* 270). It is also why he ridiculed the stream-of-consciousness novelists for "the death-rattle in their throats," for "dying in a very long-drawn-out fourteen-volume death-agony, and absorbedly, childishly interested in the phenomenon. 'Did I feel a twinge in my little toe, or didn't I?' asks every character in Mr Joyce or Miss Richardson or Monsieur Proust" (*STH* 151).

On his part, Joyce returned the ill opinion in repeated condescension toward Lawrence's work. In one letter he mockingly calls Lawrence's book *"Lady Chatterbox's Lover,"* and in a later letter says of *"Lady Chatterli's* [*sic*] *Lover"*: "I read the first 2 pages of the usual sloppy English which is a piece of propaganda in favour of something which, outside of D.H.L.'s country at any rate, makes all the propaganda for itself."[4] Joyce's derisive parodies of Lawrence's title convey the same sort of judgment (or misjudgment) as Lawrence's derisive parody of the stream-of-consciousness character's obsession with his own sensations. But the real clue to Joyce's judgment of Lawrence is his charge against *Lady Chatterley's Lover* of "propaganda," an accusation related to Stephen Dedalus's declaration, in chapter 5 of *A Portrait of the Artist as a Young Man,* that "pornographical or didactic" arts, which excite "kinetic" feelings of "desire or loathing," are "improper arts."[5] As Richard Ellmann comments,

3. The question of the impact of *Ulysses* on Lawrence's novel is argued persuasively by Jackson, in *"Lady Chatterley's Lover:* Lawrence's Response to *Ulysses?,"* 410–16. Lawrence's remark to Mackenzie is quoted in Compton Mackenzie, *My Life and Times, Octave Five,* 167. Mackenzie contends, in *On Moral Courage,* that Lawrence, "gnawed by jealousy," wanted to show that he could use words as boldly as Joyce but in a purifying rather than corrupting freedom (118), in order to snatch Bloomsbury's laurel wreaths from Joyce's head (135–36).

4. The two letters, both to Harriet Shaw Weaver, dated respectively 27 September 1930 and 17 December 1931, are in *Letters of James Joyce,* 1:294, 309. For a defense of the first two pages of *Lady Chatterley's Lover,* see the unsigned review "A Man in His Senses," *Times Literary Supplement* (London), 4 November 1960, 708. The author calls these pages "exemplary" and the novel "an extremely deliberated work."

5. Joyce, *A Portrait of the Artist as a Young Man,* 205; hereafter cited parenthetically in the text as *Portrait.*

Joyce "was anxious that his books should not commit propaganda, even against institutions of which he disapproved."[6]

Yet both Joyce and Lawrence employed scenes of the type that Joyce called "epiphany" and Lawrence called "visionary experience," although they arrived at these scenes by different routes and from opposing theoretical positions. The theory set forth in *A Portrait of the Artist* is a classical, mimetic view in which "the esthetic emotion" "arrests the mind" because "the tragic emotion is static. . . . The mind is arrested and raised above desire and loathing." "Beauty expressed by the artist," Stephen declares, "cannot awaken in us an emotion which is kinetic or a sensation which is purely physical." Rather, it should awaken or induce "an esthetic stasis, an ideal pity or an ideal terror, a stasis called forth, prolonged and at last dissolved by what I call the rhythm of beauty" (*Portrait* 204–6).

Lawrence recognized the validity of classical theory for certain types of literature. His statement in "Poetry of the Present" that the "poetry of the beginning and the poetry of the end" have a "finality" and a "perfection" "conveyed in exquisite form" fits Joyce's aesthetic theory and practice. "But," Lawrence suggests, "there is another kind of poetry: the poetry of that which is at hand: the immediate present. In the immediate present there is no perfection, no consummation, nothing finished. The strands are all flying, quivering, intermingling into the web, the waters are shaking the moon. . . . If we try to fix the living tissue, as the biologists fix it with formalin, we have only a hardened bit of the past, the bygone life under our observation" (*CP* 181–83).

Joyce in *A Portrait of the Artist* and Lawrence in "Art and the Individual" set forth the theories in which their views of art are rooted, although both go beyond these theories in their artistic practice. Stephen Dedalus's celebrated aesthetic theory in the fifth chapter of *A Portrait of the Artist* is drawn, of course, from the teachings of Saint Thomas Aquinas on the three principles required for beauty, "*integritas, consonantia, claritas*," which Stephen translates as "*wholeness, harmony and radiance*," qualities that, he believes, "correspond to the phases of apprehension." The "synthesis of immediate perception," as the object is first seen as a unified image, "self-bounded and selfcontained" against the background of all that is not it (*integritas*), is followed by the "analysis of apprehension," as the image is seen to be "complex, multiple, divisible, separable, made up of its parts, the result of its parts and their sum" (*consonantia*). Finally, having rejected as "literary talk" the idea that

6. Ellmann, "On Joyce's Centennial," 29.

radiance is "the artistic discovery and representation of the divine purpose" or universality of the object, Stephen concludes that having perceived the object's wholeness and having analyzed its form, "you make the only synthesis which is logically and esthetically permissible. You see that it is that thing which it is and no other thing" (*claritas*), which Stephen takes to be identical with "the scholastic *quidditas*, the *whatness* of a thing" (*Portrait* 212–13).

In "Art and the Individual," a youthful essay of the Croydon period, Lawrence's concept of "two schools of aesthetic thought," the intellectual and mystic school and the emotional and material school, prefigures his later theory of the two kinds of poetry, that of the beginning and the end and that of "the immediate present." In the first, "Beauty is the expression of the perfect and divine *Idea*." In the second, "Art is an activity . . . springing from sexual desire and propensity to play—and it is accompanied by pleasurable excitement." In Lawrence's interpretation, "Harmony is the name we give to a certain emotional state roused by certain blended components" (*STH* 139). "The delight of form in art is said to be largely physical. The movement of the eye is grateful and pleasing along certain curves" (*STH* 142). Despite his differences from Joyce, Lawrence's definition of *harmony*, in the first version of this essay, using the example of a swan, as approval of "the silken whiteness, the satisfying curve of line and mass" (*STH* 226), is compatible with Stephen Dedalus's definition of *consonantia* as the "analysis" that follows *integritas* as "you pass from point to point, led by [the object's] . . . formal lines; you apprehend it as balanced part against part within its limits; you feel the rhythm of its structure" (*Portrait* 212). But whereas Joyce relies on Aristotle and Aquinas, Lawrence's idea of art depends on Johan Friedrich Herbart's "classification of interests," from which Lawrence arrives at categories according to the source of the interest and arranges these in ascending order from the concrete to the universal (empirical, speculative, aesthetic, sympathetic, social, religious) (*STH* 136–37). "Remark how the scale of Interests rises," Lawrence says, "The Aesthetic and the Religious are the highest in their two groups" (*STH* 138). The aesthetic image in Lawrence's work may be seen as incorporating all six planes on ascending levels of experience. To these six interests he "humbly" adds a seventh: "action—doing something" (*STH* 137). In the essay Lawrence gives no example of the kinetic effects of art, but the position of "action" on his scale of interests is roughly comparable to "stasis" in Joyce's aesthetics.

Before turning to Lawrence's visionary scenes and images, I want to consider first the distinguishing characteristics of what Joyce

called epiphany, then some types of literary epiphany. Joyce originally used the term to refer to the genre of some seventy short prose
pieces he wrote between 1900 and 1904, recording actual experiences and moods.[7]

As Joyce explains Stephen Dedalus's use of the term in *Stephen
Hero,* "By an epiphany he meant a sudden spiritual manifestation,
whether in the vulgarity of speech or of gesture or in a memorable
phase of the mind itself. He believed that it was for the man of
letters to record these epiphanies with extreme care, seeing that
they themselves are the most delicate and evanescent of moments."[8]
This statement is clearly the source of Morris Beja's definition of
epiphany as a "sudden spiritual manifestation, whether from some
object, scene, event, or memorable phase of the mind—the manifestation being out of proportion to the significance or strictly logical
relevance of whatever produces it."[9] Dorothy Van Ghent refers to
Joyce's epiphanies as "[t]hose moments in the dialectical process
when a synthesis is achieved, when certain phrases or sensations or
complex experiences suddenly cohere in a larger whole and a meaning shines forth from the whole. . . . The epiphany is an image, sensu-
ously apprehended and emotionally vibrant, which communicates
instantaneously the meaning of experience."[10] In a critical exchange
with Robert Scholes, Florence Walzl comments that "the term *epiphany* has several meanings in current Joyce criticism. It may refer to
an early prose type, to a spiritual and intellectual illumination of
the nature of a thing, and also, by extension, to the artistic insights
and means by which such a revelation is achieved."[11] George Ford,
recognizing Lawrence's widespread use of the technique in presenting the effect of the transforming experience on the beholder, sees
the essential quality of his epiphanies as intensification by the juxta-
position of contrasting elements: light and darkness, love and hate,
life and death.[12] Whereas Beja barely mentions Lawrence, Ann
Shealy treats Lawrence's epiphanies in light of the second and third
meanings of the term as given by Walzl.[13]

7. Forty extant examples of these epiphanies are published by Scholes and Kain, in
The Workshop of Daedalus. Joyce, *Epiphanies,* earlier presented twenty-two epiphanies from the manuscripts in the Lockwood Memorial Library. Scholes and Kain re-
print these and add eighteen others from the Mennen Collection at Cornell University.

8. Joyce, *Stephen Hero,* 188.

9. Beja, *Epiphany in the Modern Novel,* 18.

10. Van Ghent, "On *A Portrait of the Artist,*" in *The English Novel,* 268.

11. Walzl, in an exchange with Scholes, "The Epiphanies of Joyce," 153.

12. Ford, *Double Measure,* 94–96.

13. Shealy, "Epiphany Theme in Modern Fiction," in *The Passionate Mind,* 3–27.

Irene Hendry Chayes, in her seminal essay "Joyce's Epiphanies," correctly observes that "the epiphany is not peculiar to Joyce alone":

> Virtually every writer experiences a sense of revelation when he beholds a fragment of his ordinary world across . . . 'psychic distance'—dissociated from his subjective and practical concerns, fraught with meaning beyond itself, with every detail of its physical appearance relevant. It is a revelation quite as valid as the religious; in fact, from our present secular viewpoint, it perhaps would be more accurate to say that the revelation of the religious mystic is actually an esthetic revelation into which the mystic projects himself—as a participant, not merely as an observer and recorder—and to which he assigns a source, an agent and an end, called God. What Joyce did was give systematic formulation to a common esthetic experience, so common that few others—writers, if not estheticians—have thought it worth considering for its own sake.[14]

Where Lawrence is concerned, the question is not the presence in his work of revelatory experience of this kind but the breadth of the "psychic distance" across which such fragments of ordinary experience are seen in the transforming light. There is no need to rehearse Chayes's whole discussion of Joyce's work. Indeed, only two types of epiphany she discusses are in accord with Lawrence's practice.[15]

In one type, "although *claritas* is ultimately generated by *quidditas,* we are first aware of an effect on the beholder—Stephen, or ourselves through Stephen—not of an objectively apprehensible quality in the thing revealed." For Joyce this method may have been regressive when seen against his aesthetic goal of refining the artist's personality out of existence, but it had the advantage, Chayes says, "of realizing the three principles, *integritas, consonantia,* and *claritas,* in a single image" (209). For Lawrence, whose third-person narratives often center in the consciousness of a focal character, this method is predominant, especially in scenes that emphasize the importance of a visionary experience in the character's education into instinctual or sensual being. Examples of this type of epiphanic

---

14. Chayes, "Joyce's Epiphanies," 206; hereafter cited in the text as "Chayes."

15. Two of Chayes's types of epiphany are largely irrelevant to Lawrence's work: the achievement of *claritas* "through an apparently trivial incident, action, or single detail which differs from the others . . . only in that it illuminates them, and gives them meaning"; and the emergence of *claritas* from *quidditas* as "character is sacrificed to the *integritas* of the esthetic image," which resynthesizes the generalities of the individual.

scene include Ursula Brangwen's encounter with the horses near the end of *The Rainbow,* her recognition of the meaning of Gerald Crich's brutal subjugation of the Arab mare and of Rupert Birkin's stoning of the moon's reflection in *Women in Love,* and Lou Witt's vision of the "mysterious fire" of St. Mawr's body in *St. Mawr.*

In the other type, *quidditas* has the function "to identify rather than to abstract." The character, "broken down into its separate parts," is then reduced to an image associated with him. "Only one or two of the detached 'parts'—'the vulgarity of speech or of gesture,' . . . a detail of figure or expression, an item of clothing"—are recombined to create the individual *quidditas,* a technique that "represents the ultimate in 'objective' characterization, 'revealing' an individual essence by means of a detail or an object to which it has a fortuitous relation"; for example, Father Dolan's pandybat or Mr. Casey's "three cramped fingers." Through this "epiphany technique (in which *claritas* is a tiny, perfunctory flash, all but absorbed by *quidditas*) we can trace out a virtual iconography of the characters, like the systematic recurrence of emblems and attitudes among the figures in sacred art" (Chayes 216–18).

There are emblems aplenty in Lawrence—Will Brangwen's phoenix butter-mold, Count Dionys's ladybird, Ramón Carrasco's "eye of Quetzalcoatl," or even Anna Brangwen's gargoyle faces, Ursula's rainbow, and Aaron Sisson's flute. But these deliberate emblems, except perhaps for the last one, are not the same as the metonymic images with which Joyce's characters have a "fortuitous relation." A nearer example in Lawrence can be found in the clothes imagery by which characters throughout his work are defined—William Morel's collar, Gudrun Brangwen's stockings, Gerald Crich's elegant robe, Hermione Roddice's feathered hat.[16] But this epiphany technique is perhaps most evident in the close association Lawrence evokes between a character and an image that clearly objectifies his essential quality as a human being—Henry Grenfel and the fox, Jill Banford and the dead tree, or Sir Clifford Chatterley and the motorized wheelchair. Lawrence's identification of character with iconographic image, however, cannot often be called the "ultimate" in objectivity. It must be said also that his insight is never a "perfunctory flash" of meaning absorbed in the "whatness" of the object, but a clear metaphorical statement in which the image, rather than merely "standing for" the character, is so interpenetrated with his essential quality that it effectively becomes him: Sir Clifford's motorized chair *is* his very being.

16. See Hinz, "D. H. Lawrence's Clothes Metaphor," 87–113.

Both Joyce and Lawrence employ epiphanic scenes to present ideas by means of revelation rather than by thematic statement. But because Lawrence's narrative technique involves more discursive statements about the characters and less aesthetic or psychic distance from them than is typical of Joyce, Lawrence has not often been described an as epiphanic writer. Dorothy Van Ghent comments that "[t]he major epiphanies" in *A Portrait of the Artist* "occur as the symbolic climaxes of the larger dialectical movements constituting each of the five chapters." She cites Hugh Kenner's suggestion that out of initially "warring impressions," "each develops toward an emotionally apprehended unity; each succeeding chapter liquidates the previous synthesis and subjects its elements to more adult scrutiny in a constantly enlarging field of perception and develops toward its own synthesis and affirmation."[17] While Connie's perception develops in a similar process of growth, destroying an outworn homeostasis in order to affirm a new synthesis, Lawrence's chapters are not organized aesthetically in the Joycean manner and his epiphanies do not have quite the same narrative function. The first three chapters of *Lady Chatterley's Lover,* written from the point of view of an assumed narrator relating a general history, lack the artistic objectivity necessary to the Joycean epiphanic style. Rather, the technique corresponds to Stephen Dedalus's definition of the "epical form" (*Portrait* 214), mediating between artist and reader through the narrative point of view. But the scenes present what usually happens in the ongoing relationship, and the potential for epiphanic distillation inherent in the dramatic situation and a few concrete details is undercut by Lawrence's inveterate explanations. In contrast, the opening chapter of *A Portrait of the Artist,* although it also has an expository function, is fully visualized, concrete, specific, and not interpreted by a narrator.

It would be a mistake to claim more for Lawrence's epiphanic mode than the text can support. In chapter 4 of *Lady Chatterley* the discussion of the "mental lifers" who visit Wragby parallels in several ways that of the Christmas-dinner scene in chapter 1 of *A Portrait of the Artist.* Both involve a dramatic situation in which a group of people, family and visitors, engage in a lively discussion that is registered on the perceiving consciousness of one member of the family (Stephen and Connie) who takes little part in the discussion but whose perceptions of the discussants and the issues involved motivate a change in the observer. Whereas Joyce uses Mr. Casey's "three cramped fingers" as an epiphanic identification of his char-

17. Van Ghent, 270.

acter, Lawrence, in his brief sketch of the Wragby visitors, associates the first two with institutional abstractions—Tommy Dukes with the army, Charles May with the science of the stars—only in the case of Arnold B. Hammond identifying and distilling the character by means of an epiphanic image: "a tall thin fellow with a wife and two children, but much more closely connected with a typewriter" (*LCL* 34). Joyce's judgment of Dante Riordan for the narrowness of her religious politics in supporting the Irish clergy even in their treatment of Parnell is clear if unstated. Similarly, when Tommy Dukes compares the sexual and property instincts in terms of the "craving for self-assertion and success," when Charles May speaks of sex as "just an interchange of sensations instead of ideas" (*LCL* 34–35), or when Arnold Hammond, in Graham Holderness's phrase, "equates sexual emotions with excretory functions,"[18] Lawrence's judgment of them is clear.

The violent rhetoric of the Christmas-dinner scene in *A Portrait of the Artist* brings to vivid life the "nets" of family, church, and nation that the soul of the youthful artist will later determine to "fly by." The ostensibly intellectual conversation of the "mental lifers" in *Lady Chatterley* embodies, in its emotional vacuity and its desperate wit, the triviality and deadness that the instinctual self, in order to live at all, will have to escape. Joyce maintains Stephen's point of view throughout; the epiphanic experience is registered on his consciousness from the beginning to the end of the scene, when "Stephen, raising his terrorstricken face, saw that his father's eyes were full of tears" (*Portrait* 39). Lawrence begins in a general, historical perspective, moves to a concrete dramatization, and brings the potential for epiphanic insight to the surface by returning increasingly to Connie's point of view. The reader of both scenes is conscious not so much of "meaning" as of an "effect" registered on an observer. Connie says nothing at first but "put another stitch in her sewing" (*LCL* 38), an ironic link with the faithful Penelope, since Connie's thoughts reveal her real attitude of contempt for both the "suitors" and the returned soldier husband. The men discuss Plato and Socrates, Bolshevism and capitalism, and the meaninglessness of sex. They ignore Connie's presence, but Lawrence does not let the reader forget that the scene is being played out on her consciousness. When Dukes speaks of Renoir's saying that "he painted his pictures with his penis" and confesses, "I wish I did something with mine. God! when one can only talk," Connie responds to his despair: "There are nice women in the world," thus revealing how closely she has been attending the conver-

18. Holderness, *Who's Who in D. H. Lawrence*, 49.

sation (*LCL* 44). Connie's disillusionment with this kind of mental life is comparable to the disillusionment with Irish patriotism motivated by Stephen Dedalus's experience of the Christmas-dinner scene. The potential for epiphany is inherent in the dawning realization of sterility and death that precede rebirth and growth, but it is not realized in the kind of objective synthesis that Stephen experiences or the revelation that Connie will experience later.

Chapter 5 of *Lady Chatterley* begins, appropriately, with an objective statement: "On a frosty morning with a little February sun, Clifford and Connie went for a walk across the park to the wood. That is, Clifford chuffed in his motor-chair, and Connie walked beside him" (*LCL* 45). The shift from the generalized historical perspective of the first three chapters to the dramatic scene of the fourth chapter and thence to the concrete narrative mode of the fifth establishes the necessary context not only for the contrast between Clifford and Mellors introduced in this chapter but also for several important epiphanic images.

One of these is the denuded knoll: "The chair chuffed slowly up the incline, rocking and jolting on the frozen clods. And suddenly, on the left, came a clearing where there was nothing but a ravel of dead bracken, a thin and spindling sapling leaning here and there, big sawn stumps showing their tops and their grasping roots, lifeless. And patches of blackness where the woodmen had burned the brushwood and rubbish" (*LCL* 46). The narrative explanation as Connie surveys the wasteland scene directs without stating the interpretation: "This was one of the places that Sir Geoffrey had cut during the war for trench timber. The whole knoll, which rose softly on the right of the riding, was denuded and strangely forlorn. On the crown of the knoll where the oaks had stood, now was bareness; and from there you could look out over the trees to the colliery railway, and the new works at Stacks Gate. Connie had stood and looked, it was a breach in the pure seclusion of the wood. It let in the world. But she didn't tell Clifford" (*LCL* 46). Considered in the light of the Fisher King motif in the novel, the war has caused both the sexual maiming of Clifford (the Fisher King) and the destruction of the phallic trees of Wragby (his kingdom): Both have been reduced to lifeless stumps. There is even an echo of T. S. Eliot's imagery: As in *The Waste Land,* where the question "What are the roots that clutch?" (line 19) is ultimately answered in "And other withered stumps of time" (line 104),[19] so in this passage from *Lady Chatterley's Lover* question and answer are combined in the image of "big sawn stumps

19. Eliot, *The Complete Poems and Plays,* 38, 40.

showing their tops and their grasping roots, lifeless." The explanation for this destruction lies, for Lawrence, in the war that followed
the rise of industry, which already encroached upon the landscape:
Sir Geoffrey had cut the trees "during the war for trench timber."
The progression of imagery leads as inevitably as the colliery train
to "the new works at Stacks Gate."

The denuded knoll is not only a symbolic image but an epiphanic
one as well, a self-contained microcosm of the waste land over which
Sir Clifford Chatterley presides, though its meaning is revealed at
different levels to the two observers. To Clifford, in anger, it conveys
the destruction by the War of a legacy of the heart of "the Old
England," which had been entrusted to the stewardship of his generation to keep inviolate. To Connie, in pathos, it is "a breach in the
pure seclusion of the wood," an assault on the private self and on
organic nature. That for both it is also linked with the destruction of
Clifford's potency is signaled by their conversation, in this context,
on Clifford's inability to sire a son and his suggestion that Connie
might have a child by another man. But the mechanistic quality of
Clifford's love of tradition and his wish for paternity is exposed by
the difference between his attitude and Connie's toward the prospect. "I don't believe very intensely in fatherhood," he says in a
Laurentian blasphemy,[20] and refers to the hypothetical heir as an
"it," not as a person. He does not think it matters much who the
father is. Connie, already an organicist, wonders "how could she
know what she would feel next year?" and says that while she agrees
with Clifford theoretically, "life may turn quite a new face on it all."
It is at this point, as if in response to Connie's prophetic statement,
that Oliver Mellors, the gamekeeper, emerges with his symbolic red
mustache, dark green velveteens, and phallic gun (*LCL* 48–51).

Another major epiphanic image introduced in this chapter is Clifford's motorized wheelchair. Clifford, who has chuffed into the wood in

20. This statement may be compared with one reported by Jessie Chambers, in
D. H. Lawrence: A Personal Record, 208: " 'Fatherhood's a myth,' Lawrence declared.
'There's nothing in it. . . . There's no such thing as fatherhood.' " In context, Lawrence
is commenting sardonically on the attitude of a friend (George Henry Neville) toward
the illegitimate child he had fathered (see Lawrence, *Letters* 1:373–74). In the background, too, is Lawrence's attitude toward his own father. That he places the negative
sentiment in the mouth of Clifford Chatterley instead of Mellors, who embodies many
of the positive qualities that Lawrence later found in his devalued father imago, is in
keeping with the change in attitude. Through Clifford, Lawrence is also rejecting a
side of himself that he finds shallow. As Frieda commented in 1955, "The terrible
thing about Lady C. is that L. identified himself with both Clifford and Mellors; that
took courage, that made me shiver, when I read it as he wrote it." (Frieda Lawrence,
Frieda Lawrence: The Memoirs and Correspondence, 389.)

the chair, calls to Mellors to "turn the chair round and get it started." Mellors, "curiously full of vitality, but a little frail and quenched," pushes "the chair up the steepish rise of the knoll in the park." Set in opposition to the wood, the chair symbolically embodies all of the forces that account for the denuding of the knoll (*LCL* 51–53).

The chair is the focal image in a recurrent pattern culminating in the long scene in chapter 13 in which the motor stalls and Mellors is again called to help. The mindless war of machine against nature is set forth in admirable, uninterpreted specificity as the chair puffs slowly on: "Connie, walking behind, had watched the wheels jolt over the wood-ruff and the bugle, and squash the little yellow cups of the creeping-jenny. Now they made a wake through the forget-me-nots." An epic simile presents the chair, "washed over with blue encroaching hyacinths," as the ship of Western civilization, and Clifford, with an ironic allusion to Whitman's Lincoln, as its mock-heroic captain: "Oh last of all ships, through the hyacinthian shallows! Oh pinnace on the last wild waters, sailing in the last voyage of our civilisation! Whither, Oh weird wheeled ship, your slow course steering! Quiet and complacent, Clifford sat at the wheel of adventure: in his old black hat and tweed jacket, motionless and cautious. Oh captain, my Captain, our splendid trip is done!" (*LCL* 220–21). The simile of the ship identifies the chair with Clifford's mines, for Mrs. Bolton has told him: "Oh, there's been some money made in Tevershall. And now the men say it's a sinking ship, and it's time they all got out. . . . It seems soon there'll be no use for men on the face of the earth, it'll be all machines" (*LCL* 123).

Throughout the novel, the chair is compared, sometimes directly, sometimes subtly, to Clifford's sexual being, which is held in contrast to that of the organicist Mellors, who confesses his incompetence "about these mechanical things." In chapter 13 (*LCL* 224–28), Lawrence employs a number of sexual double entendres. Clifford's attempts to force the wheelchair to go are compared to masturbation. Connie warns him, "You'll only break the thing down altogether, Clifford, . . . besides *wasting your nervous energy.*" Calling for Mellors to examine the motor, Clifford asks pointedly, "Have you looked at *the rods underneath?*" Grimly determined, "[Clifford] began *doing things* with his engine, running her fast and slow as if to get some sort of tune out of her. . . . Then he put her in gear with a jerk, having *jerked off* his brake." Use of the feminine pronoun to refer to the mechanism most closely associated with Clifford's phallic self suggests his feeling that his sexual being has become anomalous. Finally, he turns to the gamekeeper: " 'Do you mind *pushing her home,* Mellors!' he said in a cold, superior tone." The irony of the question escapes Clifford, but Lawrence does not allow it to escape the reader.[21] As Mellors pushes the wheelchair home, he takes Connie's wrist in a caress behind Clifford's back, and she bends to kiss Mellors's hand (*LCL* 230). Clifford is identified and defined throughout the novel by the metonymic image of the wheelchair, which is as much a part of Clifford as Mellors's penis is of Mellors. As an epiphanic image, this motorized chair distills his whole mechanistic being, a mechanical contrivance that he possesses instead of a self.

In chapter 6, Connie, walking in the old wood, from which comes "an ancient melancholy, somehow soothing to her" (*LCL* 74), comes upon the gamekeeper's cottage. Because the scene presents the major epiphany of the novel, I should like to quote it in full and to examine its development in Lawrence's conception:

> She turned the corner of the house and stopped. In the little yard two paces beyond her, the man was washing himself, utterly unaware. He was naked to the hips, his velveteen breeches slipping down over his slender loins. And his white slim back was curved over a big bowl of soapy water, in which he ducked his head, shaking his head with a queer, quick little motion, lifting his slender white arms, and pressing the soapy water from his ears, quick, subtle as a weasel playing with water, and utterly alone. Connie backed away round the corner of the house, and hurried away to the wood. In spite of herself, she had had a shock. After all, merely a man washing himself; commonplace enough, Heaven knows!
>
> Yet in some curious way it was a visionary experience: it had hit her in the middle of the body. She saw the clumsy breeches slipping down over the pure, delicate, white loins, the bones showing a little, and the sense of aloneness, of a creature purely alone, overwhelmed her. Perfect, white, solitary nudity of a creature that lives alone, and inwardly alone. And beyond that, a certain beauty of a pure creature. Not the stuff of beauty, not even the body of beauty, but a lambency, the warm, white flame of a single life, revealing itself in contours that one might touch: a body! [*LCL* 75–76]

---

21. The emphasis throughout this paragraph has been added to call attention to the thematic use of sexual puns employing slang usage current in Lawrence's day. See, for example, the definition "*[t]o jerk one's juice or jelly* (also *to jerk off*) = to masturbate," in Farmer and Henley, *Slang and Its Analogues*, 4:47 (abrgd. rprt., 243). See also Stoehr, " 'Mentalized Sex' in D. H. Lawrence," 101–22, which discusses Lawrence's attitude toward masturbation in the context of the sexual mores and literature of his time.

Lawrence's revisions of the scene in the three versions of the novel show clearly the evolution of his thinking. In *The First Lady Chatterley,* the epiphanic vision, although not so well-structured aesthetically, is interpreted directly as a showing forth of the god, a revelation of the "divine body." Having discovered Parkin with his shirt off washing himself, ducking his head in the water like an animal, Connie retires to the wood: "But in the dripping gloom of the forest, suddenly she started to tremble uncontrollably. The white torso of the man had seemed so beautiful to her, splitting the gloom. The white, firm, divine body with that silky firm skin! Never mind the man's face, with the fierce moustache and the resentful hard eyes! Never mind his stupid personality! His body in itself was divine, cleaving through the gloom like a revelation" (*FLC* 17).

In *John Thomas and Lady Jane,* the increased emphasis on beauty moves the second version of the scene closer to the Joycean conception of such an epiphany, but the intensification of emphasis on the divinity of the body shows that Lawrence's conception remains thoroughly religious rather than secular or aesthetic:

> The white torso of the man had seemed so beautiful to her, opening on the gloom. The white, firm, divine body, with its silky ripple, the white arch of life, as it bent forward over the water, seemed, she could not help it, of the world of the gods. There still was a world that gleamed pure and with power, where the silky firm skin of the man's body glistened broad upon the dull afternoon. Never mind who he was! never mind what he was! She had seen beauty, and beauty alive. That body was of the world of the gods, cleaving through the gloom like a revelation. And she felt again there was God on earth, or gods. [*JTLJ* 43–44]

The emphasis on power, divinity, and, in particular, the "gleaming whiteness" of the body suggests a biblical source that is appropriate to Lawrence's purpose. In the liturgical calendar, in addition to the feast of the Epiphany, which commemorates the visitation of the three wise men to the Christ child, there is another epiphanic feast day, the Transfiguration, which commemorates the event and the vision that took place when Jesus took the disciples Peter, James, and John up to a high mountain and was there, with Elijah and Moses, "transfigured before them": "And his raiment became shining, exceeding white as snow; so as no fuller on earth can white them" (Mark 9:3). Because "the broad, gleaming whiteness" of the man's body "had touched her soul," Connie cherishes the vision not merely as an aesthetic but as a transfigurative experience: "A great soothing came over her heart, along with the feeling of worship. The sudden sense of pure beauty, beauty that was active and alive, had put worship in her heart again. Not that she worshipped the man, nor his body. But worship had come into her, because she had seen a pure loveliness, that was alive, and that had touched the quick in her. It was as if she had touched God, and been restored to life. The broad, gleaming whiteness! It was the vision she cherished, because it had touched her soul" (*JTLJ* 44). The effect of the experience on Connie is profound: "When she was home again, she seemed haunted by another self inside herself. It was a self which had seen powerful beauty, seen it alive, and in motion, seen it as the greatest vision of her life" (*JTLJ* 46). The language, "herself" and "another self," recalls that of Lawrence's letter to Edward Garnett (5 June 1914) about "The Wedding Ring": "You mustn't look in my novel for the old stable ego of the character. There is another ego, according to whose action the individual is unrecognisable, and passes through, as it were, allotropic states . . ." (*Letters* 2:183). The first self sees only the man's face and the external trappings of his working-class position. It is "another self," the "soul" touched by the epiphanic image, that responds to the divinity in the man's body, not to worship the body, Lawrence makes clear, but to worship the divinity that shines through this matter as a revelation.

In the third version of the novel, *Lady Chatterley's Lover*, Lawrence omits the direct references to God, the world of the gods, and revelation of the divine and concentrates instead on the human quality of Connie's visionary experience. The contrast between "herself" and "another self" is made more concrete in the distinction between mind and womb: "Connie had received the shock of vision in her womb, and she knew it. . . . But with her mind she was inclined to ridicule" (*LCL* 76). The shift from "the vision . . . had touched her soul" (*JTLJ* 44) to "the shock of vision in her womb" (*LCL* 76) is a greater change than it may at first appear. In the former, the visionary experience is still spiritual, opening to Connie "the world of the gods," putting "worship in her heart again" (*JTLJ* 44). In the latter, the experience is fully human without being "social." It is concerned not with "personality" but with "the warm, white flame of a single life, revealing itself in contours that one might touch: a body!" (*LCL* 76). Lawrence was possibly already considering the idea of a risen man, a Christ figure returning to the fulfillment of instinctual being through sexuality instead of to fulfillment of spiritual mission through sacrifice. Thus, in the second version, the effect of Connie's vision of Parkin's body is "as if she had touched God, and been restored to life" (*JTLJ* 44), an allusion to the healing by faith of the woman with the "issue of blood" who had touched Christ's garment (Mark 5:25–34). But perhaps concerned that readers might be misled by such comparisons to Christian divinity, Lawrence discarded most of these allusions in the third version and reserved the fuller treatment of the risen-man theme for *The Escaped Cock*.[22] The significant biblical allusions that remain in *Lady Chatterley's Lover* use biblical language with revisionist meaning to present the theme of rebirth through phallic experience: "Go ye into the streets and byways of Jerusalem, and see if ye can find *a man*" (*LCL* 73); "Ye must be born again! I believe in the resurrection of the body! Except a grain of wheat fall into the earth and die, it shall by no means bring forth" (*LCL* 98); "Lift up your heads o' ye gates, that the king of glory may come in" (*LCL* 252).[23] These allusions support a consistent movement in the third version from the divine to the human, from the spiritual to the carnal.

In the third version, the bathing scene combines aesthetic and religious vision. It may be instructive to compare it to a scene in Joyce's *Portrait of the Artist* that parallels it in both subject matter and structure—the "bathing girl" epiphany at the end of chapter 4, which I shall also quote in full:

> A girl stood before him in midstream, alone and still, gazing out to sea. She seemed like one whom magic had changed into the likeness of a strange and beautiful seabird. Her long slender bare legs were delicate as a crane's and pure save where an emerald trail of seaweed had fashioned itself as a sign upon the flesh. Her thighs, fuller and softhued as ivory, were bared almost to the hips where the white fringes of her drawers were like featherings of soft white down. Her slateblue skirts were kilted boldly about her waist and dovetailed behind her. Her bosom was as a bird's soft and slight, slight and soft as the breast of some darkplumaged dove. But her long fair hair was girlish, and girlish, and touched with the wonder of mortal beauty, her face.
>
> She was alone and still, gazing out to sea, and when she felt his presence and the worship of his eyes her eyes turned to him in quiet sufferance of his gaze, without shame or wanton-

22. This interpretation was suggested to me by Dennis Jackson. See also his "Progression Toward Myth and Ritual in the Three Versions of D. H. Lawrence's *Lady Chatterley's Lover*," 10–13.

23. See Terry, "Aspects of D. H. Lawrence's Struggle with Christianity," 112–29; and Sheerin, "John Thomas and the King of Glory: Two Analogues," 297–300.

ness. Long, long she suffered his gaze and then quietly withdrew her eyes from his and bent them towards the stream, gently stirring the water with her foot hither and thither. The first faint noise of gently moving water broke the silence, low and faint and whispering, faint as the bells of sleep, hither and thither: a faint flame trembled on her cheek.

—Heavenly God! cried Stephen's soul, in an outburst of profane joy. [*Portrait* 171]

If Vivian de Sola Pinto and F. Warren Roberts are correct in their suggestion that Joyce's "bathing girl" epiphany was a source for Lawrence's poem "The Man of Tyre,"[24] then possibly the same scene also influenced Connie's "visionary experience" of Mellors bathing. For Wayne Burns, the two passages are contrasted in that even if Lawrence's scene "qualifies as an epiphany, in Joyce's sense of 'epiphany,' its effect is altogether different—primarily because, in Lawrence, such scenes are not the 'set pieces' that they are in Joyce." Lawrence's presentation of visionary experience, it is true, is dynamic and does not convey the sense of perfected finality of vision that he associated with the poetry of the end. In Burns's view, such scenes "are but feelings in the developing relationship between the man and the woman."[25] From the characters' viewpoint, as Connie's religious and aesthetic response shows, the experience is more than that. From a critical perspective, the care Lawrence took in the composition and revision of the scene in three successive versions of the novel to achieve the poetic effect from which his meaning derives requires that his artistic mastery be recognized.

Although I have found no evidence that Lawrence had read *A Portrait of the Artist,* there are significant parallels between the two scenes, which show that both writers used similar intense epiphanic experiences as prime motivating forces for change in their characters' lives. In both Joyce and Lawrence, the point-of-view character, beset with personal difficulties (Stephen confronting a choice of vocation, Connie experiencing spiritual and physical atrophy) and walking outdoors in a state of mind that represents a crisis of conscience and personal psychology, comes upon a person of the opposite sex

24. In the notes to *Complete Poems of D. H. Lawrence,* 1018, Pinto and Roberts suggest that the middle stanza of "Man of Tyre" bears some striking resemblances to Joyce's "bathing girl" epiphany. Smailes, "Lawrence's Verse: More Editorial Lapses," 465–66, refutes this idea and contends that Lawrence based the third stanza of the poem on his own experience rather than the scene in Joyce's novel.

25. Burns, "D. H. Lawrence: The Beginnings of a Primer to the Novels," in *Towards a Contextualist Aesthetic of the Novel,* 204.

who is alone and self-absorbed in a ritual of bathing and whose image passes into the consciousness of the observer in a revelatory experience. In both scenes, the figure is isolated in a setting that symbolically parallels the character's sense of nullity and desolation, Stephen amid "a waste of . . . brackish waters and . . . veiled sunlight" (*Portrait* 171), Connie in a "dying," "grey," "inert," "hopeless" world, itself in need of renewal. Both figures are compared to animals in grace, the bathing girl to a dove, Mellors to a weasel, and their motion in the water is emphasized. The girl's thighs are "bared almost to the hips," where her skirts are kilted about her drawers and "dovetailed" behind her. Mellors is "naked to the hips," where his breeches have slipped down "over the pure, delicate, white loins, the bones showing a little." In both scenes, the sexual content of the figure's half-nudity is sublimated into quasi-religious epiphany, with the observer's attitude of worship a common element of the scenes in both *A Portrait of the Artist* and *John Thomas and Lady Jane*. In both images, the color white is prominent, although in Joyce's it is not predominant. In both scenes, the observer sees the figure of the other as a "flame" body: Stephen observes that "a faint flame trembled on her cheek," and Connie discovers "the warm white flame of a single life" in the "contours" of the man's body. There is, however, one apparent difference between the two scenes: in Joyce's epiphany, "her image had passed into his soul," whereas in Lawrence's final conception of the scene, Mellors's image "had hit her in the middle of the body"—"Connie had received the shock of vision in her womb, and she knew it . . ." (*LCL* 75–76). As a result of their experiences, both Stephen and Connie take a new direction, toward life, and the difference between "soul" and "womb" as the organ of reception may be attributable to the distinction in aim between Stephen's move toward his true vocation as an artist and Connie's move toward liberation of her instinctual and psychological being. As Richard Ellmann points out, however, Stephen "receives a *call*, hears 'a voice from beyond the world,' but what it summons him to is not the priesthood but life, including sexual love, and an art that would content body and soul alike."[26] Connie is also summoned toward an awakening, in the sexual relationship with Mellors, of a new life of body and soul together.

The difference in means by which the image impresses itself upon the consciousness of the observer is an aesthetic difference that has its source in the opposing aesthetic theories from which the two scenes emerge. Aesthetically, Joyce's epiphany follows the

26. Ellmann, "On Joyce's Centennial," 29.

pattern of Stephen Dedalus's artistic theory drawn from Saint Thomas Aquinas. It moves from the *integritas* of the isolated figure of the girl standing before Stephen in midstream, through the *consonantia,* the analysis of the rhythm and harmony of the component parts of the figure (legs, thighs, drawers, skirt, bosom, hair, face), and thence, in the reintegration of the image, to the *quidditas,* or "whatness," of the unique object, from which the *claritas* of vision is registered on the observer's consciousness in the perception of the radiance of the bather's image. Lawrence's visionary experience, on the other hand, follows aesthetically from his conception, as stated in "Art and the Individual," of the blending of "the mystical and the sensual ideas of Art." Sensually, the "approval of Harmony" is presented in the observation of Mellors's figure, which, no less than the observation of the bathing girl's figure, moves from the integrity of the image in aloneness as Mellors washes himself "unaware," through analysis of the "harmony" of the parts that make up the image (loins, breeches, back, head, arms), and finally to the reintegration of the image in the "solitary nudity," from which the "visionary experience" is registered on the observer's consciousness. The culmination of the epiphanic scene in Lawrence is not, as in Stephen Dedalus's theory, an ideal stasis, although Stephen's ecstatic cry and his movement "On and on and on and on!" suggest that the immediate effect of his epiphany, in practice, is not entirely static either. Whereas Stephen rejects the "literary" idea of radiance as the artistic representation of "divine purpose" (*Portrait* 213), Lawrence accepts a blending of the "mystical" conception of beauty, "the shining of the idea through matter," and the "sensual" conception of beauty, the expression of "pleasurable emotion." In his later poetic theory, these ideas emerge in the distinction between the poetry of the beginning and the end and that of "the immediate present," a poetic distillation of experience characterized by vital energy and relationship rather than by "perfection" or "consummation," as equal components of art. The order that Lawrence's images express is not the finality of stasis but the vitality of dynamic equilibrium, and the "morality" which they embody is "that delicate, forever trembling and changing *balance* between me and my circumambient universe, which precedes and accompanies a true relatedness" (*STH* 172).

The epiphanic vision of Mellors bathing propels Connie back to Wragby, where, at the beginning of chapter 7, she goes up to her bedroom for a critical examination of her own body, "naked in the huge mirror": "what a frail, easily hurt, rather pathetic thing a human body is, naked; somehow a little unfinished, incomplete!"

What the lamp illuminates is a formerly "good figure," now "out of fashion," deprived of sun and warmth and "[d]isappointed of its real womanhood." "Instead of ripening its firm, down-running curves, her body was flattening and going a little harsh." Connie takes note of her rather small, unripe breasts; her slack, thin belly; her "flat, slack, meaningless" thighs: "She was old, old at twenty-seven, with no gleam and sparkle in the flesh" (*LCL* 79–80). A consequence of what the mirror reflects in her deliberate examination of her own body, Connie's dawning "sense of injustice, of being defrauded" (*LCL* 82) is motivated by the vision of Mellors bathing, and it leads, in turn, to her continuing visits to the wood. These visits increase her organicism, her identification of herself with nature, and establish the condition for the development of her psychological and sexual potential in the relationship with Mellors.

Nature imagery in chapter 8 reveals the change that is taking place in Connie, the newly awakened vision that frees her to recognize the natural manifestation of sexuality, fecundity, and life. The following passage, presented from Connie's point of view, provides an example of how this visionary experience transforms her way of seeing:

> Constance sat down with her back to a young pine-tree, that swayed against her with curious life, elastic and powerful, rising up. The erect, alive thing, with its top in the sun! And she watched the daffodils turn golden, in a burst of sun that was warm on her hands and lap. Even she caught the faint, tarry scent of the flowers. And then, being so still and alone, she seemed to get into the current of her own proper destiny. She had been fastened by a rope, and jagging and snarring like a boat at its moorings; now she was loose and adrift. [*LCL* 99]

No great powers of perception are required to recognize the phallic symbolism that associates the pine tree as fully with Mellors as with Connie, for as Lawrence emphasizes, the tree is "rising up" in elasticity and power, "erect" and "alive." More important is what the phallic symbolism itself signifies. Placed in the context of other nature symbolism (the sun, the daffodils), the pine tree becomes emblematic of far more than Mellors's sexual potency; it suggests the mythic powers that Lawrence evokes in "Pan in America" in the figure of the pine tree at Kiowa Ranch,[27] gathering up "earth-power

27. For a photograph of this tree, see the *D. H. Lawrence Review* 5, no. 3 (Fall 1972): 133. The same tree became the subject of Georgia O'Keeffe's painting *The Lawrence Tree*, which is reproduced in O'Keeffe, *Georgia O'Keeffe*, plate 57.

from the dark bowels of the earth, and a roaming sky-glitter from above. And all unto itself, which is a tree, woody, enormous, slow but unyielding with life, bristling with acquisitive energy, obscurely radiating some of its great strength." "It vibrates its presence into my soul, and I am with Pan" (*P* 25). While this kind of symbolism is far from Joyce's carefully ordered and objectified concrete imagery, the organicism of the new life of the body to which Connie is just awakening comes to her, as Stephen Dedalus's earliest education in poetic imagery does, through the immediacy of sensory experience. Since Connie assumes Lawrence's own characteristic posture in writing the manuscript "at the Villa Mirenda, . . . sitting on the grass under a tree,"[28] the image conveys something of both the origin and the organicist philosophy of the novel. Connie could say, with Lawrence, "I have become conscious of the tree, and of its interpenetration into my life" (*P* 25).

The change in Connie is also signaled by her conversation with Clifford on her return home:

> ". . . Look, aren't the little daffodils adorable! To think they should come out of the earth!"
> "Just as much out of the air and sunshine," he said.
> "But modelled in the earth," she retorted, with a prompt contradiction, that surprised her a little. [*LCL* 100]

Whereas Clifford's emphasis on air and sunshine suggests the transcendent male forces of spirit and intellect, Connie's emphasis on the earth affirms the female generative function of incarnation. In contradicting Clifford, Connie is not only elevating her own femaleness and herself as a person but also signaling that she has come into relationship with transpersonal forces that allow her to affirm incarnation and mutability captured in the life cycle as equipotential to transcendental forces outside time and change. Her development to this point has prepared her for the recognition that to live in time as an individual woman with someone else who lives in time as an individual man is the ontological affirmation of being in the world. This developmental change in Connie's character prepares for her visionary experience of the pheasant chick and what it leads to.

In chapter 10, a justly admired scene takes place at the chicken

---

28. Orioli, *Adventures of a Bookseller*, 233. The Villa Mirenda tree was an olive tree. For a photograph of Lawrence sitting under it with his back against the trunk, see Moore and Roberts, *D. H. Lawrence and His World*, 105.

coop, where Mellors draws a peeping chick from under the mother hen and places it in Connie's hand:

> "There!" he said, holding out his hand to her. She took the little drab thing between her hands, and there it stood, on its impossible little stalks of legs, its atom of balancing life trembling through its almost weightless feet into Connie's hands. But it lifted its handsome, clean-shaped little head boldly, and looked sharply round, and gave a little "peep."
> "So adorable! So cheeky!" she said softly. [*LCL* 134–35]

Joyce's presentation of Thomas Aquinas's theory of beauty in the fifth chapter of *A Portrait of the Artist,* although not the basis for this kind of scene in Lawrence's work, is a statement of principles so universal that the theory is applicable not only to certain Joycean epiphanies, such as the "bathing girl" scene, but also, with allowances for stylistic and thematic differences, to many scenes by other writers presenting the recognition of what in the largest sense must be called beauty. So it is that Connie's perception of the chick, like her visionary experience when she sees Mellors bathing, corresponds structurally to the Thomist theory elaborated by Stephen Dedalus, moving from the initial wholeness of the image (the chick in Mellors's hand), to the harmony of the parts of the image ("its impossible little stalks of legs," "its almost weightless feet," "its handsome, clean-shaped little head"), to the unique individuality of the reconstituted image (the chick's "peep" of "cheeky" defiance). It is from this reintegrated image that radiance emerges.

The keeper, squatting beside Connie, sees "a tear fall on her wrist." Suddenly "aware of the old flame shooting and leaping up in his loins, that he had hoped was quiescent for ever," Mellors stands away, but at his recognition of her forlornness, his compassion flames for her: "At the back of his loins the fire suddenly darted stronger. . . . Her face was averted, and she was crying blindly, in all the anguish of her generation's forlornness." Crouching beside her, Mellors returns the chick to the hen. "He laid his hand on her shoulder, and softly, gently, it began to travel down the curve of her back, blindly, with a blind stroking motion, to the curve of her crouching loins." The first of their sexual encounters begins with his quiet suggestion: "Shall you come to the hut?" (*LCL* 135–36).

Connie's tears and Mellors's flame reveal that the experience has been epiphanic for both of them. Although from a Joycean perspective they lead to kinetic action rather than ideal stasis, these images at once recall the beginning and foreshadow the end of the novel.

Connie's tears, in part for her own barren condition, both as a potential mother and as a potential creative human being, and in part for the vision of impossible vulnerability and indomitable bravery which the chick shows forth, are a catharsis that few experience in this forlorn generation, of which the narrator says in the opening sentence of the novel: "Ours is essentially a tragic age, so we refuse to take it tragically" (*LCL* 1). Mellors's flame, which leaps in his body as his heart melts "like a drop of fire," will become "the forked flame" between him and Connie that constitutes the Pentecostal creed of his belief (*LCL* 364). Because of his reverence for life, even this tiny life, and his compassion for her, Connie recognizes Mellors as the man with whom mutual affirmation of earthly being is possible. Because her reaction reveals an equal reverence for life in a sense of tragedy that includes a recognition of the necessity of a fall into time and incarnation, Mellors recognizes Connie as the woman, unlike Bertha Coutts, with whom this mutual affirmation of earthly being is possible. For both, the pheasant chick evokes a vision of life, vulnerable and without defenses, except for its defiant selfhood.

As the scene continues in the hut, immediately after the epiphany of the chick, the medium through which Connie's growth in sensual consciousness is realized shifts from sudden visionary experience to touch and direct sexual experience.[29] After chapter 12, especially, the focus of the story shifts from Lady Chatterley to her lover and the working out of the realistic and symbolic details of their life together. There are still occasional insights through visual perception— Connie's sight of Mellors's "erect phallus rising darkish and hot-looking from the little cloud of vivid gold-red hair" (*LCL* 251); Connie's journey with her sister Hilda to Venice as a tour in hell (chapter 17)—but little that could be called epiphanic. A scene such as the one in chapter 15 in which Connic and Mellors dance naked in the rain, then decorate their pubic hair with forget-me-nots, Mellors's penis with creeping jenny, and their bodies with campion and bluebells, although certainly conducive to growth, involves acting out rather than "sudden spiritual manifestation."

In *Lady Chatterley's Lover*, epiphany or visionary experience is the principal means by which Connie's development in consciousness progresses only in the first half of the novel. In Lawrence's concep-

---

29. Torgovnick, *Visual Arts, Pictorialism, and the Novel*, 154, comes by a different route to a similar conclusion: "Visual appreciation is . . . a crucial step for Connie toward the reawakening of her being, but it is a step that the novel leaves rather quickly behind. Once lovers, Connie and Mellors rely on tactile sensation, not visual sensation. . . ."

tion, insight alone is not enough. The shift from insight to direct experience of what has been envisioned clearly suggests the function of the epiphanic mode in his work. Lawrence's thematic purpose required that the individual accept responsibility for moving toward meaningful change. In the second half of *Lady Chatterley's Lover,* Connie must undertake the life tasks of living out the implications of what has been epiphanically illuminated and of developing, through internal transmutation of this experience, the integrity that allows her to come to some basic decisions in reordering her life. The radical nature of the change Lawrence suggests, which is no less than the death of the old self and the "resurrection of the body" that Connie says she believes in, emerges in *The Escaped Cock* in the revision of religious, cultural, and individual consciousness that the man who had died undertakes.

12

Allusions and Symbols
in *The Escaped Cock*

Wishing to bring the "trembling balance" of life to both religious experience and sexual love, D. H. Lawrence sought in his last years to revitalize what he considered to be the sterile and misdirected religious practice of modern man by reestablishing contact with pagan mythology. By denying the flesh and emphasizing the spirit, Christianity had misunderstood love and promoted an imbalance that was detrimental to life. In Christian society, love—even sexual love—had been abstracted as an intellectual ideal. Because it did not take account of buried but powerful feelings, the pale concept of Christian love was without realistic basis in the deep wellsprings of being. "The wild creatures are coming forth from the darkest Africa inside us," Lawrence says (*STH* 202). The response of evangelical big-game hunters like Billy Sunday was to hunt them down with elephant guns, while Christian society attempted to tame the emotions like domesticated animals. "Now we have to sow wild seed again. We have to cultivate our feelings" (*STH* 204). To correct the imbalance, Lawrence pleaded for a reassertion of "the blood" as a source of both love and religious experience.

In the short novel *The Escaped Cock* (published in England and America under the title *The Man Who Died*), "the death" has already taken place. Lawrence presents an imagined version of the revitalizing experiences of Jesus in "the resurrection," a version vastly different from biblical accounts of Christ's appearances after death.[1] Although numerous parallels to the Gospels clearly establish the life, and death, from which the man who died has been liberated, Lawrence never calls the character "Jesus" but presents him as a universal figure for the risen man. His body has been taken down from the cross and laid in the tomb, but the man's death had been spiritual rather than physical. His old missionary life as teacher and savior is dead within him, and he is free to seek the true sources of human happiness in a more vital life than he has lived before. He realizes that he has been saved from his own salvation, that he has neglected the needs of his own body to pursue a spiritual mission. Forsaking that mission, he decides to use his healing powers as a physician and to follow a life in which his own wounds, as much psychic as physical, will be healed. Leaving his former followers, he finds, in a temple of Isis, the fulfillment for which he has been searching. Although it is more difficult to love sexually than it had been to die, he learns, through his relationship with the priestess, what human love is and recognizes that he has offered and asked only "the corpse of love" before. In telling his story of the resurrection in *The Escaped Cock,* Lawrence employs both traditional symbols and biblical and mythic allusions, which I want to examine in the context of his reassertion of the values of feelings, wildness, and instinct through the metaphor of pagan religious mythology in an effort to correct the imbalance on the side of abstract religious concepts, domestication of feelings, and spiritual idealism that he thought Christianity promoted.

The central symbol in part 1 is a young gamecock owned by a poor peasant. The cock "[looks] a shabby little thing, but . . . [puts] on brave feathers as spring [advances], and [is] resplendent with an arched and orange neck, by the time the fig-trees" are putting out leaves. Cutting a splendid figure in that dirty yard, the cock learns to arch his neck and crow shrill answers to the faraway, unseen cocks crowing beyond the wall. The peasant, fearing that his prized bird will fly away, ties him to a post. But one day, with a mighty burst of strength, the rooster snaps the string that holds him and flies over the wall. At the same moment, a man awakens "from a long sleep in which he [has been] tied up" (*EC* 13, 15).

In these few opening paragraphs, Lawrence, through the meta-

1. See Matthew 28, Mark 16, Luke 24, and John 20 and 21. All references to The Holy Bible in my text are to the King James Version. Additional literary analogues are discussed in Thompson, "The Christ Who Didn't Die," 19–30.

phor of the gamecock, foreshadows the nature of the new life to which
the man is awakening and refers back to the old life he has left
behind. The gamecock is a fitting thematic image; it heralds both
Jesus' death and the man's rebirth, both Peter's denial of Christ (John
18:15–27) and the risen man's self-affirmation through instinctual
experience. Thematically, the idea of male sexuality is effectively
presented in the image of the cock, which, besides being the male of its
species, suggests the phallic connotations of its name in slang usage.
From the moment when both the man and the cock break the fetters
that bind them (the bandages wound around the buried man and the
string attached to the cock's spur), the man is identified with the cock.
It is clear that the man will break not only the physical bonds of death
but also the metaphorical fetters of sexual repression that have prevented his living so vital a life as the cock.

Lawrence graphically illustrates the aggressive gamecock's sexuality as both dominant and tender. Even when fettered, the young
cock crows with a voice "stronger than chagrin" out of "the necessity
to live, and even to cry out the triumph of life." Watching him the
man sees "not the bird alone, but the short, sharp wave of life of
which the bird [is] the crest" (*EC* 21). When he throws "a bit of bread
to the cock, it [calls] with an extraordinary cooing tenderness, tou-
sling and saving the morsel for the hens." But when his favorite hen
comes near him, "emitting the lure," he pounces "on her with all his
feathers vibrating." Watching "the unsteady, rocking vibration of
the bent bird," the man who had died sees "not the bird . . . , but one
wave-tip of life overlapping for a minute another, in the tide of the
swaying ocean of life" (*EC* 22). The man sees in the life of the gamecock a more vital existence than he has known before in the life of
the spirit. "Surely," he says, "thou art risen to the Father, among
birds" (*EC* 28). But it is clear that he uses the phrase to denote an
earthly, instinctual life that he himself has not yet learned to live,
rather than the heavenly, spiritual life denoted by the phrase in
biblical usage (see John 20:17). When he decides to go out in search
of the new, vital life, he buys the cock from the peasant. But there is
a difference between this purchase and the one by which Jesus had
been betrayed (see Matthew 26:14–16), for the man who had been
sold into imprisonment and death buys freedom and life for the bird.
By this time the cock has become a symbol of virtue for him, and the
life of the cock the good life.

When the risen man meets two of his followers along the way (in
Lawrence's version of Jesus' appearance after resurrection to Cleo-
pas and another follower on the road to Emmaus [Luke 24:13–35]),
this conversation ensues:

"Why do you carry a cock?"
"I am a healer," he said, "and the bird hath virtue."
"You are not a believer?"
"Yea! I believe the bird is full of life and virtue." [*EC* 33]

This dialogue has no parallel in the gospel source, which aims at verifying the resurrection as a warrant of belief and reveals the presence of Christ through his celebration of the communion. According to Evelyn J. Hinz and John J. Teunissen, Lawrence here identifies the risen man with Asclepius, the god of healing and patron of medicine, who was associated with both serpent and cock and to whom cocks were sacrificed by those who had been healed. "The conversion of the man who died from his mission as 'savior' to his role as 'healer' consists largely of . . . a movement away from the Christian and plebeian toward a pagan and elitist attitude to regeneration and away from an ego-centric to a self-sufficient concept of deity."[2]

The man's disposition of the gamecock illustrates the shift from salvation to self-sufficiency. When he comes to an inn, where the cock engages in a fight with the innkeeper's cock, the man, indicating his growing willingness to risk all for life, prevents the innkeeper from stopping the fight by promising that he may have the gamecock to eat if he loses or keep him for his hens if he wins. When the gamecock wins, the man who has died says to it, "Thou at least hast found thy kingdom, and the females to thy body" (*EC* 33). The speech, which parallels Jesus' words to Pilate, "My kingdom is not of this world" (John 18:36), illustrates again the change in the risen man's attitude toward life: No longer looking to be more than human, he now wishes to be what is even more difficult for him to be—an integrated man.

The gamecock, of course, is the central symbol in part 1 of *The Escaped Cock,* but there are other symbols and other allusions in this section of the novella that point up the contrast between the old life and the new and illustrate the risen man's changing attitude as he emerges into the rich, vital life of the blood.

The coming change is marked in Lawrence's demythologizing of Jesus' followers by comparison with the simple, ignoble peasants who offer the risen man the shelter of their humble cottage, where he is taken after arising from the tomb. Still numb with pain and "the great void nausea of utter disillusion" (*EC* 18), he has no desire, even for food and drink. Nevertheless, he moistens a bit of bread in

2. Hinz and Teunissen, "Savior and Cock," 287.

water and eats it. At his "last supper" Jesus had had his twelve disciples with him; but at what might be called his "first breakfast" the risen man has with him only a poor peasant and his wife. But whereas three of the disciples had fallen asleep as Jesus prayed in the Garden of Gethsemane and one had thrice denied him (see Matthew 26:36–75), these peasants, though "limited, meagre in their life, without any splendour of gesture and of courage," offer the man shelter at the risk of their own lives. "They [have] no nobility, but fear [makes] them willing to serve" (*EC* 19).

The sun, another major symbol in the first section, in its suspension in the sky has phallic significance, thus foreshadowing the risen man's subsequent identification with Osiris, who is often represented as a sun god.[3] More important, the sun appears here in its function as a health-renewing, life-giving force. When the peasant departs for work in the vineyard of his master, the man who had died asks to lie in the yard in the sun. This he does again for the following two days. As Hinz and Teunissen point out, in Asclepian medicine "health was not merely physical well-being, but the condition of harmony between the body and the mind." Hence, "the cock and the sun work together to heal the psychic and physical 'scars' of the man," a cure symbolized thematically "in his assumption of the Asclepian role as the 'healer' associated with the cock."[4]

This means inevitably a revisionist view of his former role as savior. Looking at the stupid, dirty peasant, the man thinks to himself: "Why then should he be lifted up? Clods of earth are turned over for refreshment; they are not to be lifted up. Let the earth remain earthy, and hold its own against the sky. I was wrong to seek to lift it up. It was wrong to try to interfere. . . . No man can save the earth from tillage. It is tillage, not salvation . . ." (*EC* 22–23). The allusion to Jesus' statement about his own crucifixion and glorification, "And I, if I be lifted up from earth, will draw all men unto me" (John 12:32), illustrates the man's changing attitude toward all humanity, including himself.

Lawrence's version of the conversation between the risen man and Madeleine in *The Escaped Cock* differs in several ways from biblical accounts of the encounter between the risen Jesus and Mary Magdalene at the sepulchre (see Matthew 28:9–10, Mark 16:9, and John 20:14–18). In John's account, Jesus says to Mary Magdalene, "Touch me not; for I am not yet ascended to my Father: but go to my brethren, and say unto them, I ascend to my Father and your Father; and

3. Frazer, *The Golden Bough*, 1 vol. abridged ed., 446–47.
4. Hinz and Teunissen, 284, 289.

to my God, and your God" (John 20:17). But in Lawrence's version, the man says, "Don't touch me, Madeleine. . . . Not yet! I am not yet healed and in touch with men" (*EC* 23). The change of phrase from "ascended to my Father" to "in touch with men" indicates a shift in allegiance on the part of the risen man from the spiritual forces of heaven to the physical forces of earth. Later in the conversation, Madeleine asks him, "And will you come back to us?" And he answers, "What is finished is finished. . . . For me that life is over" (*EC* 24). This part of the conversation has no parallel in the gospel accounts, but the man's statement recalls Jesus' final words on the cross as recorded by John: "When Jesus therefore had received the vinegar, he said, It is finished: and he bowed his head, and gave up the ghost" (John 19:30). In Lawrence's version, what is "finished" is the man's spiritual mission. As he goes on to explain, "The teacher and the saviour are dead in me; now I can go about my own business, into my own single life" (*EC* 24). Once Jesus' parents had found him, at the age of twelve, teaching the elders of the temple: "And he said unto them, How is it that ye sought me? wist ye not that I must be about my Father's business?" (Luke 2:49). The radical change in regard to whose "business" he is concerned with makes any reference to Lawrence's character as "the Christ"[5] inappropriate: He has clearly rejected his former messianic mission.

In Lawrence's revisionist rendering of Christian symbols, even the sacrament of the Eucharist is redirected from spiritual to earthly needs as bread itself is deconsecrated. Obtaining a little money from Madeleine, the man who had died returns to the cottage and gives it to the peasant's wife. "Take it!" he says. "It buys bread, and bread brings life" (*EC* 27). Once when Jesus had fasted for forty days and forty nights in the wilderness, the devil had tempted him: "If thou be the Son of God, command this stone that it be made bread. / And Jesus answered him, saying, It is written, That man shall not live by bread alone, but by every word of God" (Luke 4:2–4). Since Christ's rejection of the temptation of the bread reverses Adam's yielding to the temptation of the forbidden fruit, it therefore reverses the effect of the Fall. Hence, the risen man's offering money to the peasant woman for nonsacramental bread suggests an acceptance of the fallen, that is, the human, world as natural and appropriate to earthly life.

Thinking over the changes that have been wrought in him by

5. See, for example, LeDoux, "Christ and Isis," 133. Most critics have referred to the man as Christ or Jesus, but Lawrence's text, though it employs many reverse parallels to the Gospels, provides no authority for the name.

death, he says to himself, "Now I belong to no one, and have no connection, and my mission or gospel is gone from me. Lo! I cannot make even my own life, and what have I to save? I can learn to be alone" (*EC* 29). In effect, he accepts the task implied by the mocking words of the chief priests as Jesus hung on the cross: "He saved others; himself he cannot save" (Mark 15:31).

Another reordering of priorities occurs when the man who had died, aware of the vital forces of life going on around him, reconsiders the primacy he had formerly given to the word over the flesh: "The Word is but the midge that bites at evening. Man is tormented with words like midges, and they follow him right into the tomb. But beyond the tomb they cannot go. Now I have passed the place where words can bite, and the air is clear, and there is nothing to say, and I am alone within my own skin, which is the walls of all my domain" (*EC* 30). Jesus had told a parable about the sower and the word (Mark 4:14–20). And once when many of his followers had deserted him, he had said to his twelve disciples, "Will ye also go away?" Simon Peter had answered him, "Lord, to whom shall we go? thou hast the words of eternal life" (John 6:67–68). Now the man thinks that these "words" lead not to "eternal life" but to "the tomb," beyond which "they cannot go." By this change Lawrence revises the Christian tradition that he had criticized as early as the unpublished "Foreword to *Sons and Lovers*" (1913), in his rejection of St. John's doctrine that "[t]he Word was made Flesh" (John 1:1–14): "For what was Christ? He was Word, or He became Word. What remains of Him? No flesh remains on earth, from Christ. . . . He is Word. And the Father was Flesh. For even if it were by the Holy Ghost His spirit were begotten, yet flesh cometh only out of flesh" (*Letters,* ed. Huxley, 98). In *The Escaped Cock* Lawrence attempts to restore the natural order that he thinks John had reversed.

The man who had died also revises his definition of immortality. The Apostle Paul wrote to Timothy that "our Saviour Jesus Christ . . . hath abolished death, and hath brought life and immortality to light through the gospel" (2 Timothy 1:10). But the risen man, Lawrence says, "healed of his wounds, and enjoyed his immortality of being alive without fret. . . . For in the tomb he had left his striving self . . ." (*EC* 30). Now for the first time, in the interest of preserving his self inviolate, he elevates phenomenology above spirituality as he decides to venture forth "among the stirring of the phenomenal world": "Strange is the phenomenal world, dirty and clean together! . . . And life bubbles everywhere, in me, in them, in this, in that. But it bubbles variously. Why should I ever have wanted it to bubble all alike?" (*EC* 30–31). From this new perspective he arrives at the insight that he had been executed because his preaching had closed the fountains of the phenomenal world.

In part 2 of *The Escaped Cock,* Lawrence introduces the Osiris-Isis myth as a thematic device. The section opens at the temple of Isis in Search, which stands on a peninsula, "a little, tree-covered tongue of land between two bays," facing southwest toward Egypt, toward "the splendid sun of winter as he [curves] down towards the sea" (*EC* 35). As the man watches, two half-naked slaves, a boy of about seventeen and a girl, dress pigeons for the evening meal, making of the process the ritual of a sacrifice. When the girl lets one of the pigeons escape and fly away, the boy beats her with his fist until she slips to the ground, "passive and quivering": "He twisted her over, intent and unconscious, and pushed his hands between her thighs, to push them apart. And in an instant he was in to her, covering her in the blind, frightened frenzy of a boy's first coition. Quick and frenzied his young body quivered naked on hers, blind, for a minute. Then it lay quite still, as if dead" (*EC* 36–37).

An aura of eroticism pervades the entire passage. Sexuality emanates not only from the detailed description of the sex act but also from the carefully chosen phallic symbols (the peninsula, the sun, the trees, the pigeons) and the yonic symbols (the temple, the two bays, the sea); indeed, from the sensuous phrasing itself: "radiance flooded in between the pillars of painted wood," "the light stood erect and magnificent off the invisible sea, filling the hills of the coast," "on the rocks under which the sea smote and sucked," "a high wall, inside which was a garden" (*EC* 35), and from the presentation of orgasm as the "little death." From the perspective of an enlightened modern consciousness, Janice Hubbard Harris offers some well-taken objections to the scene, and to the elitist reaction of the priestess.[6] But the naturalistic description of naïve primitive sexual behavior modulates into the sexual symbolism, which Lawrence employs effectively to introduce the pagan religious consciousness embodied in the myth of Isis and Osiris.

The priestess serves the goddess Isis—not Isis, Mother of Horus, or Isis Bereaved, Lawrence makes clear, but Isis in Search. After the evil brother Set had torn Osiris's body into fourteen pieces and scattered them abroad, the goddess sailed throughout the marshes in search of the pieces, burying each one as she found it, although she never found the genitals.[7] A few obvious parallels between Christ

6. Harris, *Short Fiction of D. H. Lawrence,* 242 and 305 nn. 62, 63.
7. Frazer, abrgd. ed., 421–24.

and Osiris make the Osiris myth a particularly appropriate choice to hold in balance with the Christ myth. Both performed seeming miracles, Osiris introducing the treading of grapes and Christ turning water into wine. Both were betrayed by men who called themselves brothers. Both were slain. And both were deified: Osiris, like Christ, was "a god of the dead, assuring personal resurrection to man."[8] One essential difference between them, of course, is that Christ was celibate and Osiris was not. Lawrence's purpose in establishing the parallel is to introduce to modern Christianity a vitalism lacking in the Christ myth, or more specifically, through the risen man's assumption, at least temporarily, of the role of Osiris, to view the spiritual message of Christianity from the critical perspective of the pre-Socratic vitalism of the Osiris myth.

In *The Escaped Cock*, Christianity and the Osiris myth are brought together when the risen man asks shelter at the temple of Isis in Search. Continuing the reversal of Christian tradition, Lawrence here takes up the plan first proposed to Satan by Belial, "the dissolutest Spirit that fell, / The sensualist," in John Milton's *Paradise Regained:*

> "Set women in his eye and in his walk,
> Among daughters of men the fairest found;
> Many are in each Region passing fair
> As the noon Sky; more like to Goddesses
> Than Mortal Creatures, graceful and discreet,
> Expert in amorous Arts, enchanting tongues
> Persuasive, Virgin majesty with mild
> And sweet allay'd, yet terrible to approach,
> Skill'd to retire, and in retiring draw
> Hearts after them tangl'd in Amorous Nets."
> [2:153–62][9]

In Milton's sexual pun, women have such power to "Enerve," "Draw out with credulous desire, . . . / As the Magnetic hardest Iron draws," that they beguiled even Solomon "And made him bow to the Gods of his Wives." In his reply, Satan, cautioning that Belial ever judges others by his own fabled lechery, rejects the proposal: "But he whom we attempt is wiser far / Than *Solomon*"; no woman can be found, "Though of this Age the wonder and the fame," on whom a man of

---

8. LeDoux, 146 n. 10.

9. Milton, *Paradise Regained,* in *Complete Poems and Major Prose,* 497–98. Subsequent references will be cited parenthetically in the text by book and line numbers.

such "exalted mind" would cast "an eye / Of fond desire" (2:205–11). The difference is that in Milton Belial proposes to use woman as a means of tempting Christ to his downfall, whereas in Lawrence woman becomes the means of consummation and fulfillment for the man who had died. Although I have found no specific references to *Paradise Regained*, Lawrence, who was familiar with Milton, may have had this passage in mind in his description of the risen man's mating with the priestess of Isis, who, it may be said, is "more like to Goddesses / Than Mortal Creatures," "Expert in amorous Arts," "yet terrible to approach," and able to "Enerve," "Draw out with credulous desire" the "hardest Iron" in concrete terms and lead the risen man to bow to her god.

The emergence of the risen man's fully human sexuality is foreshadowed by the moral inversion of the traditional valuation of goats, which Christ at the Judgment will metaphorically separate from the faithful sheep and consign "into everlasting fire" (Matthew 25:32,41). The cave of the goats where the priestess allows the man to sleep becomes a place of rebirth for him, as the stable of Jesus' nativity (Luke 2:1–20), with its association with sheep and shepherds, is ironically replaced by one of the haunts of Pan associated with satyrlike goats. The cave also compares with the tomb from which the man arose at the beginning of the novella. Both the sepulchre, "the rocky cavity from which he had emerged" (*EC* 16), and the cave, a dark place, "absolutely silent from the wind," with "a little basin of rock where the maidenhair fern [fringes] a dripping mouthful of water" at its descriptively yonic entrance, are, in context, womb symbols. But whereas the man's emergence from the sepulchre marks a physical rebirth, his emergence from the cave, as the "faint odour of goats" (*EC* 41) indicates, marks the rebirth of long repressed sexuality.

As "[t]he all-tolerant Pan [watches] over them" (*EC* 48), the coming together of the risen man and the priestess enacts a ritual whereby Lawrence brings into creative balance the myths of Christ and Osiris. The priestess, who has seen the man's nail-scarred hands and feet as he slept, believes, on the basis of his "beauty of much suffering" (*EC* 43), that he is the lost Osiris. Greatly attracted to him sexually, she invites him to the temple, detaining him for a second night. Pan's influence is apparent in the man's saying to himself, "Unless we encompass it in the greater day, and set the little life in the circle of the greater life, all is disaster" (*EC* 50). He agrees to come to the priestess again, but before he goes he meditates on the "destinies of splendour" that await him, admitting to himself, "I am almost more afraid of this touch than I was of death.

For I am more nakedly exposed to it" (*EC* 52). (Compare with Matthew 26:39.) When he goes to her, wanting now desperately to be healed in flesh and spirit, he is still afraid, still repressed and inhibited sexually. "It has hurt so much!" he says. "You must forgive me if I am still held back." But at her gentle suggestion, he removes his clothes and walks naked toward the idol, where, like Solomon (1 Kings 11:1–8), he prays to the woman's god, in this case Isis: "Ah, Goddess, . . . I would be so glad to live, if you would give me my clue again" (*EC* 54).

The sexual union is presented as an act of sacramental healing. "Let me anoint you!" the woman says to him softly. "Let me anoint the scars!" As the priestess chafes the risen man's feet "with oil and tender healing" (*EC* 54), he remembers another woman, a former prostitute (Mary Magdalene), who had washed his feet with her tears, dried them with her hair, and poured precious ointment on them (Luke 7:36–38). Suddenly it dawns on him why he was put to death: "I asked them all to serve me with the corpse of their love. And in the end I offered them only the corpse of my love. This is my body—take and eat—my corpse—" (*EC* 55). This revisionist view of the Last Supper (see Matthew 26:26–28, Mark 14:22–23, Luke 22:19–20) is followed by a radical psychoanalytic interpretation of Judas's kiss of betrayal: "I wanted them to love with dead bodies. If I had kissed Judas with live love, perhaps he would never have kissed me with death. Perhaps he loved me in the flesh, and I willed that he should love me bodilessly, with the corpse of love—" (*EC* 55).[10]

With the risen man's new self-knowledge, "a new sun [is] coming up in him" under the woman's tender ministrations. The healing ritual also alludes to both myths: "Having chafed all his lower body with oil, his belly, his buttocks, even the slain penis and the sad stones, having worked with her slow intensity of a priestess, . . . suddenly she put her breast against the wound in his left side, and her arms around him, folding over the wound in his right side and she pressed him to her, in a power of living warmth. . ." (*EC* 56). The Christian allusion is to the disciple Thomas's insistence on empirical evidence of Jesus' resurrection: "Except I shall see in his hands the print of the nails, and put my finger into the print of the nails, and thrust my hand into his side, I will not believe" (John 20:25). When Jesus later appears in their midst in a closed room, "Then saith he to Thomas, Reach hither thy finger, and behold my hands; and reach hither thy hand, and thrust *it* into my side, and be not faithless, but

10. Lawrence's ambivalent attitude toward Judas is examined in detail in Thompson, "D. H. Lawrence and Judas," 1–19.

believing" (John 20:27). The structural repetition of the action in the priestess's pressing her breast against the wound in the risen man's side shifts the meaning from empirical evidence of his overcoming mortality to the means of his healing. According to Larry V. LeDoux, "The image of the priestess as a healing girdle around his body is a direct representation of bas-relief pictures of Osiris rising from the dead from between the outstretched wings of Isis."[11]

In simplest terms, the man's mission shifts from establishing the church to establishing his life. Touching the woman, he says, "On this rock I build my life!" (*EC* 57). The allusion to Jesus' words to Simon Peter—"And I say also unto thee, That thou art Peter, and upon this rock I will build my church; and, the gates of hell shall not prevail against it" (Matthew 16:18)—emphasizes the contrast between the old life and the new. No longer interested in the spiritual world or its human institutions, he now wants only to build a solid life for himself and the woman he loves in the sacramental communion of flesh with flesh. Crouching to her, he feels "the blaze of his manhood and his power rise up in his loins, magnificent," and he declares: "I am risen!" (*EC* 57). Lawrence's multileveled pun presents erection as the metaphorical equivalent of resurrection, but it also has a more general phallic significance: he is "risen" with the "new sun" of the vital life of the blood. Marking his release from sexual inhibition, "Father! he [says]—Why did you hide this from me?"

Revisions of the biblical associations with "mansion" and "hour" mark the shift in emphasis from death to life. Responding for the first time to "the deep, interfolded warmth, warmth living and penetrable, the woman, the heart of the rose," the man who had died says to himself, "My mansion is the intricate warm rose, my joy is this blossom!" (*EC* 57). The phrasing recalls Jesus' words to his disciples: "In my Father's house are many mansions: if it were not so, I would have told you" (John 14:2). The risen man recognizes that there is one "mansion" that the "Father" has hidden from him! "My hour is upon me, I am taken unawares—" (*EC* 58), he thinks. The allusion to Jesus' words to his mother, "mine hour is not yet come" (John 2:4), and later to Andrew and Philip, "The hour is come that the Son of man should be glorified" (John 12:23), Lawrence places at the exact moment of the first sexual experience of the man who now lives, thus altering the meaning from "hour of death" to "hour of life."

After the sexual union, Lawrence signals the nature of the contact

11. LeDoux, 138. LeDoux cites a reproduction in Campbell, *Hero with a Thousand Faces*, 209.

accomplished between the two myths in the responses of the two principal figures. The priestess is ecstatic: "I am full of Osiris. I am full of the risen Osiris!" The man is meditative: "This is the great atonement, the being in touch" (*EC* 58). For her, the risen man has supplied the missing phallus of Osiris; for him, the priestess of Isis, through the sexual relation, has given new meaning to the Christian concept of atonement. The contrast with St. Paul's view that atonement with God is mediated by Christ's sacrifice (Romans 5:11) reveals Lawrence's opposition to the Pauline direction taken by Christianity since the time of Christ.

A short time later, the priestess discovers that she is pregnant, and she is afraid that her mother and her mother's slaves will make trouble for her and her lover. "Let not your heart be troubled!" he says. "I have died the death once" (*EC* 60). The quotation of Jesus' words to his disciples, "Let not your heart be troubled: ye believe in God, believe also in me" (John 14:1), is here given a new dimension: he wants the woman to believe in him not as a savior but as a lover and a man committed to life. Then he tells her, "I must go now soon. Trouble is coming to me from the slaves. But I am a man, and the world is open. But what is between us is good, and is established. Be at peace. And when the nightingale calls again from your valley-bed, I shall come again, sure as spring" (*EC* 60). The "trembling balance" of life is now established in the transformation of the Christian myth by contact with the Osiris myth. This passage contains allusions to both religions. The biblical reference is to Christ's words to his disciples: "I will come again, and receive you unto myself; that where I am, there ye may be also" (John 14:3) and "Peace I leave with you, my peace I give unto you: not as the world giveth, give I unto you. Let not your heart be troubled, neither let it be afraid" (John 14:27). The promise and the benediction are both enhanced by the references to the Osiris myth: Osiris, who "travelled over the world, diffusing the blessings of civilisation and agriculture wherever he went," is, in his aspect as a corn god, closely identified with the cycle of the seasons and the subject of popular rites of the Egyptian harvest in the spring.[12] In addition, the sexual connotations of such words as "nightingale," "valley-bed," and "I shall come again" invests the passage with the phallic significance of Lawrence's "religion of the blood."

As I have tried to show, the biblical allusions in *The Escaped Cock* serve as reference points in the dialectic that Lawrence sets up be-

---

12. Frazer, abrgd. ed., 421, 431.

tween the self-denying life of the spirit and the self-affirming life of the blood. Words that in their biblical context state basic tenets of orthodox Christianity are made applicable to the "religion of the blood" in the unorthodox meanings that the context of Lawrence's novella gives them. Lawrence's ultimate thematic purpose must be further explored.

As Janice Harris notes, criticism of the novella is "divided not on the issue of quality but on the 'heretical' nature of the work."[13] The question, then, is whether Lawrence seeks to revitalize the established Christian religion or to substitute in its place a pre-Socratic religion founded on pagan vitalism. The answer is not a simple one. In Hinz and Teunissen's view, "What is revitalized in the story is pre-Christian symbolism." Since "there is no possible way of reconciling" the opposites, "the healing of the man who died is essentially a healing of the duality that is the Platonic and Christian inheritance."[14] But in Laurentian terms, the healing of the duality does not lie in the triumph of either side but in the polarity between them. In rejecting spiritual interference with the peasants' souls, the risen man says, "Let the earth remain earthy, and hold its own against the sky" (*EC* 22). But in terms of Lawrence's dualism, does not the reverse, in principle, also apply? What if the lion really annihilated the unicorn, Lawrence asks in "The Crown." "Would not the lion at once expire, as if he had created a vacuum around himself? Is not the unicorn necessary to the very existence of the lion, is not each opposite kept in stable equilibrium by the opposition of the other" (*RDP* 253)? For Lawrence, the answer lay neither in annihilation of the sensual by the spiritual, as in Miriam's self-sacrificial sexual submission, nor in destruction of the spiritual by the sensual, as in the black African statuary that Birkin contemplates. Lawrence's homeostasis required that the opposites of flesh and spirit be held in a "trembling balance" in which the energies of both were available for life affirmation rather than the dead end of absolute reduction on either side. In Lawrence's controlling metaphor, "The crown is upon the perfect balance of the fight, it is not the fruit of either victory" (*RDP* 262).

On the other hand, to speak of the relation that Lawrence establishes between the two myths as a "fusion," as I did in an earlier

13. Harris, 302 n. 55.

14. Hinz and Teunissen, 279, 296. The duality is embodied for them in the opposites of Christ as Savior and a bronze icon in the Vatican museum, "a composite of a phallus, a cock, and the head and shoulders of a man," entitled "The Saviour of the World" (293).

study, is equally inexact, although this wording is common in criticism of the novella.[15] There is, undeniably, a coming together, a touching, a creative balance of the two myths; but the merger is purposefully incomplete. LeDoux is surely correct in his observation that although the priestess of Isis three times "identifies him as the embodiment of Osiris, . . . the man who died never questions his own identity and never credits her identification," even when he acquiesces, by his conditional "If you will" (*EC* 53), in "ritualistically supplying the missing part of the god."[16] Lawrence's ridicule of "merging" in the "Whitman" essay (*SCAL* 169–70) provides clear evidence of his attitude on "fusion." In his discussions of dualism, he repeatedly insists that there be no confusion of the opposites. His comments in *Twilight in Italy* are still applicable to *The Escaped Cock:*

> [There] are two Infinites, twofold approach to God. And man must know both.
>
> But he must never confuse them. They are eternally separate. The lion shall never lie down with the lamb. The lion eternally shall devour the lamb, the lamb eternally shall be devoured. Man knows the great consummation in the flesh, the sensual ecstasy, and that is eternal. Also the spiritual ecstasy of unanimity, that is eternal. But the two are separate and never to be confused. To neutralize the one with the other is unthinkable, an abomination. [*TI* 58]

Lawrence suggests in "The Crown" that any revelation of God is manifested only in the physical, temporal world: "The revelation is a condition in the whole flux of time. When this condition has passed away, the revelation is no more revealed." It exists only in memory as the "perpetuation of a momentary cohesion in the flux." Because modern man hates the "imprisoning memory," he seeks war to annihilate it, preferring to destroy the old revelations rather than "create a new revelation of God" (*RDP* 304–5).

Christ's passion was a revelation imprisoned in the memory of orthodox Christianity. As Lawrence says in his review of Tolstoy's *Resurrection*, "We have all this time been worshipping a dead Christ: or a dying." But the mystery of the resurrection is an on-

---

15. See Cowan, "Function of Allusions and Symbols in D. H. Lawrence's *The Man Who Died*," 251; Fiderer, "D. H. Lawrence's *The Man Who Died:* The Phallic Christ," 95–96; and Lacy, "Commentary," in Lawrence, *The Escaped Cock*, 124.

16. LeDoux, 138–39.

going revelation: "the Cross was only the first step into achievement. The second step was the tomb. And the third step, whither?"
In Western Christianity as represented by Tolstoy, "the stone was
rolled upon him" (P 737), leaving Christ a God of death and spirit,
not of life and flesh. In "The Risen Lord," Lawrence declares: "the
Churches insist on Christ Crucified, and rob us of the fruit of the
year," for in the liturgical calendar, all the months from Easter to
Advent belong to "the risen Lord" (P II 571):

> If Jesus rose from the dead in triumph, a man on earth
> triumphant in renewed flesh, triumphant over the mechani-
> cal anti-life convention of Jewish priests, Roman despotism,
> and universal money-lust; triumphant above all over His
> own self-absorption, self-consciousness, self-importance; tri-
> umphant and free as a man in full flesh and full, final experi-
> ence, even the accomplished acceptance of His own death; a
> man at last full and free in flesh and soul, a man at one with
> death: then He rose to become at one with life, to live the
> great life of the flesh and the soul together, as peonies or
> foxes do, in their lesser way. If Jesus rose as a full man, in
> full flesh and soul, then He rose to take a woman to Himself,
> to live with her, and to know the tenderness and blossoming
> of the twoness with her; He who had been hitherto so limited
> to His oneness, or His universality, which is the same thing.
> [P II 575]

In *The Escaped Cock*, Lawrence brings modern Christianity,
which he finds to be overintellectualized and therefore sterile, into
contact with the instinctual experience of flesh-and-blood sexuality
through allusions to the Osiris-Isis myth. For it is modern, Western
civilization, not historical, primitive Christianity, to which Lawrence addresses himself. Through the vehicle of the risen man's
relationship with the priestess of Isis, he attempts to reconcile the
Christian religion in which he was brought up with an imagined
religion of the blood based on pre-Socratic vitalism.

In his review of *Georgian Poetry: 1911–1912*, Lawrence wrote:

> I worship Christ, I worship Jehovah, I worship Pan, I worship
> Aphrodite. But I do not worship hands nailed and running
> with blood upon a cross, nor licentiousness, nor lust. I want
> them all, all the gods. They are all God. But I must serve in
> real love. If I take my whole, passionate, spiritual and physi-
> cal love to the woman who in return loves me, that is how I

serve God. And my hymn and my game of joy is my work. [*P* 307]

The Escaped Cock is a hymn to the resurrection of the body, not the glorified body of Christianity but the instinctual body of physical being. The symbolism in the novella often has phallic significance; but if it is carnal, it is never licentious. It is, rather, the religious imagery through which Lawrence evokes the sacramental mystery of sex. "Rare women," the philosopher tells the priestess of Isis in Search, "wait for the re-born man" (*EC* 39). And through sexual union with her, the man who died, in an entirely different sense than Jesus intended in his words to Nicodemus (John 3:3), is "born again," not to the stasis of eternal life but to the trembling of the balance. Written as a parable for contemporary Christian society, the novella sets forth one of D. H. Lawrence's major themes: rebirth of the whole man through tenderness in the sexual relationship.

13

The Trembling of the Balance

The "trembling balance" is a figure for health in the self and in the self's relationship to the external environment. It is not, however, an abstract ideal. The trembling of the balance keeps it from being that.

This study has considered Lawrence's conception of balance on widely varied levels and from seemingly disparate approaches. But in whatever form the concept emerges in Lawrence's work, it is distinguished from more mechanistic systems of balance by the dynamic homeostasis and the potential for growth that it shares with organic life. This is true even of Lawrence's comparatively abstract concept of dualism, since his Dionysian element, like that in Nietzsche's late work, finally contains both opposites in an organic polarity. Because his artist theme is biologically based and because the artistic identity he struggles with is masculine, Lawrence locates the aesthetic balance he seeks to establish between blood consciousness and spiritual consciousness in the image of the male body. Melville is the "true artist" as myth-maker, reconciling Christian and pagan consciousness in an organic symbolism rooted in unconscious experience. The cinema, however, is a false art, depending on assemblage rather than organic balance and exploiting psychic division by appealing to childish fantasy and stereotypes of beauty. Lawrence's theory of the unconscious balances voluntary and sympathetic body centers, and the etiology of illness lies in organic homeostatic imbalance rather than in the mechanistic malfunctioning of separable anatomical parts. Touch, which activates instinctual motives rather than mentally derived ideas, is central to human reconciliation and bonding. In psychic imbalance, even in such cases as phobia, sexual experience and self-acceptance can lead to psychological growth. Lawrence adopts the phoenix not as a static symbol for Christian resurrection but as a personal emblem for rebirth through creative change, which is projected as the theme of his last novels. In *The Plumed Serpent*, the pattern of imagery that I have related to the occult system of balance and transformation in alchemy provides both a mythic substratum for dualistic structure and a thematic paradigm for religious transformation. In *Lady Chatterley's Lover*, dynamic visionary experience as opposed to the ideal stasis of Joycean epiphany becomes a motive for change. In *The Escaped Cock*, traditional Christianity is brought into creative balance with the fertility myth of Isis and Osiris in a revisionist view of Christian resurrection. The "trembling balance" in Lawrence's work, considered either as theoretical system or in its phenomenological form, is characterized by the dynamic qualities of interrelatedness and flux.

In his essay "The Novel," Lawrence says that "the novel inherently is and must be"

1. Quick.
2. Interrelated in all its parts, vitally, organically.
3. Honorable. [*STH* 186]

The "quick" of life is a recurrent theme in Lawrence's work, from Paul Morel's turning sharply away from his depression at the end of *Sons and Lovers* to walk "quickly" toward the town (*SL* 492), meaning both rapidly and with enlivened spirit, to the priestess's feeling "touched on the quick at the sight of a man, as if the tip of a fine flame of living had touched her" in *The Escaped Cock* (*EC* 43). The great merit of the novel, Lawrence says, is that it "can't exist without being 'quick.'" "The man in the novel must be 'quick.' And this means . . . he must have a quick relatedness to all the other things in the novel" (*STH* 183). Novelists who write to propound a "philosophy" or "purpose" may consciously violate this principle, but unconsciously, "[i]n their passional inspiration, they are all phallic worshippers" (*STH* 180). This is why the real hero in every great novel is "[n]ot any of the characters, but some unnamed and nameless flame behind them all" (*STH* 182). If the novelist is faithful to his own character, this flame will come through in the dynamic "trembling balance" of his art.

Honor, for Lawrence, is concerned not with allegiance to external codes or abstract ideals but with fidelity to the "inner meaning" of one's own instinctual being: "A man's manhood is to honour the flames in him, and to know that none of them is absolute" (*STH* 189). Even sex, though of central significance, is both relative and relational, and Lawrence adopts no phallic absolute: Burning "against every absolute" and "deeper than functional desire," sex "is a deep reserve in a man, one of the core-flames of his manhood" (*STH* 189–90). Lawrence's definition of character encompasses growth and change on a continuum of the individual life flame, which changes continually yet remains single and separate (*STH* 186). While Dante or Petrarch might worship from afar the changeless ideal of Beatrice or Laura, Lawrence insists on being involved in time with the changing beloved, who "startles me into change and defies my inertia" (*STH* 196).

Lawrence, aiming at no ideal stasis in art, expected none in life. He was a self on the move. One is at first inclined to give assent when he says, "My yea! of today is oddly different from my yea! of yesterday"; but when he adds, "My tears of tomorrow will have nothing to do with my tears of a year ago" (*STH* 196), one's response is more dubious. The injuries to his self sustained in early childhood are too well known. They reverberate throughout his life, and his work simultaneously proclaims and encodes, exhibits and conceals, expresses and defends the self he was.

Many of Lawrence's characteristic ideas were formed or expressed in ongoing cultural dialogue with psychoanalysis. Lawrence's conception of life as a "trembling centre of balance" about which opposites sway and oscillate (*STH* 173) describes a concern with process and relationship, not with moral or philosophical categories or fixed scientific entities. This conception placed him in the same arena with Sigmund Freud, who challenged established scientific categories from a dissident position in psychiatry but who employed scientific formulations of physical energy and physiological development as concrete metaphors in his psychological theories. Lawrence, who did not have the same professional reason to bring his ideas into line with established science, turned more frequently to myth, including occult science, primitivism, and pre-Socratic cosmology, for his metaphors in a view of human development that saw tentativeness, interrelatedness, and flux as normal conditions. His understanding of psychoanalysis, though seldom without basis, was limited and sometimes erroneous. For him, such psychoanalytic concepts as repression, sexual complexes, and sublimation were fixed and basically negative categories. Viewed from the outside, the psychoanalytic interpretation of unconscious motives based on infantile sexual wishes and blocked instinctive drives seemed reductively mechanistic. Lawrence saw both psychoanalytic terminology and the psychoanalytic process as illegitimate attempts to fix and stabilize the balance. But psychoanalysis was the modern science that probed the same areas, psychosexual development, human relationships, psychic structure, and the unconscious, that most concerned D. H. Lawrence.

As a conclusion to this study, a further consideration of Lawrence's relation to Freud and psychoanalysis will reveal both uneasy affinities and intense differences, based as much on nearness as on philosophical distance. In this dialogue, Lawrence consistently returns to and illuminates the metaphor of the "trembling balance." He assumes a dissident position on reductive drive theory and becomes a significant early spokesman for a view of the self and its relationships that would emerge most fully in the subsequent psychoanalytic theories of interpersonal relations, object relations, and self psychology.

Lawrence's interest in psychoanalysis was, of course, in part personal. At times, for example, he was able to recognize his travels as an attempt to escape the self and its conflicts: "It is all a form of running away from oneself and the great problems: all this wild west and the strange Australia" (*Letters* 4:313). More often he was a self in transition, with the ego strength and courage of resilience, though his conception of the change required was more radical than Frederic Flach's resilience hypothesis: "One has oneself a fixed conscious entity, a self, which one has to smash. We are all like tortoises who have to smash their shells and creep forth tender and overvulnerable, but alive" (*Letters* 2:426). While Lawrence's many statements of this sort may seem to advocate the kind of deconstruction proposed in psychoanalysis, he has in mind nothing so deliberate as uncovering unconscious motives and making them conscious. Lawrence saw his art as an act of health in attempting to deal with his injuries creatively. He recognized the personally therapeutic function of the repetition in art of his experiences in life: "one sheds ones sicknesses in books—repeats and presents again ones emotions, to be master of them" (*Letters* 2:90). While this process, like psychoanalysis, has the restorative purpose not merely of ventilating but also of working through and understanding, the repetition in the text is inherently different from repetition in the transference. The artist recreates his internal objects in the text, which is intended as a synthesis of his experience. The psychoanalytic patient recreates them in the transference relationship, which becomes the subject of the analysis.

Lawrence's criticism of science in general is that its method of analysis rather than synthesis emphasizes the disintegrative rather than integrative functions of the mind. In "Why the Novel Matters," Lawrence again criticizes the scientist for functioning only as a pathologist at a postmortem examination of slide sections of tissue after the quick is gone: "He puts under the microscope a bit of dead me, . . . and says first one piece, and then another piece, is me" (*STH* 195). Lawrence flatly rejects the implied fragmentation into so many separable parts: "The whole is greater than the part," he says. "I am man alive, and as long as I can, I intend to go on being man alive" (*STH* 195).

In these terms, the new science of psychoanalysis comes under similar attack. In his familiar letter to Edward Garnett (19 November 1912), Lawrence, without referring to Freud, asserts a clearly Freudian theory of oedipal conflicts as the source of Paul Morel's split between sexual and spiritual love in *Sons and Lovers* and sees the Oedipus complex as "the tragedy of thousands of young men in England" (*Letters* 1:477). Motivated by the autobiographical impulse to come to terms with his own life and being, Lawrence produced the first great psychoanalytic novel in English. Ivy Low wrote enthusiastic postcards to friends: "Be sure to read *Sons and Lovers.*" "This is a book about the Oedipus complex!"[1] And so it was received by the London psychoanalytic community. But Lawrence wrote to Gordon Campbell: "I am not Freudian and never was—Freudianism is only a branch of medical science, interesting" (*Letters* 2:218). Although psychoanalysis as "the talking cure" had grown out of clinical practice, Freud himself saw psychoanalysis in a larger psychological, humanistic, and cultural context. In "The Question of Lay Analysis" (1926), he strongly opposes requiring psychoanalysts to take the medical degree and says it is undesirable for psychoanalysis to be "swallowed up by medicine" as a subsidiary method in psychiatry.[2] In 1913, Lawrence had not read Freud (*Letters* 2:80), and any Freudian influence on the novel probably came during his final revision of it by way of Frieda

1. Ivy Low Litvinoff, "A Visit to D. H. Lawrence," *Harper's Bazaar,* October 1946, 411–18 (reprinted in *D. H. Lawrence: A Composite Biography,* 1:215). Mme. Litvinoff's aunt, Barbara Low, and her uncle by marriage, David Eder, M.D., were both London psychoanalysts.

2. Freud, "The Question of Lay Analysis," *Standard Edition 20:247–48.* Among the prominent "lay analysts" who would have disagreed with Lawrence's statement are Melanie Klein, Hans Sachs, James Strachey, Anna Freud, and Lawrence's friend Barbara Low.

from Otto Gross, with whom she had an affair during her first marriage.[3] Lawrence wrote to Barbara Low that he hated Alfred Booth Kuttner's article on *Sons and Lovers* in the *Psychoanalytic Review*. His conscious objection to Kuttner's "Freudian Appreciation" was to having his art reduced to the terms of a case history: "You know I think 'complexes' are vicious half-statements of the Freudians. . . . When you've said Mutter-complex, you've said nothing—no more than if you called hysteria a nervous disease. Hysteria isn't nerves, a complex is not simply a sex relation: far from it.—My poor book: it was, as art, a fairly complete truth: so they carve a half lie out of it and say 'Voilà.' Swine!" (*Letters* 2:655) Two weeks later, he extends the objection to psychoanalysis in general: "I can't help hating psychoanalysis. I think it is irreverent and destructive" (*Letters* 2:659). Kuttner, in a report to Mitchell Kennerley on the manuscript of "The Wedding Ring" (10 November 1914), finds the psychology monotonous and, particularly in the men (the Brangwens, Skrebensky, Birkin), a repetition of Paul's psychology in *Sons and Lovers*. Kuttner correctly perceives that his kind of "analytical criticism" would be "bewildering" to Lawrence, since "his productivity is conditioned by such extreme subjectivism." Pained by the evidence of "deterioration . . . in a gifted writer, knowing as I do that it is of neurotic origin," Kuttner ventures his opinion: "A rigorous Freudian analysis would make Mr. Lawrence both a happier man and a greater artist. But as mere strangers we have no business to invade his personality to that extent."[4]

In *Psychoanalysis and the Unconscious* (1921), Lawrence uses Freud as a "straw man" in mounting his attack on psychoanalysis for bringing to light the "unspeakable horror" of "maniacal repressions, sexual complexes, faecal inhibitions, dream-monsters" (*PU* 5)—all of which, incidentally, appear in Lawrence's own fiction. Following an ironic strategy of carrying Freud's theoretical formulation to its literal extreme, Lawrence argues that since the complexes that Freud exposed as part of the normal unconscious are not, as psychoanalysis claims, dissolved by sublimation when brought to light, their overt expression is inevitable: "Once . . . you accept the incest-

---

3. A brilliant but decidedly outré member of the early Freudian circle, Gross was addicted to cocaine and opium, was referred by Freud for treatment by Jung, who ultimately diagnosed the young physician's illness as dementia praecox. See Freud and Jung, *The Freud/Jung Letters*, 141, 151, 152, 155–57.

4. See Kuttner, *"Sons and Lovers:* A Freudian Appreciation," 295–317. The article is an expansion of Kuttner's earlier review, *"Sons and Lovers," New Republic*, 10 April 1915, 255–57. Kuttner's subsequent comments are quoted from his "Report and Letter on 'The Wedding Ring,' " in Appendix III to Lawrence, *The Rainbow*, 483–85.

craving as part of the normal sexuality of man, you must remove all repression of incest itself. In fact you must admit incest as you now admit sexual marriage, as a duty even" (*PU* 7). This reasoning, which is inconsistent with Lawrence's emphasis on the value of getting in touch with one's feelings, becomes specious in its failure to distinguish between unconscious feelings and overt acting out.

In "The Novel and the Feelings" (1925), Lawrence clarifies his position on both the feelings and psychoanalysis. Modern man, having deliberately set out to tame himself, has lost the power of control from within himself and so looks for control from without. But, Lawrence says, in "the dark continent of myself, I have a whole stormy chaos of 'feelings.' . . . Some of them roar like lions, some twist like snakes, some bleat like snow-white lambs, some warble like linnets, some are absolutely dumb, but swift as slippery fishes, some are oysters that open on occasion" (*STH* 202). One can choose to respond, or not to respond, to the feelings as they make their presence known in "the blood." One cannot consciously call up and direct these instinctual promptings, but listening and answering to them puts one in touch with one's core self and engenders the kind of growth that can correct the imbalance. Lawrence asserts that psychoanalysis shows "the greatest fear of all, of the innermost primeval place in man" by seeking to tame the feelings (*STH* 204).

Lawrence's understanding of Freud's topographical and developmental theories was limited, and of the structural theory possibly nonexistent.[5] Freud's dictum on ego autonomy, "Where id was, there ego shall be," is founded on the emergence of the reality principle, which employs the secondary process to become the governing force of personality, controlling and modifying the pleasure principle and repressing its primary process. The formulation, however, is conditioned upon Freud's conception that the ego is itself a portion of the id, which remains the most important part of the personality and expresses through its drives the fundamental aims of the individual organism's life. The ego derives its energy from the id, and, on the whole, carries out the id's intentions by directing the expression of its drives into realistic channels. But a partial basis for Lawrence's

5. Lawrence would probably have known something of Freud's concepts of repression and sublimation through his friend Barbara Low, a lay analyst whose book *Psycho-Analysis* includes chapters on "Mental Life—Unconscious and Conscious" and "Repressions." In 1925, Lawrence was probably unfamiliar with the structural theory, which was first presented in Freud's *Das Ich und Das Es,* originally published in German (Leipzig, Vienna, and Zurich: Internationaler Psychoanalytischer Verlag, 1923), and first published in English translation as *The Ego and the Id,* trans. Joan Riviere (London: Hogarth Press, 1927).

charge is shown in Freud's employing a similar metaphor of wildness and tameness: "To adopt a popular mode of speaking, we might say that the ego stands for reason and good sense while the id stands for the untamed passions."[6]

Lawrence's argument distorts Freud's position as "the perverted vision of the degenerate tame: tamed through thousands of shameful years": "So great is the Freudian hatred of the oldest, old Adam, from whom God is not yet separated off, that the psychoanalyst sees this Adam as nothing but a monster of perversity, a bunch of engendering adders, horribly clotted" (*STH* 204–5). Surprisingly less tolerant than the psychoanalysts of these "engendering adders" of the id, Lawrence may resist uncovering the particulars of his own repressions by psychoanalytic means, but he is not being simply obtuse. He did not think of the feelings to which he listened as repressed material kept by moral prohibitions from entering consciousness but as deep unconscious impulses that link us with the biological, inhuman world of which we are a part.

In an effort to get in touch with "that which is physic—nonhuman, in humanity," Lawrence was ready to abandon the conventionally humanistic values that cause one "to conceive a character in a certain moral scheme and make him consistent." As he writes to Edward Garnett about "The Wedding Ring" (5 June 1914), he was not interested in "what the woman *feels*" in her conscious, social ego but in "what she *is*, inhumanly, physiologically, materially . . .: what she *is* as a phenomenon (or as representing some greater, inhuman will), instead of what she feels according to the human conception" (*Letters* 2:182–83). The distortion of Freud, it becomes clear, is predicated on Lawrence's view of feelings as the expression of basic organic instincts deriving from a pristine "carbon" self ("another ego"), prior to consciousness, and his rejection of sublimation, which he sees as a mechanism of the social persona ("the ego") and antithetical to this core identity.

Whatever Lawrence may have thought, he and Freud shared some ideas and goals, though they pursued these purposes by different methods. Daniel J. Schneider sees a correspondence between "Lawrence's sympathetic impulse and Freud's Eros" as unifying forces, and "a remote kinship . . . between Lawrence's idea that life always seeks a balance of sympathetic and voluntary impulses and Freud's 'principle of conservation,' the idea that life strives for equilibrium." Schneider suggests that Lawrence's conception of "two kinds of

---

6. For Freud's restatement of the structural theory, see his "Dissection of the Psychical Personality," in *New Introductory Lectures on Psycho-Analysis, Standard Edition*, 22:57–80. The quotations are from pp. 80 and 76.

dreams: body dreams and soul dreams," is "subtler" than Freud's idea of the dream as wish fulfillment, later modified to include anxiety dreams.[7] But Freud's original theory of the wish-fulfillment dream is revised and further elaborated throughout his work, and his later theory of the anxiety dream[8] roughly corresponds to Lawrence's simpler conception of the "distress dream" as expressing "the *reverse* of the soul's desire" (*FU* 198).

As two of the chief spokesmen for sexual freedom in the first third of the twentieth century, Freud and Lawrence were opponents of conventional morality while espousing a more profound ethic. Neither advocated promiscuous behavior, and neither could be called a libertine. Freud, whose strong personal morality was derived from "a sense of justice and consideration for others," writes to James J. Putnam (8 July 1915), "Sexual morality as defined by society, in its most extreme form that of America, strikes me as very contemptible. I stand for an infinitely freer sexual life, although I myself have made very little use of such freedom. Only so far as I considered myself entitled to."[9] Lawrence, similarly, says, "I want men and women to be able to think sex, fully, completely, honestly and cleanly." But he asserts, "Ours is the day of realization rather than action." Like Freud, he wanted to free the mind of inhibitions: "The mind has an old grovelling fear of the body and the body's potencies. It is the mind we have to liberate, to civilize on these points" (*P II* 489, 490, 491).

For both Freud and Lawrence, however, the phallus was the bridge to mental and emotional liberation through genital sexuality. Freud elucidates the multiple meanings of the bridge symbol in dreams: "First it means the male organ, which unites the two parents in sexual intercourse"; thus, secondarily, it refers to "the crossing from the other world (the unborn state, the womb) to this world (life)," or conversely to "something that leads to death," conceptualized "as a return to the womb (to the water)"; "and finally, at a further remove from its original sense, it stands for transitions or changes in condition generally."[10] Lawrence's statement that "the bridge to the future is the phallus" evokes both the original and the transitional, or transformational, sense of the image, but his vision of phallic regeneration is more radical than Freud's: "For the new

7. Schneider, *D. H. Lawrence: The Artist as Psychologist*, 249–50, 253.

8. See Freud's discussion of his "news from the front" dream in Freud, *The Interpretation of Dreams, Standard Edition*, 558–60.

9. Freud, *Letters of Sigmund Freud*, 308.

10. Freud, "Revision of the Theory of Dreams," in *New Introductory Lectures on Psycho-Analysis, Standard Edition*, 22:24.

impulse to life will never come without blood-contact; the true, positive blood-contact, not the nervous negative reaction. And the essential blood-contact is between man and woman, always has been so,
always will be" (*P II* 508).

Although they had some affinities, Lawrence, as Frederick J. Hoffman pointed out some time ago, did have a "quarrel" with Freud.
Commenting that the two men were agreed on "at least one
particular—that the normal sex life of man had been disastrously
repressed and neglected," Hoffman delineates the differences between Lawrence and Freud in seven principal terms. Since "vital
life" depends on "the spontaneous functioning of the non-cerebral
self," consciousness should not interfere with such vital areas of
unconscious life as the mother-child relationship, child rearing, and
sexuality. Lawrence saw the Freudian concepts of infantile sexuality
and bisexuality as "scientific myth." In adult sexuality, "man should
go beyond the crucial union of egos" in coition, which becomes "the
source of renewal," serving "to drive him forward into creative group
life."[11]

A more important difference, on which the others depend, is their
conceptions of the nature of the unconscious. The Freudian unconscious is a vast region, accessible only obliquely through dreams,
fantasies, and free associations, and containing not only the id and
its impulses but large portions of the ego and superego as well.
Conflicts between id impulses and superego prohibitions mobilize
ego defenses of repression and resistance, which both prevent the
instinctive drive from entering consciousness and defend against its
uncovering. The healthy Laurentian unconscious is not, as Lawrence persists in seeing the Freudian unconscious, merely a repository of forbidden erotic wishes but the wellspring of vitality and
creativity. Psychic imbalance, therefore, has its etiology not in these
creative unconscious processes themselves but in their weakening
and perversion by repression, as in Gudrun Brangwen and Gerald
Crich, Dollie Urquhart and Cathcart.

In his conception of human personality, Lawrence was not a drive/
structure theorist but a relational/structure theorist. Jay R. Greenberg and Stephen A. Mitchell suggest that these two divergent models of human psychology embody two major traditions within Western
thought. The first, taking "as its premise that human satisfactions
and goals are fundamentally personal and individual," is represented
by Hobbes and Locke, who emphasize man's private pursuit of power,

11. Hoffman, "Lawrence's Quarrel with Freud," in *Freudianism and the Literary
Mind*, 157, 166–67.

pleasure, or happiness. The second, holding that "[h]uman nature is completely realized only in relationship, interaction, participation with others," is represented severally by Rousseau, Hegel, and Marx, who emphasize that "[m]eaning in human life is possible only through social fulfillment."[12] When these two traditions are elaborated in psychoanalytic models, Lawrence, strong romantic individualist though he may be in some respects, is more fully in the tradition of the relational/structure model of Trigant Burrow (group- or phylo-analysis theory), Harry Stack Sullivan (interpersonal relations theory), W. R. D. Fairbairn and D. W. Winnicott (object relations theory), and Heinz Kohut (psychoanalytic self psychology), than in the tradition of the drive/structure model of Sigmund Freud (topographical and structural theory of psychoanalysis), Heinz Hartmann (ego psychology), and Jacques Lacan (deconstructionist psycholinguistic theory). For the drive theorists, the self was not a basic psychic structure but a set of internalized representations to be reduced to the original drive impulses, and their prohibition, by means of analysis (deconstruction). For the relational theorists, psychoanalysis was concerned with the developing structure of the self and its relation to the object world.

Fantasia of the Unconscious presents a theory not only of intrapsychic but also of intersubjective balance. Despite the conscious oedipal conception underlying *Sons and Lovers,* Lawrence came to feel that modern man's problems, including his own, centered in the blockage not of object-instinctive drives but of what he called the "primeval societal instinct." I have earlier quoted his statement in a letter to Trigant Burrow, "There is no repression of the sexual individual comparable to the repression of the societal man in me, by the individual ego, my own and everybody else's" (*CL* 989–90). As Schneider comments, "The deepest agreement between the two lies in their recognition that egoistic individualism is a severance from organic 'primary identification.' " In Burrow's phylobiology, this unity was based naturally in a preconscious "homogeneous matrix," and the unnatural separation was artificially induced by society, which encourages the formation of a false "I-persona."[13] Freud, who did not tolerate deviations from classical psychoanalytic drive theory by Jung or Adler, did not endorse the independent Baltimore analyst's pioneer work in group therapy. Lawrence's friend the American Imagist poet H. D. (Hilda Doolittle, former wife of Richard Aldington) says that in one of her analytic sessions, "Freud said it showed the state of

12. Greenberg and Mitchell, *Object Relations in Psychoanalytic Theory,* 400–403.
13. Schneider, 256.

the UC-N [unconscious] of D.H.L. that he should have hit on Burrow, of all people."[14] The reasons for the attraction are obvious. Burrow posited a preconscious flow of the self toward others that had been interrupted and destroyed by society. Lawrence emphasized the need for a "nourishing creative flow" with others, though as Schneider points out, this "unconscious striving for identity entails sundering as well as union."[15] In one sense, Rananim was an extension of the therapeutic group as utopian colony designed to facilitate maintenance of the "trembling balance."

Literary response, for Lawrence, was relational, always involving a personal interaction with the book. As I suggested in the Introduction, textual reading of any kind places the reader in an object relation to the author. That is why Lawrence saw criticism as a matter of the critic's becoming aware of how he employed his own feelings in the act of reading. As Lawrence writes in "John Galsworthy":

> Literary criticism can be no more than a reasoned account of the feeling produced upon the critic by the book he is criticising. Criticism can never be a science: it is, in the first place, much too personal, and in the second, it is concerned with values that science ignores. The touch-stone is emotion, not reason. We judge a work by its effect on our sincere and vital emotion, and nothing else. [STH 209]

Bruce Steele observes that the first draft of "John Galsworthy" is marked by a "concomitance of ideas—even of phrasing" to two papers by Trigant Burrow, which the psychoanalyst sent to Lawrence just before he began the Galsworthy essay in February 1927.[16]

For all his effort to articulate the "trembling balance," Lawrence was not always able to achieve and maintain a healthy balance in his own life and being. When one tries imaginatively to make empathic contact with Lawrence's self as it developed in childhood, a few recurrent "identity themes," to borrow Holland's term, summarize the most problematic areas of his early object world. Both his

14. Letter to Bryher (Winifred Ellerman), 11 May 1933, in Beinecke Library, Yale University. Quoted in Robinson, H. D., 282.

15. Schneider, 257.

16. Steele, "Introduction" to Lawrence, Study of Thomas Hardy and Other Essays, lii. The first essay Burrow sent to Lawrence, "Psychoanalysis in Theory and in Life," 209–24, was later incorporated as the first chapter of his The Social Basis of Consciousness, which Lawrence reviewed in Bookman (November 1927). On 7 February 1927, Burrow also sent Lawrence another essay, "The Reabsorbed Affect and Its Elimination," 209–18.

strengths and his dependency needs derive from his relationship with his mother. He was tied to his mother for too long, slept with her at times, merged with her, and it left him with a lifelong fear of merging, of being swallowed up. His father did nothing to protect him from that danger. His mother actively participated in the destruction of his father's status as a viable paternal object and the man's internal exile from the family. The son couldn't idealize his father, and he spent the rest of his life searching for a man he could. When he grew to young manhood, he couldn't get spiritual and sensual love together. Sexually he seemed to need an older woman, and sometimes he seemed to need a quasi-homoerotic relationship with a stronger man.

Such consistent object choices may explain why many critics, as well as Lawrence himself at first, thought his problems were oedipal.[17] They weren't, at least not in their earliest etiology. Despite the undeniable importance of oedipal conflicts in Lawrence's development, they do not account for the major problem areas of his adult life. That is to say, his underlying difficulties were not primarily a matter of instinctive drives, repressed by oedipal prohibitions but emerging in neurotic symptoms. They were located earlier in the preoedipal period, though they were later sexualized and activated oedipal disturbances. Lawrence was correct in finally identifying his injuries as "wounds to the soul, to the deep emotional self" (*CP* 620). They really had to do with nurturance, in the formation of his archaic nuclear self, not with triangular sexual competition in the "family romance." The impact on his work of early injuries to his developing self can scarcely be estimated. That is why Lawrence's fictional themes, with few exceptions, do not center on oedipal guilt but on male autonomy, and sometimes on shame and male nurturance. The ambivalence of the son who struggled for independence from the strong mother, whom he loved but whose overwhelming possessive love served her own need for sustenance more than his need for normal psychological growth and development, is echoed in the ambivalence toward women and struggles for male autonomy on the part of protagonists like Rupert Birkin or Aaron Sisson. The shame of the little boy at having to go on Fridays to pick up his father's pay from the colliery paymaster, or at having to endure the ridicule of cruel schoolmates who called him "mard-arsed" and jeered that he "played with the wenches," reemerges in the over-

17. See especially Weiss, *Oedipus in Nottingham;* and Cavitch, *D. H. Lawrence and the New World.*

whelming shame that follows Bachmann's phobic failure to climb the rampart, in Aaron Sisson's savage sense of worthlessness after he has sexual relations with Josephine Ford, and in Parkin's sexual demoralization. The unmet need of the son for fatherly support and nurturance, a need nonetheless real despite his severe disappointment in his own devalued father, is answered in the nurturance provided by the leader like Rawdon Lilly or Ramón Carrasco.[18] But Lawrence's wariness that even fatherly love may become devouring is evident in Richard Lovat Somers's resistance to Kangaroo's Jehovah-like embrace as a threat to put him in his pouch. Lawrence's lifelong elemental anger, or, in Heinz Kohut's term, his narcissistic rage, is attributable to these deficits. It reverberates in his flirtation with violent revolution, in Jack Callcott's and Cipriano Viedma's killings, in the awaited sacrifice of "the woman who rode away," and in Sir Clifford Chatterley's spiteful stories and class arrogance.

As an adult, Lawrence thought he could resolve his conflicts, especially the split between spiritual and sensual love, as Birkin tries to do, by establishing two kinds of irrevocable love relationships, star-polarity with a woman and blood brotherhood with a man. He liked having disciples, and he kept wanting to escape to a faraway place and establish a utopian colony called Rananim where they could all be happy; but his Rananim could exist only, and imperfectly, in the fantastic and invented Mexico of Ramón's Quetzalcoatl revolution. Lawrence wanted to be free sexually, and to free the world as well, but finally, with the physical debilitation of advancing pulmonary tuberculosis and attendent psychogenic symptoms of depression and anxiety, he couldn't function sexually himself. He invested both the heroic sexual ideal of his wish fulfillment and the demoralized sexual self of his depressive position in the twin portraits of Oliver Mellors and Sir Clifford Chatterley.

In his voracious need, Lawrence wanted things he couldn't have, like Birkin's "two kinds of love," and Frieda told him so. Yet she stayed with him. He alone of the significant men she had loved and slept with—a thoroughly conventional professor, an erratic psychiatrist, an opportunistic captain—was an artist. That was his strength. Like Keats, he was an empathic artist. Keats said of

18. My view of Lawrence's psychology is in substantial agreement with Judith Ruderman's emphasis, in *D. H. Lawrence and the Devouring Mother,* on the pre-oedipal origins of Lawrence's own psychological problems (9–10). Ruderman suggests that a major function of the leader in Lawrence's leadership novels is not simply to lead the masses but to provide the male nurturance that will prevent the man's being devoured by woman in her Magna Mater role (174–75).

himself, "If a Sparrow come before my Window I take part in its exist[e]nce and pick about the Gravel."[19] Frieda recalled, "When Lawrence first found a gentian, a big single blue one, I remember feeling as if he had a strange communion with it, as if the gentian yielded up its blueness, its very essence, to him. Everything he met had the newness of a creation just that moment come into being."[20] Lawrence, like Shiva dancing, is surprised by the joy of his own creation. With few lapses, Lawrence maintains empathy with his creation in a shifting point of view fully invested now in one, now in another, of his characters. And this empathy carries him to unexpected dimensions of quickness, pregnant with the potential for further transformation and change. By putting the reader in touch with the affective wellsprings of his being, Lawrence engenders in him a recognition of his own capacity for continued growth. In so doing, Lawrence becomes the "true artist."

Lawrence attributes the mechanistic elements of psychoanalysis to the rationalism or "idealism" that he sees as the mechanistic basis of modern medical science in general. The implied narrator of St. Mawr, sounding very much like D. H. Lawrence, has little use for psychoanalysis, which he likens to the pathologist's dissection: "If anatomy pre-supposes a corpse, then psychology pre-supposes a world of corpses. Personalities, which means personal criticism and analysis, pre-supposes a whole world-laboratory of human psyches waiting to be vivisected" (St. M 44). Lawrence's charge, again not without basis, sounds like a complementary identification with Freud's similar metaphors from the anatomy laboratory, as in the title of his restatement of the structural theory: "The Dissection of the Psychical Personality." If there is a distortion in Lawrence's statement, it is in the implication that psychoanalysis is a deathly process. For him, "post-mortem effects" (SCAL 165) could neither account for the "quickness" of "man alive" nor allow for the dynamic process of change.

Lawrence's reservation that psychoanalysis is too scientific, though not based on personal experience, is a reasonable concern. Contemporaneous evidence from two of Lawrence's women friends suggests that, however scientific the theoretical formulations of psychoanalysis might be, its therapeutic action derived at least as much from the analyst's empathy as from his impersonal interpretations. While H. D. has reservations about Freud's interpretation of penis envy, she attests to the human quality of his interaction with her, and

19. Keats, The Letters of John Keats, 1:186.
20. Frieda Lawrence, "Not I, But the Wind . . . ," 35.

Freud's warm, affectionate letters to her confirm it.[21] It is not Freud's theories that she found curative; it is her empathic relationship with the Professor himself.[22] Similarly, Ethel Mannin's memoir depicts another of Lawrence's friends, the psychoanalyst David Eder, as a lovable, kindly, honest, thoroughly knowledgeable man of genuine humility, whose "wisdom and understanding" provided the strength that enabled her to emerge from the "dark tunnel" into which she found herself "so unexpectedly and horrifyingly plunged." Dr. Eder, she says, listened more than he talked, but delivered his subtle psychoanalytic interpretations with warmth and profound conviction.[23]

Lawrence's concern is surely related to his sense that the etiology of his own illness lay not in the mechanism's "working wrongly" but in "wounds to the soul, to the deep emotional self" (CP 620). This too is a legitimate self issue, but one that would not be adequately addressed theoretically for another generation or two, and controversially even then. It is clear that from the beginning the therapeutic action of psychoanalysis depended more on the empathic connection than on the specific intellectual content of the psychoanalytic interpretations. The psychoanalyst Margaret I. Little's account of her own analysis with the classical Freudian drive theorist Ella Freeman Sharpe (1940–47) depicts the relationship as "one of constant struggle between us, she insisting on interpreting what I said as due to intrapsychic conflict to do with infantile sexuality, and I trying to convey to her that my real problems were matters of existence and identity: I did not know what 'myself' was. . . ." Dr. Little's description of her subsequent analysis with the object relations theorist D. W. Winnicott (1949–55, 1957), which involved a harrowing regression and an intense relationship with him, presents an almost diametrically opposite picture of empathic connection that demonstrates clearly why the latter analysis was therapeutically successful while the former was not.[24] W. R. D. Fairbairn, who replaced Freud's instinct theory with object relationships, voices the same objections to

21. H. D., Tribute to Freud, 95–104. Freud's letters to H. D. are on pp. 189–94.

22. For four more detailed discussions of H. D.'s analysis with Freud, see Guest, "19 Bergasse Strasse," Herself Defined: The Poet H. D. and Her World, 207–22; Holland, "H. D. and the 'Blameless Physician,' " 474–506; Friedman, "A Most Luscious Vers Libre Relationship: H. D. and Freud," 319–43; and Friedman, "Against Discipleship: Collaboration and Intimacy in the Relationship of H. D. and Freud," 89–104. Beginning 5 March 1933, their one-hour sessions for five days a week continued, with one interruption, for a total of five months in 1933 and 1934. While it is clear that " 'deep' material was reached," Holland thinks the analysis was as much didactic as therapeutic.

23. Mannin, "Dr. David Eder," in Confessions and Impressions, 222, 224.

24. Little, "Winnicott Working in Areas Where Psychotic Anxieties Predominate," 15. Discussion of her analysis with Winnicott is on pp. 19–41.

scientific psychoanalysis that Lawrence did. As Fairbairn told the psychoanalyst Harry Guntrip, during the latter's analysis with him: "You can go on analysing for ever and get nowhere. It's the personal relation that is therapeutic. Science has no values except scientific values, the schizoid values of the investigator who stands outside of life and watches. It is purely instrumental, useful for a time but then you have to get back to living." Guntrip believes that "psychoanalytic therapy is not a purely theoretical but a truly understanding personal relationship."[25]

Even in the midst of his denunciation of Freudianism in *Psychoanalysis and the Unconscious,* Lawrence was capable of a brief tribute to what Freud himself regarded as his major achievement: ". . . who could remain unmoved when Freud seemed suddenly to plunge towards the origins? Suddenly he stepped out of the conscious into the unconscious, out of the everywhere into the nowhere, like some supreme explorer. He walks straight through the wall of sleep, and we hear him rumbling in the cavern of dreams. The impenetrable is not impenetrable, unconsciousness is not nothingness" (*PU* 5).

In the early months of her analysis with Freud (1933–34), H. D. talked extensively about Lawrence with Freud and transferred to the analyst many of her feelings about Lawrence: "I asked him how he was and he smiled a charming, wrinkled smile that reminded me of D. H. Lawrence." To her, Freud at seventy-seven "is like D. H. Lawrence, grown old but matured and with astute perception. His hands are sensitive and frail. He is midwife to the soul."[26] She kept Lawrence's photograph with her and read his letters in the Huxley edition to recapture the period of her relationship with him.[27] Freud admired the ending of one of Lawrence's books: "Lawrence impressed him as 'being unsatisfied but a man of real power.' "[28]

At this time, H. D. either discussed or planned to discuss with Freud Lawrence's *Man Who Died (The Escaped Cock)*. Stephen

25. Guntrip, "My Experience of Analysis with Fairbairn and Winnicott," 448. Guntrip, who, like Margaret I. Little, found in his subsequent analysis that D. W. Winnicott had a greater "capacity for natural, spontaneous 'personal relating' " than his first analyst did, even with his agreeable theory, concluded that much depends on the "natural fit" between the two persons involved. Fairbairn clarified his views on "psychoanalysis and science" in two papers: "Theoretical and Experimental Aspects of Psycho-Analysis," *British Journal of Medical Psychology* 25 (1952): 122–27; and "Observations in Defence of the Object-Relations Theory of the Personality," *British Journal of Medical Psychology* 28 (1955): 144–56.

26. H. D., 128, 116.

27. Robinson, 279–83.

28. H. D., 144.

Guest, who had given her the book, had told her that Lawrence had written it for her and that she was the priestess of Isis.[29] Since their infatuation in 1916–17, intense as it was, was apparently an affair primarily of the mind and spirit, this seems unlikely. The complete truth is difficult to ascertain. Robinson charges that "it was covered up" by Aldington, who destroyed evidence of the affair and influenced its suppression in the Moore and Nehls biographies. Robinson even suggests that, as the risen man had fathered the priestess's unborn child, Lawrence may have been the unacknowledged father of H. D.'s daughter.[30] That possibility is interesting but again unlikely. But the Asclepian values and themes of Lawrence's novella inform her moving tribute to Freud as a modern Asclepius:

> It was Asklepios of the Greeks who was called the *blameless physician*. He was the son of the sun, Phoebos Apollo, and music and medicine were alike sacred to this source of light. This half-man, half-god (Fate decreed) went a little too far when he began actually to raise the dead. He was blasted by the thunder-bolt of an avenging deity, but Apollo, over-riding his father's anger, placed Asklepios among the stars. Our Professor stood this side of the portal. He did not pretend to bring back the dead who had already crossed the threshold. But he raised from dead hearts and stricken minds and maladjusted bodies a host of living children.[31]

Their theories and methods were far apart. But for all their differences, Freud, the heir to the Enlightenment, and Lawrence, the heir to Romanticism, both traced their roots to older traditions than either. In Freud's study, H. D. admired his treasured collection of sculpture from Mediterranean antiquity. In *Last Poems,* in such poems as "The Greeks Are Coming!," "The Argonauts," "Middle of the World," "For the Heroes Are Dipped in Scarlet," "Maximus," "The Man of Tyre," and "They Say the Sea Is Loveless," Lawrence returns to the Mediterranean world of Dionysus, Odysseus, Hermes. Each man in his way saw healing as an Asclepian art.

Lawrence's "religion of the blood" was a metaphor by which to evoke the original divinity of the body: "In the oldest of the old

29. Ibid., 134, 141.
30. See Robinson, 142–80. Covering the same ground somewhat less speculatively, Firchow, "Rico and Julia: The Hilda Doolittle-D. H. Lawrence Affair Reconsidered," 51–76, concentrates on the literary effects of the affair in works by H. D., Lawrence, Aldington, and John Cournos.
31. H.D., 101.

Adam, was God: behind the dark wall of his breast, under the seal of the navel" (*STH* 205). And through his art he sought to restore the balance by awakening in man an awareness of this inner divinity by putting him in touch with the feelings that called from the deepest instincts of his body: "the primeval, honorable beasts of our being, whose voice echoes wordless and forever wordless down the darkest avenues of the soul, but full of potent speech. Our own inner meaning" (*STH* 205).

The light of the mind and the dark of the blood, the voices of spirit and beast: Lawrence knew and honored both, and he tried to right the balance between them. It had to be a trembling balance, stable but dynamic, allowing for creative change and growth. Depending on one's own empathic abilities, Lawrence at times puts one in touch with his or her deepest self, with what he calls one's "own inner meaning." This enables the empathic reader to discover the inner strength of resilience, the courage to destroy a habitual but no longer useful psychological homeostasis and to create a new and more adaptive one. That alone is enough to justify the effort to understand him. If I can understand Lawrence, I can also understand the self he puts me in touch with. That's not a matter of identification, nor solely a question of identity. It is a means of affirming "the acceptance of one's own and only life cycle and the people who have become significant to it as something that had to be and that, by necessity, permitted of no substitutions." That, in Erik Erikson's sense of the term, is a question of integrity.[32]

32. Erikson, *Identity and the Life Cycle*, 98–99. For Erikson, the choice between *integrity* and *despair* is the major task of the last stage of the life cycle.

Bibliography

Works by D. H. Lawrence

———. *Aaron's Rod*. Edited by Mara Kalnins. Cambridge: Cambridge University Press, 1988.

———. *Apocalypse and the Writings on Revelation*. Edited by Mara Kalnins. Cambridge: Cambridge University Press, 1980.

———. *The Collected Letters of D. H. Lawrence*. Edited by Harry T. Moore. 2 vols. New York: Viking Press, 1962.

———. *The Complete Plays of D. H. Lawrence*. London: William Heinemann, 1965.

———. *The Complete Poems of D. H. Lawrence*. Edited by Vivian de Sola Pinto and F. Warren Roberts. New York: Viking Press, 1971.

———. *The Complete Short Stories of D. H. Lawrence*, vol. 3. London: William Heinemann, 1955; reprinted 1958.

———. *D. H. Lawrence: Ten Paintings*. Redding Ridge, Conn.: Black Swan Books, 1982.

———. *England, My England and Other Stories*. Edited by Bruce Steele. Cambridge: Cambridge University Press, 1990.

———. *The Escaped Cock*. Edited by Gerald M. Lacy. Los Angeles: Black Sparrow Press, 1973.

———. *Etruscan Places*. In *Mornings in Mexico* and *Etruscan Places*. London: William Heinemann, 1956.

———. *Fantasia of the Unconscious*. In *Psychoanalysis and the Unconscious* and *Fantasia of the Unconscious*. New York: Viking Press, Compass Books, 1960.

———. *The First Lady Chatterley*. New York: Dial Press, 1944.

———. "Foreword to *Sons and Lovers*." In *The Letters of D. H. Lawrence*. Edited, and with an Introduction, by Aldous Huxley, 97–104. New York: Viking Press, 1932; reprinted 1936.

———. *John Thomas and Lady Jane*. New York: Viking Press, 1972.

———. *Kangaroo*. London: William Heinemann, 1955.

———. *The Ladybird*. In *Four Short Novels by D. H. Lawrence*. New York: Viking Press, Compass Books, 1965.

———. *Lady Chatterley's Lover*. New York: Grove Press, 1959.

———. *Letters from D. H. Lawrence to Martin Secker, 1911–1930*. [London]: Privately printed, 1970.

———. *The Letters of D. H. Lawrence*. Edited, and with an Introduction, by Aldous Huxley. New York: Viking Press, 1932; reprinted 1936.

———. *The Letters of D. H. Lawrence*. Vol. 1: *September 1901–May 1913*. Edited by James T. Boulton. Cambridge: Cambridge University Press, 1979.

———. *The Letters of D. H. Lawrence*. Vol. 2: *June 1913–October 1916*. Edited by George J. Zytaruk and James T. Boulton. Cambridge: Cambridge University Press, 1981.

———. *The Letters of D. H. Lawrence*. Vol. 3: *October 1916–June 1921*. Edited by James T. Boulton and Andrew Robertson. Cambridge: Cambridge University Press, 1984.

———. *The Letters of D. H. Lawrence*. Vol. 4: *June 1921–March 1924*. Edited by Warren Roberts, James T. Boulton, and Elizabeth Mansfield. Cambridge: Cambridge University Press, 1987.

———. *The Letters of D. H. Lawrence*. Vol. 5: *March 1924–March 1927*. Edited by James T. Boulton and Lindeth Vasey. Cambridge: Cambridge University Press, 1989.

———. *The Lost Girl*. Edited by John Worthen. Cambridge: Cambridge University Press, 1981.

———. *Movements in European History*. Edited by Philip Crumpton. Cambridge: Cambridge University Press, 1989.

———. *Paintings of D. H. Lawrence*. Edited by Mervyn Levy. New York: Viking Press, A Studio Book, 1964.

———. *Phoenix: The Posthumous Papers of D. H. Lawrence*. Edited by Edward D. McDonald. New York: Viking Press, 1936, reprinted 1968.

———. *Phoenix II: Uncollected, Unpublished, and Other Prose Works by D. H. Lawrence*. Edited by Warren Roberts and Harry T. Moore. New York: Viking Press, 1968.

———. *The Plumed Serpent*. Edited by L. D. Clark. Cambridge: Cambridge University Press, 1987.

———. *The Prussian Officer and Other Stories*. Edited by John Worthen. Cambridge: Cambridge University Press, 1983.

———. *Psychoanalysis and the Unconscious*. In *Psychoanalysis and the Unconscious and Fantasia of the Unconscious*. Introduction by Philip Rieff. New York: Viking Press, Compass Books, 1960.

———. *The Quest for Rananim: D. H. Lawrence's Letters to S. S. Koteliansky, 1914–1930*. Edited by George J. Zytaruk. Montreal and London: McGill–Queen's University Press, 1970.

———. *The Rainbow*. Edited by Mark Kinkead-Weekes. Cambridge: Cambridge University Press, 1989.

———. *Reflections on the Death of a Porcupine and Other Essays*. Edited by Michael Herbert. Cambridge: Cambridge University Press, 1988.

———. *Sons and Lovers*. Edited, with an Introduction and Notes, by Keith Sagar. Harmondsworth, Middlesex, U.K.: Penguin Books, 1981, reprinted 1986.

———. *St. Mawr and Other Stories.* Edited by Brian Finney. Cambridge: Cambridge University Press, 1983.

———. *Studies in Classic American Literature.* New York: Viking Press, Compass Books, 1961.

———. *Study of Thomas Hardy and Other Essays.* Edited by Bruce Steele. Cambridge: Cambridge University Press, 1985.

———. *The Symbolic Meaning: The Uncollected Versions of "Studies in Classic American Literature."* Edited by Armin Arnold. New York: Viking Press, 1964.

———. *The Trespasser.* Edited by Elizabeth Mansfield. Cambridge: Cambridge University Press, 1982.

———. *Twilight in Italy.* New York: Viking Press, 1958.

———. "Vin Ordinaire." *English Review* 17 (June 1914): 298–325.

———. *The White Peacock.* Edited by Andrew Robertson. Cambridge: Cambridge University Press, 1983.

———. *Women in Love.* Edited by David Farmer, Lindeth Vasey, and John Worthen. Cambridge: Cambridge University Press, 1987.

Books

Alldritt, Keith. *The Visual Imagination of D. H. Lawrence.* Evanston, Ill.: Northwestern University Press, 1971.

Arvin, Newton. *Herman Melville.* New York: Viking Press, Compass Books, 1957.

Bachofen, J. J. *Myth, Religion, and Mother Right: Selected Writings of J. J. Bachofen.* Translated by Ralph Manheim. Bollingen Series 84. Princeton, N.J.: Princeton University Press, 1967.

Baker, Paul G. *A Reassessment of D. H. Lawrence's "Aaron's Rod."* Studies in Modern Literature, no. 31. Ann Arbor, Mich.: UMI Research Press, 1983.

Beebe, Maurice. *Ivory Towers and Sacred Founts: The Artist as Hero in Fiction from Goethe to Joyce.* New York: New York University Press, 1964.

Beja, Morris. *Epiphany in the Modern Novel.* Seattle: University of Washington Press, 1971.

Bell, Clive. *Art.* New York: Frederick A. Stokes, [1913].

Bell, Michael. *Primitivism.* London: Methuen, 1972.

Bersani, Leo. *A Future for Astyanax: Character and Desire in Literature.* Boston and Toronto: Little, Brown, 1976.

Black, Michael. *D. H. Lawrence: The Early Fiction: A Commentary.* Cambridge: Cambridge University Press, 1986.

Brett, Dorothy. *Lawrence and Brett: A Friendship.* Philadelphia: J. B. Lippincott, 1933.

Britton, Derek. *"Lady Chatterley": The Making of the Novel.* London: Unwin Hyman, 1988.

Brown, Norman O. *Life against Death.* New York: Vintage Books, 1959.

Brownlow, Kevin. *The Parade's Gone By . . .* New York: Ballantine Books, 1968.

Burns, Wayne. *Towards a Contextualist Aesthetic of the Novel.* Edited by James Flynn, Gerald Butler, and Evelyn Butler. Seattle, Wash.: Genitron Books, 1968.

Burrow, Trigant. *A Search for Man's Sanity: The Selected Letters of Trigant Burrow, with Biographical Notes.* Prepared by the Editorial Committee of the Lifwynn Foundation: William E. Galt, Chairman. Foreword by Sir Herbert Read. New York: Oxford University Press, 1958.

Bibliography

Butler, Gerald J. *This Is Carbon: A Defense of D. H. Lawrence's "The Rainbow"*
against His Admirers, with an Introduction by Jerry Zaslove. Seattle, Wash.:
Genitron Press, 1986.
Bynner, Witter. *Journey with Genius: Recollections and Reflections Concerning the*
D. H. Lawrences. London: Peter Nevill, 1953.
Campbell, Joseph. *The Hero with a Thousand Faces.* 2d ed. Princeton, N.J.: Princeton
University Press, 1968.
———. *The Masks of God: Creative Mythology.* New York: Viking Press, 1968.
Cannon, Walter B., M.D. *The Wisdom of the Body.* 2d ed., rev. and enl. New York:
W. W. Norton, 1939.
Capra, Frank. *The Name Above the Title: An Autobiography.* New York: Macmillan,
1971.
Carter, Frederick. *D. H. Lawrence and the Body Mystical.* London: Denis Archer,
1932.
Cavitch, David. *D. H. Lawrence and the New World.* New York: Oxford University
Press, 1969.
Chambers, Jessie. *D. H. Lawrence: A Personal Record.* By E. T. New York: Knight
Publications, 1936.
Clark, L. D. *Dark Night of the Body: D. H. Lawrence's "The Plumed Serpent."* Austin:
University of Texas Press, 1964.
Clarke, Colin. *River of Dissolution: D. H. Lawrence and English Romanticism.* New
York: Barnes and Noble, 1969.
Collins, Joseph. *The Doctor Looks at Literature: Psychological Studies of Life and*
Letters. New York: George H. Doran, 1923.
Compton, Susan, ed. *British Art in the 20th Century: The Modern Movement.* Munich:
Prestel-Verlag, 1986.
Cowan, James C. *D. H. Lawrence's American Journey: A Study in Literature and*
Myth. Cleveland, Ohio, and London: Press of Case Western Reserve University,
1970.
D. H. [Hilda Doolittle]. *Tribute to Freud: Writing on the Wall, Advent.* Boston: David
R. Godine, 1974.
Daleski, H. M. *The Forked Flame: A Study of D. H. Lawrence.* Evanston, Ill.: North-
western University Press, 1965.
Delany, Paul. *D. H. Lawrence's Nightmare: The Writer and His Circle in the Years of*
the Great War. New York: Basic Books, 1978.
Delavenay, Emile. *D. H. Lawrence: The Man and His Work, The Formative Years,*
1885–1919. Translated by Katharine M. Delavenay. Carbondale and Ed-
wardsville: Southern Illinois University Press, 1972.
Derrida, Jacques. *Dissemination.* Translated, with Introduction and Additional Notes,
by Barbara Johnson. Chicago and London: University of Chicago Press, 1981.
Dervin, Daniel. *A "Strange Sapience": The Creative Imagination of D. H. Lawrence.*
Amherst: University of Massachusetts Press, 1984.
Eisenstein, Sergei. *Film Form: Essays in Film Theory.* Edited and Translated by Jay
Leyda. New York: Harcourt, Brace, Jovanovich, Harvest Book, c. 1949.
Eliot, T. S. *The Complete Poems and Plays.* New York: Harcourt, Brace, 1952.
Ellis, David, and Howard Mills. *D. H. Lawrence's Nonfiction: Art, Thought, and*
Genre. Cambridge: Cambridge University Press, 1988.
Erikson, Erik H. *Childhood and Society,* 2d rev. ed. New York: W. W. Norton, 1963.
———. *Identity and the Life Cycle: Selected Papers.* Published as *Psychological Issues,*
1, no. 1 (New York: International Universities Press, 1959): 1–171.
Fabricant, Noah D., M.D. *Thirteen Famous Patients.* New York: Pyramid Books, 1960.

Farmer, John S., and W. E. Henley. *Slang and Its Analogues: Past and Present*, vol. 4. [London]: Printed for Subscribers Only, 1896. Reprinted in abridged form as *A Dictionary of Slang and Colloquial English*. London: George Routledge and Sons; New York: E. P. Dutton, 1912.

Fernald, Dodge. *The Hans Legacy: A Story of Science*. Hillsdale, N.J., and London: Lawrence Erlbaum, 1984.

Fitzgerald, F. Scott. *Tender Is the Night*. In *Three Novels of F. Scott Fitzgerald*. New York: Charles Scribner's Sons, 1953.

Ford, George H. *Double Measure: A Study of the Novels and Stories of D. H. Lawrence*. New York: Holt, Rinehart, and Winston, 1965.

Frazer, James George. *The Golden Bough*, vol. 2. 3d ed. London: Macmillan, 1911.

———. *The Golden Bough*. 1 vol. abridged ed. New York: Macmillan, 1951

Freeman, Mary. *D. H. Lawrence: A Basic Study of His Ideas*. Gainesville: University of Florida Press, 1955.

Freud, Sigmund. *An Autobiographical Study; Inhibitions, Symptoms and Anxiety; The Question of Lay Analysis; and Other Works* (1925–26). Vol. 20 of *The Standard Edition of the Complete Psychological Works of Sigmund Freud*. Translated under the general editorship of James Strachey, in collaboration with Anna Freud, assisted by Alix Strachey and Alan Tyson. 24 vols. London: Hogarth Press and the Institute of Psycho-Analysis, 1962.

———. *Early Psycho-Analytic Publications* (1893–1899). Vol. 3 of *The Standard Edition of the Complete Psychological Works of Sigmund Freud*. Translated under the general editorship of James Strachey, in collaboration with Anna Freud, assisted by Alix Strachey and Alan Tyson. 24 vols. London: Hogarth Press and the Institute of Psycho-Analysis, 1962.

———. *The Ego and the Id and Other Works* (1923–1925). Vol. 19 of *The Standard Edition of the Complete Psychological Works of Sigmund Freud*. Translated under the general editorship of James Strachey, in collaboration with Anna Freud, assisted by Alix Strachey and Alan Tyson. 24 vols. London: Hogarth Press and the Institute of Psycho-Analysis, 1962.

———. *The Interpretation of Dreams (Second Part) and On Dreams* (1900–1901). Vol. 5 of *The Standard Edition of the Complete Psychological Works of Sigmund Freud*. Translated under the general editorship of James Strachey, in collaboration with Anna Freud, assisted by Alix Strachey and Alan Tyson. 24 vols. London: Hogarth Press and the Institute of Psycho-Analysis, 1962.

———. *Letters of Sigmund Freud*. Edited by Ernst L. Freud. Translated by Tania Stern and James Stern. New York: Basic Books, 1960.

———. *New Introductory Lectures on Psycho-Analysis and Other Works* (1932–1936). Vol. 22 of *The Standard Edition of the Complete Psychological Works of Sigmund Freud*. Translated under the general editorship of James Strachey, in collaboration with Anna Freud, assisted by Alix Strachey and Alan Tyson. 24 vols. London: Hogarth Press and the Institute of Psycho-Analysis, 1964.

———. *Totem and Taboo and Other Works* (1913–1914). Vol. 13 of *The Standard Edition of the Complete Psychological Works of Sigmund Freud*. Translated under the general editorship of James Strachey, in collaboration with Anna Freud, assisted by Alix Strachey and Alan Tyson. 24 vols. London: Hogarth Press and the Institute of Psycho-Analysis, 1955; reprinted with corrections, 1958.

———. *Two Case Histories ("Little Hans" and the "Rat Man")* (1909). Vol. 10 of *The Standard Edition of the Complete Psychological Works of Sigmund Freud*. Translated under the general editorship of James Strachey in collaboration with Anna Freud, assisted by Alix Strachey and Alan Tyson. 24 vols. London: Hogarth Press and the Institute of Psycho-Analysis, 1962.

———, and C. G. Jung. *The Freud/Jung Letters: The Correspondence between Sigmund Freud and C. G. Jung*. Edited by William McGuire. Translated by Ralph Manheim and R. F. C. Hull. Bollingen Series 94. Princeton, N.J.: Princeton University Press, 1974.

Fry, Roger. *Vision and Design*. London: Chatto and Windus, 1924. Reprinted New York: Peter Smith, 1947.

Garnett, David. *The Flowers of the Forest*. New York: Harcourt, Brace, 1956.

———. *The Golden Echo*. New York: Harcourt, Brace, 1954.

Gay, Peter. *Freud: A Life for Our Time*. New York and London: W. W. Norton, 1988.

Gilbert, Sandra M. *Acts of Attention: The Poems of D. H. Lawrence*. Ithaca, N.Y., and London: Cornell University Press, 1972.

Gish, Lillian, with Anne Pinchot. *The Movies, Mr. Griffith, and Me*. New York: Avon Books, 1970.

Goldberg, Arnold. *A Fresh Look at Psychoanalysis: The View from Self Psychology*. Hillsdale, N.J., Hove and London: Analytic Press, 1988.

Goodheart, Eugene. *The Utopian Vision of D. H. Lawrence*. Chicago: University of Chicago Press, 1963.

Gordon, David J. *D. H. Lawrence as a Literary Critic*. New Haven, Conn., and London: Yale University Press, 1966.

Graves, Robert. *The Greek Myths*. 2 vols. New York: George Braziller, 1959.

Gray, Henry. *Anatomy of the Human Body*. Edited by Warren H. Lewis. 20th ed., rev. Philadelphia and New York: Lea and Febiger, 1918.

Greenberg, Jay R., and Stephen A. Mitchell. *Object Relations in Psychoanalytic Theory*. Cambridge, Mass., and London: Harvard University Press, 1983.

Greenson, Ralph R. *The Technique and Practice of Psychoanalysis*. Vol. 1. New York: International Universities Press, 1967.

Gregory, Horace. *D. H. Lawrence: Pilgrim of the Apocalypse: A Critical Study*. New York: Viking Press, 1933; reprinted New York: Grove Press, Evergreen Books, 1957.

Guest, Barbara. *Herself Defined: The Poet H. D. and Her World*. Garden City, N.Y.: Doubleday, 1984.

Gutierrez, Donald. *The Maze in the Mind and the World: Labyrinths in Modern Literature*. Troy, N.Y.: Whitston, 1985.

Hardy, George, and Nathaniel Harris. *A D. H. Lawrence Album*. New York: Franklin Watts, 1986.

Harris, Janice Hubbard. *The Short Fiction of D. H. Lawrence*. New Brunswick, N. J.: Rutgers University Press, 1984.

Harvey, Paul, ed. *The Oxford Companion to Classical Literature*. Oxford: Oxford University Press, 1955.

Hayles, N. Katherine. *The Cosmic Web: Scientific Field Models and Literary Strategies in the Twentieth Century*. Ithaca, N. Y., and London: Cornell University Press, 1984.

Hillman, James. *Archetypal Psychology: A Brief Account, Together with a Complete Checklist of Works*. Dallas, Texas: Spring Publications, 1983.

Hoffman, Frederick J. *Freudianism and the Literary Mind*. 2d ed. Baton Rouge: Louisiana State University Press, 1957.

Holderness, Graham. *Who's Who in D. H. Lawrence*. New York: Taplinger, 1976.

Holland, Norman N. *The Dynamics of Literary Response*. New York: Oxford University Press, 1968.

————. *5 Readers Reading*. New Haven, Conn., and London: Yale University Press, 1975.

Holroyd, Michael. *Lytton Strachey: A Critical Biography*. Vol. 2: *The Years of Achievement (1910–1932)*. New York: Holt, Rinehart and Winston, 1968.

Hough, Graham. *The Dark Sun: A Study of D. H. Lawrence*. New York: Macmillan, 1957.

Howe, Marguerite Beede. *The Art of the Self in D. H. Lawrence*. Athens: Ohio University Press, 1977.

Jackson, Dennis. "The Progression Toward Myth and Ritual in the Three Versions of D. H. Lawrence's *Lady Chatterley's Lover*." Ph.D. diss., University of Arkansas, Fayetteville, 1978.

Janik, Del Ivan. *The Curve of Return: D. H. Lawrence's Travel Books*. English Literary Studies Monograph Series, no. 22. Victoria, B.C., Canada: University of Victoria, 1981.

Joyce, James. *Epiphanies*. Introduction and Notes by O. A. Silverman. Buffalo, N. Y.: University of Buffalo, Lockwood Memorial Library, 1956.

————. *Letters of James Joyce*. Vol. 1. Edited by Stuart Gilbert. New York: Viking Press, 1957; rev. 1966.

————. *A Portrait of the Artist as a Young Man*. New York: Penguin Books, 1982.

————. *Stephen Hero*. London and New York: Jonathan Cape, 1944.

Jung, C. G. *Alchemical Studies*. Vol. 13 of *The Collected Works of C. G. Jung*. Translated by R. F. C. Hull. Bollingen Series 20. Princeton, N. J.: Princeton University Press, 1967.

————. *Mysterium Coniunctionis: An Inquiry into the Separation and Synthesis of Psychic Opposites in Alchemy*. Vol. 14 of *The Collected Works of C. G. Jung*. Translated by R. F. C. Hull. Bollingen Series 20. New York: Pantheon Books, 1963.

————. *Psychology and Alchemy*. Vol. 12 of *The Collected Works of C. G. Jung*. Translated by R. F. C. Hull. Bollingen Series 20. New York: Pantheon Books, 1953.

————. *The Structure and Dynamics of the Psyche*. Vol. 8 of *The Collected Works of C. G. Jung*. Translated by R. F. C. Hull. Bollingen Series 20. New York: Pantheon Books, 1960.

————. *Symbols of Transformation: An Analysis of the Prelude to a Case of Schizophrenia*. Vol. 5 of *The Collected Works of C. G. Jung*. 2d ed. Translated by R. F. C. Hull. Bollingen Series 20. Princeton, N. J.: Princeton University Press, 1967.

Kaufmann, Walter. *Nietzsche: Philosopher, Psychologist, Antichrist*. Cleveland and New York: World Publishing Co., 1966.

Keats, John. *The Letters of John Keats*, 2 vols. Edited by Hyder Edward Rollins. Cambridge, Mass.: Harvard University Press, 1958.

Kerényi, C. *Asklepios: Archetypal Image of the Physician's Existence*. Translated by Ralph Manheim. Bollingen Series 65, vol. 3. New York: Pantheon Books, 1959.

Klein, George S. *Psychoanalytic Theory: An Exploration of Essentials*. New York: International Universities Press, 1976.

Klein, Melanie. *The Selected Melanie Klein*. Edited by Juliet Mitchell. New York: The Free Press, 1986.

Knight, Arthur. *The Liveliest Art: A Panoramic History of the Movies*. New York: Macmillan, 1957.

Kohut, Heinz, M.D. *The Analysis of the Self: A Systematic Approach to the Psychoanalytic Treatment of Narcissistic Personality Disorders*. Monograph Series of the Psychoanalytic Study of the Child, Monograph no. 4. New York: International Universities Press, 1971.

———. *How Does Analysis Cure?* Edited by Arnold Goldberg, with the collaboration of Paul Stepansky. Chicago: University of Chicago Press, 1984.

———. *The Search for the Self: Selected Writings of Heinz Kohut: 1950–1978.* 2 vols. Edited with an Introduction by Paul H. Ornstein. New York: International Universities Press, 1978.

Langer, Susanne K. *Philosophy in a New Key.* New York: New American Library, Mentor, 1956.

Lawrence, Frieda. *Frieda Lawrence: The Memoirs and Correspondence.* Edited by E. W. Tedlock, Jr. New York: Alfred A. Knopf, 1964.

———. *"Not I, But the Wind . . .".* New York: Viking Press, 1934.

Low, Barbara. *Psycho-Analysis: A Brief Account of the Freudian Theory.* Introduction by Ernest Jones, M.D. London: George Allen and Unwin, 1920.

Luhan, Mabel Dodge. *Lorenzo in Taos.* New York: Alfred A. Knopf, 1932.

Mackenzie, Compton. *My Life and Times, Octave Five: 1915–1923.* London: Chatto and Windus, 1966.

———. *On Moral Courage.* London: Collins, 1962.

Mannin, Ethel. *Confessions and Impressions.* Garden City, N.Y.: Doubleday, Doran, 1930.

Margulies, Alfred, M.D. *The Empathic Imagination.* New York: W. W. Norton, 1989.

Masterman, C. F. G. *England after the War.* London: Hodder and Stoughton, 1922.

Masters, William H., and Virginia E. Johnson. *Human Sexual Response.* Boston: Little, Brown, 1966.

Melville, Herman. *Billy Budd, Sailor* (reading text). Edited by Harrison Hayford and Merton M. Sealts, Jr. Chicago and London: University of Chicago Press, 1962.

———. *Moby-Dick, or The Whale.* Edited, with Historical Note, by Harrison Hayford, Hershel Parker, and G. Thomas Tanselle. Evanston and Chicago: Northwestern University Press and Newberry Library, 1988.

Merrild, Knud. *With D. H. Lawrence in New Mexico: A Memoir of D. H. Lawrence.* London: Routledge and Kegan Paul, 1964.

Meyers, Jeffrey. *D. H. Lawrence and the Experience of Italy.* Philadelphia: University of Pennsylvania Press, 1982.

———. *The Enemy: A Biography of Wyndham Lewis.* London and Henley: Routledge and Kegan Paul, 1980.

———. *Homosexuality and Literature, 1890–1930.* Montreal: McGill-Queen's University Press, 1977.

———. *Painting and the Novel.* Manchester: Manchester University Press; New York: Barnes and Noble, 1975.

———Miko, Stephen J. *Toward "Women in Love": The Emergence of a Lawrentian Aesthetic.* New Haven, Conn., and London: Yale University Press, 1971.

Miller, Henry. *The Wisdom of the Heart.* Norfolk, Conn.: New Directions Books, 1941.

Millett, Kate. *Sexual Politics.* Garden City, N. Y.: Doubleday, 1970.

Millett, Robert W. *The Vultures and the Phoenix: A Study of the Mandrake Press Edition of the Paintings of D. H. Lawrence.* Philadelphia: Art Alliance Press; London and Toronto: Associated University Presses, 1983.

Milton, Colin. *Lawrence and Nietzsche: A Study in Influence.* Aberdeen, U. K.: Aberdeen University Press, 1987.

Milton, John. *John Milton: Complete Poems and Major Prose.* Edited by Merritt Y. Hughes. New York: Odyssey Press, 1957.

Mizener, Arthur. *The Far Side of Paradise: A Biography of F. Scott Fitzgerald.* Boston: Houghton Mifflin, 1949, reprinted 1950, 1951.

Moore, Harry T. *The Priest of Love: A Life of D. H. Lawrence.* New York: Farrar,
 Straus, and Giroux, 1974.
Moore, Harry T., and Warren Roberts. *D. H. Lawrence and His World.* New York:
 Viking Press, 1966.
Nehls, Edward, ed. *D. H. Lawrence: A Composite Biography.* Vol. 1, *1885–1919.* Madi-
 son: University of Wisconsin Press, 1957.
———, ed. *D. H. Lawrence: A Composite Biography.* Vol. 2, *1919–1925.* Madison:
 University of Wisconsin Press, 1958.
———, ed. *D. H. Lawrence: A Composite Biography.* Vol. 3, *1925–1930.* Madison:
 University of Wisconsin Press, 1959.
Neville, G. H. *A Memoir of D. H. Lawrence (The Betrayal).* Edited by Carl Baron.
 Cambridge: Cambridge University Press, 1982.
Nixon, Cornelia. *Lawrence's Leadership Politics and the Turn against Women.* Berke-
 ley, Los Angeles, and London: University of California Press, 1986.
Ober, William B., M.D. *Boswell's Clap and Other Essays: Medical Analyses of Literary
 Men's Afflictions.* Carbondale and Edwardsville: Southern Illinois University
 Press, 1979.
O'Keeffe, Georgia. *Georgia O'Keeffe.* New York: Viking Press, 1976.
Orioli, Giuseppe. *Adventures of a Bookseller.* New York: McBride, 1938.
Otto, Rudolf. *The Idea of the Holy.* London, New York, and Toronto: Geoffrey Cum-
 berlege, Oxford University Press, 1946.
Otto, Walter F. *Dionysus: Myth and Cult.* Translated by Robert B. Palmer. Blooming-
 ton and London: Indiana University Press, 1965.
Ovesey, Lionel, M.D. *Homosexuality and Pseudohomosexuality.* New York: Science
 House, 1969.
Pace, Billy James. "D. H. Lawrence's Use in His Novels of Germanic and Celtic Myth
 from the Music Dramas of Richard Wagner." Ph.D. diss., University of Arkan-
 sas, Fayetteville, 1973.
Parmenter, Ross. *Lawrence in Oaxaca: A Quest for the Novelist in Mexico.* Salt Lake
 City, Utah: Gibbs Smith, Peregrine Smith Books, 1984.
Pearson, John. *The Sitwells: A Family's Biography.* New York and London: Harcourt,
 Brace, Jovanovich, Harvest/HBJ, 1978.
Posenet, George. *A Dictionary of Egyptian Civilization.* Translated by Alix MacFar-
 lane. London: Metheun, 1962.
Racker, Heinrich. *Transference and Countertransference.* New York: International
 Universities Press, 1968.
Ragussis, Michael. *The Subterfuge of Art: Language and the Romantic Tradition.*
 Baltimore, Md., and London: Johns Hopkins University Press, 1978.
Rhode, Eric. *A History of the Cinema from Its Origins to 1970.* New York: Hill and
 Wang, 1976.
Rieff, Phillip. *The Triumph of the Therapeutic: Uses of Faith after Freud.* New York:
 Harper and Row, 1966.
Robinson, Janice S. *H. D.: The Life and Work of an American Poet.* Boston: Houghton
 Mifflin, 1982.
Rogin, Michael Paul. *"Ronald Reagan", the Movie, and Other Episodes in Political
 Demonology.* Berkeley, Los Angeles, and London: University of California
 Press, 1987.
Ruderman, Judith. *D. H. Lawrence and the Devouring Mother: The Search for a
 Patriarchal Ideal of Leadership.* Durham, N.C.: Duke University Press, 1984.
Sagar, Keith. *D. H. Lawrence: A Calendar of His Works, with a Checklist of the*

Manuscripts of D. H. Lawrence by Lindeth Vasey. Austin: University of Texas Press, 1979.

Salgādo, Gāmini, ed. *D. H. Lawrence: "Sons and Lovers."* Casebook Series. Nashville, Tenn., and London: Aurora Publishers, 1969.

Sandler, Joseph, ed. *Projection, Identification, Projective Identification.* Papers of the first conference of the Sigmund Freud Center of the Hebrew University of Jerusalem, May 27–29, 1984. Madison, Conn.: International Universities Press, 1987.

Schickel, Richard. *D. W. Griffith: An American Life.* New York: Simon and Schuster, 1984.

Schmertz, Jack. *A Reinterpretation of "A Phobia in a Five Year Old Boy."* Notre Dame, Ind.: Foundations Press, 1984.

Schneider, Daniel J. *D. H. Lawrence: The Artist as Psychologist.* Lawrence: University Press of Kansas, 1984.

Scholes, Robert, and Richard M. Kain. *The Workshop of Daedalus: James Joyce and the Raw Material for "A Portrait of the Artist as a Young Man."* Evanston, Ill.: Northwestern University Press, 1965.

Segal, Hanna. *Introduction to the Work of Melanie Klein.* 2d ed. New York: Basic Books, Harper Torchbooks, 1973, reprinted 1974.

Shone, Richard. *The Century of Change: British Painting Since 1900.* Oxford, U.K.: Phaidon, 1977.

Shumaker, Wayne. *The Occult Sciences in the Renaissance: A Study in Intellectual Patterns.* Berkeley, Los Angeles, and London: University of California Press, 1972.

Sitwell, Edith. *Taken Care Of: The Autobiography of Edith Sitwell.* New York: Atheneum, 1965.

Sitwell, Osbert. *Penny Foolish: A Book of Tirades and Panegyrics.* London: Macmillan, 1965.

Spilka, Mark. *The Love Ethic of D. H. Lawrence.* Bloomington: Indiana University Press, 1955.

Squires, Michael. *The Creation of "Lady Chatterley's Lover."* Baltimore, Md., and London: Johns Hopkins University Press, 1983.

Swigg, Richard. *Lawrence, Hardy, and American Literature.* London: Oxford University Press, 1972.

Tedlock, E. W., Jr., ed. *D. H. Lawrence and "Sons and Lovers": Sources and Criticism.* New York: New York University Press, 1965.

Tindall, William York. *D. H. Lawrence and Susan His Cow.* New York: Columbia University Press, 1939.

Torgovnick, Marianna. *The Visual Arts, Pictorialism, and the Novel: James, Lawrence, and Woolf.* Princeton, N. J.: Princeton University Press, 1985.

Van Ghent, Dorothy. *The English Novel: Form and Function.* New York: Holt, Rinehart and Winston, 1953.

Vivas, Eliseo. *D. H. Lawrence: The Failure and the Triumph of Art.* Evanston, Ill.: Northwestern University Press, 1960.

Walker, Alexander. *Rudolph Valentino.* New York: Penguin Books, 1977.

Weiss, Daniel A. *Oedipus in Nottingham: D. H. Lawrence.* Seattle: University of Washington Press, 1962.

Whistler, James A. M. *The Gentle Art of Making Enemies, as Pleasingly Exemplified in Many Instances, Wherein the Serious Ones of Earth Carefully Exasperated, Have Been Prettily Spurred on to Unseemliness and Indiscretion, While Overcome by an Undue Sense of Right.* London: William Heinemann, 1890.

Widmer, Kingsley. *The Art of Perversity: D. H. Lawrence's Shorter Fictions.* Seattle: University of Washington Press, 1962.

Wilde, Oscar. *The Artist as Critic: Critical Writings of Oscar Wilde.* Edited by Richard Ellmann. New York: Random House, 1969.

Woolf, Virginia. *The Common Reader.* First Series. New York: Harcourt, Brace, Harvest Books, 1953.

Articles and Other Short Pieces

Abolin, Nancy. "Lawrence's 'The Blind Man': The Reality of Touch." In *A D. H. Lawrence Miscellany,* edited by Harry T. Moore, 215–20. Carbondale: Southern Illinois University Press, 1959.

Amon, Frank. "D. H. Lawrence and the Short Story." In *The Achievement of D. H. Lawrence,* edited by Frederick J. Hoffman and Harry T. Moore, 222–34. Norman: University of Oklahoma Press, 1953.

Apter, T. E. "Let's Hear What the Male Chauvinist Is Saying: *The Plumed Serpent.*" In *Lawrence and Women,* edited by Anne Smith, 156–77. London: Vision Press; Totowa, N. J.: Barnes and Noble, 1978.

Arnold, Armin. "D. H. Lawrence and Max Mohr." In *The Modernists: Studies in a Literary Phenomenon, Essays in Honor of Harry T. Moore,* edited by Lawrence B. Gamache and Ian S. MacNiven, 126–39. Rutherford, N. J.: Fairleigh Dickinson University Press; London and Toronto: Associated University Presses, 1987.

Barry, Sandra. "Singularity of Two; the Plurality of One." *Paunch,* no. 26 (April 1966):34–39.

Britton, Derek. "Henry Moat, Lady Ida Sitwell, and *John Thomas and Lady Jane.*" *D. H. Lawrence Review* 15, nos. 1–2 (Spring–Summer 1982):69–76.

Brown, W. Langdon, M.D., M.R.C.P. "The Return to Aesculapius." In *Medical Pamphlet No. 4,* 11–27. N.p.: C. W. Daniel, 1932.

Burrow, Trigant, M.D. "Psychoanalysis in Theory and in Life." *Journal of Nervous and Mental Disease* 64 (September 1926):209–24.

———. "The Reabsorbed Affect and Its Elimination." *British Journal of Medical Psychology* 6, part 3 (1926):209–18.

"Can Great Books Make Good Movies? Seven Writers Just Say No!" *American Film* 12, no. 9 (July/August 1987):36–40.

Cannon, Walter B., M.D. "Croonian Lecture. The Physiological Basis of Thirst." *Proceedings of the Royal Society B* 90 (1917–19):283–301.

———. "Organization for Physiological Homeostasis" (1925). In *Homeostasis: Origins of the Concept,* edited by L. L. Langley, 250–82. Stroudsburg, Pa.: Dowden, Hutchinson and Ross, 1973.

———. "Physiological Regulation of Normal States: Some Tentative Postulates Concerning Biological Homeostatics." In *À Charles Richet: ses amis, ses collègues, ses élèves, 22 Mai 1926,* edited by Auguste Pettit, 91–93. Paris: Les Éditions Médicales, 1926. Reprinted in *Homeostasis: Origins of the Concept,* edited by L. L. Langley, 246–49. Stroudsburg, Pa.: Dowden, Hutchinson and Ross, 1973.

———. "Some General Features of Endocrine Influence on Metabolism." *American Journal of Medical Science* 171 (1926):1–20.

———, and A. Querido. "The Rôle of Adrenal Secretion in the Chemical Control of Body Temperature." *Proceedings of the National Academy of Science* (Washington, D. C.) 10 (1924):441–54.

————, and A. L. Washburn. "An Explanation of Hunger." *American Journal of Physiology* 29 (1912):441–54.

Chamberlain, Robert L. "Pussum, Minette, and the Africo-Nordic Symbol in Lawrence's *Women in Love.*" *PMLA* 78 (September 1963):407–16.

Chayes, Irene Hendry. "Joyce's Epiphanies." In *Joyce's "Portrait": Criticisms and Critiques,* edited by Thomas E. Connolly. New York: Appleton-Century-Crofts, 1962.

Clark, L. D. "The D. H. Lawrence Festival, Kiowa Ranch, New Mexico, September 30–October 4, 1970." Photographs by LaVerne H. Clark and Judith R. Cowan. *D. H. Lawrence Review* 4, no. 1 (Spring 1971):44–60.

Conrad, Joseph. "Preface" to *The Nigger of the "Narcissus,"* xxxvii–xlii. New York: Harper and Brothers, 1951.

Cowan, James C. "The Function of Allusions and Symbols in D. H. Lawrence's *The Man Who Died.*" *American Imago* 17, no. 3 (Fall 1960):241–53.

Cushman, Keith. "D. H. Lawrence at Work: 'Vin Ordinaire' into 'The Thorn in the Flesh.'" *Journal of Modern Literature* 5 (February 1976):46–58.

————. "'I am going through a transition stage': *The Prussian Officer* and *The Rainbow.*" *D. H. Lawrence Review* 8, no. 2 (Summer 1975):176–97.

Delavenay, Emile. "Lawrence and the Futurists." In *The Modernists: Studies in a Literary Phenomenon, Essays in Honor of Harry T. Moore,* edited by Lawrence B. Gamache and Ian S. MacNiven, 140–62. Rutherford, N. J.: Fairleigh Dickinson University Press; London and Toronto: Associated University Presses, 1987.

Eliot, T. S. "'The victim and the sacrificial knife': T. S. Eliot on Lawrence, a Review of *Son of Woman* by J. M. Murry." In *D. H. Lawrence: The Critical Heritage,* edited by R. P. Draper, 241–47. New York: Barnes and Noble, 1970.

Ellis, David. "Lawrence and the Biological Psyche." In *D. H. Lawrence: Centenary Essays,* edited by Mara Kalnins, 89–109. Bristol, U. K.: Bristol Classical Press, 1986.

Ellmann, Richard. "On Joyce's Centennial." *New Republic* 186 (17 February 1982):28–31.

Fairbairn, W. R. D. "Observations in Defence of the Object-Relations Theory of the Personality." *British Journal of Medical Psychology* 28 (1955):144–56.

————. "Theoretical and Experimental Aspects of Psycho-Analysis." *British Journal of Medical Psychology* 25 (1952): 122–27.

Fiderer, Gerald. "D. H. Lawrence's *The Man Who Died:* The Phallic Christ." *American Imago* 25 (1968):91–96.

Firchow, Peter E. "Rico and Julia: The Hilda Doolittle–D. H. Lawrence Affair Reconsidered." *Journal of Modern Literature* 8, no. 1 (1980):51–76.

Flach, Frederic, M.D. "The Resilience Hypothesis." *Psychiatric Times* 5, no. 5 (May 1988):5–6.

Ford, George H., Frank Kermode, Colin Clarke, and Mark Spilka. "Critical Exchange: On 'Lawrence Up-Tight': Four Tail-Pieces." *Novel: A Forum on Fiction* 5 (Fall 1971):54–70.

Friedman, Paul. "The Phobias." In *American Handbook of Psychiatry,* 3 vols. Edited by Silvano Arieti; vol. 1, 293–306. New York: Basic Books, 1959.

Friedman, Susan Stanford. "Against Discipleship: Collaboration and Intimacy in the Relationship of H. D. and Freud." *Literature and Psychology* 33, nos. 3–4 (1987):89–104.

————. "A Most Luscious *Vers Libre* Relationship: H. D. and Freud." *Annual of Psychoanalysis* 14 (1986): 319–42.

Gajdusek, Robert E. "A Reading of 'A Poem of Friendship,' A Chapter in Lawrence's *The White Peacock.*" *D. H. Lawrence Review* 3, no. 1 (Spring 1970):47–62.

Greenson, Ralph R. "Empathy and Its Vicissitudes." In *Explorations in Psychoanalysis,* 147–61. New York: International Universities Press, 1978.

Guntrip, Harry. "My Experience of Analysis with Fairbairn and Winnicott (How Complete a Result Does Psycho-Analytic Therapy Achieve?)." In *Essential Papers on Object Relations,* edited by Peter Buckley, M.D., 447–68. New York and London: New York University Press, 1986.

Hardy, G[eorge] W. "Short Communication—*The Lost Girl.*" *Journal of the D. H. Lawrence Society* (England) 1, no. 2 (1977):23.

Heywood, Christopher. "African Art and the Work of Roger Fry and D. H. Lawrence." In *Papers on African Literature,* edited by Christopher Heywood, 102–13. *Sheffield Papers on Literature and Society,* no. 1 (1976).

———. " 'Blood-Consciousness' and the Pioneers of the Reflex and Ganglionic Systems." In *D. H. Lawrence: New Studies,* edited by Christopher Heywood, 104–23. New York: St. Martin's Press, 1987.

Hinz, Evelyn J. "The Beginning and the End: D. H. Lawrence's *Psychoanalysis* and *Fantasia.*" *Dalhousie Review* 52 (Summer 1972):251–65.

———. "D. H. Lawrence's Clothes Metaphor." *D. H. Lawrence Review* 1, no. 2 (Summer 1968):87–113.

———, and John J. Teunissen. "Savior and Cock: Allusion and Icon in Lawrence's *The Man Who Died.*" *Journal of Modern Literature* 5, no. 2 (April 1976):279–96.

Holland, Norman N. "H. D. and the 'Blameless Physician.' " *Contemporary Literature* 10, no. 4 ["Special Number on H. D.": *H. D.: A Reconsideration*] (Autumn 1969):474–506.

Howarth, Herbert. "D. H. Lawrence from Island to Glacier." *University of Toronto Quarterly* 37 (April 1968):215–29.

Humma, John B. "D. H. Lawrence as Friedrich Nietzsche." *Philological Quarterly* 53 (January 1974):110–20.

———. "Lawrence's 'The Ladybird' and the Enabling Image." *D. H. Lawrence Review* 17 (Fall 1984):219–32.

———. "Melville's *Billy Budd* and Lawrence's 'The Prussian Officer': Old Adams and New." *Essays in Literature* 1 (1974):83–88.

Jackson, Dennis. "*Lady Chatterley's Lover:* Lawrence's Response to *Ulysses?*" *Philological Quarterly* (Summer 1987):410–16.

———. "Literary Allusions in *Lady Chatterley's Lover.*" In *D. H. Lawrence's "Lady": A New Look at "Lady Chatterley's Lover",* edited by Michael Squires and Dennis Jackson, 170–96. Athens: University of Georgia Press, 1985.

Kernberg, Otto F., M.D. "Projection and Projective Identification: Developmental and Clinical Aspects." *Journal of the American Psychoanalytic Association* 35, no. 4 (1987):795–819.

———. "Projection and Projective Identification." In *Projection, Identification, Projective Identification,* edited by Joseph Sandler, 93–115. Papers of the first conference of the Sigmund Freud Center of the Hebrew University of Jerusalem, May 27–29, 1984. Madison, Conn.: International Universities Press, 1987.

Kramer, Peter, M.D. "What Hurts," in "Practicing" column. *Psychiatric Times* 5, no. 8 (August 1988): 3, 33.

Kuttner, Alfred Booth. "Report and Letter on 'The Wedding Ring,' " In Appendix III in *The Rainbow,* edited by Mark Kinkead-Weekes, 483–85. Cambridge: Cambridge University Press, 1989.

———. "*Sons and Lovers:* A Freudian Appreciation." *Psychoanalytic Review* 3 (July 1916):295–317.

LeDoux, Larry V. "Christ and Isis: The Function of the Dying and Reviving God in *The Man Who Died.*" *D. H. Lawrence Review* 5, no. 2 (Summer 1972):132–48.

Little, Margaret I. "Winnicott Working in Areas Where Psychotic Anxieties Predominate: A Personal Record." *Free Associations* 3 (1985):9–41.

MacDonald, Robert H. " 'The Two Principles': A Theory of the Sexual and Psychological Symbolism of D. H. Lawrence's Later Fiction." *D. H. Lawrence Review* 11 (Summer 1978):132–55.

McLean, Celia. "The Entropic Artist: Lawrence's Theory of Art in *Women in Love.*" *D. H. Lawrence Review* 20, no. 3 (Fall 1988): 275–86.

"A Man in His Senses." *Times Literary Supplement* (London), 4 November 1960, 708.

Margulies, Alfred, M.D. "Toward Empathy: The Uses of Wonder." *American Journal of Psychiatry* 141, no. 9 (September 1984):1025–33.

Meissner, W. W., S.J., M.D. "A Note on Projective Identification." *Journal of the American Psychoanalytic Association* 28 (1980):43–67.

———. "Projection and Projective Identification." In *Projection, Identification, Projective Identification,* edited by Joseph Sandler, 27–49. Papers of the first conference of the Sigmund Freud Center of the Hebrew University of Jerusalem, May 27–29, 1984. Madison, Conn.: International Universities Press, 1987.

Mohr, Max. "David Herbert Lawrence." *Vossische Zeitung* (Berlin), 21 March 1930.

Moody, H. L. B. "African Sculpture Symbols in a Novel by D. H. Lawrence." *Ibadan,* no. 26 (February 1969):73–77.

Morris, Inez R. "African Sculpture Symbols in *Women in Love.*" *D. H. Lawrence Review* 16, no. 1 (Spring 1983):25–43.

Morrison, Kristin. "Lawrence, Beardsley, Wilde: *The White Peacock* and Sexual Ambiguity." *Western Humanities Review* 30 (1976):241–48.

Oates, Joyce Carol. "Lawrence's Götterdämmerung: The Apocalyptic Vision of *Women in Love.*" In *Contraries: Essays,* 141–70. New York: Oxford University Press, 1981.

Owen, Frederick I. "D. H. Lawrence and Max Mohr: A Late Friendship and Correspondence." *D. H. Lawrence Review* 9, no. 1 (Spring 1976):137–56.

Pearson, S. Vere, M.D., M.R.C.P. "The Psychology of the Consumptive." *Journal of State Medicine* 40 (August 1932):477–85.

Poe, Edgar Allan. "The Fall of the House of Usher." In *Tales and Sketches, 1831–1842.* Vol. 2 of *Collected Works of Edgar Allan Poe.* Edited by Thomas Ollive Mabbott, with the assistance of Eleanor D. Kewer and Maureen C. Mabbott, 397–422. Cambridge, Mass., and London: Belknap Press of Harvard University Press, 1978.

Poesch, Jessie J. "The Phoenix Portrayed." *D. H. Lawrence Review* 5, no. 3 (Fall 1972):200–237.

Richardson, John Adkins, and John I. Ades. "D. H. Lawrence on Cézanne: A Study in the Psychology of Critical Intuition." *Journal of Aesthetics and Art Criticism* 28 (Summer 1970):441–53.

Rossman, Charles. "Four Versions of D. H. Lawrence." *D. H. Lawrence Review* 6, no. 1 (Spring 1973):47–70.

Sandler, Joseph. "The Concept of Projective Identification." In *Projection, Identification, Projective Identification,* edited by Joseph Sandler, 13–26. Papers of the first conference of the Sigmund Freud Center of the Hebrew University of

Jerusalem, May 27–29, 1984. Madison, Conn.: International Universities Press, 1987.

Schoenberner, Franz. "More about My Collaborators: D. H. Lawrence Is Shocked." In *Confessions of a European Intellectual,* 282–92. New York: Macmillan, 1946.

Scholes, Robert, and Florence L. Walzl. "The Epiphanies of Joyce." *PMLA* 82 (March 1967):153.

Scott, James F. "D. H. Lawrence's *Germania:* Ethnic Psychology and Cultural Crisis in the Shorter Fiction." *D. H. Lawrence Review* 10, no. 2 (Summer 1977):142–64.

Shealy, Ann. "The Epiphany Theme in Modern Fiction: E. M. Forster's *Howards End* and D. H. Lawrence's *Sons and Lovers.*" Part 1 of *The Passionate Mind: Four Studies, Including "Julia Peterken: A Souvenir,"* 3–27. Philadelphia: Dorrance, 1976.

Sheerin, Daniel J. "John Thomas and the King of Glory: Two Analogues to D. H. Lawrence's Use of Psalm 24:7 in Chapter XIV of *Lady Chatterley's Lover.*" *D. H. Lawrence Review* 11, no. 3 (Fall 1978):297–300.

Sitwell, Osbert. "A Visit with D. H. L." *New York Herald Tribune,* 20 December 1960.

Smailes, T. A. "Lawrence's Verse: More Editorial Lapses." *Notes and Queries,* n.s., 17 (December 1970):465–66.

Solecki, Sam. "D. H. Lawrence's View of Film." *Literature/Film Quarterly* 1, no. 1 (Winter 1973):12–16.

Spilka, Mark. "Lawrence's Quarrel with Tenderness." In *Critical Essays on D. H. Lawrence,* edited by Dennis Jackson and Fleda Brown Jackson, 223–37. Boston: G. K. Hall, 1988.

———. "Lawrence Up-Tight, or the Anal Phase Once Over." *Novel* 4 (Spring 1971):252–67.

Stewart, Jack F. "Lawrence and Gauguin." *Twentieth Century Literature* 26, no. 4 (Winter 1980):385–401.

———. "Primitivism in *Women in Love.*" *D. H. Lawrence Review* 13, no. 1 (Spring 1980):45–62.

Stoehr, Taylor. " 'Mentalized Sex' in D. H. Lawrence." *Novel: A Forum on Fiction* 8, no. 2 (Winter 1975):101–22.

Tansey, Michael H., Ph.D., and Walter F. Burke, Ph.D. "Projective Identification and the Empathic Process." *Contemporary Psychoanalysis* 21, no. 1 (1985):42–69.

Terry, C. J. "Aspects of D. H. Lawrence's Struggle with Christianity." *Dalhousie Review* 54, no. 1 (Spring 1974):112–29.

Thompson, Leslie. "The Christ Who Didn't Die: Analogues to D. H. Lawrence's *The Man Who Died.*" *D. H. Lawrence Review* 8, no. 1 (Spring 1975):19–30.

———. "D. H. Lawrence and Judas." *D. H. Lawrence Review* 4, no. 1 (Spring 1971):1–19.

Weaver, Raymond. "Narcissus and Echo." *Bookman* (New York) 58 (November 1923): 327–28.

———. "What Ails Pegasus?" *Bookman* (New York) 52 (September 1920):57–66.

Wheeler, Richard P. "Intimacy and Irony in 'The Blind Man.' " *D. H. Lawrence Review* 9, no. 2 (Summer 1976):236–53.

Woodman, Leonora. " 'The Big Old Pagan Vision': The Letters of D. H. Lawrence to Frederick Carter." *Library Chronicle of the University of Texas at Austin,* n.s., no. 34 (1986):39–51.

Zytaruk, George J., ed. "The Last Days of D. H. Lawrence: Hitherto Unpublished Letters of Dr. Andrew Morland." *D. H. Lawrence Review* 1, no. 1 (Spring 1968):44–50.

Audiotapes

Brown, Malcolm. *Psychological Genius of D. H. Lawrence.* Audio Tape Recordings in
    the Forum of Human Potentiality and Human Growth. San Rafael, Calif.: Big
    Sur Recordings, no. 4620 1 1/2, 1971.
Spender, Stephen. *D. H. Lawrence.* "Literary Criticism of Stephen Spender" Series.
    Cincinnati, Ohio: McGraw-Hill, Sound Seminars, no. 75910, n.d.

Index